DATE			

BIG GAME,
SMALL WORLD

BIG GAME, SMALL WORLD

A Basketball Adventure

ALEXANDER WOLFF

WARNER BOOKS

An AOL Time Warner Company

Grateful acknowledgment is given for the following:

Photographs on pages xi, xv, 3, 18, 65, 76, 123, 384 by Heinz Kluetmeier.
Used by permission.

Photograph on page 90 by Miguel Angel Forniés. Used by permission.

Map on page 136 courtesy of University of Kansas Office of University Relations. Used by permission.

Photograph on page 173 courtesy of Appalachian State University Office of Sports
Information. Used by permission.

Parts of this book originally appeared in *Sports Illustrated*, *Sports Illustrated for Women*,
PhillySport, *Princeton Alumni Weekly*, and *Attaché* magazines.

Warner Books, Inc., 1271 Avenue of the Americas, New York, NY 10020

Visit our Web site at www.twbookmark.com.

For information on Time Warner Trade Publishing's online program, visit www.ipublish.com.

W An AOL Time Warner Company

Printed in the United States of America

First Printing: January 2002
10 9 8 7 6 5 4 3 2 1

Library of Congress Cataloging-in-Publication Data

Wolff, Alexander.
    Big game, small world : a basketball adventure / Alexander Wolff.
        p. cm.
    ISBN 0-446-52601-0
    1. Basketball. 2. Wolff, Alexander—Journeys. I. Title.

GV885 .W62 2002
796.323—dc21   2001026116

For Vanessa—
and with her

CONTENTS

PROLOGUE xi
CALLED FOR TRAVELING xv

FALL: *Founding Myths, Conflicting Cultures*
1. Almonte, Ontario: Duck on a Rock 3
2. Lithuania: Forest Brothers in Short Pants 18
3. Poland: The Sultans of Złoty 33
4. Switzerland: Please Do Not Air Your Dirty
   Laundry 52
5. Celebration, Florida: Communities of Three 65
6. Italy: Strength vs. Virtue 76
7. Sarajevo Airport: Prisoners of War 90
8. Bosnia: The Woman Who Sells Men 108

WINTER: *The American Game and Her Far-Flung Offspring*
9. Peoria, Illinois: Crossover Dreamers 123
10. Eastern Kansas: Driving Mister John 136
11. El Paso: The Bear in Winter 148
12. Whiteriver, Arizona: Shoots from the Sky 163
13. Boone, North Carolina: Mayberry Friends 173
14. Ireland: To Build a Gym 186
15. Israel: The Long Arm of the Law of Return 200

16. The Philippines: Madness and Mimicry 219
17. China: Qiao Dan, Celestial Citizen 235

SPRING: *The Game Within*
18. Philadelphia: Quaker Meeting House 253
19. Brazil: Women of the Laughing Blood 267
20. Des Moines: Unguarded Moments 282
21. Japan: A Journey of a Thousand Miles,
    Begun with a Single Shot 292
22. Bhutan: Gross National Hoopiness 311

SUMMER: *Fast Break to the Future*
23. Washington, D.C.: Going to the Next Level 337
24. France: The "I Love This Game" Theory of
    Conflict Prevention 351
25. Angola: Lasme's Plane Will Be Arriving Shortly . . . 360
26. Kansas City: To Rest, Rather Than to Mischief . . . 384
27. Princeton, New Jersey: Through the Back Door . . . 393

EPILOGUE 403
ACKNOWLEDGMENTS 415

When the individual was permitted to move about anywhere, so long as he did not have the ball, the game became spirited and kaleidoscopic.
　　　　　　　　　　　　　—DR. JAMES NAISMITH

There is no truth but in transit.
　　　　　　　　　　　　　—RALPH WALDO EMERSON

PROLOGUE

The café shimmered with chrome and glass. Like so much of modern Shanghai, the decor seemed to hold in contempt anything more than a few years old. But the man seated across from me appeared immune from the cutting-edge scorn of the place, even as his appearance evoked a time long past.

Bai Jinshen has one of those furrowed faces that tend to soak up and neutralize their surroundings. Lineage grounded him, too: During the 19th century an ancestor lived in Beijing's Forbidden City, serving in the court of an emperor of the Qing dynasty. Bai himself had learned basketball from American missionaries while growing up in Tianjin during the 1930s before going on to play for and coach the Chinese national team when it suited up for the greater glory of Mao Zedong and the revolution. If basketball in China has a birthplace, Tianjin is it: The Tianjin YMCA was the site of the first game played in the Middle Kingdom, and a factory in that northeastern city produced the country's first basketball.

"A basketball has eight slices," Bai was telling me. "Four slices belong to yin and four slices belong to yang. We call the yang side hardware. Hardware includes body strength, skills, psychology, and teamwork. We call the yin side software. Software includes coaching, development of young players, support staff, and education. Four and four. Eight things."

If I'd handed him a basketball just then, Bai might have picked up a knife and peeled the ball's pebblegrain rind into a seamless coil.

"Because a basketball is like the earth, it spins every day. And because it spins, it must develop. And for it to develop, those of us involved with the game must think forward—think progressively. And if we think progressively, we can control the game's progress. In our life and work, if we think, we gain insight. Everybody has curiosity. Which leads to interest. And if we devote ourselves to that interest, our ability increases.

"So you see, it all starts with thinking."

Despite his blood ties to the Qing dynasty, Bai did not look back fondly on its reign. "The Qing eliminated the Ming reforms and spoke of the 'foreign devil' at the very time the West was quickly developing. Yes, the Qing united the country. But during its rule China was left behind.

"I am 66 years old. I once learned from my parents and teachers. Now I learn from young people like my son. They understand things more quickly than I do, and they're more tolerant than I am. In the past dozen years the Chinese people have opened their eyes and started to accept different ways of thinking. Of course, buying Air Jordans and Bulls T-shirts aren't really ways of thinking. But one of the motivations of human beings is to pursue things in their heads—to imagine. Some of these imaginings are just illusions, but others can keep you going. And during the 1990s, after Chinese television bought the rights to the NBA, that's what started to happen here. On the surface, you could see kids trying to copy Michael Jordan. But at a deeper level, when children open their minds to fantasies, their minds are being conditioned. They become more receptive to other things as well."

A basketball court sits just beyond the Tiananmen Gate in central Beijing, on the threshold of the Forbidden City, the very ground where Bai's ancestors once trod—a court from which NBC broadcaster Ahmad Rashad and a crew, filming a segment for *NBA Inside Stuff*, had recently been chased away by guards who mistook cue cards for propaganda. I asked Bai how he felt about the game to which he had devoted his life, as player and coach and philosopher, having a place in his country's hallowed seat of power.

"It makes me happy," he said.

In Shanghai that evening, listening as a man told me how the simplest of games was changing the world, I lost his words in a contentment of my own. Kierkegaard, the favorite philosopher of a more familiar basketball thinker, Dean Smith, once remarked that a man is no happier than when his wish coincides with his duty. I was that man. Wish and duty had fused into a compulsion, one that had carried me half a world from home, and would take me many other places as well.

CALLED FOR TRAVELING

I had bought the Russian nesting dolls from a street vendor in St. Petersburg. Over the years, as they peered at me from a shelf in the study of my Manhattan apartment, I'd come to appreciate their tidy hierarchy. The Michael Jordan figurine enclosed the Magic Johnson. The Magic Johnson enclosed the Larry Bird. For an argument over where these basketball greats rank you once had to flick on sports-talk radio or go down to the corner bar. Yet here some faceless Russian artisan had thrown in his two kopecks' worth and underscored for me a truth: Scarcely a century after basketball's invention in Springfield, Massachusetts, by an aspiring clergyman, NBA iconography and school-yard dreamers are commonplace in virtually every country on earth.

Midlife crises come in many guises, but mine, after two decades spent writing about the game and nearly twice that long playing it, took the form of an imperative. I needed to do what ballplayers do. I needed to move, to pick up, to go—to watch and play and puzzle out basketball wherever I found it. Just as removing the top of each doll revealed another inside, I would set out in search of the truths at the core of the game.

As a student at Princeton during the late 1970s, I learned much from two teachers, each of whom grew up in eastern

Pennsylvania under hardscrabble circumstances. As it happened, the two—sociology professor Marvin Bressler and basketball coach Pete Carril—were friends, drinking buddies who could often be found at a tavern on the edge of campus, as likely to be discussing international trade policy as the best way to break a zone trap. Carril's class I only audited, watching his teams as they won a couple of Ivy League championships. But I actually took Bressler's course on the sociology of education. As plans for this book took shape I ran into him on campus, and there he told me a story.

It seemed that Bressler had just shared dinner with E. D. Hirsch Jr., the academic whose book *Cultural Literacy* stipulates what every educated American should know. As the evening progressed, Bressler brought the conversation around to basketball. He told Hirsch how, one preseason toward the ends of their careers, an interviewer approached Magic and Larry separately with the same questions. "How do you motivate yourself after all these years? How do you get yourself ready for one more season?"

"I think of Magic," Larry replied. "Wherever he is, I know how hard he's working."

"It's Larry," said Magic. "Larry Legend. I'd *better* be working hard, 'cause I sure know he is."

"Each one was bound to the other," Bressler told his dinner companion. "Like Ahab and the whale."

Hirsch caught the *Moby Dick* reference. But he looked at Bressler blankly and said, "Who are Magic and Larry?"

Preparing to light out for the country of basketball, I could think of few places where Hirsch's response would fail to cause consternation. Ever since the NBA Dream Team's appearance at the 1992 Olympics in Barcelona, the game had become a global lingua franca. When NBA commissioner David Stern paid a visit to a remote Chinese province at the height of the reign of Jordan and the Chicago Bulls, a local VIP came alive with recognition upon learning of Stern's identity. "Ah!" he said. *"The Red Oxen!"*

But basketball's ascendancy was most evident among young

people the world over. According to a study of middle-class teenagers conducted during the mid-1990s, no sport more passionately engaged adolescents internationally, not even soccer. Some 71 percent either played the game or watched it, including nearly two of every three girls on the planet. Despite all the passions soccer can still unleash, that game is world-historical in pace and analog in structure—ill suited for the Information Age. Basketball is quick-cutting, digital, perfectly adapted for a generation eager to supplicate itself to music videos, computers, and other manifestations of American cultural power. In 1995 a boy named Tomasz was among a dozen people pulled from an avalanche in an Icelandic fishing village. After spending 24 hours buried in snow, he had three questions: Where am I? Is there school today? And who won that game between the Orlando Magic and the Philadelphia 76ers?

My father is an immigrant who left Germany in 1948 to study chemistry at Princeton. After earning his Ph.D. he took a research job with RCA just outside town. Growing up, I did not toss a baseball with my dad in the backyard. He had broken his nose three times playing field hockey as a schoolboy in Bavaria, and his eagerness to assimilate never overcame a vow to swear off ball games of all types. But our family pediatrician told my American-born mother that, for orthopedic reasons, he preferred basketball to other sports, and my mom channeled doctor's orders into a subtle encouragement to play hoops.

At the same time, Bill Bradley was installing himself as a local hero. He would be written up at great and approving length in the pages of the *New Yorker,* a publication that held truck in our household. Studious, clean-cut, and churchgoing, Bradley appeared to be wholly admirable, and though my parents were baffled by his devotion to a sweaty game, it seemed to be part of a larger, disciplined approach to life, and for basketball they were prepared to excuse him. One of my earliest memories dates to December 1964, when I was put to bed so my parents could watch Bradley and Princeton hook up with Cazzie Russell and Michigan on TV in the finals of the ECAC Holiday Festival. This has stuck in my head, I think, not so much because of my disappointment at missing the game, but because I don't recall my parents ever again accommodating their lives to a televised sporting event.

As a result of the unlikely status basketball held in our home, my parents hadn't removed the hoop put over the garage by the previous owners. And so I found myself spending many hours alone beneath it. I played even when the net, rigid from rain and cold, would catch my shot fast, and I'd have to whack the ball free with a broom handle after each basket. Nevertheless, in the act of trying to send a ball through a hoop I found hours of solitary pleasure. At an annual summer carnival in town I discovered that I could sink a shot better than most kids my age. Even after my father left RCA for Xerox and we moved to a suburb of Rochester, New York, I ignored the vogue for ice hockey in our new neighborhood and went on to become a decent high school player on a decent high school team. But I wasn't good or big enough to play at the summit of the Ivy League. So upon returning to Princeton for college I began covering campus news for the *Trenton Times,* an evening paper down Route 1.

I took a front-row seat in Carril's lecture hall, sometimes typing out a skeletal play-by-play for the sports information office. For that duty—for coming up with pithy gems like SOWINSKI 15-FT JUMP and OMELTCHENKO 2 FT, GOOD, GOOD—I received $15 a game and a taste of my future profession. My greatest failure as a player had always been a reluctance to mix it up, and this extracurricular choice would complete my transit from participant to observer. From time to time I regretted not having tried out for the team. This wasn't because I believed I could have made it, much less made any contribution. It was because to watch Princeton play was to be reminded repeatedly of why I loved the game.

Yes, I adored basketball for its style and argot, its racial ecumenism, its jaunty, loose spirit. But the Tigers under Carril pulled off something just as appealing. Canny, throwback, almost pious in their respect for each possession, they seemed to share an intuitive understanding of Newton's third law. Their offense flowed away from the ball, with players moving in opposition to defensive pressure. The transcendent Princeton moment—the Tigers' earthbound answer to the alley-oop dunk—was the backdoor layup, the play available when the balance of an opponent has tipped irretrievably away from the goal he's supposed to defend. Think of the reverse commuter at rush hour, or the martial artist well-practiced at jujitsu. The overdefended player cuts to the basket, then takes a teammate's pass for two easy points. If its constituents can all pass, move, and shoot, and no one cares who ultimately scores, a team running a backdoor offense will press against the limit of its potential, while the opposition suffers death by a thousand back cuts.

Treated regularly to so artful a display of the game, I was hardly able to abandon its practice. For my first two years on campus I drifted over to musty Dillon Gym in the afternoons to play pickup. I abandoned college after my sophomore year, kiting off to Switzerland to spend a season with a club team there. To my parents' relief I eventually came back to school. But the summer after junior year, a buddy and I threw a ball into the trunk of a car and vagabonded around the U.S. in search of the perfect pickup game, then wrote up an account of our journey called *The In-Your-Face Basketball Book*.

So to me notions of movement have always attended the game. Indeed, basketball owes its very existence to human mobility: It was invented in Springfield, Massachusetts, by a Canadian immigrant, Dr. James Naismith, at the International YMCA Training School, which was chartered to groom missionaries. When Bradley won two NBA titles with the New York Knicks, he catalyzed the team as a hyperkinetic forward, helping to enshrine perpetual motion as one of the great virtues of offensive play. Today there is still no greater crime against the game than to "stand around"; no compliment—not "nice pass," not "good shot"—gladdens a player's heart more than "sweet move."

Princeton had been the site of my childhood fascination with the game. It had indulged my affection when I was a college student there. Now, nearly 20 years out, the school figured in my summons. During the 1996 NCAA tournament, Pete Carril made his final victory a 43–41 upset of defending national champion UCLA, with the Tigers winning on their signature play in the game's dying seconds. Then, two years later, Princeton spent most of the season in the Top 10, losing only twice. The Tigers had long been regarded as a "visit to the dentist" team that would numb opponents with the novocaine of 10, 15, 20 passes or more before applying the drill. Yet here they were drilling patients without anesthesia. They'd never passed so deftly, cut so hard, or scored so audaciously. With play so selfless that in one game each of its 21 baskets came on an assist, Princeton drew the attention of every segment of the mainstream media and won legions of new followers, all curious to know how a school that couldn't offer athletic scholarships consistently found wide-open layups against national powers.

At times that season Princeton hardly seemed to need a coach. During their all-assist game, at the ECAC Holiday Festival, the Tigers found themselves momentarily bamboozled after Niagara jumped into a zone defense. The man who had succeeded Carril, Bill Carmody, called timeout to tell his players nothing more than this: "You're smart guys. You figure it out." In that long-ago Holiday Festival final my parents hadn't let me see, Princeton lost a lead and ultimately the game after Bradley fouled out. Thirty-three years later the Tigers scored those 21 assisted baskets in the very same tournament. Having evolved from a gross dependency on a single player to a consummate interdependency, this time they won the Holiday Festival, in as fine an example as any of basketball virtue rewarded.

Princeton's remarkable year set me to wondering whether the Tigers didn't embody a kind of hoops metaphysics. Carmody hinted that something Eastern sat at the heart of the team's approach. "We run a lot of yin stuff," he said at one point during

that season. "Oak tree, willow tree—you know." Carril had preferred to sound a note more in keeping with Western moral
philosophy. "Guys who come around to the ball just feed greed
and ignorance," he once told me. Whatever their provenance,
Princeton's precepts worked, and I tried applying them when I
took the court for my regular Wednesday night run in a rented
gym on the Upper West Side. I vowed to pass and cut away, and
never to come around to the ball—to spread love rather than
greed and ignorance. Of course, in the hurly-burly of a pickup
game this made me the crank screaming "Repent!" in Times
Square at rush hour, and I quickly reverted. But I was at least
looking at basketball with a heightened consciousness.

And then, during the second half of Princeton's game with
Brown that February, I had my epiphany. From where he dribbled to the right of the key, one of the Tigers' seniors, Mitch
Henderson, saw a teammate bolt toward the basket from the
opposite wing. In a trice the ball left his hands and found its
way, on a bounce, through a bramble of bodies in the lane and
into the hands of another senior, James Mastaglio, for a layup.
Or so I believed; I wasn't sure that what I thought I'd seen was
even possible. I checked with one of the people who had by
now flocked to follow the Tigers. The bard of the ballparks,
Washington Post columnist George Will, sat next to me on press
row, and confirmed that Henderson had indeed whipped a pass
through and past most of the players on the floor. My neighbor
wasn't wearing his usual bow tie, but if he had been it might
have spun cartoonlike on the top button of his Oxford shirt. It
occurred to me: If George Will could write rhapsodic essays on
the Jeffersonian origins of the infield-fly rule, surely there was a
thing or two worth saying about hoops.

"The appeal of basketball is that it is a game easy to play, but
difficult to master," Doc Naismith once said. In that lacuna
between just playing—"piddling at it," as Naismith put it—and
perfection, people could get blissfully lost and pull off wonderful things. Mitch Henderson's crosscourt backdoor bounce
pass through traffic had been one of those wonderful things. It
moved me like a prod.

I prepared to set out in the fall of 1998 under what might have seemed like inauspicious circumstances. The NBA and its players were mired in a small-minded and rancorous labor dispute. Basketball's greatest player ever had just taken what appeared to have been his last shot. Standards of sportsmanship lagged at every level of the game. But I was not setting out in search of basketball only at its competitive summit, or even primarily in its sunlit uplands. I wanted to discover it elsewhere, too—in places from which it bubbled up and others to which it filtered down. I wanted to see how far the bird that is the TV satellite had carried the game's seed. If something of Naismith's original vision still held, basketball would be gaiting the young in their striving, annealing the spirit of the poor, and connecting people of all races and genders, able-bodied and disabled alike, regardless of nationality. But if commercialism, racism, nationalism, and other noxious isms had won out, I was prepared to reckon with that, too. Regardless of what I found, by journey's end I hoped to have taken the measure of the game, and much of the world, and maybe even my sorry, settle-for-the-jump-shot self.

Mine wouldn't be an entirely contiguous route. But my movements would reflect the spliced-together essence of the sport and its multiple misdirections. Even as I tried to keep in mind the distinction between basketball Stateside and the game abroad, the barrier was blurring: There had never been so many non-Americans on rosters of NBA and college teams. FIBA, the international basketball federation, was about to pass a rule abolishing all restrictions on nationality in its club competitions. This meant a top European team like Panathinaikos Athens or Real Madrid could, if it wanted, suit up an entire roster of players from the U.S., the country of basketball's invention, propagation, and, with the NBA, apotheosis. As my odyssey would take me, in turn, around America and overseas, I was sure to feel sometimes as if I were simultaneously home and away.

Finally, I'd take along a traveling companion. Among those who chronicle the game for a living, it has become a cliché to survey the sprawling reach and saltatorial sallies of modern basketball and ask, "What would Naismith say?" I decided to apply that question wherever possible, but more than proverbially. I would enlist Doc Naismith's sensibility, reflected in comments he made and writings he left behind, as my conscience.

Back in the mid-1980s I spent an evening with the late Jack McMahon. An assistant coach and scout for the Philadelphia 76ers, he was the man who had bird-dogged Andrew Toney and Maurice Cheeks, the guards who helped lead the Sixers to their 1983 NBA title. We met up at a game between Oklahoma and Missouri in Columbia, Missouri, which McMahon had come to scout despite a blizzard that left tractor-trailers jackknifed the length of his drive along Interstate 70 from the St. Louis airport.

McMahon impressed on me two things that night. One was the importance of seeing a game in person. McMahon's very presence, despite the weather, testified to that point. Scores of fine pros had never appeared on TV as collegians, and McMahon took the time to ferret out Toney and Cheeks, NBA All-Stars both, from a couple of backwater schools, Southwestern Louisiana and West Texas State. The Sixers drafted each in the first round based on what their top scout believed to be predictors of NBA success—basketball skills, to be sure, but also ostensibly trivial things that can only be judged up close: expression, carriage, spirit, even pigeon-toedness (the more the better, McMahon believed). In Toney, McMahon had been struck by a kind of ruthlessness, a quality that reminded him of Iago, the villain from *Othello*, on whom he had written a long-ago high school essay; in Cheeks, he saw an almost implacable knack for getting to the basket no matter how hard or often he'd get knocked down en route. That was the standard by which McMahon judged guards: whether they could find their way to the basket. "When you go to the hole, you either score, or pass off to someone who scores, or get fouled," he told me. "Only good things happen when you go to the hole."

McMahon died of a heart attack within several years of our meeting, very likely from the toll of the road—one too many high-cholesterol, sodium-saturated room-service meals, or stressed-out dashes to catch a last flight for a last chance to see what just might be the last piece in the Sixers' player-personnel puzzle. But I'll always associate a single verb with him. It was on my mind as I hit the road, and it hinted at a unified field theory of this game of constant motion. Go. Go to the basket, go to the game. Only good things happen when you go.

FALL

Founding Myths, Conflicting Cultures

ONE

Almonte, Ontario
Duck on a Rock

As I made my way toward Canada and the birthplace of basketball's inventor, an oversized Massachusetts mill town beckoned from alongside Interstate 91. I stopped, but not for the purpose most tourists do, to slog through Springfield's Naismith Memorial Basketball Hall of Fame. Rather, I stopped to see Bob Jennings.

I'd first found him about 15 years ago at Dunbar Community Center, the recreation hall he ran in the city's blighted Hill-McKnight district. Jennings was a trim and courtly black man who had eased into his sixties with an even temper and an ever-open door. Dunbar was once the First South Church of Christ, and Mister J—everyone called him Mister J—used it to minister to a variety of the neighborhood's needs. The old nave had been given over to a basketball court, which indicated one need prime among them. In the late afternoons the best ballplayers in western Massachusetts gathered at Dunbar's procrustean court to jostle one another for elbow room. The cramped quarters required a stout heart, and so the Dunbar parquet was known for miles around as Death Valley.

On that visit Mister J had recited the wagon train of local stars to rumble through Death Valley. He told of an intern he once supervised, an undergrad from the University of Massachusetts in nearby Amherst known as Julius (Doctor J) Erving. And Mister J described what it took to get himself to set aside his duties as a surrogate father to the local kids and pull on his sneakers to play. Not much, it turned out. "They'll say, 'Run with us, Mister J.' I'll wake up the next morning a little stiffer. But I won't play half-court. You stand around too much."

That last comment had particularly endeared him to me. So, though I hadn't been in touch for years, I drove out State Street on a brilliant fall afternoon. I ducked into Dunbar and asked to see Bob Jennings.

"Mister J's passed a few years now," a young man told me.

Doctor James, Mister J, and Doctor J made up a kind of holy trinity at Dunbar, whose court sat closest to the very first one. Now two of those three icons were dead. I spun the three blocks to Winchester Square, site of the old YMCA Training School at the northeast corner of Sherman and State, and found it gone, too—replaced by a shopping center parking lot commanded by that international symbol of spoilage, a McDonald's.

I'd been told that a plaque marked the sacred spot. But I could find only a drive-thru lane and a few NO LOITERING signs. I asked a fry-slinger if he could direct me to any commemoration of the game's invention.

"There's a sign over there, but I think it's for some guy," he said.

"Naismith?"

"Yeah. That's the guy."

I crossed the street to a traffic island with a monument, but it turned out to be a war memorial. So I went back to Mickey D's.

"It's a sign?" I pressed. "I didn't see any sign. What kind of sign?"

"Well, in this neighborhood, somebody probably stole it."

Necessity may be the mother of invention, but eccentricity is the inventor's mistress. Benjamin Franklin believed you could fend off flatulence by drinking perfume. Leonardo da Vinci used a shorthand of his own devising to take 5,000 pages of notes, all backward. Thomas Edison tried to get people to say "ahoy" when answering the telephone, an effort that mercifully foundered on the shoals of "hello."

The originator of basketball stands proudly in this tradition. First let it be said that James Naismith invented more than just hoops. He came up with various other games, whose names (hy-lo, vreille) hint at why they never caught on. In the fall of 1891, he jerryrigged what's believed to be the first football headgear, a chamois skullcap secured by a chin strap.

But even if Naismith had never invented anything, he sometimes seemed like a man at least a free throw short of a three-point play. Certainly his wife, Maude, must have found him a constant entertainment. He slept only four hours a night. He was so absentminded that he would regularly drive to work, then at the end of the day hitch a ride or hop a streetcar home, thereby marooning the family Model T. Upon returning from World War I, where he served 19 months as a YMCA chaplain in France, he declared that he stood two inches shorter from all the walking he'd done. And while we aren't sure that Naismith actually believed you could make an athlete run faster by feeding him rabbit, as athletic director at the University of Kansas he hired a coach who did.

When his youngest son, Jimmy, was three days old, Naismith took him into a classroom at Kansas and, to illustrate points on child development, plopped him down naked and marked him up with red and blue chalk. The good doctor was so enamored of data that he took 19 measurements of every entering freshman male, from height and weight to breadth of shoulders and girth of chest, and added notations about more private bodily regions—which led his daughter, Annie, in remarks made years later to his biographer, to call Papa Jim's records "a mid-Victorian *Kinsey Report*." In the throes of his preoccupation he was forever making notes like this: "Man dribbling. Defense holds out arm. Dribbler runs into arm. On whom the foul?"

I suppose we'd all be forgetful if pondering such essential questions.

Naismith had received his divinity degree from McGill University in Montreal, and he enrolled at the Training School in the fall of 1890 to begin work on his master's in physical education because he wanted to reconcile a love of sports with Christian rectitude. But one of his assignments turned into a test of faith. In December 1891 he took over what, were the Y not such a pious place, would surely have been called the Phys Ed Class from Hell. Two other instructors had tried and failed to bring some order to this incorrigible group of 18 future YMCA executive secretaries, most of them out-of-season rugby and football players who chafed under the regimen of leapfrog and tumbling that passed for sport during the winter.

As it happened, Naismith had already begun wondering why there wasn't a game better suited to his athletic beau ideal, a specimen somewhere between the rugger and the runner—"the tall, agile, graceful, and expert athlete," he would write, "rather than the massive muscular man on the one hand, or the cadaverous greyhound type on the other." The characteristic act of his invention—the arched throw of a ball at an elevated goal—would come from an obscure children's game popular in Ontario's Ottawa valley, which young Jim had played in the hamlet of Bennies Corners. In the game, called duck on a rock, players knocked a fist-sized rock off a boulder by pelting it from a distance with smaller stones. If the thrower missed the target, he had to retrieve his stone before another player, designated "it," could tag him. Naismith recalled how finesse was at least as important as force, for the thrower had to balance the objective of hitting the duck with the need to retrieve his stone if it were to miss. Thus players learned to throw in an optimal arc. Station the goal overhead, Naismith concluded, and his new game would further reward skill over force.

Naismith stayed up late drafting the original 13 rules, and the next morning asked the Training School janitor, whom history records as one James Stebbins, to fetch a couple of boxes. Stebbins famously produced instead two half-bushel peach baskets, which he hung from the 10-foot-high balcony circling the basement gym. The inaugural game ended with a YMCA executive secretary-to-be named William Chase having scored basketball's first—and the first game's only—basket, a throw from 25 feet away.

As Training School graduates fanned out on missions around the world, and Naismith shared his game with anyone who showed an interest, basketball spread rapidly and widely—so widely that before his death in 1939, the inventor had collected translations of the rules in almost 50 languages and dialects. But in its first blush of life, no one gave any consideration to where basketball might go. The game had been a stopgap, and it had worked: The class was brought to heel. But consider for a moment. What if Stebbins had come back with two lengths of stovepipe? What if the balcony had been 12 feet high instead of 10? A colleague of Naismith's at the Training School would invent a different sport involving a ball and a net; had he done so sooner—had William Morgan come up with volleyball in 1890 instead of 1895—missionaries might have packed its rules with their Bibles, and there might be volleyball nets, not basketball hoops, in gyms and parks and schoolyards the world over. You might be reading a book called *The Golden Spike: By Rail through the Country of Volleyball.*

By 1898 the Naismiths had settled in Lawrence, Kansas, where the good doctor, having now added a degree in medicine to those in divinity and phys ed, took on three duties at the university: as athletic director, chapel director, and the entire faculty of the department of health and phys ed. As an afterthought, he served as the school's first basketball coach.

In 1905, Naismith's best player was an angular young man from Missouri named Forrest (Phog) Allen. That fall officials at a small college near Lawrence contacted Naismith to ask if they might hire Allen as a part-time basketball coach. Naismith laughingly mentioned the offer to Allen.

"What's so funny about that?" Allen wanted to know.

"Why, you can't coach basketball," replied Naismith, who rarely even traveled with his team. "You just play it!"

The exchange may be apocryphal, but the sentiments behind it were real enough. For years the two would spar over their philosophical differences. Allen came to regard Naismith as something of a fuddy-duddy, scoffing at his habit of counseling any student with a problem who stopped by his office, as if Naismith were some early-century Mister J. By contrast, Allen hitched his ambitions to the game. He took that job, and by 1907 had replaced Naismith as the Jayhawks' coach. (It's often noted that Naismith is the only losing basketball coach Kansas has ever had.) After two seasons Allen left to study osteopathy, but a decade later he returned, first taking over as hoops coach from the man who liked to serve rabbit as a training meal, and, in 1924, in the great humiliation of Naismith's professional career, accepting an appointment from the chancellor to replace the Basketball Man himself as head of phys ed.

Over the years Allen showed Naismith many kindnesses, offering to help him avoid foreclosure on his house and launching a campaign to send him to Berlin in 1936 for basketball's Olympic debut. Naismith would, with no apparent begrudgement, sign a photograph for Allen with the inscription: "From the father of basketball to the father of basketball coaching." But none of this altered Naismith's conviction that his game should be for the masses, not an entertainment spectacle played by the competitive elite. In notes appended to the first edition of the rules, published in 1892, he wrote, "At a picnic the baskets may be hung on a couple of trees and the game carried on as usual." He even envisioned goals being stuck at either end of a football field, and as many as a hundred people playing with several balls at once. To Naismith, in the midst of a noble contest the true sportsman shouldn't have some nonparticipant telling him much more than "You're smart guys. You figure it out." Indeed, in 1910 the rules committee, on which Naismith still sat, banned coaching during games, and not until 1949, a decade after the inventor's death, were coaches allowed even to talk to players during timeouts. Naismith believed the purpose to which he had devoted his life—the development of muscular Christianity through sport—was best served when players were taught the basics of a game and left to themselves.

This conflict, almost as old as basketball itself, seemed to me an essential one. Of course there was a place in the game for coaching. But to whom did basketball really belong? The players? The coaches? Or the heirs to Doc Naismith and Mister J, ministers of the game who taught a kid self-reliance and responsibility long before the limelight found him, just in case it never did?

The next morning, looking up from the foliage that lingered in the floodplain of the Connecticut River, I saw flocks of Canada geese heading south. But like Doc Naismith I was going to be something of an odd duck and continue north.

All sorts of incongruities awaited. In the upper reaches of New York State, just beyond the ferry from Vermont, yard signs touted a candidate for sheriff named Lawliss. Across from a Mohawk tribal office near Hogansburg, a Conestoga-style hutch peddled Sof-Serv under a sign reading CUSTARD'S LAST STAND. But I came across the starkest contrast later that day, after Highway 374 carried me unawares into a forlorn farming village a few miles from the Canadian border: the juxtaposition of Doc Naismith with McGill's second most famous basketball graduate.

For some reason the name of Chateaugay, New York, had stuck in my head, and I soon remembered why. It's the hometown of a coach named Kevin O'Neill. O'Neill, who was then carrying a clipboard for Northwestern, had a few too many clicks on the odometer to qualify as what wags call "an up-and-comer." But he happened to be working his first head coaching job, at Marquette, when three underfunded filmmakers put together a documentary called *Hoop Dreams*. Because O'Neill would sign to a scholarship one of the film's two subjects, Chicago high school star William Gates, the coach found himself with several fleeting minutes of screen time in the three-hour movie, including a visit to the Gates family's apartment in the Cabrini-Green housing project. *Hoop Dreams* depicted O'Neill as a reasonable if businesslike guy, not the unctuous procurer who as an assistant coach at Arizona some years earlier had cultivated a reputation as such a ruthless recruiter that he said, "When I walk into a gym, I want everybody to say, 'That asshole's here.'"

When *Hoop Dreams* was finally finished—after the filmmakers spent eight years maxing out credit cards and negotiating every circle of development hell—the movie met an improbable fate. In the rarest of receptions for a documentary, it won a theatrical release and rave reviews, even touching off a revolt among critics when the Academy failed to nominate it for Best Documentary. Throughout its long gestation, director Steve James had told the families of Gates and costar Arthur Agee that the film probably wouldn't make money, but if it did, the families would get their fair shares. When James sat down to write them checks, he also offered sums to 45 others with a speaking part in the film, with the money apportioned according to screen time. For permitting the filmmakers to document his sales call in the Gates family living room, O'Neill was to receive $887.31, with the possibility of almost $2,000 more depending on future revenues—not all that much, but $887.31 more than convention requires documentarians to pay their subjects.

But James soon heard from a lawyer representing O'Neill. Alone among those to appear in the film, the coach—who by then was making some $350,000 a year from his salary, endorsements, TV show, and camp as coach at Tennessee—wanted more. Almost $50,000 more. James pointed out that the formula was designed so every supporting player would be treated the same way, whether player, coach, or minister of the game. In response he received a note from O'Neill that read, "Steve: Let's move on this and get it cleared up. It's not going to go away."

Fortunately, it did go away. O'Neill dropped the matter. Yet here I found myself in the town that had nurtured such a charitable specimen of humanity. I skulked into the gym in which O'Neill had rung up 30 points a game for the Chateaugay High Bulldogs before heading up to McGill for college. I picked his mug shot out of the hallway photo board from the class of '75. (He rather looked like a kid whose ambition in life was to piss people off.) And I recalled how Naismith, McGill class of 1887, had replied to the question of whether he regretted not making a penny off the game. "It would be impossible for me to explain my feelings to people who ask this," the good doctor wrote shortly before his death. "My pay has not been in dollars, but in satisfaction of giving something to the world that is a benefit to masses of people."

Sometimes the place you find yourself tells you exactly where you need to go. Chateaugay was just such a place. I left in a hurry. Soon I was speeding over the St. Lawrence River, bound for Doc Naismith's birthplace.

Southeastern Ontario was flat and aflame. It pushed to the horizon with yellows and reds and rusty browns, like Vermont with a rolling pin put to it. Almonte was once known as Little Manchester, after the mills that attracted British immigrants like Naismith's Scottish father, John. In 1870 John and his wife, Margaret, left Almonte with their three children for a lumber camp on the Quebec shore of the Ottawa River. But a typhoid outbreak swept through the camp that fall, killing John and, three weeks later, on young Jim's ninth birthday, Margaret, too. Jim and his two siblings were shipped back to Almonte, to live with Margaret's brother, Pete Young, just outside town in the stone farmhouse in which Margaret and Pete had grown up.

The orphaned Jim took eagerly to the outdoor life. He dropped out of high school at age 15, and for four years found work in lumber camps and on Uncle Pete's farm. According to

Bernice Larson Webb's biography of Naismith, *The Basketball Man,* as a lumberjack Naismith "learned to swear and drink, and began to wear heavy boots." There is no Pythonesque mention of his having put on women's clothing, but he did hang around in bars—a biographical detail that doesn't entirely conform with the eulogy read at his funeral, which asserted that "In no sense was he the reformed unclean liver preaching to others. Clean living seemed to have been the passion of his life youth up."

In fact, clean living only kicked in at age 20, if we're to believe a story Doc Naismith told over the years. After one hard day of lumberjacking, he sat down in an Almonte saloon and ordered a whiskey.

"Ye're Margaret Young's son, aren't ye?" said a man sitting next to him.

"Aye," Naismith replied.

"She'd turn over in her grave to see ye."

He set the glass down, pushed it away, and never took a drink again.

James returned to high school that year, and in the fall of 1883 took a scholarship to enroll at McGill. For seven years he studied there, first earning a B.A. and then that master's in divinity. But he made his mark in gymnastics, soccer, and rugby, too, and his peers twice named him the school's best all-around athlete.

During Naismith's final year at McGill, at a 6 A.M. rugby practice, a teammate let slip a curse. "Sorry, Jim," he quickly added. "Forgot you were here." Naismith had heard much worse in the lumber camps. But the incident persuaded him that a righteous man could have an influence on the athletic field, which was then regarded as a seedbed of ruffianism. He decided to pass up the ministry to pursue the career in phys ed that would bring him to Springfield.

Naismith's decision left his professors scandalized. They had prayed for his soul since the Sunday he delivered a sermon while sporting shiners on each eye. Back in Almonte, Uncle Pete and Jim's sister, Annie, were just as disappointed. They had reluctantly supported his decision to go to McGill because they imagined him someday mounting a pulpit, and now he was devoting his life to games. Pete and Annie cited Luke 9:62, accusing him of looking back after putting his hand to the plow. Over the years Jim would patch things up with his uncle. But his sister, who spent the rest of her days in that stone farmhouse, never forgave him.

As I cruised up Provincial Highway 15, the Young-Naismith farmstead appeared on the right, just past the Almonte turnoff. Scottish immigrant stonemasons had built it to last, and I was cheered to note the hoop over the garage. But the farmhouse was now a private home, and so the Visitors Centre of the Naismith International Basketball Centre and Foundation lay a half mile back from the highway, in a tiny structure that could have been made of gingerbread. On many days—especially long, cold, dark, Canadian winter ones—no one turned off at the ambiguously marked signpost and followed the access road to where I found John Gosset.

John was director, curator, archivist, landscaper, janitor, flamekeeper, and chief propagandist of the Naismith Foundation and its affiliated Canadian Basketball Hall of Fame. Every chore of preserving the Canadian chapters of the Naismith legend fell to him. Several years earlier, after hours of searching, he had discovered the tumbledown graves of Naismith's parents in the cemetery adjoining Auld Kirk Presbyterian Church, and each year he—for no direct survivors still lived in Almonte—scrubbed the marble headstones to keep moss from accumulating anew. He staged an annual fund-raiser in downtown Almonte, something called the Running of the Balls (No Bull!), in which Almonteans bought up the rights to each of hundreds of plastic mini-basketballs, then rolled them all down the Mill Street hill for a jackpot prize. Over the years John had fielded scores of queries from journalists, historians, and tourists, including an indignant one from a woman from North Carolina who emerged from her car to ask, "Yer not claimin' the game was in-*vin*-ted here, are yew?"

Out front of the Visitors Centre sat the very boulder at which young Jim and his buddies used to play the stone-throwing game that was basketball's progenitor. For centuries the sacred duck's rock had remained where Naismith would have remembered it, about a mile away, in a yard fringed with maple trees by the old Bennies Corners blacksmith's shop. When a woman bought the shop as a residence, she had the rock pushed to the edge of the lot by the road. Sensing history in peril, John arranged for it to be packed in sand and trucked on a flatbed to the Visitors Centre. One of the movers was amused by the boulder's sudden status as fragile historical arti-fact. "I've driven a snowplow for 30 years and hit that rock I don't know how many times," he said. "Never cracked then. Sure isn't gonna crack now."

Almonte was content to cede basketball itself to Springfield. But the town wanted to honor Naismith the man and recognize the migration of his invention beyond the United States. In his most optimistic moments, John Gosset envisioned moving the Naismith Foundation to the old town hall, a limestone Victorian that sits at the head of Almonte's business district. Tourists would have no problem finding the place, and the downtown would get a sorely needed boost. "You're starting to see some vacant storefronts," John told me. "This may be a ghost town if the community doesn't get on board." But the Naismith Foun-dation wasn't the only organization eyeing that space, and my visit to Almonte coincided with a public forum on how the old town hall ought to be used. The following evening John invited me along.

Citizens made their pitches in an auditorium at the new municipal offices, as portraits of hoop-clueless Windsors gazed quizzically from the walls. One woman pleaded that the space be converted into a lending library for toys. Another argued for a performing arts center. When a man proposed a diorama to commemorate the Almonte train wreck in 1942, a calamity that killed 42 people, I wasn't the only person who regarded his idea as a bit ghoulish. "What," a man next to me stage-whispered, "and perform reenactments every hour?"

After the Naismith Foundation president made his pitch, the chairwoman of the town council called for public comment. Before I knew it, I was on my feet in this room full of strangers.

I had no standing to be standing, I began. But as a visitor in this entirely reasonable country and thoroughly hospitable community, I might have a perspective not available to anyone else. "I've spent the past two days in Almonte," I said. "I can vouch that you do hospitality well. The Visitors Centre could be better marked, but if I'd taken a wrong turn off Highway 15, I don't doubt that whichever door I'd knocked on, someone would have cheerfully steered me in the right direction.

"But I speak tonight not just as a tourist, but on behalf of basketball. It's a great game, but it's suffering right now. It's suffering from misplaced emphasis and too much money and poor sportsmanship. More people play it and love it and know about it in more parts of the world than ever before, but the spirit in which Doctor Naismith conceived the game is being forgotten. There's a world beyond Almonte that needs to be reminded of where basketball comes from, and why it's with us, and you're in a better position to do this than anyone else."

Perhaps any visitor saying kind things about their hometown would have pleased the people in that room. Maybe a majority really did want to see the old town hall turned into a shrine to the good doctor and one of his good works. All I know is, many others spoke that evening, and only I got an ovation.

The next afternoon John took me by the old Young-Naismith farmstead to meet the current occupants. Greg Smith and his Swiss-born wife, Marianne, had four boys, two horses, sundry chickens, several dogs, a barn, and the same granary in which young Jim used to hole up to cry over the loss of his mother. Deer, wolves, geese, skunks, lynx, and coyotes still gamboled on the adjacent acreage. In the summer, tourists turned into the

Smiths' driveway four or five times a day. Usually they mistook the historical marker out front as a come-on for the Visitors Centre. "You can always tell the basketball people," Greg told me. "They turn in really slowly. The dogs start to bark. And I'm usually on a long-distance call."

But the Smiths were honored to be living on hallowed ground. They understood that pilgrims to the childhood home of the inventor of basketball weren't worth snapping at. Greg had even served a term as president of the Naismith Foundation.

I mentioned idly that I wanted to go over to the Visitors Centre to play duck on a rock. At that, Greg's 11-year-old son Colin abandoned plans to go horseback riding. Soon he was astride his bike, bolting through the fields that led back from the highway.

I hopped in my car and shadowed him. Halfway down the dirt access road I looked left. At first I could see nothing but an empty field, tawny in the goldening light. But Colin soon appeared from behind a row of maples, pumping madly to keep up. Beyond him, at the fringe of another field, a doe flashed a tuft of tail and disappeared, her movement for a wonderful instant in perfect sync with Colin's.

We met at the famous rock, plinthed there in front of the Visitors Centre. We agreed that we wouldn't play a formal game, for we didn't have the numbers to do it justice. Instead we'd test our aim with target practice. I scavenged around the parking lot, gathering a dozen stones of various sizes, a cache of ammo with which to fire from 10 paces away.

Colin took a different approach. He hunted for a single stone, but just the right one. "I want to use the same stone so I can get the feel of its shape and weight," he explained. It didn't bother Colin that he would have to retrieve this stone after each toss.

As we placed the duck on the rock to begin, it occurred to me that in Colin I was catching a glimpse of James Naismith as a boy. Here in rural Ramsay Township, Colin hadn't been raised to take the easy way out. He didn't have that Nintendency to become instantly bored. He knew the land and the animals that lived off it, and to him a high-tech contraption was the bike on which he had just ridden over. Like young Jim, he could amuse himself with nothing more than rocks and stones.

Late in his life Naismith confessed bafflement at the spell a ball and a hoop could cast. "I remember walking across the gym floor one day and seeing a boy toss the ball toward the basket, recover it, and toss it again," he wrote. "An hour later, as I came back through the gym, the same boy was still at his play. For some time I had been trying to discover what there was about goal-throwing that would keep a boy at it for an hour. I stopped and asked him why he was practicing so long. The boy answered that he did not know, but that he just liked to see if he could make a basket every time he threw the ball."

Once, at Colin's age and in my own driveway, the same simple act—easy to perform, difficult to master—had bewitched me, too, and for much the same reason. I didn't mind picking up that broom handle to knock the ball free from the net on cold or rainy days. And so I identified with my new Canadian friend. But I was a little jealous of him, too. In my jet-age, big-city life, it was harder than ever to find time for getting lost in that repetitive but soothing exercise of shooting hoops.

Both the story of basketball's beginnings and the key to mastering the shot lie with the Protestant work ethic, and the Protestant work ethic has a distinctly North American cast. Yet there's a third place, far from Almonte and Springfield, where the game is more central to national identity than it is in Canada—more so, even, than in the U.S.

TWO

Lithuania

Forest Brothers in Short Pants

Though his hands gripped the wheel, it wasn't really the flesh-and-blood Liudas Rimkus driving me at 85 radar-immune miles an hour through the Lithuanian countryside. Piloting a late-model Ford Mondeo was Liudas's memory—recollections of interminable childhood trips over this same route in a glorified Matchbox toy.

A former player on the junior national team, Liudas was 22, clean-cut and business-schooled, with fluency in English and computers. Today, as guy Friday to Šarūnas Marčiulionis, the NBA guard turned Baltic business and basketball mogul, life was good. But back in the 1980s a family trip to the Baltic Sea was an eight-hour ordeal. The Rimkuses would leave their home in Vilnius at dawn, stopping repeatedly to let the two-stroke engine of their Russian-made Zaz cool. It would be midafternoon by the time they reached the coastal city of Klaipėda and made the ferry crossing to the beaches of Neringa. After half an hour of sunning and swimming, they'd pile back into the car for the multistage schlep back to Vilnius. First thing next morning, the Zaz went into the shop.

But there was no dawdling on the way to Neringa this morning, not in the new Lithuania. For every minute frittered away then Liudas seemed determined to make up two minutes now, and so he turned the A-1 highway into a blur of freshly built convenience stores, lone trees in open pastureland, and billboards for joints serving *cepelinai,* the blimp-shaped potato dumplings that are Lithuania's national dish.

On a long descent just past Kaunas, the radar detector came alive. Liudas hit the brakes with several incriminating pumps. Too late: A policeman was already striding across the median at the bottom of the hill, motioning for us to pull over. We scrambled to hide the fuzzbuster.

"You have a radar detector," the cop said.

"No," Liudas said.

"I can tell by the way you stopped. You have a radar detector."

"No, no," Liudas said, with a little less conviction.

The cop examined the registration, which identified the car as a steed out of the stable of the Hotel Šarūnas in Vilnius. His tone softened as he addressed Liudas once again.

"Don't lie to me."

Liudas fessed up, but he was spared having to fork over either the radar detector or the $70 fine. "In the old days I would have had to pay him off," he said as we resumed our trip. "Now he just wants you to pass along greetings to Šarūnas."

My trip to Lithuania had begun in Manhattan, shortly after returning from Ontario. Šarūnas was passing through town, and my wife and I had him over for dinner. Marčiulionis is a man best judged by his business card, which is plastered with more logos than a NASCAR Chevy. One represents the Hotel Šarūnas. Another is for the Šarūnas Marčiulionis Basketball School (motto: "Be a master of strength and a slave to honesty!"). Others stand for the Lithuanian Basketball League he serves as president, and the brand of potato chips he endorses; soon his card would add the logo of the Northern European Basketball League (NEBL), which he was in the throes of founding. But the most telling insignia is that of the foundation that administers his charitable interests, including the Šarūnas Lithuanian Children's Fund. It depicts a lone man in silhouette, straining to lift a boulder above his head. As hard as Marčiulionis had worked on behalf of a fledgling Lithuania, he seemed as much Sisyphus as Atlas. "He has now maybe eight responsibilities," Liudas would tell me. "Hotel. School. League. Children's fund. He is sports ambassador for foreign ministry, too. Even he agrees this is too many."

Marčiulionis won a gold medal with the Soviet Union's last Olympic team at the 1988 Games in Seoul. Then he took his six feet four inches and sudden first step to the NBA, where he spent eight seasons slashing through defenses for the Golden State Warriors, Seattle SuperSonics, and Denver Nuggets. After his country won its independence in 1991, it wasn't enough for him to join 7'2" center Arvydas Sabonis, who would eventually become a Portland Trail Blazer, on the Lithuanian team that won a bronze medal at the 1992 Olympics in Barcelona. In the first blush of freedom, Marčiulionis all but assembled that team. He picked out the uniforms. He hammered out a sneaker deal. He rounded up sponsors ranging from Bank of America to the Grateful Dead, which prevailed on one of its licensees to design the tie-dyed T-shirt that became as prized a souvenir of the end of the cold war as a chunk of the Berlin Wall.

Šarūnas did all this in his usual manner, a style a Deadhead might call Not Fade Away. Three times before turning 10 he had won Lithuanian age-group tennis titles, doing so by switching his racquet from right hand to left, swatting nothing but forehands—a detail that says much about his personality. Growing up, his sister Zita found her little brother so starkly different from their mother, a genial geography teacher, and their father, an engineer with a winsome manner, that she sought out an astrologer for an explanation. He's a Gemini, she was told: He wants to be in motion and with people.

That evening in Manhattan, Šarūnas spotted a print on the wall of our apartment that depicts Napoleon's fateful Russian campaign over the winter of 1812–13. The cartographic equivalent of a triple double, the map not only traces, with an ever-narrowing band of color, the route the French took and the thinning of their ranks, but also plots their progress against both date and plunging temperature. Šarūnas was fascinated. He fixed his finger on Vilnius, the city through which Napoleon's army advanced with 450,000 troops and retreated with 8,000. Watching Šarūnas step back, I wondered what had moved him more: Sympathy with this piece of paper that seemed to have as many things going on at once as he did? Or the concept of attrition, to which he was being introduced for the first time in his life?

I'd gone to Vilnius in the fall of 1992, shortly after those Barcelona Olympics, to find Marčiulionis afflicted with a kind of elated exhaustion. Surely no Olympian who had won gold at a previous Games was ever so happy with a bronze. "They were two completely different things," he told me then. "Most athletes finish their careers after winning the gold, because it's a dream. But our bronze was like a beginning, a new era. The gold in '88 was for each of us as individuals. But the bronze—we knew who we were playing for."

Over dessert I asked Šarūnas why basketball was such a big deal in his homeland. He could scarcely conceal his contempt for so silly a question.

"Because of the history!" he said.

And so, a little ashamedly, I spent the days before departure studying up. I started with the national anthem, the first two lines of which are, "Lithuania, my homeland, land of heroes! Let your sons draw strength from the past!" I read about Steponas Darius, a Lithuanian-American aviator who, before perishing in a crash 650 miles short of completing a New York–to–Kaunas nonstop flight in 1933, spread the gospel with his book *The Basketball Game*. (Imagine the glory reflected on basketball in North America if Doc Naismith had also piloted the *Spirit of St. Louis*.) And I learned about a man named Frank Lubin.

Lubin lived more or less his entire life in Los Angeles until his death in 1999 at age 88. After playing the pivot for the gold-medal-winning U.S. team at the 1936 Olympics in Berlin, he expected to return to his job as a $50-a-week stagehand in Hollywood, and perhaps play a little amateur ball on the side. But the studios, angry that he had abandoned the backlots to participate in the Nazi Olympics, refused to rehire him. So in the fall of 1936 Lubin left California for his ancestral home, which was enjoying a 20-year interregnum of independence before the Soviet jackboot would replace the tsar's.

For three years, as Pranas Lubinas, Frank Lubin ruled Lithuanian basketball. As a coach he introduced ball movement and the fast break, distinctly American concepts that would come to characterize the Baltic game. And as a 6'7", 235-pound center he led Lithuania to the 1937 European Championship, scoring the last basket of a 24–23 defeat of Italy in the final.

Two years later Lithuania had the right to defend its European crown at home, and the government hastily built a new sports hall in Kaunas. By then so many European countries were trying to pass off hyphenated American nationals as indigenous talent that FIBA, the international federation, moved to limit eligibility to native-born players. The Lithuanian Basketball Federation produced a creased birth certificate with Cyrillic characters stipulating that Lubinas had been born in a village near Kaunas on a particular day in 1911. Skeptical, FIBA cabled the U.S., asking the Amateur Athletic Union to check its records. Lithuania had already defended its European title, with a 37–36 defeat of Latvia, when the AAU's reply arrived at the FIBA offices in Geneva: Frank Lubin had indeed been born on that date—in Los Angeles.

World War II forestalled any further investigation or punishment, and Lithuania's most durable modern myth—the country's supremacy in the game of *krepšinis*—also went unchallenged. Ever since, Lithuanians have used the word "Lubinas" the way others refer to a Goliath or a Leviathan. Indeed, Lithuanians still bemusedly point out that the Latvian government lodged a diplomatic protest after the final, not because of doubts about Lubinas's eligibility, but because it believed he was so huge that his very participation violated the spirit of sportsmanship. To this day, Latvia regards itself as 1939 Normal-Sized European Champions.

Frank Lubin returned to Southern California before World War II broke out, resuming work as a grip on TV soundstages. But by the time he left he had taught the game to a generation of young players, who would in turn coach Marčiulionis, Sabonis, and their contemporaries. With Sabonis at center, and the clever point guard Vitoldas Masalskis directing play, Lithuania's flagship club team, Žalgiris Kaunas, so captivated the public during the 1980s that every clerk in every liquor store knew: If a customer asked for a Sabonis, he wanted a big bottle of vodka; if he asked for a Masalskis, he wanted a small one.

Žalgiris won three Soviet championships in that decade, each time defeating CSKA Moscow, the Soviet Red Army team that represented the nation's occupiers with its very name. Émigrés celebrated each title as the next best thing to liberation, while Lithuanians still living under Soviet rule savored the victories as much as political conditions allowed. In the diaspora and at home, Lithuanians loved to point out that their countrymen scored all but 20 of the Soviet national team's points in its 82–76 defeat of the U.S. on the way to the 1988 Olympic gold in Seoul.

After independence in 1990, Lithuanians knew only one way to celebrate their national identity: to resurrect the country's last mark on the international stage, that 1939 European basketball title. At the 1992 Olympics, Lithuania's first accomplishment as a new nation was another hoop exploit, a defeat of the Soviet Union, rechristened the Commonwealth of Independent States, for the bronze. Basketball had bridged more than 50 years between two incarnations of the independent state, and citizens honored the game by exalting its place in their lives. Politicians regularly trotted out basketball analogies in parliament and on the stump. Lithuanians played in firemen's leagues, accountants' leagues, and leagues for bank clerks and civil servants. As Liudas liked to say, "We have three and a half million people, and half of them are coaches."

But that hoopheadedness came at a price. "If the national

team finishes in fourth place in any competition—with no medal—it is a national tragedy," Algimantas Pavilonis, manager of the Lithuanian team, would tell me. "But we have no choice. This is the best way to express Lithuania to the world. People understand that, and that's why they adore basketball. But it's not easy being a saint. Eventually, even saints die."

At the time of my visit Šarūnas was still in the States, scaring up sponsors for the NEBL. So he had vouchsafed me to Liudas, who was under orders to show me the country's greatest natural feature. "You must see Neringa!" Šarūnas had said with such enthusiasm that I imagined the logo of the tourism ministry muscling its way onto that business card.

Known to English speakers as the Couronian Spit, Neringa is a 60-mile long sandbar on the country's west coast, never more than several miles across, that the winds and tides of the Baltic have sculpted over eons into a pristine ecosystem of sand, water, and woods. Fishermen pull eel, flounder, and pike from the lagoon, and in Nida, Neringa's main village, you can buy a specimen of that morning's catch smoked to delectation. "In some places the lagoon is no more than two meters high," Šarūnas had said. "Sabonis could walk across it!"

By this he meant that a seven-footer could ford the lagoon, not literally walk atop it. But it's not inconceivable that a Lithuanian basketball hero would be credited with hydroper-ambulatory powers. This was the last European country to adopt Christianity, and a strong strain of paganism persisted among the people, including a mystical belief in the power of trees. Marčiulionis and Sabonis were known as the Lithuanian Oaks, and they'd both been garlanded with oak leaves upon returning from Barcelona. The solitary trees I'd seen during our drive were oaks given wide berth by reverent farmers. The forest had harbored the partisan Forest Brothers, who waged an eight-year guerrilla war against the Soviets until a general amnesty following Stalin's death.

Soon after we disembarked the ferry to Neringa, I saw forest as I'd never seen it before. Pines mingled with deciduous trees in full autumn finery, while a spackle of moss, Day-Glo green, covered the forest floor. In Nida we picked up some take-away fish, then doubled back for the port city of Klaipėda, where the home team, Neptūnas, would be hosting Marčiulionis's old club, Lietuvos Rytas.

The game took place in a flyblown firetrap, with a balcony the architect hardly should have bothered with, for it accommodated only a few rows of seats. With their Betty Sue outfits and first names heat-transferred to the backs of their sweaters, the cheerleaders appeared to have been lifted from the fifties. The brightest touch was the Neptūnas mascot, King Neptune himself, a hook-nosed, white-haired, trident-wielding monarch. But the basketball outdid its trappings. Lithuanians play the game with range, agility, and guile. American hoops chauvinists often deride European players as "mechanical" or "soft," but that seemed to me a slander. At a time when many Americans are supple and showy but wouldn't know a fundamental if it reverse-pivoted in their face, we should all be so mechanical. The players I saw in Klaipėda could all pass, defend, box out, and, most of all, shoot.

As for softness, a place on this court wasn't for the weak of heart. In the game's waning moments, with victory for the home team secure, a Neptūnas player broke away for a layup. Lietuvos Rytas's star guard, Šarūnas Jasikevičius, who had played the previous few seasons at Maryland, gave chase and knocked his rival hard to the floor, touching off a cry of "Rapist!" from one fan. The bump and grind of the Atlantic Coast Conference, and the invective of the Duke student section and Jasikevičius's own college coach, the tungsten-tongued Gary Williams, couldn't have been any tougher than this.

Jasikevičius had returned to Lithuania after his collegiate sojourn in the States, but Marius Janulis, a former Neptūnas star who played for Syracuse, was more representative of the career path traced by talented young Lithuanian players. Neptūnas had developed Janulis from the time he was in grade school, and the club had counted on him for this season. But after bottoming out a jumper to win an NCAA tournament game for the Orangemen, Janulis took a job with a computer company outside Boston. This was how the generation that was supposed to succeed Marčiulionis and Sabonis was being picked clean: Young Lithuanians eagerly enrolled at any American college, and even if they made no progress as ballplayers, the value of a degree kept them there. "Parents want to be able to tell their neighbors that their kid is going to school in the U.S., getting an education, and learning English," Šarūnas had told me. "So kids go even to junior colleges or Division II or III schools where there's no real basketball competition. Last year we had 25 candidates for the junior national team leave for the States, and a lot of them just disappeared. It hurts."

In a bookshop in Vilnius's Old Town I spotted an English copy of *Petersen's Sports Scholarships and Athletic Programs in the U.S.A.* ("Over 300 listings!"). It was kept up front by the register, to discourage anyone from giving it a furtive thumbing-through. But it spoke to Šarūnas's point. In this new nation, gaining a secure foothold in an uncertain future was more important than grasping at any hoop dream. Vilnius-raised Nobel laureate Czesław Miłosz points out that the Balts, as essentially peasant people, possess both peasant virtues, like thrift and diligence, and peasant faults, like stinginess and obsessive worry about the future. It was within their nature to choose the surer thing, and the surer thing wasn't a flyer on a pro basketball career.

I asked Liudas about this on the drive back. By my lights, the back injury that had ended his career was a blessing. He had picked up his marketing degree and hooked on as Šarūnas's aide-de-camp. Liudas conceded the point, but assured me that becoming a basketball professional was still a respectable goal. "In Lithuania today, if you have money, you have no reputation, because your money is black money. If you have reputation, you are teacher, scientist, artist—but you have no money. Only basketball player has money *and* reputation."

We pulled into the parking lot of the Hotel Šarūnas by

10 P.M. In a single day we'd crossed the country, touched the Baltic, seen a spirited game of hoops, and returned to Vilnius without, Liudas proudly noted, requiring the services of a mechanic. The Ford needed only a fumigator, to get rid of the smell of smoked flounder.

One of my goals in coming to Lithuania was to find someone with living memory of the exploits of the late 1930s, whether a player, coach, or eyewitness fan. Unfortunately, most of the players on those two European title teams were Lithuanian-Americans who, like Lubin, reemigrated after 1939 and lived out their lives in the States. Of the few who stayed, all but a handful wound up casualties either of World War II or the Stalinist purges that followed, and the last survivor had passed away in Kaunas four years earlier. But just as I was beginning to despair of finding any link to the past, I discovered one in the unlikeliest place.

I had talked basketball with a head of state only once, in 1993, when the White House suddenly granted a long-standing request to plumb Bill Clinton's passion for the Arkansas Razorbacks. The most sobering thing I learned in that session was that the leader of the free world sometimes yelled back at the image of Dick Vitale on his TV set—an admission that probably ought to constitute grounds for invoking the 22nd Amendment. I've always believed I got that interview because of the quickening rapids of the Whitewater scandal, and talking hoops served the White House's purpose as a diversion. So perhaps all the business then before Valdas Adamkus, the 71-year-old president of Lithuania, accounted for my being ushered through the metal detector in the foyer of the Presidential Palace, up a balustraded staircase, past gilt-edged mirrors, and into an office that was decidedly non-oval. Never mind that Adamkus was to leave shortly for a visit with Clinton in Washington, or that Russia and the ruble were going all kerblooey. Word had come from a friend of a journalist friend: If the subject were hoops, the president could make time.

It turned out Adamkus had the perfect pedigree to lead an independent Lithuania. In 1939, at grave risk to his standing in grade school, he had skipped class and snuck into the Kaunas Sports Hall for the European final against Latvia. A few years later he fled with his family to Chicago, where he waited out most of the Nazi and Soviet occupations, first as an autoworker, then as a civil engineer, and for nearly 30 years as an official with the Environmental Protection Agency before repatriating himself in 1993 to enter the hurly-burly of postindependence Lithuanian politics. (There's a tantalizing, decade-long entry in his official bio: "1960–69, owner-operator of summer resort in Sodus, Mich." Any Lithuanian on the street will tell you, with a nudge and a wink, that Adamkus spent this period helping the CIA interrogate captured Soviet spies.) He had won election the previous January despite his opponent's attempt to paint him as a carpetbagger—"a bigger fan of the Chicago Bulls than of the Lithuanian national team."

In fact, from Chicago, Adamkus followed Lithuanian hoops with a get-a-lifer's passion. If Žalgiris Kaunas played a Soviet league game against Red Army Moscow, he would tune into Voice of America to catch the score. If someone at the *Tribune* or the *Sun-Times,* so help him, referred to Sabonis or Masalskis as "a Russian," Adamkus would place an indignant call to the sports desk. In 1939, from the window of his family's Kaunas apartment, he had watched the frantic, round-the-clock construction of the Sports Hall in advance of the European Championships. He snuck into the final, he would tell me, because "it was difficult to get a ticket, and I didn't have the money."

The day before I met with the president, Liudas had reached Šarūnas in San Diego and told him of my appointment, then handed me the cell phone. "Be sure to tell Adamkus about the NEBL!" Šarūnas said. "Tell him how important it is! As a country, we have no oil, no computers, no *nothing!* We have only basketball!"

I couldn't quite bring myself to quote him exactly, but I did mention Šarūnas's latest ball in the air to Adamkus, and the president made clear that he supported the new league, which was to be headquartered in Vilnius and feature two Lithuanian teams.

"My entire life I've believed that basketball and Lithuania are synonymous," he said. "I've never doubted it, not even when we were forced to play for the Soviet Union. During the occupation, for 50 years, basketball was the expression of freedom. The entire country was trying to beat the Russians, to show that we were supreme in that respect. The game reflected our will to win against our oppressors and sustained our hope and resolve. Even in Seoul, winning the gold medal—how could you call it the Soviet Union when there were four Lithuanians on the court in the final? If Lithuania plays the game at the highest level today, winning Olympic medals, it's just the continuation of that tradition."

Just west of Vilnius's Old Town stands the unlikeliest of monuments: a bust of Frank Zappa, rendered by a sculptor whose oeuvre otherwise consists of heads out of the Communist pantheon. With much of the world having become aware of Lithuanian basketball thanks to the Grateful Dead, I wondered if shrines to other rock acts were in the offing—to Led Zeppelin, perhaps, in honor of what a *cepelinas* feels like in the pit of the stomach.

They served those starchy dirigibles at Men's Joy, the basement sports bar I'd ducked into, even as most of the patrons preferred liquid sustenance. Tonight was EuroLeague night, and the Žalgiris game on TV offered an engaging subplot. Gintaras Einikis, the starting center for Lithuania's national team and a former stalwart with Žalgiris, now played for Autodor Saratov, the Russian club that would be Žalgiris's host.

Both Saratov and its team emblematized the anarchy into which Russia was then slipping. According to the papers, conditions in Saratov were medieval. The beds in Žalgiris's hotel didn't reach six feet. Heat was rare and electricity even more so. The Autodor owner had made his money in oil, and for a player he had just paid a transfer fee to a Latvian club with the most stable currency available to him—three railroad cars of crude. When the Žalgiris delegation reached the border, Russian customs agents had thoughtfully offered to confiscate everybody's cell phones, pointing out that, with no phone service, they'd be of no use.

For some reason, three years earlier Einikis had chosen to leave Kaunas for this misbegotten outpost on the Volga. Perhaps he was won over by the solicitude of the people, who had made him an honorary citizen; maybe, exasperated by all the attention a ballplayer in Lithuania gets—particularly a publicly hard-drinking, seven-foot-tall one—he simply wanted to be left alone. In Saratov no one bothered him, and he could while away his days at the local casino.

But around the cellar tables in Vilnius, patrons advanced darker theories to explain why Einikis would forsake Žalgiris for Autodor. One fan suggested that Autodor had failed to pay Einikis all he was due a year earlier and issued a threat. "I am sure of it," the man said. "They say, 'Stay, and you see the rest of your money. Go, and we don't know what happens to you.' Deal with guys like that, it is like the dark side of the moon. I see no other reason for Einikis to choose to play in Saratov. You think it is good to play there? It is like a *prison*."

When Einikis did get paid, it was in wads of ruble notes. In the two months since the season began, the value of the ruble had tumbled, from four to the dollar to 80. So he and his teammates treated their salary as if it were lettuce. On paydays they stuffed it into suitcases and lugged it by train to Moscow, 400 miles away, to convert it into hard currency before it could go bad.

The crowd had other reasons to pick on Einikis besides his decision to play in Russia. Two months earlier, just before the World Championships in Athens, he had been kicked off the Lithuanian national team for excessive drinking. The coach brought him back only after Einikis signed a pledge not to imbibe until the competition was over. After Lithuania lost to Russia at the Worlds, on its way to a shameful seventh-place finish, he was seen sharing a cigarette and a laugh with several Russian players. Šarūnas had witnessed the scene, and it disgusted him. "If we lost to the Russians in the quarterfinals of the Worlds," he had told me, "Sabonis and me would have *cried all day!*"

The broadcast began. A pregame tease morphed the word *EuroLyga,* or EuroLeague, into *EuroLiga,* which means Euro-Sickness. Images of medicine bottles and hospital beds drove home the point: Lithuanians regarded Thursday Night Basketball with the same addled devotion that Americans once did Monday Night Football. The quality of the TV feed was primitive, with Cyrillic graphics and no visible clock, and the camera angle cut off play at the near sideline, but I could follow the action well enough. Though Žalgiris started three former NBA players—onetime Oklahoma star Anthony Bowie and ex-UCLA teammates Tyus Edney and George Zidek—only the ungainly Eurelijus Žukauskas, the neckless center who didn't begin playing the game until age 17, was having any success controlling Einikis. Žukauskas blocked several of his shots early, much to the delight of the crowd.

"Einikis, you're an asshole!" one patron cried.

But over the course of the game Einikis consistently got the better of Zidek, the plodding Czech whom Žalgiris had signed after Einikis turned the club down. Žalgiris pulled within a basket in the final minutes. But Zidek failed to bottom out a critical hook shot, Einikis finished with 30 points, and Autodor won, 87–82.

During my visit to the Presidential Palace, I had asked Adamkus whether it bothered him that the center on his country's national team played for a Russian club. The president fell silent for a beat, and I sensed an interlude during which a diplomatic point is either made, or made a mess of. Adamkus figuratively took a deep breath and bent his knees before launching a shot. "No, it doesn't bother me," he said. "If we really believe in the principles of democracy, we should be free to choose in every part of our lives. You could turn the question around and ask if it hurts me to see Sabonis play for the Portland Trail Blazers, or [Žydrūnas] Ilgauskas play for the Cleveland Cavaliers. It simply shows that we can contribute internationally, that our players can play at the highest levels. And that gives recognition to Lithuania and our school of basketball. Freedom of choice is part of what democracy is."

In their more reflective moments, the patrons at Men's Joy might have accepted so finely drawn an answer. But given that they'd spent the game getting oiled up, these weren't those moments. Nonetheless, as chairs scraped the floor and the bar slowly emptied, the fans had a last laugh of sorts, a satisfaction that could be credited to nothing more than their country's freedom. No, it isn't easy being a saint. But Lithuanian basketball still stood for Lithuanian independence, which beat what had come before. And tonight these fans had paid their tabs in Lithuanian litas. Tomorrow Einikis would still be lugging a suitcase full of rubles.

THREE

Poland
The Sultans of Złoty

At $15, the bus from Vilnius to Warsaw might be Europe's best deal on wheels. It might also be the worst, for the ride lasts 11 hours and the driver finds sport in passing on blind curves. On the outskirts of the Polish capital prostitutes clustered in the stark light of late afternoon, some leaning against crucifixes planted along the roadside.

This was not America. Nevertheless, an American friend was trying to make a go of it as a coach in a midsized town a half hour out on the commuter line from Warsaw's Central Station. Pruszków features Catholic churches, quiet residential neighborhoods, and, if you don't mind muddy streets without sidewalks, walkable dimensions. I could see why Mike McCollow would take a job there, given that he had debt to pay off and a family to support, and he'd spent eight years kicking around mid-major college and minor-league pro ball in the States.

On the other hand, Pruszków is the Palermo of Poland. Some ill-shaven man in a track suit can supply any illicit commodity, be it sex, drugs, a hot stereo, or smuggled liquor. Pekaes, the club team Mike was to coach, had won two of the previous three Polish titles, and as the club attracted more and more of the limelight, Pruszków's wiseguys came out from the shadows to share in it. Pekaes had lost the seventh game of the Polish championship series the previous spring, and to a number of influential members of the town's business community the team might as well have turned down an offer it couldn't refuse. In the still of Pruszków's *hala sportowa*, as those final seconds ticked away and the opposition prepared to celebrate, spectators could hear the squeal of tires outside and knew exactly where they came from: the Mercedes of a fan known as Big Jarek, patching furiously out of the parking lot.

Pruszków wasn't an easy place to play, but it was an even harder one in which to coach. Pekaes had gone through three coaches in four years, firing one shortly after he led the team to the 1997 Polish title. Still Mike had taken the job, even as he knew that a championship might not be enough to keep it.

I'd gotten to know Mike when he was a carefree undergraduate hoophead, eager to help me track down the best pickup basketball courts in America for the sequel to *The In-Your-Face Basketball Book*. Now he regarded the game with complete seriousness. He was 32, coiled in both physique and temperament, with a wife and two preschool-age kids. He wore a ring from a season spent in the Continental Basketball Association as an aide to Flip Saunders, with whom he had led the La Crosse (Wisconsin) Catbirds to the 1992 CBA title before Saunders moved on to become coach of the NBA's Minnesota Timberwolves. Mike had been a graduate assistant at Oklahoma State, then a full-fledged one at North Texas, when his daughter, Meg, was diagnosed with a rare cancerlike disease called histiocytosis. The particular strain of the disease turned out to be a self-healing one, but the McCollows moved back to the Twin Cities to be near a specialist at the University of Minnesota. Mike signed on as head coach and virtually the entire front office of the St. Paul Slam of the International Basketball Association, but the gig ended after a single season in a rancorous mess, with the club being sold even as the old owner owed him what Mike figured to be $70,000. He was able to recover only $1,000, and at the time Pekaes came calling he was working part-time scouting potential sites for a golf course entrepreneur, while his wife, Katie, designed patterns for needlepoint kits.

After Mike's misadventure with the Slam, anxious relatives pressed him about his new post. "You have a *signed contract,* right?" they asked. He reassured them with what had reassured him—testimony of his assistant with the Slam, a former Pekaes player, that the club had never shorted anyone so much as a złoty. In his optimistic moments, Mike permitted himself to imagine winning a Polish title, moving on to a better-paying job in Italy or Greece, climbing out of debt, then making a down payment on a house back in the Twin Towns.

Mike had grown up in the Minneapolis suburb of Bloomington, but "Minnesota nice" didn't get him right. Most basketball coaches lack the irony gene, for irony isn't a useful trait when you're trying to get players to believe that life itself depends on chasing down the next loose ball. But Mike could drift into sarcasm. Lampooning the hypocrisies and pomposities of the coaching trade, he sometimes seemed repelled by the profession even as he wanted to make his mark in it.

At the same time, Mike could pull on a letter sweater from the old school. He was still the holler guy who had been a star guard in high school and at Avila College, an NAIA school in Kansas City. Pekaes's management seemed to have ambition to match his, and Mike liked that. He could have suited up the same players who had nearly won a title the season before, but he was determined to install a new offense and instill a new attitude. "Like in *Hoosiers,*" he told me, sounding as removed from ironic as a coach could be. "Break 'em down, then build 'em back up."

Poland was no incubator of basketball talent. Since the 1936 Olympics, where the Poles nearly won a medal and Doc Naismith declared their style the most appealing one he saw, the Polish game had regressed sharply. Only one player, a forward at Providence during the 1980s named Jacek Duda, had made a mark in the U.S., and that was because teammates called him "Zippity." Pekaes nonetheless fielded four players from the national team, including Dominik Tomczyk, a 6'9" small forward likened to Croatia's Toni Kukoč, the NBA veteran. Tomczyk collected $150,000 a year in a country where the average citizen made $3,000. "Nobody here is a basketball genius," Mike had told me over the phone, shortly after he arrived in Pruszków. "But he's a three man who can play the two or the four, and the closest thing you'll find to a complete player."

As for Americans, Mike had three—or at least two going on three. One was a 6'3" guard fresh out of Texas Christian named Mike Jones. M.J. didn't do one thing superbly, but he could do a range of things very well—defend, rebound, pass, and shoot. His fiancée, Stacie Terry, was playing for Polonia, a women's team in Warsaw, so stability marked both M.J.'s game and his life, which was good given the notorious instability of another one of Pekaes's Americans.

Richard Dumas, a 6'7" forward with a chiseled physique, had scored 25 points for the Phoenix Suns in Game 5 of the 1993 NBA Finals, dunking on Michael Jordan, Scottie Pippen, and Bill Cartwright in a single quarter. He still carried a videotape of that game around with him like a rosary. But Dumas's life before and after that moment had been marked by chronic substance abuse, and he returned to cocaine and liquor as quickly as he had up and shone in that one game. Yet Dumas had now cleared detox. He came vouched for, and he came cheap. Because of his past, Pekaes was able to sign him to a $7,000-a-month contract, nonguaranteed and renewable each month. He was a risk, but if he really had cleaned up, he'd be a steal. Mike had called a dozen basketball people he knew and respected, virtually pleading with each to talk him out of agreeing to take the gamble. "Richard stood for everything I'm against," Mike had told me. "And virtually everyone I spoke to said, 'You know, he's awful talented.'"

The half mercenary was Steve Wojciechowski, the 5'10" point guard from Duke who, surname notwithstanding, was 100 percent American. Because of Polish league rules restricting teams to two non-Europeans each, Wojo couldn't play if Dumas and M.J. suited up. The only Polish he knew was "Krzyzewski," and you had to go back to great-grandparents on his father's side to find anyone born in the old country. Still, as a result of Mike's spadework, Pekaes was able to bring Wojo over on a two-month trial, to see how he liked Poland and how Poland liked him, and whether the club or its influential friends could push through his bid for Polish basketball citizenship. For now, the name looked good and Wojo's hustling style enlivened practice.

"Wojo's exactly what the team needs," Mike had told me. "Our Polish players have a lot of talent, but zero passion and fire. M.J. doesn't have superstar talent—he's not a break-you-down-and-score-20-on-his-own kind of player. But he's a hard-working, solid character. If Dumas is who Dumas can be, we'll be fine. And if the Wojo citizenship thing comes through, it's a bonus. In a lot of ways, this is the perfect job. There are a lot of talented, decent guys. All they need is some coaching."

But the last time I'd spoken with Mike, from Springfield a month into the season, everything had changed. "We've lost four in a row," he said. "Dumas has fallen off the wagon with an earth-shattering thud. Nobody on our team has been paid in three months. Which means I haven't received one cent, my wife is an emotional wreck, and our players are threatening to strike. Last week we were up nine in the final minutes against a Latvian team at home. We locked up against a zone and lost by a point. I've never seen more finger-pointing than after that one."

Dumas had found his old friends, or rather they'd found him—no surprise, for they lurked on every street corner in Pruszków. The Polish Kukoč hadn't played a minute yet because of injuries. Meanwhile the club's sponsor, a bus and trucking firm, did 60 percent of its business in Russia, and the ruble's slide had pinched the company's balance sheet. The Pekaes Corporation was in no mood to make up the shortfall after the club lost its secondary sponsor, a Polish soft drink company that Coke and Pepsi were muscling aside. Though Pekaes had earmarked $1 million for basketball during the fiscal year, management refused to free up that money until the club found an additional patron.

"With the salary thing, I've tried to make like Lech Wałęsa, solidarity and all that, but it's fallen on deaf ears," Mike said. "The guys have no idea what it means to play hard. And they have no idea that they're not talented enough to win *unless* they play hard. Our second-division team and our reserves routinely win scrimmages in practice, and that tells me everything I need to know. When you're more talented and you don't win, you're coasting.

"It's not that they're individualistic. It's that they're blasé. They don't play for the love of the game. We grew up playing in the park or the gym, winners hold the court. You sat if you didn't win, so you played hard if you wanted to play at all. Over here, there's a select group of Poles skilled enough to play at this level, and no one's pushing to replace them. And my piss and vinegar just doesn't seem to go over."

Mike had tried pushing every button he could think of. His sister-in-law had come over to visit and spent a day with Katie at Auschwitz, and the two had returned with chilling stories just before Pekaes was to play a German team, Ratiopharm Ulm. Trying to shake his players out of their self-pity, Mike mentioned the war and the camps in his pregame remarks. "Just mentioned how a lot of people in the world have it worse, and how that country had oppressed theirs. I'm sure the guys thought I was crazy. They were just looking down at their shoes. Then we went out and played our worst half of the year.

"Tomorrow we play on the road against a team that's 4-1, and if we don't win, we're cooked. My luck's gotta change. I'm Irish."

Having been incommunicado in Lithuania for a week, I called Mike the moment I checked into the Warsaw Marriott.

The team's fortunes had taken a turn. In their make-or-break game—on the road against that 4-1 team—Pekaes had won, 77–74. Mike had taken one look at Dumas on game day and concluded he'd be a waste. So he suited up Wojciechowski as one of his Americans instead, and Wojo sank all four of his three-pointers. The Polish Kukoč, playing for the first time all season, sealed the victory with a couple of free throws.

Before heading for Cyprus for their next game, the players had declared that if money didn't appear in their bank accounts within three days, they'd quit and start shopping themselves around as free agents. In Nicosia they won again, and when they returned to Pruszków on the eve of the deadline, the president of Pekaes, without waiting for the approval of his board, dipped into company coffers to pay the Polish players two of the three months' salary due them. The Americans, coach McCollow included, got one month apiece.

Then, the night before my arrival, Pekaes had scored its biggest success of the season. Pruszków defeated Nobiles Anwil Włocławek, the unbeaten team at the top of the standings, at home and on national TV with a shot at the buzzer. Mike had found Dumas in town a few hours before the game, intercepting him at a hooch kiosk before he could get a buzz on. "It's time to play," he had told him. "Time to give us one game of Richard Dumas basketball, or we're gonna have to send you home."

That night Dumas shot 8 for 12, threw down six dunks, and sank a signal three-pointer. But the play in the final minutes of three others—M.J. and a couple of Poles—cheered Mike even more. "It was perfect," Mike said. "Our three guys with heart won our biggest game." He had both a victory and an object lesson for the rest of the team.

After losing four in a row, Pekaes had now won four straight. The streak relieved the pressure on Mike, as did news of the sponsor's fiscal woes, which had spilled into the papers and provided an alibi for the team's earlier struggles. But losing and winning in equal measure weren't what the town of Pruszków was accustomed to, and Mike already felt redoubled pressure to make up for the sputtering start. "There are daily talks to find that second sponsor," he said. "But we're still teetering on the brink."

At least he had gotten a measure of protection from the local racketeers. One day Mike and Katie were walking along one of Pruszków's pedestrian-unfriendly streets, pushing a stroller with their kids. A BMW sedan nearly clipped them as it roared by.

"Hey!" Mike yelled, adding an internationally recognized gesture.

The car jolted to a stop. The driver backed up. The passenger-side window rolled down, and a tracksuited foot soldier shot Mike a look out of a Scorsese movie.

"My kids," Mike said imploringly.

The driver nodded. Soon Mike and Katie heard that the word was out: Watch out for the American coach and his family.

I took the train out to Pruszków the next morning. The distensions of urban Warsaw gave way quickly to tidy houses attached to small plots of beets and potatoes. Pruszków itself hardly existed until World War II, when the Nazis razed Warsaw and refugees fled to settle there. With the end of the cold war, organized crime soon followed. The town's sinister reputation complicated Pekaes's search for a second sponsor. Yet even if mobsters were among the team's most passionate fans, Mike was sure the club itself was clean. It had to be, he figured, or everyone would have been paid in full by now, and some civil servant who knew what was good for him would have waved Wojo's bid for citizenship through.

At the station I handed Mike a copy of the *USA Today* of Poland, *Gazeta Wyborcza*, which featured an advance on Pekaes's game that night with Spartak Moscow. The paper was billing it as the Battle of the Bankrupt Clubs, for the Russians had gone seven months without a paycheck. A color profile shot of *amerykanie trener Mikea McCollowa* dominated the story. "Let's see if we can find the words 'embattled,' 'beleaguered,' or 'fired' anywhere," said Mike, who knew just enough Polish to spot something unflattering. "The New York tabloids don't have anything on these Polish pit bulls."

We walked from the station to the townhouse where the club was putting the McCollows up. After three months, Mike still hadn't received most of the perks in his contract—no car;

no cell phone; no reimbursement for plane fare over. That morning he had gotten into a shouting match with Janusz Wierzbowski, the Pekaes general manager. Countless times Mike and Katie had pleaded for someone to cut the grass around their place, where they were essentially marooned with two toddlers, so their kids could have space to play. Mike regarded this as the simplest of requests. He pleaded for a lawnmower so he could do the job himself. But to Janusz, a besieged executive with no money and very nearly no team, this seemed like a peevish demand. "You have a game today, and you're obsessed about the grass?"

Mike could see Janusz's point, but resented it just the same. "We hear 'You must wait' all the time. Doing anything here requires patience, and I guess patience is a virtue I do not have. Wojo and M.J. and I want to have T-shirts made up that say YOU MUST WAIT. Only we don't have the money."

I tagged along to the team's shootaround, where the Pekaes trainer asked Mike to wait some more: The Polish Kukoč had reinjured his knee and would be out for six more weeks.

Wojciechowski was stretching on the sideline. He had arrived in Pruszków two months earlier, on his 22nd birthday. He had yet to cash a paycheck or find his own place to live, and his quest for a hoop green card was going nowhere. Every meeting on the subject ended with someone suggesting he simply marry a Pole, and he was sick of hearing it. "That's not happening," he said. "My mother would go nuts."

So Wojo was left to sleep on the couch in M.J. and Stacie's apartment, wondering why he was in Poland at all when he could be in grad school, or pick from among job offers from ESPN and Wall Street, or get started in a coaching career of his own. "Last year at this time I was on the cover of *Sports Illustrated* and in a make-believe world," he said. "Here it's real, and not one thing has gone right. I wish there was something I could hang on to. Either the citizenship thing, or the money, or a bed to sleep on. Something. I guess we're just the Bad News Bears of Poland. One day I hate the world. The next day M.J. does. So we balance each other out."

Wojo shot a look down at the far end of the court. "And then there's Richard, who hates the world every day."

Dumas was shooting lazy jump shots in his old Phoenix Suns jersey, which gave prominence to the tattoo on one biceps reading BEWARE DOOM BOOM/STILL LETHAL. That tattoo was intended to make opponents cower. Instead it was looking more and more like a warning label on a toxic substance. Dumas lived in a townhouse opposite the McCollows, and the day the strike was averted, Mike had looked out his window to see a stream of Pruszkówian characters filing in to party with a freshly paid Doom Boom.

From his time on the staff at Oklahoma State, where Dumas went to college, Mike had known of his player's extravagant reserves of potential and maddening determination to squander it. "People told me he looked good, that he'd gotten off cocaine," Mike said. "And when I talked to Richard, he said all the right things. 'I know this is my last chance'—the usual routine. But he was out of shape when he got here, and I could tell within two days that he was drinking again."

Mike urged Janusz to send him home. Janusz declined, and in retrospect, that struck Mike as the first sign that the club was bankrupt: Pekaes couldn't get rid of Dumas, because it couldn't replace him—because a replacement would actually insist on getting paid. "But if we don't make a change," Mike said, "we may find ourselves too far out in the league."

A month earlier, Dumas had confessed to Mike that he had never gone without at least a couple of beers a day since he was 14. He didn't feel he had anywhere to turn; he could live with his mother back in Oklahoma, but an ex-wife would be hassling him for payments. Watching Dumas's mood swings, seeing the behavioral tic that caused him to touch his hand to his mouth repeatedly, Mike suspected that Doom Boom had a range of psychological problems, perhaps the result of some childhood trauma.

"It wasn't until this year that I got a full idea of how bad his situation is," Mike said. "We can't be doing him any kind of favor keeping him here when he should be getting his life straightened out. Oklahoma State, Phoenix, Philly, teams in

Venezuela and France, they've all tried to live with him. Why we thought it would be any different here, I don't know. In the end he's like Satan. He tempts you with unbelievable things, but he always gets you in the end."

That night in the *hala sportowa*, just before tip-off against Spartak, Mike turned to the Pekaes official at the scorer's table.

"How do you say aggressive in Polish?"

"Agresywny," came the reply.

"Agresywny!" Mike said as he returned to the huddle. *"Agresywny!"*

Perhaps his players took him too literally, and that's why Pekaes was whistled for fouls on five straight possessions during the first half. Then again, the same official made all five calls.

"Check his passport!" Mike yelled.

Mike would find out later that no one from Pekaes had given the referees a ride in from the airport, a pointless snub given all the stories he'd heard about Polish officiating. "I've been told 75 percent are on the take, if only for a bottle of vodka," he would say. "And that one guy looked like an extra in every Indiana Jones movie."

Agresywny Pekaes nonetheless was. With 13 minutes to play, Dumas had already fouled out. Four minutes later a center joined him on the bench. Then another one of Pekaes's post players took a seat.

It was Churchill who said, "There are few virtues that the Poles do not possess, and there are few errors which they have ever avoided." Mike might have argued with the first half of that statement as it applied to basketball, but I thought I saw the truth of its entirety as Pekaes pushed gamely through its foul trouble. To my eyes, the team was playing hard—so hard that it made a mess of just about every two-on-one and three-on-two opportunity. Still, somehow, Pekaes won, 88–74. To be shorted seven months' pay was apparently more dispiriting than missing three and a half.

Mike flapped his tie at the dozen journalists gathered for the postgame press conference. He had worn the same neckwear through all five of Pekaes's recent victories. "All you guys who think I'm a terrible coach, listen up," he said. "I was just picking out the wrong tie."

The writers had their angle. No one asked a question about Dumas, who had failed to score a field goal. Even the press was beginning to give up on him.

At breakfast the next morning I saw a newspaper headline that read SZCZEŚLIWY KRAWAT. I guessed that *krawat* meant tie. But *szcześliwy* was one place I did not have the courage to go. I showed the story to my waitress, pointing at the word and giving her an inquiring look.

"Happy!" she said with a smile.

Pekaes's next date, a road game in the badlands of southern Poland, lay a few days off. If a single prospect could chill the blood of even the most hardened CBA veteran, it was surely a road game in Silesia. I told Mike I'd meet up with the team for the game that weekend, and left Warsaw for a couple of days to tour more fetching parts of the country.

Much about Poland had left Mike and Katie enchanted. They'd made several good friends and loved to meander through Warsaw's Old Town. One day, having taken their kids to a park in Pruszków, the McCollows watched Meg wordlessly play with a girl who eventually motioned her over to a nearby apartment building. The girl's mother had put two apples in a basket, and she was lowering it by rope from an open window.

But at other times the place seemed like the far rim of a yawning cultural chasm. The language was such a hunter's stew of unpronounceable gristle that whenever Katie cracked open her copy of *Teach Yourself Polish*, she said, "I want to cry." Mike called the country "an Al Bundy dreamworld," and he didn't mean this approvingly. "The guys are all overweight and in sweatshirts and sweatpants, and the women dress to kill," he said. "Turn on the TV and you wouldn't believe some of the stuff you see." Both were still trying to figure out what to make of the coaching tips Mike got via e-mail from Marzena, a teenage moll-in-training whose cyberaddress was "lolita." But Mike most stubbornly resisted the Polish custom of paying to pee. At first he simply refused to pony up, feigning ignorance and striding past the stout babushkas who stationed themselves outside every public toilet. Eventually he gave in, and now tithed regularly at the Church of the Urge.

I sympathized with Mike's disdain for what he called "the one-złoty potty." At a café in Kraków I found myself with nothing but a 20-złoty note, which I duly presented to the attendant upon exiting. She couldn't break it, and so trundled off in a cloud of gibbered consonants, returning after an interval to shower me with a 10-złoty bill and a spray of coins. I was ready to conclude that there's nothing quite so discomfiting as performing a financial transaction with a 70-year-old woman moments after stowing oneself. Then I made a day trip to Auschwitz.

About Auschwitz there is nothing to say but this: If Mike had gone there, he never would have mentioned it pregame in Ulm.

On Saturday I took the train from Kraków to Sosnowiec, where Pekaes was to play a mid-standings team called Zagłębie. After the grandeur of Kraków, Silesia looked like a coal yard with zoning. Graffiti on one wall of the Sosnowiec station read ZAGŁĘBIE HOOLIGANS.

Mike had left Dumas at home, officially because of a stress fracture. But even if he had been healthy, Mike told me, Dumas wouldn't have made the trip. Dropping by Doom Boom's town-house the night before, Mike had found him shirtless, with pants unzipped, working a cigarette—"just the picture of the Greek ideal of an athlete. I didn't want him around the team." Wojo would suit up instead.

Zagłębie's two American mercenaries included a flighty young guard named Darryl Moore. Early in the game he embarrassed the Pekaes guards by leaking out for a couple of breakaway dunks. Then, midway through the half, Moore pump-faked from the top of the circle, swanned past Mike's gawking players, and bolted down a dunk that set the crowd off. Pekaes trailed by only eight at the half, but I now knew what left Mike so exasperated. His players had surrendered 45 points. In the locker room he lost it.

"You tell me how, in a professional basketball game, someone can shot-fake from the three-point line, dribble through the entire defense, go up for a dunk, and nobody—*nobody*—comes over to stop him! And it's *really* horseshit when you don't even go to the offensive boards, and they *still* get layups at the other end!

"They're kicking your ass. And you know why? Because they're playing harder! And because you're fucking soft! *You do not play hard!* I see it, the fans see it, the writers see it, everyone watching on national TV sees it! That team is ahead of you right now, and they should be, *because they're playing harder!*"

When Katie arrived from Minneapolis after Mike had already been with the team for a month, she was startled to find her husband speaking pidgin English. Straining to be understood, he had throttled back on his native tongue. But here Mike shifted into another gear. Suddenly he sounded like those American tourists who, sensing they're not getting through, try speaking English louder.

"We could play zone, we could put seven guys out there, but you're *still* gonna get your ass kicked because *you're not playing hard!* And it ain't gonna be zone, it ain't gonna be trapping—it's gonna be man-to-man!"

From his college coach Mike had learned that if a team is playing poorly, there's nothing like stripping the game down to its elements. "Man-to-man defense and motion offense," he would tell me. "The age-old conflict of man versus man. Keep it simple, and you can see who's winning and who's losing each little battle and work from there."

Pekaes left the locker room. "All right, let's go," Mike said, trying to strike an encouraging note. "Everybody has a job to do."

Nobody did it. Within the first minute of the second half, Moore riveted a corkscrew dunk on a breakaway, then airplaned his way back downcourt, tipping his wings in an aeronautic nod to the crowd. If failure to hustle was the Polish flu, it had infected even Wojo, who missed a three from the left of the key, then let a Zagłębie guard escape for a bunny. Pekaes wound up losing 101–90. Those five straight wins hardly mattered anymore.

When Mike walked into the crypt that was the Pekaes locker room, all he said was, "Practice at the old gym when we get back. Be there taped at nine tonight, ready to go."

The four-hour ride back to Pruszków should have been funereal. But within an hour someone had cued up a video of a sitcom featuring a befuddled police officer, played by an actor who looked like a Polish Jim Carrey. Laughter soon filled the bus. After the driver stopped at a McDonald's by a freeway interchange, the Polish players sequestered themselves at one end of the restaurant. M.J., Mike, and I took our food to the opposite end. Wojo ate by himself.

For the rest of the ride, Mike vented about his team and his lot. "If this doesn't work out, I don't think Katie'll let me stay in the business. And I can't blame her. She's gotten nothing but goose eggs out of this. It's one thing to be a coach's wife, putting up with the road, the late hours, hearing people call your husband names. But what we've been through here has been far beyond the call of duty."

I asked him if he'd ever consider taking a high school job. Mike was sharp and conscientious. After Pruszków he'd be worldly, too. He knew that college coaching was an oily business, and that pro coaching put you only one chippy player away from unemployment. He had to know he'd be a catch for any school looking for a teacher and a coach. But Mike only wanted to coach where the game really mattered, and he didn't think basketball mattered enough at the typical high school.

We got back to Pruszków, swung by Mike's townhouse, then returned to the old gym just before nine. M.J. sat alone on a bench, pulling on his shoes. No one else could be seen. Then a custodian summoned Mike to take a phone call.

It was Janusz, the G.M., on the line. The players were

refusing to practice. Over their Big Macs they'd plotted a revolt. Janusz said he'd be over to the gym in 10 minutes. Mike didn't seem the least bit fazed. "It'll be interesting to see which side management comes down on," he said.

Given the circumstances, I excused myself and headed back to the Marriott, leaving Mike to put down the McDonald's Mutiny by himself.

Pekaes never did practice. Having failed to pay them what they were owed, Janusz could hardly dictate to the players. Instead, Mike told me when he called later that night, "We ended up having a bit of a fireside chat."

The Polish players were pissed about the extra practice, and pissed that their American teammates weren't carrying more of the load. Janusz was pissed that the blowout on national TV had set back his search for a second sponsor. Wojo was pissed that everyone was pissed, looking to assign blame rather than accept responsibility. "By the time we were finished," Mike said, "there was maybe some recognition that we're all the problem."

He agreed that the team needed more scoring from its Americans. But he had been particularly stung by the criticism of Mike Jones. "M.J. is leading us in assists, steals, and scoring. He's second on the team in rebounding and third in blocks, and he's our friggin' *two* guard. They don't understand the contributions he makes. They want black Americans to jump and dunk. It's almost like the racist old days: 'Sing, happy Negro, sing.'"

At the same time, Mike blamed himself. He had signed off on what had turned out to be a terribly fragile team. Dumas had to score inside, so the guards could find open shots outside, so M.J. could tend to the details and the Polish Kukoč could emulsify the mix by driving and dishing. As things stood now, two of those principals weren't even suiting up. "Maybe my mistake was not doing the status quo thing," Mike said. "Maybe I should have just taken the team and the offense they had and won the games and moved on. It was a multipart plan, with each part depending on the others being in place. I'd counted on Dumas being sober, on Tomczyk not getting hurt, on our players getting paid and playing hard.

"And, you know, this thing still hasn't completely fallen apart. Last year Zepter Wrocław lost eight in a row in the middle of the season. For some reason they didn't fire their coach. And they got back to the finals and beat Pekaes for the title."

The next morning Mike and his family took the train into Warsaw, where I'd invited them for a taste of home at the Marriott's brunch buffet. Over waffles, Mike told me of a dream he had every few months. It recurred whenever he became discouraged, and he had dreamed it again the previous night.

He was back at Bloomington's Kennedy High, lacing up his shoes again for the last time, against St. Paul Central for third place in the Minnesota Class AA tournament. In reality, Kennedy had lost that game by a point on a last-second shot, after Mike, trying to dribble out the clock, was whistled for a five-second violation. The dream never lasted long enough for Mike and his teammates to overturn the result; his reverie usually petered out after layup lines and a few bars from the pep band. But as he described it to me I could tell that, even if high school ball didn't mean enough to others, it surely meant a lot to him. As unlikely as it seemed, Mike and Doom Boom had something in common—only Mike's answer to Richard's Game 5 was an unrequited achievement, a game that had been video-transferred onto his subconscious, where it played again and again.

"There's probably some Freudian explanation," he said. "Or maybe it's just that I love basketball, and that was the time in my life when the game was purest. I was in control of things. I wasn't a coach, relying on other people. I think that's why I love to play golf so much—why coaches in general love golf. It's your ball. You play the course. You're not dependent on anyone else, not even officials. Nobody can really screw you but yourself."

After brunch I followed Mike out to Pruszków for practice.

Wojo was waiting in the gym, dressed, taped, and ready to go. He wasn't wearing the look of a guy hunting for a Polish bride.

"You know, it isn't easy or fun to dive for a loose ball," he said. "If I stepped back and looked at it, I'd say the difference is the same one between capitalism and socialism. The best of these guys are national team players. You can't cut them or trade them. They want to be given something, not work for something, and that's the way it's always been. They've never fully grasped the concept of having to dig and scrap."

I asked him if he thought his comments the previous night had gotten through.

"No. Winning and teamwork, they're habits. And a habit is something you grow up with, not something you suddenly adopt."

Dumas wasn't around, whether due to infirmity or intoxication no one seemed to know, much less care. But today another American would be suiting up for practice. To make a point, Mike sometimes ran with the team, and when he did, the side he played for almost always won. He rolled his five feet nine inches out of the bleachers, the waffles still sloshing around inside his gut. He made sure that Wojo and M.J. joined his five, to help hammer home his point that the Americans weren't the problem. And he picked up Pete Szybilski, the captain, to help the lesson take and pull the Poles along.

With Mike's type-A temperament setting the tone, his team won five games in a row. "I don't know why," he said afterward. "But we played harder in practice today than we did yesterday in the game."

Still, as we left the gym, something had changed. Mike usually added a grace note of optimism after enumerating his gripes. Here he didn't. "The guys are tuning me out," he said. "To them I'm just background noise now."

I went to hear the Warsaw Philharmonic the night before I left. The program included the Third Symphony of a Polish composer named Henryk Górecki. Spare and lugubrious, Górecki's Third has no beat and you can't dance to it, but it had been a huge hit—a pop hit, even—in Europe. As I sat in the Filharmonia that evening, listening to evidence of how distinct from ours the Continental character really is, I was reminded that Mike's problems had much more to do with culture than personality. In Pruszków, he would sooner pronounce *szczęśliwy* than be happy. Here the game surely mattered, as it mattered in the States—but not in the same way and not for the same reasons. I knew this both from what I'd witnessed over the previous week and from personal experience, for I'd once been a basketball mercenary in Europe, too.

The following afternoon I saw Mike and the team to the airport. They were going to Barcelona to play Joventut Badalona, which was having no apparent trouble meeting its multimillion-dollar payroll.

I was headed for Switzerland, where 21 years earlier I'd spent a season as the first American to play for the club team in the lakeside city of Lucerne. I wanted to lighten my load.

"Here," I said, pulling a few stray złoty from my pocket and handing them to Mike. "This should subsidize a few trips to the bathroom."

FOUR

Switzerland

Please Do Not Air Your Dirty Laundry

No discerning person would have mistaken Stadtturnverein Luzern for a basketball team, even though in the late 1970s STL was a member in good standing of the third division of the Swiss national league. Three times a week we practiced with a "trainer," who led us in calisthenics and herded us into layup lines. Each weekend we played a game, for which we were turned over to a "coach," who called timeouts and made substitutions. It hadn't occurred to anyone that handsome advantages accrue to a team that vests both of these responsibilities in the same person.

Only a few years before my arrival, a game tied at the conclusion of regulation would simply end, the concept of overtime apparently being at odds with the Swiss imperative to keep to a schedule. Whenever the ball went anywhere near the nether regions of a player's leg, a cry would go up: *"Fuss!"*—foot, to indicate a kicking violation, regardless of whether the instance had been intentional, which is the test of when the rule should be applied and a whistle blown. Always, a whistle blew. Indeed, the entire Swiss conception of the game seemed to lie in a single distinction: In basketball you use your hands but not your feet; in soccer you use your feet but not your hands. I could hear the guy over in marketing: "Hey Urs, I've got it! 'Play Basketball: *It's Not Soccer!*'"

Before my account of Swiss hoops circa 1977 begins to sound too snarky, I should make clear that, in me, STL had no great catch. When he went to the train station to pick me up, our general manager, André Porchet, must have been crestfallen to come upon a scraggly, acne-pocked 20-year-old who had stopped out of college because of a vague late-adolescent restlessness. I stood barely six feet, weighed 145 pounds, and played in dark-framed glasses secured by a Velcro strap, an accessory that Kurt Rambis hadn't yet made fashionable. My only credentials were the co-captaincy of a very suburban high school team, and a recommendation from a dual-national childhood friend who played for the Swiss champions.

Nonetheless, we won more games that season than STL had ever won since its promotion to the third division. Swiss basketball was so abjectly underdeveloped that I averaged 17 points a game and led the league in free-throw shooting. We even finished ahead of all three of our rivals from the Ticino, Switzerland's Italian-speaking canton, where basketball was merely bad, not horrible. Lastly—and given the Swiss esteem for thrift, not leastly—I came virtually free. The club put me up with Winu Küster, president of STL's basketball section, and I took meals in his home. André later told me that I had set the club back only $300, the cost of a subsidy to Winu for food, plus the fee for my license from the Swiss federation.

My biggest nemesis proved to be the economic policies of the Carter administration, which kept the dollar plunging against the franc and what little savings I had from going anywhere. Even the *International Herald Tribune* was a luxury beyond my means. I soon learned how to loiter by a news kiosk and perform a sort of mental origami-in-reverse. I'd unfold that day's paper in my head as it sat quartered in its rack, to determine roughly where the NBA standings were. Then I'd quickly lift the appropriate corner to sneak a peak before the kiosk minder could shoo me away.

So I filled the days: skulking along the Alpenquai by Lake Lucerne; dipping into a copy of *Teach Yourself German*, though it couldn't help me decipher the phlegmy dialect spoken by the

Swiss; and sniffing ineffectually—as only a scraggly, acne-pocked, 20-year-old college stopout could do—around the city's American Fashion School in Switzerland, where Stateside sugar daddies sent their daughters to do doctoral work in runway modeling. I picked up the odd franc refereeing games in the cantonal league, making sure to whistle every *"Fuss"* to keep the locals happy. But there was no denying the stark truth. I was a basketball bum.

Then, several months into the season, I caught a break. André worked for an agronomical consulting firm, and he found me a completely alingual job in his office, coloring maps to indicate soil aptitudes. I took to it with the enthusiasm of a kindergartner suffering from attention surplus disorder. At the end of any given workday I could expound on the fecundity of topsoil in the Neuchâtel valley or the Engadine wolds. I had left an Ivy League school to crayon for hire, but I was living in Alpine splendor, playing ball, and earning 15 Swiss francs an hour, every last one of which the agronomical consulting firm laundered through a member of the STL directorate who slipped me a wad of bills twice a month. I soon moved out of Winu's place and into an apartment of my own, with a view of a switching yard full of punctual trains, and there contemplated my new freedom.

Only my freedom wasn't much greater than that accorded most other Swiss apartment dwellers, which is drastically attenuated. Often, no showers are permitted between 10 P.M. and 7 A.M. No toilets may be flushed during those hours, either. When relieving themselves, men are expected to sit. (Is it the likelihood of an errant drop that so offends? Or the clangorous tinkle?) One day I was accosted by a neighbor, an elderly woman furious that I'd left my soiled socks on the balcony to air after practice.

Perhaps you've heard of Christoph Meili. He's the young security guard at Union Bank of Switzerland who in 1997 saved from the teeth of the shredder a pile of documents that traced riches seized by the Nazis from Jews during World War II. Meili turned his find over to Jewish organizations so they could press for restitution, and for this act he was fired from his job, denounced by his employer, and subjected to death threats. I wasn't entirely surprised by what he experienced, for I'd learned long ago that the Swiss aren't very keen on the airing of dirty laundry in public.

For as long as Americans have gone abroad to play basketball, they've struggled with life off the court. Even I felt a certain amount of cultural dislocation in Switzerland, and I had every reason not to, given that I was an amateur at the lowest level of European basketball, with one German-born parent and several trips to the Continent already behind me. But Americans who play for pay abroad, particularly African-Americans, have long labored under the extravagant expectations of elite clubs and their fans. I'd sensed those expectations in Pruszków in the way people reacted to Richard Dumas and Mike Jones—the attitude that Mike McCollow called "Sing, happy Negro, sing." Every now and then an American could turn his distinctiveness to his advantage. He might learn the language, perhaps marry a local woman, maybe become an entrepreneur, a coach, or a broadcaster. But far more often mercenary Yanks struggled in proportion to their size, their blackness, and their unfamiliarity with European life. Such was the case of Fessor (Moose) Leonard that 1977–78 season.

The Swiss call them *saisonniers,* the Italians and Turks and Yugoslavs who emigrate temporarily, find menial work, then remit most of their earnings to families back home. *Saisonniers* fix Swiss roads and collect Swiss trash, and most citizens, if they see one working on a bridge in a bright orange jumpsuit, look right through him, another dago in Day-Glo. Leonard was a *saisonnier,* too, only in a different line of work. He was a 6'11" center, a former star at Furman who played for Federale Lugano, a Ticinese club then trying to win its fourth straight Swiss first-division title. Waiting back home in Georgia for a share of his $30,000 salary was an extended family that included a younger half-brother, Sam Mitchell, who would go on to play for the Minnesota Timberwolves.

Like many of the Americans who played in Lugano that season, Leonard hung out at the Gestibar on the via Zurigo. He often wore a brightly colored visor that made him look like an exotic croupier. He sometimes carried a boom box, which led teammates to call him Gemetti, after the Ticinese electronics company. But those were the only hints of loudness about Leonard, who was otherwise every bit the small-town southerner. James Baldwin, in his essay "Stranger in the Village," described the lot of the black interloper in a Swiss town: "Wherever I passed . . . a wind passed with me—of astonishment, curiosity, amusement, and outrage." Given Leonard's size, that wind must have been a gale.

Just before Christmas, apparently unprovoked, Leonard accosted and kicked an elderly woman on a Lugano street. Or so went the official account, carried in the local papers. But shortly after the incident Dan Stockalper, a Swiss-American who was playing that season for Viganello, another Ticinese club, told me a different story. He said that the woman in question had been previously hospitalized for a phobia about someone wanting to steal her purse. "Moose was just the unlucky guy who walked by her when she grabbed him and started screaming," Stockalper said. "The newspapers and people of Lugano were pretty tough on him. He got threats on his life for 'beating up' this old woman, and I'm certain that's how his problems began. But he kicked her only when he saw a man run out of a store at him with a hatchet."

For three days Leonard was detained by the police. He refused to answer their questions. The cops finally released him and referred him to a psychiatrist, who prescribed Valium.

One Saturday that February, Leonard didn't show up until several minutes into Federale's game with crosstown rival S.P. Lugano. The Federale coach sent him into the lineup anyway. Leonard quickly drew a technical foul for hanging on the rim after a dunk and eventually fouled out. "It was as if he wanted to foul out," recalled Bob Marty, another Viganello player, who was in the stands that day. By now exasperated, Federale officials arranged for Leonard to fly home the following Wednesday.

On the intervening Monday two friends—Jim Frei, a teammate, and Viganello's Ken Brady—swung by Leonard's studio apartment in a Lugano suburb and knocked on the door. There was no answer. Then one of them noticed the smell of smoke, and Brady, a former star forward at Michigan, used his shoulder to force the door open. There they found Leonard, dead, with an empty bottle of Valium alongside his body. The coroner ruled that Leonard hadn't died of an overdose, but from inhaling the smoke from a pyre of basketball posters, magazines, and clippings—many documenting his own career—that he had apparently collected in a wastebasket and set ablaze.

In the aftermath of his death, Federale officials insisted that Leonard had always been free to leave. Stockalper told me differently: "The team pressed him to keep playing because they were battling for a fourth title. I know Moose just wanted to get back to familiar surroundings, to get himself together. Moose would still be alive if Federale had let him go home when he wanted to."

An editorialist for the Swiss weekly *Semaine Sportive* pronounced a cause of death of his own. "Leonard died of misery," he wrote. "Misery, and the complete indifference of others."

Unless you happen to be a tourist with a Platinum card, Switzerland can be an unwelcoming place. The government turned Jews away at the border during World War II, insisting that "the boat is full." More recently, Switzerland's halting response to the Nazi gold scandal underscored the country's ill ease with even the scrutiny of outsiders, let alone their presence. Fortunately I hadn't found this feature among my teammates, least of all in the former STL player who was putting me up on this visit.

Pius Portmann was a Swiss mensch. He had grown up a baker's son in Entlebuch, a whistle stop outside Lucerne on the railroad line to Bern. Pius (pronounced PEE-oos) didn't see his first basketball game until 1972 when, at age 16, he watched the Olympic final from Munich. He couldn't figure out why teams sometimes received two points for a basket and at other times only one. He thought it might have to do with whether or not a shot hit the backboard.

André Porchet, STL's G.M.-to-be, was then a biology teacher and coach at the *Kantonschule* in Lucerne. He spotted Pius's 6'6" frame in the hallway one day and cajoled him into trying out the game. Pius liked it so much that he clambered onto the roof of his father's bakery to rig up an antenna, hoping to pull in Ticinese TV so he could watch the finals of the Italian league. Basketball favored him back: Pius had supple hands and a knack for playing with his back to the basket. Within a few years he had become STL's best player and earned a spot on the Swiss national team. Like any young player anywhere in the world, he scrawled his name and address on his basketball, but like no kid anywhere else that name and address read PIUS PORTMANN, BAKERY, ENTLEBUCH.

Pius was retired now, but he and a handful of STL alums still gathered for a regular Friday run, and on my first night back in town he took me by the gym. He could still wheel in the post with either hand, and his Poindexter glasses had given way to contact lenses. Afterward I joined him and Bruno Dünner, STL's old point guard, at a pizzeria, to see how many of 21 years we could catch up on.

Pius and Bruno quickly launched into a catalog of all the American mercenaries who had followed me. Two of the earliest, Rick Taylor and Blake Taylor, though no relation, had both starred at Arizona State. But they'd come in the early 1980s, when STL still wasn't paying its players.

"Rick worked as a plumber's assistant and pumped gas," Pius said. "Blake washed dishes."

"Then there was Chris Lockhart," said Bruno. "He shot this funny jumper where he spread his legs apart in midair. He said he didn't want to come down on a defender's foot and sprain an ankle."

A jump shot is such a complex biomechanical undertaking that most players would let a concern like that slide. But this was just the kind of punctilious habit the Swiss could warm up to—unlike the tic of another STL ringer, an ex-CBA player named Randy Johnson.

"Randy was from Kansas," said Pius. "He liked to chew tobacco. During practice he'd spit tobacco juice in the corners of the *Kantonschule* gym."

So Pius and Bruno went on. They told of one American who started a computer business while in Switzerland, and now shuttled between offices in Zug and the U.S., a multimillionaire; of another who would quaff a bottle of cough syrup before a game, kick butt in the first half, then nod off in the second; and of a seven-footer who, Pius said, "looked great stretching during warmups. But that's about all he could do. He runs a vineyard in Bordeaux now."

Most of these Americans came cheap. But in 1982, after STL qualified for the top league and had to lay out real money, the team performed so miserably in its first season in the top division that it should have been sent right back down. Yet STL avoided what would have been a merciful fate because, at the end of that season, two other top-level clubs merged and a third folded. So STL got a second crack at competing among Switzerland's basketball elite, however oxymoronic that phrase may have been. The club hired a Yugoslav coach named Milan Dokić, who had led a team in Göttingen to a German championship.

"The first day of practice Dokić told us we were going to win the Swiss title," Pius said. "That's when we got suspicious. I mean, we'd won *two games* the year before."

"We got even more suspicious when in the preseason he had us run up steps carrying each other on our backs and everybody started to get injured," said Bruno. "And when Nyon full-court pressed us in our first game, and he told us to just dribble through it."

STL lost its first six games. Yet the coach continued to devote practice to nothing but drills and scrimmages, never once breaking anything down tactically. So one day Pius decided to call the club in Göttingen to ask about the legendary Milan Dokić, mastermind behind a German title.

"We've never won any title," said the guy who answered the phone. "I know, because I'm on the team." Pius asked if he would put his statement in writing and fax him a copy.

As it happened, Dokić had called a team meeting for the next day to address his players' unwillingness to fulfill his prophecy. The coach had even invited a journalist to sit in as he delivered his motivational philippic. "Some people in this room don't believe we can become Swiss champions!" he thundered. "Their attitude is bringing us down! I've proved it can be done—proved it in Göttingen!"

That's when STL's own Christoph Meili blew the whistle. Dokić stammered his protestations. But the journalist in the meeting contacted the Yugoslav Basketball Federation, which had no record of Dokić, either. Soon *l'affaire Dokić* was all over the papers.

That wasn't the end of the story. The events had unfolded while both André and STL's president were off doing the compulsory annual military duty that makes Switzerland the world's most incongruously pacifist nation. Neither was pleased when journalists began leaving messages for them at the barracks. Instead of showering Pius with gratitude for ridding the team of a hornswoggler, the club suspended him for two weeks. "Not for what you did," André told Pius, "but for the way you did it"—even though Dokić, not Pius, had invited the journalist to the team meeting. STL management said it would shorten the suspension if Pius submitted a written apology. He refused. "If I had to do it all over again," he told the papers then, as he told me now, "I'd do the same thing."

Dokić conformed with a stereotype widely held in Switzerland that Yugoslav immigrants are con men and bicycle thieves. (The Swiss have a joke: Did you know the triathlon was invented by a Yugoslav? He ran to the swimming pool one day and rode home on a bike.) But the way STL treated Pius played into an equally unflattering stereotype of the Swiss: that they are a people who pay more honor to petty procedure than larger principle. It may be unfair to second-guess what happened in the final minutes of Swissair Flight 111, which crashed in September 1998 in the Atlantic off Nova Scotia. But investigators developed a theory that, despite the copilot's attempts to talk him out of it, the pilot insisted on following a procedural checklist to the letter, which called for a detour out over the water to dump fuel before trying an emergency landing—a delay he had no time for.

"So, after all that, what'd you guys do?" I asked.

"Lose," Pius said.

Pius and I returned to the apartment he shared with his wife and son. It's an aerie on the north side of the lake, with a view of Mount Pilatus that silences anyone who sees it. Before turning in for the night, I asked him if he remembered Moose Leonard.

"Yes," he said. "Max Frisch, one of our most famous writers, once said, 'We expected workers, and people came.' The case of Moose Leonard may have been an example of just that. We expected basketball players, and people came.

"You know, Dokić may have been a bad guy, but I know lots of other Yugoslavs, and every one of them is a good guy. After this recent controversy with the Jews, I think fewer of us here have the attitude that 'the boat is full.' We have such a high standard of living. Who are we not to share?"

The Lucerne I returned to was alive with Proustian sensations. The smell of roasted chestnuts on the promenade by the Reuss, the rustle-and-clang of the streetcars, the filtering whim of the clouds, which permitted random sections of Pilatus to come in and out of focus as if you were looking at some Alpine screensaver—I savored each of these more on this visit, I think, than I had on any one day during my entire season in Switzerland.

But much about the city had changed, too, and on Saturday, when I joined Pius, Bruno, and André to watch STL's game with Geneva Pâquis, I saw evidence everywhere. I'd played with guys named Otto and Klaus and Max; now the names in the game program—Jean-Paul Stojanov, Sipho Mabona, Hakim Kratou, Mirko Razzi—bespoke a country in transition. Two decades ago, when my teammates and I invaded a schoolyard on a balmy day to play pickup, people stared at us as if we were urinating in public. Now Lucerne was a stop on the Adidas Streetball European tour. This very gym had no breakaway rims when I'd played in it in 1978, for they would have been like lifeguards at a wading pool. Now STL's Bosnian-born center threw down dunks during warmups.

As gangly kids in NBA gear loped in, I spotted one Generation Xer who couldn't have been more than 25. His head was entirely shaved, except for a pompadour in front. He wore a Dominique Wilkins jersey and a pair of sweatpants. His name was Ernesto Rea, André told me, and he was going to coach the team dressed exactly like this. André assured me that Ernesto—coach *and* "trainer"—ran STL's practices, too.

Bruno and Pius returned to their reminiscing, and I realized that I'd been derelict in Pruszków not to get more of the Polish players' perspectives. Later in the 1980s my friends had jumped crosstown to another club, which had a couple of pricey Americans—Willie White, who played briefly for the Denver Nuggets, and Don Robinson. "They each made at least $130,000," Bruno said. "Yet I had to bring the ball upcourt and play defense for Willie, and Pius had to defend the other team's American. We were doing the dirty work on the court, practicing four times a week and working full-time and not earning a thing from the club, and we had to listen to Willie and Don complain about how bad we were.

"But you know, after those two years in the top league with STL, even after only six wins total, Pius and I were like brothers. Even though, after every one of those 54 losses, I was furious."

Pius nodded. "I would put my hand in the fire for any of the guys I played with," he said. "You have to understand: For 15 years basketball was our life. Bruno and I took no vacations, no ski trips on weekends. But at the same time we had a chance to play the game in a way that wasn't exaggerated. Today, starting at 14, kids practice five times a week. And by 20 or 22 they say, 'Oh, I'm not going to make it big. I quit.' Growing up I had to make my own TV antenna out of coat hangers to see the Italian championship with snow on the screen. Now they can see four or five NBA games a week. They're just spoiled."

Looking around, I could see what Pius meant. Clearly, no one here had seen his first basketball game at age 16. As STL went through warmups, one player stepped off the floor to use his cell phone. The club's youth section now served 140 kids, and the pipeline was pumping more talent, Pius told me, with more individual skill than ever. But he didn't believe the players' understanding of the game or sense of team play had advanced at all. It was as if a generation had swallowed whole the modern NBA ethos, good and bad.

STL had found its own level over the past two decades, shuttling between the Swiss second and third divisions. Its American of the moment, Rob Wesley, had married a Swiss woman and moved to her hometown, near Baden, where he taught phys ed at an international school. Although the team now had a title sponsor, McDonald's, one thing remained the same: Wesley didn't get a franc from STL, other than reimbursement for taking the train to practice three times a week.

Geneva raced out to an early advantage, as Wesley's teammates seemed out of sorts trying to find him. In the second half the home team deployed a 1-3-1 half-court trap, and I beamed. We had played that defense in high school, and 21 years ago I'd prevailed on my Swiss coach to let us try it. I jabbed André with an elbow.

"Eins-drei-eins, oder?"

André smiled, perhaps a little more broadly because the trap was actually beginning to gouge a chunk out of the Geneva lead. I felt like the irrigation engineer who, years after a turn in the Peace Corps, returns to the savannah to find fields of tender kumquats ripening in the sun.

Then one of STL's reserves, a 5'5" refugee from Kosovo, sank a long three-pointer. A teammate bottomed out another to draw the home team even. Moments later that Bosnian center dropped in two free throws, and my old team, after trailing virtually the entire game, had won 90–88.

Back in the late seventies, the very idea that two Swiss teams would have had the basketball wits to score 178 points in 40 minutes would have been unentertainable. Most impressively, STL had won without its American, who had sat out most of the second half with a bad knee.

I found Wesley after the game and wished him good luck.

"Be safe," he replied. "You're in the real world. I'm in Disneyland."

I knew exactly what he meant. When I'd gone Disney two decades earlier, I knew vaguely that Swiss basketball was bad. Exactly how bad I would discover upon returning to campus the following fall, when a buddy I'd usually beaten one-on-one regularly took me to school. But none of that mattered, for the season had been a gas. What I loved most about the game in Switzerland was the same thing Pius and Bruno loved about it—the very thing that, up in Poland, was driving Mike McCollow crazy. I loved the low key it was played in. I savored the way each comic absurdity snuck up on you like a blind pick. Swiss basketball had an "at a picnic" quality that would have delighted Doc Naismith, and it sent me back to college with a smile.

Or so I was thinking when, for the first time in a week, I logged on to the Internet. The subject line in an e-mail from Mike did not bode well. "The Polish Ziggy" alluded to Dick Vitale's term for the one thing coaches dread most. "Amazing but true!" the message read. "I got fired today as coach of Pekaes Pruszków."

FIVE

Celebration, Florida
Communities of Three

In the spring of 1978, I returned from that season in Switzerland in need of a summer job. I found one supervising a playground in Woodstock, the tidy Vermont town that provides the backdrop for those Budweiser Christmas commercials in which Clydesdales clomp placidly through the snow. My boss, Chuck, turned out to be a like-minded hoophead and another transplanted New Yorker, and we both bridled at where we found ourselves—among relocated flatlanders who used "summer" as a verb, and antiqued, boutiqued, and otherwise 'iqued out a living.

Over noontime games of H-O-R-S-E, Chuck and I plotted a quiet rebellion of the imagination. We began referring to the place as "the Stock." We fantasized about renting the storefront adjacent to Who Is Sylvia?, an insufferably precious vintage clothing store, just so we could hang out a shingle reading AND WHO GIVES? We imagined a foundation called the Bad-Air Fund that would give an underprivileged country kid a chance to spend a few weeks in the Bronx to get game.

One day we hatched a plan for a huge invitational basketball tournament, open only to teams from urban centers around America, that would shake every vintage Colonial in town down to its last clapboard. Phalanxes of lean and large African-

American males would stroll over the covered bridge spanning the Ottauquechee River. The Ohio Players' anthem "Fire" would loop ceaselessly at full volume over the PA system. For one delicious weekend The Green would become Da Green, and Woodstock would play host to a hoops Woodstock.

It was all very sophomoric stuff, never to be realized. But that fantasy had never entirely left my imagination, and that's why I found myself, with a hyperactive 10-year-old to my left and a retired couple engrossed in a copy of the *National Enquirer* to my right, on a discount flight to Orlando. Lucerne may have been Disneyland, but I was going to Disney World, or at least to Disney World's adjacent bedroom community— the meticulously planned town of Celebration, Florida, which was hosting the first-ever Gus Macker All-World Three-on-Three National Championship.

From what I'd read, Celebration was what happened when an urban planner snorted a few too many lines of pixie dust. Disney had taken several hundred acres of Osceola County swampland and thrown up something that looked like the set of *The Truman Show*. A home in Mousetown came at a price, and not just a monetary one. Contractors rigorously followed Celebration's "pattern book," which prescribed standards for virtually every exterior feature, from architectural detail to color, fencing, and shrubbery. Each homeowner agreed to abide by all sorts of restrictions, including a ban on any basketball hoops visible from the street. A film screened for prospective residents boasted that Celebration was a place where "everyone has the same desires, and everyone has the same ideals." I wasn't entirely sure this was something that Celebrationites (or Celebrators, or Celebrants, or—was it too much to wish for?—Celibates) should be celebrating. Woodstock at least came by its deadening quaintness naturally. And in Vermont the snow was real; Celebration, hoping to stoke retail traffic in advance of the previous Christmas, had installed a snowmaking machine in its downtown to blow a "snowfall" of artificial flakes.

Even Celebration's criminals behaved as if they'd been drawn up in a Disney studio. Scarcely two months before my visit a man approached a Celebration resident in his garage and threatened to shoot if the victim didn't hand over his cash and credit cards. The intruder produced no gun, keeping his hand in his pocket throughout the incident. The Osceola County sheriff's office reported that the perp of the town's first holdup was "polite and apologetic and drove off in a blue Honda."

If Celebration's statutorily tidy houses embodied an architectural concept known as neotraditionalism, the One and Only Original All-World Gus Macker Three-on-Three Basketball Tournament stood for what might be called neotraditional pickup ball. The Macker was founded in 1974 in the Lowell, Michigan, driveway of Scott and Mitch McNeal, teenage brothers who decided to invite their friends from the neighborhood over to play for a few bucks tossed into a hat. As word of the tournament spread, the draw grew, and over the years the McNeals began to build freestanding basket stanchions that they stuck in the streets around their house. Soon players from all over the country were flocking to Lowell for three days of hoops each July. Imitators would take the concept and turn three-on-three into a slick production, invading big cities and cutting deals with TV networks and multinational sponsors. But over its 25 years, even as the original Macker grew into an April-to-October tour that reached more than 80 venues a year, it never strayed from its beginnings in the small-town Midwest. T-shirts and other souvenirs made an icon of the Macker Man, a cartoon-character basketball in top hat and gloves. Something called the *Mackerville Gusette* published the pairings and regulations for each event. If possible, men in the over-40 division were assigned to a court near a funeral home. Slam-dunk contestants abided by the competition's only rule: "Don't bring no weak stuff." These campy touches helped explain why places like Merrillville, Indiana, and South Sioux City, Nebraska, gave themselves over to the Macker for one weekend every summer.

Street basketball isn't afflicted by the same sociocultural chasm as, say, lacrosse, which breaks down into two stark camps—impoverished Onondaga tribesmen and preppy swells from the Baltimore suburbs. But a gulf nonetheless exists between the half-moon backboard in a small-town driveway under which the Macker was conceived, and the chain-link cages in the inner cities from which most of its champions come. The Macker somehow reconciled these extremes: Macker *macher* Scott McNeal made sure to hire black staff, and he filled the ambit of each tournament with urban contemporary music, no matter how white the community he was visiting. It's hard to concisely summarize the appeal of the Macker, but I think it derives from a kind of panracial idealism peddled lightly. McNeal himself embodied it so well that those who had never met him tended to assume he was 6'6" and black. I once asked Scott's mother, Bonnie, about this. She pointed out that her son's two favorite foods are barbecue and Yoplait yogurt. "He's a Gemini, you know," she said of Scott, who's 5'7" and white. "Split personality."

But during the tournament's salad days in Lowell, its spirit wasn't peddled lightly enough for everyone. The second time I attended a Macker, in 1985, the McNeals' next-door neighbor marched up to me and announced, with an indignation he must have thought I'd share, "Just this morning I found a spearchucker in my flowerbed!" A year later this neighbor, Larry Isenhoff, filed a lawsuit claiming that the Macker was a public nuisance, and that he had suffered "irreparable damage" from living adjacent to the McNeals. Isenhoff was smart enough not to sue on the grounds of undesired exposure to Negroes, but not so smart that he couldn't resist telling a town council meeting that he didn't like "all these blacks" around his house, and that blacks "bring problems."

Isenhoff's suit failed, but some of the ill will he sowed leached into the community. The McNeals had done their best to be considerate of their neighbors, organizing cleanup crews, hiring extra security, and throwing an annual neighbors' appreciation party. But in early 1987 the town council hindered their efforts to relocate to Lowell's downtown, and that spring the McNeals decided to move the flagship Macker the dozen miles from Lowell to Belding, Michigan, where the civic leadership was only too happy to have it.

All this suggested that Mickey Mouse and Gus Macker were in theory a pretty good match. A misanthrope like Larry Isenhoff wouldn't be attracted to a town like Celebration, which was full of people who so believed in human interaction that they'd bought closely clustered homes with porches. Still, I wasn't sure whether the burghers of Celebration really understood what a national three-on-three basketball championship would deliver. Yes, Celebration's golf course was public, and the town had no guardhouse or gate, in contrast to so many residential subdivisions in the South, which often call themselves "plantations" with no apparent awareness of the irony. But even as Disney went to great lengths to attract black residents, only one black family actually owned a home. And so I wondered if that cultures-in-collision moment I'd envisioned in Woodstock long ago—in your face, at your doorstep—had finally come.

With my body still on Lucerne time, I awoke at 5 A.M. Restless, I dressed and left my motel, then turned off the commercial strip along Highway 192, past the white polymerized vinyl picket fence that girdles the town, and the water tower that is no water tower at all, just a stagy billboard.

The citizens of Celebration still slumbered. Lit jack-o'-lanterns winked from almost every stoop, having apparently ingratiated themselves to the pattern book. Lest tourists mistake a lived-in home for a model one, house after house had a sign in its front yard reading HOME OCCUPIED/PLEASE KEEP OFF PROPERTY.

Downtown, not a person stirred. Even the Muzak hadn't yet begun to waft from the speakers visible at the bases of the palm trees. The basketball courts, 20 in all, had been meticulously laid out along the downtown streets the day before, each with its stanchion and duct tape. The storefronts echoed Woodstock's: an antique furnishings store; a café serving high-end joe; a bakery called Bread Alone. The lettering in the window of Gooding's Grocery read like parody: GROCERIES, SUNDRIES,

SUSHI. It was as if a cloud of phoniness had blown over from Disney World—as if, after EPCOT's ersatz France and stand-in Italy, Disney had decided to erect a Potemkin middle-American village as well.

The town slowly awoke. First, the croak of a heron over Celebration Lake. Then a lonely dogwalker. Soon a booth opened, offering freshly baked donuts, courtesy of the Celebration Optimists. (I would not waste my time looking for Celebration Pessimists.) That's when I spotted Scott McNeal.

There is no way to describe Gus Macker's entrance other than to say that he materializes. McNeal has shimmering blue eyes and a beard he'll stroke in the manner of a leprechaun. On many occasions I've watched Scott hear out a pissed-off player on some Macker matter, only to watch the plaintiff walk calmly away, even after a ruling has gone against him. I think it's because Gus seems bewitched somehow, possessed of a higher wisdom.

As participants began to show up, Scott cajoled them into forming a layup line on the main court. Any team finishing in the top three of any division at any Macker during the past season was eligible for these nationals, and this exercise was as much mixer as warmup, a way for players who had come from all over the country to get to know one another. Soon the queue of layuppers extended a full court and a half away.

"Ladies and gentlemen, what we have here is the world's longest layup line!" Scott announced over the PA. "And the world's shortest rebounding line!"

As play began, the music opened gently, with jazz fusion, Barry White, and Ashford and Simpson, but soon the deejay was on to Jodeci and James Brown's "Sex Machine" and George Clinton: *Why must I be like that? Why must I chase the cat? It's nothin' but the* dawg *in me.* Shirts read GAME COCKS and YO MAMA. The occasional *"Fuck!"* issued forth. Between the music, the clothing, and the language, Celebration was experiencing a three-way zoning violation. But when I asked the elderly woman volunteering at registration what she thought of all the ruckus, she surprised me. "I love it," she said. "We need a dose of reality."

Of course, the town of Celebration wasn't the only party to take a leap of faith when it contracted to bring the Macker nationals to its streets. Every participating player, if he were to pursue a loose ball with too much abandon, ran the risk of smashing a storefront window and impaling himself on a cardamom-scented candle.

Trolling through the courts, I found a team to follow. The Whitney Point Eagles came from a town of about 1,000 on the southern tier of New York State. They'd qualified for the nationals by winning the 11- and 12-year-old girls' division at the Macker in Norwich, New York, back in July. To fund their trip the Eagles had spent the intervening months raising more than $3,000 with car washes, bake sales, and raffles, and "by returning a lot of bottles and cans," according to one of the girls' moms, all of whom had made the trip. (The dads were back in Whitney Point, making do with delivered Domino's.)

Their self-funded pluck made the Eagles likable, but that wasn't why I adopted them. I followed them because not enough teams of 11- and 12-year-old girls had traveled to Florida to fill out the draw. So if they wanted to play at all, the Eagles had to move up a division, and go against 13- and 14-year-olds. Danielle, Debbie, Samantha, and Tammy—Macker rules permitted all three-on-three teams to have one substitute—had won their first two games despite giving up age and size at every position.

How did they do it? "We have pretty good outside shots," Tammy told me. "We're scrappers. And we play as a team."

"And we have plays," Debbie said. "Like Number 1. 'Danielle high.' We throw it to Danielle in the high post and basically cut behind her from the wings. People always get faked out by it."

I asked them what they liked about basketball. The question touched off a cacophony of voices. I think I sorted out all four answers:

"Teamworkplayingjusthavingfun*everything!*"

In their last game of the day, the girls lost to a ruthless team from Wisconsin that brought every bit of its puberty to bear, overpowering Danielle by sticking two players in the low post.

But the Eagles seemed happy enough with how they'd done. I asked Samantha if they'd be washing their uniforms before tomorrow, when they'd try to win their division the tough way, through the loser's bracket.

"Of course," she said.

I suggested that a lot of the boys wouldn't be washing theirs.

"Boys," Tammy said, "are *gross*."

On Sunday the Whitney Point Eagles went out. They lost to a team that included one girl with a tattoo on her biceps. But they finished third in their division, outplacing several bigger and stronger teams. And boys apparently weren't so gross that the Eagles hadn't befriended a few out by the Jacuzzi at the Comfort Suites on Highway 192: four black teenagers from Minneapolis who had the name of their team, the Wildcats, shaved into the backs of their heads. "I'm so used to seeing how poised they are on the court that it was odd to see them go all giggly in the whirlpool," one Eagle mom told me. She also noted that the Wildcats were 13 and 14. The Eagles were playing up socially, too.

With no rooting interest left, I caught up with Scott McNeal. He mentioned that a Macker Man costume languished in the back of the tournament's tractor-trailer, for want of anyone willing to wear it in the Florida heat. In the name of animanthropology—and in the spirit of Celebration's lord mayor, Mickey Mouse—I offered to suit up.

I wriggled into a plush yellow basketball costume that came down to my thighs. I pulled on white gloves and fuzzy "sneakers." Wading into the streets of Celebration, I gloried in my new identity. I posed for photos. I sang, to the tune of the Mickey Mouse theme song, "M-A-C, K-E-R, H-O-O-P-S!" And I discovered that there is virtually nothing people won't say or do when encountering a mascot in costume.

"Hey Gus, look!" yelled one kid, yanking down his pants to reveal boxer shorts festooned with the Macker Man.

So the day went.

"Nice legs!" (From a woman.)

"Give me a hug!" (From a five-year-old.)

"It must be motherfuckin' *hot* in there!" (It was.)

John Wooden, the Hall of Fame coach at UCLA and architect of the Pyramid of Success, once explained to me how very much of basketball comes down to threes. Guard, forward, center. Ball, you, man. Coaches call that moment of multiple possibilities before you've used up your dribble "triple-threat position," because you can pass, dribble, shoot. Indeed, the Chicago Bulls owed their six NBA titles to an offense, the triangle, founded on threes. You can find the number in one of the game's great successes, the three-pointer, and one of its biggest boners, the three-second violation. Why should it come as a surprise that a three-man team was the optimal basketball community? Three players can always keep the court balanced by passing, screening, cutting.

I waddled over to the main court, where the final in the top men's division was playing out. It featured teams with names that weren't ready for the pattern book: Death Row and the B-Town Dog Pound. Death Row was getting waxed. Its best player, gassed from leading his team on its long slog through the loser's bracket, conceded a layup, then stood out of bounds for a beat, catching his breath.

This caused one member of the Dog Pound to go off. "He *done gave up!*" Impounded Dog screamed. "I'm not gonna play against some chump who *done gave up!*"

Impounded Dog glared at Condemned Man and walked disgustedly away. Indignant, he motioned to a teammate to replace him. But the second Impounded Dog looked at the first as if he were crazy. "Man, *I* don't want no part of him!" he said. "*I* don't want no part of some chump who *done gave up!*"

Perhaps it was all theater, staged to humiliate a team on the verge of being finished off. Just the same, I couldn't believe what I was witnessing: two wholly amateur teammates arguing with each other over who would perform the demeaning, soul-contaminating chore of guarding a guy who *just wasn't playing hard enough.* During my visit to this place pledged to resurrecting traditional values, it took the Macker to show me the best example of one value that North Americans purport to prize as much as any—the same Protestant work ethic that had suggested itself at the Naismith homestead. If only Pekaes got its second sponsor soon, I thought: The whole team should fly over to see this.

The B-Town Dog Pound threw the switch on Death Row just in time. That weekend the East Coast had fallen back to standard time, and the gloaming stole early over the cypresses. Players dispersed with civility. As sweaty as everyone was, no one jumped indecorously into Celebration Lake—although this may have had something to do with the sign on the pier that read IT IS AGAINST FLORIDA LAW TO FEED OR HARASS ALLIGATORS.

Perhaps it took making like a Disney character on Main Street U.S.A. to adjust my attitude toward Celebration—to see, through the narrow slit of the Macker Man's eyes, basketball's all-encompassing embrace. ("Give me a hug," indeed.) But I'd come to realize that Mickey and the Macker were indeed well-suited to each other. To some of the people in town that weekend, Celebration was a New Urbanist experiment in communitarian living; to others it was a lyric from a Kool and the Gang song. But like the McNeals' streetball tournament, Celebration was trying in good faith to reconcile hokey traditionalism with a spirit of inclusion.

As for the Macker, it may be one of the great creations of the last predigital generation, those kids who grew up still having to amuse themselves by overcoming their *Lord of the Flies* instincts and choosing up teams. Like the 19th century boys and girls in Bennies Corners who conjured up duck on a rock, the McNeals and their friends invented something, too, only the Macker gang took it to a huge scale. Public-minded idealists try their hand at social engineering. Disney executives traffic in what they call imagineering. What I saw at the Celebration Macker, I think, was social imagineering.

I'd watched how conflicting cultures and competitive pressures took Fessor Leonard's life in Lugano, and Mike McCollow's job in Pruszków. In Lucerne I'd experienced how, by relieving those pressures, the game could find something approaching its rightful place. As I prepared to return to Europe, to a town divided by basketball and class, the Celebration Macker left me feeling ashamed to have entertained those ungallant fantasies about an intercultural Armageddon. Rather like Celebration's original robbery suspect, I drove off apologetically.

SIX

Italy
Strength vs. Virtue

Chaotic and surprising, the opposite of Celebration, Florida, in almost every respect, Italy often fails to work. Fortunately, the language never goes on strike. Consider the pleasures awaiting Italian speakers every day. You get to say *Prrrrrronto!* when performing the prosaic act of answering the phone. For oafishly stumbling into someone on the street you can indulge in the exquisite pleasure of saying *Mi scusi*. More than once I have set out for some shop in some Italian city, only to come upon a locked door and a sign reading CHIUSO, and later realized why I wasn't more disappointed: At least the sign didn't read CLOSED.

I scarcely speak the language and only fitfully understand it, but to my ears the two sets of fans in Bologna's Palasport Casalecchio were serenading each other with perfectly pitched arias on that Sunday afternoon. Tip-off for the game between Virtus Bologna and Fortitudo Bologna still lay an hour away, but already their followers were in full throat. Only later would their incantations be translated for me.

"We want to see you all *take a shit!*"

"*We* are Bologna!"

"You're white-and-black *bastards!*"

"Oh, and did *you* win the title?"

"Let's kill Danilović, let's sodomize Nesterović, then it's *your* turn, Forever Boys!"

"You're thinking of taking a shit! You're thinking of taking a shit!"

Stalwart tongue that it is, Italian has a word for this kind of parochial zealotry: *campanilismo*—literally, fealty to one's bell tower. The phenomenon dates from the days when Italy was divided into tiny administrative units, from city-states on down, and gets its most prominent display in Siena twice each summer at the *palio,* the ancient horse race on which 10 of that city's neighborhoods stake their honor. The difference between Sienese horse racing and Bolognese basketball is that in Bologna the passion isn't diluted 10 ways. It's divided between two huge camps of fans, all animated by the knowledge that they're cheering on one of Italy's two wealthiest and most storied teams.

Every time Fortitudo and Virtus play each other, renewing what is known as the Derby, they stir this city of 400,000 people into a froth. The teams are scheduled to meet only twice a season. But because both are among Europe's elite, they seem to run into each other at every turn. During the previous season the two hooked up a psychologically torturous 10 times. It would be strictly accurate to say that Fortitudo fared well enough, winning four of those meetings, but it would also be misleading. For while Fortitudo beat Virtus in the semifinals of the Italy Cup and went on to win that title, Virtus won both the EuroLeague and the *scudetto,* the tricolored patch emblematic of the Italian championship, at Fortitudo's expense. Always, Virtus seemed to win at Fortitudo's expense.

Virtus began as a fencing club in 1871, and its following includes Bologna's lawyers, managers, and entrepreneurs. They turn out in their Armani sweaters and Zegna slacks, with cell phones chirping in their pockets and midwinter tans hinting at ski weekends spent in the Alps. Austere and elitist, Virtus flies black and white as its colors and charges nearly twice what its rival does for season tickets. A year earlier the club won its 14th *scudetto,* a total worthy of the Boston Celtics or Žalgiris Kaunas, with a victory over Fortitudo in a decisive fifth game. That title came after Fortitudo led Virtus two games to one; after Fortitudo lost Game 4 by two points following a tantalizing missed three-pointer at the buzzer by its expensive American ringer, Dominique Wilkins; and after Virtus trailed by four points with 18 seconds to play in Game 5. Afterward, the Fortitudo players barricaded themselves in their locker room for an hour and a half. Given what and how they'd lost, it's a marvel they didn't stay holed up longer.

Catholic priests founded Fortitudo at the turn of the century as a youth center to minister to the city's working-class west side. Partisans like to say that their team still attracts students and workers, when in fact many fans turned to Fortitudo during the 1980s simply because Virtus was punching out the house. Fortitudo's hardcores, the Fossa dei Leoni, or Lion's Den, are louder, more numerous, and much more outrageous than Virtus's fan club, the Forever Boys. Ironical and self-mocking, famous for the elaborate choreography of their routines and notorious for their lapses in taste, they embody the Bolognese sense of humor and zest for life. "Fortitudo is a faith," they say. "Virtus is a fancy." And: "They say 'It is important to have.' We say 'It is important to be.'"

In Italy the epithet "Rabbit!" is a stand-in for the American "chicken," hurled at someone who's soft, weak, or ready to turn tail at the first sign of trouble. Over the years Fortitudo fans have staged all sorts of hare-raising japery, even once releasing a live rabbit on the court. (Never retrieved, it was assumed to have provided the arena's custodian with dinner.) But the Fossa dei Leoni pulled off their most inspired pageantry before a game in 1995, when Virtus was sponsored by Buckler, a nonalcoholic beer. First they unfurled a giant banner reading TO LIVE A LIFE IN BLACK AND WHITE. . . . Then they rolled out another: DRINKING NONALCOHOLIC BEER. Finally, they delivered a Fortitudian riposte to so spiritless an existence—one last banner, COLORS, followed by a cannonade of streamers of every hue, launched from the arena's top row. No one who tells this story fails to add the kicker: Fortitudo won the game by a point.

But to follow Fortitudo is to embrace the kind of fatalism

familiar to devotees of the Los Angeles Clippers. Fortitudo fans take perverse pride in their team's failures, turning each lost *scudetto* into an absent badge of honor. Following one epic Fortitudo collapse, the Forever Boys serenaded their rivals with "You never win a fucking thing!" The Fossa dei Leoni adapted this as a sort of anthem, singing it lustily for months: *Non abbiamo mai vinto un cazzo!*—"We never win a fucking thing!" When Fortitudo finally won something, the 1998 Italy Cup, many fans reacted with tortured ambivalence, as if the very purpose of the team's existence had evaporated. To some, the Cup victory is still known as "the stupid win that spoiled the song."

So it would seem that Fortitudo vs. Virtus—literally, strength vs. virtue—arrayed Bologna's working class against its upper crust. Only things weren't quite that simple, at least not as simple as they used to be. The class lines had blurred, the stereotypes softened. With its flinty comebacks the previous spring, Virtus made the case that it deserved the mantle of the city's lionhearts. Meanwhile, the hammer and sickle no longer appeared at Fortitudo games, even though the city was still ruled by Communists at the time of my visit. Indeed, when Wilkins pouted at the end of the previous season, no one was quite sure why. Was it out of shame for his role in the ignominy of Games 4 and 5? Or because the club had refused to pay the plane fare for a baby-sitter from the States?

Nowhere was this incipient role reversal more evident than in the clubs' owners. Virtus chairman Alfredo Cazzola is a bootstrapping businessman who made his fortune by staging huge auto shows. If he has any patrician reserve, it wasn't evident in the way he once responded to derisive chants from the Leoni by standing up at his seat and defiantly offering them the *scudetto* on the breast of his suitcoat. Fortitudo's own money-man, by contrast, could be a Fortitudo caricature of a Virtus supporter. Giorgio Seragnoli was born into a family of Croesusean wealth. He is said to have signed Wilkins as a birthday gift for his 10-year-old son. And after the previous season's meltdown he had made like some Giorgio Steinbrenner and cut Wilkins loose.

Seragnoli has enough rabbit in him that he rarely shows up for a Derby unless it's a Fortitudo home game. But that's what this first meeting of the season was, and that's why he sat here in the Palasport as tip-off time approached—and why the Virtus cause was taken up by fewer than 100 fans, most of them a cluster of Forever Boys confined to one corner of the arena.

The Fossa dei Leoni occupied the entire stand behind the basket at the opposite end. For a moment the Leoni stilled themselves and held aloft their blue-and-white team scarves as if they were prayer shawls. But soon enough the Fortitudo supporters were roaring again. One raised a sign reading E IL LUNEDÌ SENZA VOCE—"And on Monday I'll have lost my voice."

I considered the language this lost voice would be incapable of speaking and thought, Such a pity.

In the days leading up to the game, I immersed myself in as much of Bologna as I could. This was not duty that deserved combat pay. Nearly 22 miles of the city's sidewalks are overhung with porticoes, most impressively the arcade that snakes its way up to the Sanctuary of San Luca overlooking the city. It comprises 666 arches, a number that would seem to confirm suspicions elsewhere in Italy that this university town harbors a bit of the devil. Indeed, Bolognese attitudes have so frustrated the Vatican that an archbishop has decried the province of Emilia-Romagna, of which Bologna is the capital, as Italy's most degenerate.

The city's sensual preoccupations begin with taste. Its nickname is *la grassa*, the Fat, and the firms sponsoring Bologna's two teams over the years have included such calorie-rich concerns as Kinder (chocolate), Knorr (soups and sauces), Granarolo and Latte Sole (dairy products), Eldorado (ice cream), PAF (pasta), and the all-encompassing Mangiaebevi—literally, Eat and Drink. While shop windows celebrate the pleasures of the palate, street names glorify those of the flesh. There is a Vicolo Baciadame (Lady-Kisser Lane), even a via

Fregatette (Tit-Rub Street). The Vatican evidently fights a losing battle.

The city once bristled with nearly 200 towers, each erected by a family eager to make a show of its wealth and prominence. Of the few that remain, two stand side by side as symbols of the city. The thin aristocratic tower, the Asinelli, which has only a slight tilt to it, is said to represent Virtus, and the Garisenda— short, stout, leaning impudently to one side—Fortitudo. A 19th-century French traveler remarked that they looked like two old friends who had ventured outside the walls of the city in search of a good time and come back drunk.

I climbed the Asinelli one afternoon, hoping to spot the old basketball arena, the PalaDozza. When I couldn't, I took up the offer of a longtime Fortitudo fan named Enrico to lead me there. This being Bologna, Enrico chose a roundabout route. He took me first up the city's main drag, past movie marquees billing *Salvate il soldato Ryan, Tutti Pazzi per Mary,* and Spike Lee's *He Got Game*—the latter needing no translation, not in this town.

We passed the Sala Borsa, the old stock exchange, which until the mid-1950s doubled as Virtus's home court, where custodians cleared the floor and wheeled out baskets after a day of trading. When graffiti assaulted us as we turned a corner— VIRTUS MERDA, which means, more or less, "Virtus sucks"—I knew we were on Enrico's home turf. The gentle hills on the south side of town were home to Virtus's supporters. But this was Fortitudo country. "See?" he said, gesturing magisterially. "It *smell* of basket." I would hear that verb used this way often during my visit.

Past Bar Basket, past a men's large-size shoe store that did a lively trade with the players, past a sports bookshop run by former Virtus forward Riccardo Morandotti, we followed our noses to the PalaDozza. Known informally as *il Madison,* after Madison Square Garden, it was a low-slung roundhouse so cozily nestled in a residential neighborhood that I understood instantly both why I couldn't see it from atop the Asinelli and why old-timers rued its eclipse by the antiseptic Palasport. Where once fans could linger over a Sunday lunch and walk to the game, since 1995 they'd had to pile into cars and fight the traffic out to a spot in the southwest suburbs, hard by a shopping center and an Ikea showroom.

Enrico and I stopped at a *caffè* across from *il Madison*. To this point my guide had concealed his partisan feelings. But as he began going over painful terrain—Fortitudo's collapse on the cusp of winning the previous season's *scudetto*—the deadpan fell from his face. "Everything was set up so well," he said. "A fan dressed in an angel's costume was hiding in the overhead scoreboard at the Palasport, ready to descend and present the *scudetto* following Game 4. Back at *il Madison* there was a feast ready for everybody, just like in Siena after the *palio*. It was one of the saddest things I've seen in my life. We lost by two, after a three-point try by Dominique at the buzzer went *two times* around the rim and out. The guy in the angel costume was up there the whole game. No one knows how he got down."

Enrico stared dolefully into his espresso for what seemed like a minute. Then he turned to the future of the Derby. With the two teams playing each other so often, he feared the rivalry was losing its meaning. "Now they play always for supposedly more important things. Hearing people walk out of the Palasport after a regular-season Derby saying, 'Oh, it doesn't really count'—to me, that's sad. You see, I don't want to be Number 1 in Europe. I don't want to be Number 1 in Italy. I want to be Number 1 *in this town*.

"But there is no reason we can't be human beings about it. It bothers me to see children watching their parents screaming at the referees and the players. In Siena they fight each other so hard, neighborhood versus neighborhood, twice a year. They say their war is fought to unite everybody—that you fight your enemy because you understand your enemy, you love him, you have the same blood in common. And sure enough, after the race Siena is the most united city in the world. What they have in Siena is something I'd like to see here."

For a Fortitudo lifer, Enrico sounded almost like a statesman rehearsing his Nobel acceptance speech. Then his face clouded over. Understanding and brotherhood had their limits. "Now, why would someone drink nonalcoholic beer?" he muttered. "I mean, then *don't drink beer.*"

The next day, the Saturday before the game, I swung by the Palasport for the Virtus perspective. As the Virtus players went through light paces, the team's most respected figure tried to explain the emotional dimensions of what I'd be witnessing. A point guard who participated in 27 Derbies during a 14-year career, Roberto Brunamonti so personified the club for which he played that, upon retirement, he slid easily from the back-court into Virtus's vice presidency. Trim and balding, he had the kind of dark facial features that a receding hairline only throws into more impressive relief. "Yes, this game is worth only two points in the standings," he told me. "Yes, you can say this is a 'normal game.' But for me, none of this is true. If a player lives in Bologna, he smells this atmosphere. And I like this atmos-phere. Bologna is a university city, you see. So many ironic per-sons. The fans, when they are ironic, it is good. I play a lot of Derbies, and only sometimes what happens is what the news-papers say will happen. There are always surprises."

Both teams practiced at the Palasport, and I sensed awk-wardness as Virtus left the floor following its workout and For-titudo filed on: a few tentative handshakes, some light palaver, a forced embrace between two players. Virtus coach Ettore Messina wanted no part of it. He quickly led me into his office and jumped to the subject at hand.

He didn't like the pressure of the Derby, he said, didn't like what it did to people. "I can't stand it when I'm running in the park and somebody calls me an asshole, just because of what I do for a living."

Place him in Lexington, Kentucky, or Ann Arbor, Michigan, and Messina would be almost indistinguishable from any of a number of young American college coaches. His English is excellent. He lectures on management at the University of Milan. Having studied under Bob McKillop at Davidson and

Dean Smith at North Carolina, he emphasizes defense and ball control, and his teams know how to grow a lead, then pack it in the dry ice of a zone. He even believes in such boola-boola rituals as a postgame team meal. "It's a time for the players," he said of the spread at Brunamonti's restaurant. "I eat in another room with my staff. No one is obliged to come, but the players always do, especially after we lose. And the box score is never passed around the table."

He had spent time in and around Durham and Chapel Hill, but Messina thought the Derby made Duke–North Carolina look like intramural snooker at Eton. "Playing 10 times last year was very difficult," he said. "Both teams were built to win, and each time it was life and death. Our season is similar to an NBA season in the number of games we play, but we play three competitions at once—the EuroLeague, the Italy Cup, and for the *scudetto*. I think you in America do it better. I mean, imagine playing two NITs and the NCAAs, all at the same time. Lose two or three games in a row, and the newspapers start writing that you're 'in crisis.'"

Messina nonetheless thought he had detected a softening in the two teams' attitudes toward each other, even in their supporters' attitudes. "For a long time they were supposed to be the fighters and we were supposed to be the snobs, the no-balls team. But last year we gained respect because we won the way they'd always loved to win. We had injuries, but we relied on passion and chemistry and hard work. They looked like the old cliché of Virtus, with Dominique leading a parade of superstars. Because of that, I think they respect us more. And their fans respect us more."

Ettore Messina may have been right, but nothing I'd seen in the fevered hour before tip-off indicated that the Fortitudo fans respected Virtus at all. And once the game began, the Fortitudo players seemed to show no regard for the visiting team, either. The first eight minutes featured little more than whistles for illegal screens, and sharp commentary from the Fossa dei Leoni, both verbal and projectile. After Virtus's Alessandro Frosini got away with steps (a bad no-call), objects rained down on the floor. Fortitudo center Gregor Fučka was whistled for traveling (a good call), and more debris followed.

In the first five minutes of the second half, as Virtus pushed out to a 40–26 lead, it looked as if Fortitudo would lose to the black-and-whites once again. This time blame would fall on Arturas Karnišovas, the former player at Seton Hall who had blossomed as a scorer in Europe and this season was the bene-ficiary of Seragnoli's decision to lavish his lire on non-Ameri-cans. Karnišovas had spent the first half jumping up in the air with the ball and no clue what to do with it. Yet Fortitudo had almost imperceptibly shaved away at the Virtus lead. And here, with Virtus up by only 56–54 late in the game, right after muffing several free throws and a wide-open layup, the Lithuanian forward stepped up like a Forest Brother. He stabbed fearlessly at the air and sent a three-pointer through the net.

I could think only of Brunamonti's remark the day before: "There are always surprises." Fortitudo hadn't led since the game's opening moments. Now it was up by one. The Fortitudo fans fell into an uncharacteristic silence, perhaps because 18 seconds remained, and their memory of what had happened the last time they led Virtus with 18 seconds to play, in Game 5 a year ago, was all too fresh.

That's when events began to follow a script by Pirandello. Fortitudo hadn't yet reached its limit of team fouls, so for the remainder of the game it tried to spend the ones it had left. Once, twice, a third time the home team wasted a foul, forcing its opponent to inbound anew, and Virtus was unable to get off a last good shot. But Fortitudo had in fact exceeded the limit with this late spate of fouling. Unbeknownst to virtually everyone, after the official scorer raised the *paletta*, the red paddle indicating that a team is over the limit, a Fortitudo fac-totum sitting beside him stealthily pulled it back down.

All of this would come to light in the days following the

game. The papers would publish frame grabs from the television broadcast documenting *palettagate* with Zapruder-like precision. The offending official, a 58-year-old Sicilian named Santi Puglisi, would be barred from working a scorer's table for 45 days. Virtus's courtside counterpart would resign as a matter of honor for having failed to notice and prevent this chicanery. Cazzola, the Virtus owner, would phone a TV station and spend 10 minutes of airtime decrying "this national shame," promising "legal action," demanding "exceptional punishment." The Leoni would fete Saint Santi with a standing ovation at the team's next game and announce that they had already prepared their choreography for the second Derby of the season: 2,000 raised *palette*, all to be pulled down at once. The uproar would last for weeks. But the result, 57–56 Fortitudo, would stand.

Steamed, Messina headed off the floor for the locker room. The door to their den opened and the Leoni dashed across the court to the far end of the Palasport, to taunt and bait and gesticulate up-yourses at the few Forever Boys who hadn't begun to slink off to the parking lot.

I wondered if the Virtus delegation would still be gathering for dinner at Brunamonti's restaurant. Then I recalled what Messina had said: " . . . especially after we lose." This was Bologna, after all. There is always food and drink.

⛹

Derby Day was dissolving toward midnight. The twin towers cast their shadows as I made my way by moonlight through the university district, over fishbone pavement and past terra-cotta facings. The quiet seemed implausible after the frenzy of a few hours earlier, but it soothed somehow, took an edge off the events I'd just witnessed. I ducked into a tavern called L'Infedele, where I found Lorenzo Sani nursing a lemon liqueur in front of the bar.

Lorenzo writes for the local daily *Il Resto del Carlino*. (It says something about Bologna that the name of its *New York Times* means, more or less, "change from the cost of an espresso.") His wife, Alessandra, runs L'Infedele, a classic Bolognese *osteria,* the kind of place where students and intellectuals have gathered for centuries to imbibe and converse and make sport of the pompous and powerful. Lorenzo greeted me, then pulled an artifact from behind the bar: a Fortitudo wristwatch, stuck at 10 minutes to eight. "My friend Claudio works here," he said. "He is a Fortitudo supporter. The night Fortitudo won the Italy Cup last season, his watch just stopped. *Stopped!* Magically. Right here. He put this on the wall, and it has hung there ever since."

I realized that I was in a sort of Derby reliquary. Lorenzo produced another piece of memorabilia: a pennant with the insignia of the club team based in the Croatian city of Split. To explain its connection to Bologna, he launched into a story.

At the end of the 1990–91 season Virtus got rid of its star, Micheal (Sugar) Ray Richardson, after the former New York Knick had led the team to two titles. "Virtus insists it does this only to sign a better player," Lorenzo said. "But Sugar has had a great year and is the most popular player in town. Because it seems like such a crazy decision, there is the impression that it has to do with drugs. And because of Sugar's past"—the NBA had banned him for repeated cocaine abuse—"nobody asks Virtus to explain itself any further. Everybody accepts Virtus's version except one stupid journalist, who is me. I say if there is evidence, let's see it, and if there is no evidence, this is crazy. But there is nothing Sugar can do. He is gone. He is angry at Messina, of course. But he is most angry at Alessandro Mancaruso, the Virtus general manager, who has a very big nose.

"He is still angry when he signs with the team in Split for the next season. One month later there is a wonderful coincidence. Virtus must play Split in a European Cup game. This game is moved to La Coruña in Spain because of the war in the Balkans. I stay at Sugar's hotel, and he tells me he must make revenge. 'What can I do to best make revenge?' he asks. During the day I find the answer in a shop. It is a pair of glasses with a funny nose.

"I have the glasses in my pocket when the game begins. Sugar runs by me at courtside. He has that stutter and he says,

'Re-m-m-m-ember the n-n-nose!' And he yells at Messina about his center, who is Bill Wennington. 'H-h-h-hey, E-t-t-t-tore! W-w-w-wennington's no b-b-ballplayer! H-h-h-e's a *l-l-l-lumberjack!*' And Sugar plays great—*great*—and Split is ready to win when Sugar turns to Messina. He says, 'H-h-h-hey, E-t-t-t-t-ore! It's o-o-o-ver!' And he makes two free throws to ice the game.

"Afterward Sugar comes by me and puts on the big nose and glasses and starts to wave the STOP THE WAR IN CROATIA banner that the team takes to all its games. Then he finds Mancaruso and gets in his face and says all the swear words he has ever learned in Italian, every one of them, all together, with no logic."

Lorenzo seemed to toast himself with his *limoncello,* an impresario recalling one of his finest productions. "Virtus tried to deny me a press credential for many games after this," he said.

I examined the pennant's inscription. "Thinking to the big nose 'game.'" It was signed "Micheal R Richardson/Sugar."

Richardson never tried to pawn himself off as a rhetorician, but I liked how he had put "game" in quotes. He knew a good farce when he saw one.

I bade the Sanis good night and left L'Infedele in a rush, for my *pensione* enforced a most un-Bolognese house rule that guests be in their rooms by 1 A.M. As I made my way back, it occurred to me that Lorenzo and Micheal Ray had learned this city's lessons well. The point wasn't to trudge impassively through life. If it were, Bologna would be Bonn. The point was to push life to its limit, to infuse even the most quotidian things with all they would accept. In this city that claims to be Italy's hottest in summer and coldest in winter, if you give yourself over to *il basket,* you must surrender to the all of it, just as the Bolognese give themselves over totally to everything they do. And in the passion play I'd just seen, over Halloween weekend, each citizen had been fitted for a costume, fans and sports-writers every bit as much as players and coaches and owners.

Strength and virtue were much closer to the state of coexistence that Enrico hoped to see; Bologna was much more like Siena than anyone cared to admit. Like the two towers at the city's heart, Fortitudo and Virtus had wandered off briefly, theatrically, *campanili* indulging in *campanilismo*. But they'd helped each other make it back inside the walls, and here they'd sit, side by side, until the next Derby, when they'd go off on another bender.

I reached my *pensione* just before curfew and buzzed from the front door. Through the intercom I heard a joyful noise that made the day complete.

"*Prrrrronto!*" said the night clerk.

SEVEN

Sarajevo Airport
Prisoners of War

Head east from Italy over the Adriatic Sea, and you'll notice two differences: The basketball gets better; and the rivalries are no longer costumed ones, with streamers and rabbits and greasepaint.

Whenever I think of what has become of the former Yugoslavia, a particular face makes its way into my mind. It belongs to a Serb named Svetislav Pešić, who in 1987 coached a group of adolescent Yugoslavs to the World Junior Championship. He and I had first spoken in 1995, when three members of that team had already reached the NBA and a fourth was about to do so. But people in the Balkans were still counting their dead from the wars of Yugoslavia's destruction, and the conflict had driven wedges among his former players, Bosnians, Croats, and Serbs he had once molded into such a persuasive advertisement for teamwork.

Pešić has a little boy's ears, saturnine hollows in his cheeks, and eyes that run so deep they leave you wondering whether someone has bought up the mineral rights. When he recalled that victory his features broadened in winsome delight. And when he touched, as he couldn't help but do, on what had happened in the Balkans since, his face whipsawed back past its gloomy default setting to a despair almost beyond imagining.

The emotional amplitude of this man so haunted me that through late 1995 and early 1996 I set out to learn more about his extraordinary team. I hunted down five of the boys-turned-men who had played for him, and I spent several days with Pešić in Germany, where he was coaching Alba Berlin, one of the elite club teams on the Continent.

I hadn't seen that face for three years. But after arriving from Bologna I thought I saw it again, in the passport line at the Sarajevo Airport.

"*Herr* Pešić?" I said in German, our lingua franca.

"*Herr* Wolff!"

The next line scripted for encounters like this is normally "What are *you* doing here?" I knew better. Though born near Belgrade, Pešić had made his life in Sarajevo. He had met his wife, Vera, here. He had lived not a mile from where we stood. He had played for Bosna Sarajevo, the storied local club team, when it won the European Cup in 1979. As much as someone could, Pešić held within himself the spirit of this city, where for 500 years people of all backgrounds had lived peaceably along-side one another.

When Pešić and Bosna Sarajevo returned from France after defeating Emerson Varese for the Cup, some 10,000 people packed this very terminal to fete the team's Croatian, Muslim, and Serbian players and its Montenegrin coach. Thousands more lined the road into the city—the same road that would come to be known as Sniper Alley.

I had stumbled upon Pešić, it turned out, on the very threshold of his return to Sarajevo for the first time since the war.

In 1984, when Svetislav Pešić first took charge of the cohort that would make up Yugoslav basketball's greatest generation, the Berlin Wall still stood. Sarajevo had just welcomed the world to a Winter Olympics. The heirs to Marshal Tito still enforced the late Yugoslav strongman's call for multiethnic "brotherhood and unity," ruthlessly spackling any nationalist cracks in the socialist state as soon as they appeared.

There was no part of Yugoslavia, then a federation of five republics and two autonomous provinces, that Pešić couldn't take his team to train. For two weeks the boys bivouacked at a camp in the Serbian upcountry, where they could look out the windows of their lodge each evening and see the eyes of wolves, cold and disembodied in the darkness. But inside they felt so safe, so invulnerable, that after the coaches retired for the night they played cards, raided the kitchen, watched videos of their NBA heroes till 4, 5, 6 in the morning, a 7 A.M. summons for more training be damned.

At a camp outside Sarajevo, just a few miles from the airport, they ran the 300 steps to the top of the Olympic ski jump on Mount Igman, ran them so hard that their quaking legs balked at taking them back down. First time up they were permitted two stops to catch their breath. Second time up they could rest but once. And before they could call it a day they had to run all the way up without stopping. One of the boys, Toni Kukoč, then a bony stroke of an adolescent, tried desperately to clear his mind of the pain. "I . . . am . . . an . . . *idiot!*" he would yell, and none of his teammates could spare the breath to dispute him.

And they had assembled at a resort on Croatia's Istrian peninsula, where one night the social director cajoled them into taking part in the evening's entertainment, a variation on musical chairs. Each player was to hoist a female tourist onto his shoulders and, when the music stopped, make for a vacant seat on the poolside terrace. When only two of the boys and a single chair remained, both impishly tossed their payloads into the pool, and their teammates followed suit, heaving emcee, musicians, and tourists alike into the drink. The ringleader, a frontcourt lug named Dino Radja, did his penance in practice the next day, shuttling baseline to baseline a dozen times with a 245-pound assistant coach on his back.

They were the finest basketball players born in the Balkans during 1967 and 1968, that biennial of worldwide unrest—

"Our own Dream Team," as one of them, a long-limbed, slumbrous-eyed center named Vlade Divac, would tell me. They first mustered as 16- and 17-year-olds, and for four years they stayed together, laughing and sweating as they learned the price of victory and never failed to pony up. It would not be a stretch to say that Divac, Kukoč, and Radja went on to become stars, if not All-Stars, in the NBA. A fourth, a playmaker named Sasha Djordjević, anchored some of Europe's finest club teams and was named the continent's Player of the Year in 1994 before doing a brief turn with the Portland Trail Blazers. A fifth, Teo Alibegović, became a frontcourt star in Germany, Italy, Spain, and Turkey.

In those four years together they never lost a game in formal international competition. In 1985, as 17-year-olds, Divac and Kukoč starred for the Yugoslav team that won the European Cadet Championship; at 18 and 19 all five combined to win the 1986 European Junior title; in exhibitions and other tournaments over that span, they beat the senior national teams of Bulgaria, Turkey, even the Soviet Union. Yugoslavia's own nationals, perennially among the world's best, sometimes lost to their jayvee in training-camp scrimmages.

So it was that these young men, at 19 and 20, stepped up for what would be their valedictory, the 1987 Junior Worlds, with their sense of invincibility intact. At three in the morning on the day of the final, they stole away from their hotel to trampolines set up in the center of Bormio, the town in the Italian Alps hosting the championships. As the U.S. players rested, hoping to avenge Yugoslavia's 110–95 victory in an earlier round, the boys from the Balkans carelessly launched into somersaults. "We really didn't care," Alibegović would tell me. "We were so sure of ourselves, we never thought we could lose."

At halftime the next day Yugoslavia trailed by three points, and its post players, Divac and Radja, had picked up three fouls each. In the locker room Pešić thought for the first time he could see fear in the eyes of his boys. He flung an equipment bag violently to the floor and stalked out. It was left to Djordjević, the team's captain, to invoke what in Serbo-Croat are called *jaja*—balls. He called on his teammates to give everything "from your heels up" for 20 more minutes.

The young men who formed the core of the American team—Larry Johnson, Gary Payton, Lionel Simmons, Scott Williams, and Stacy Augmon—would go on to the NBA. But their Yugoslav counterparts hadn't sacrificed all those summers while buddies back home were taking girlfriends to the coast, hadn't given each other frightful haircuts at three in the morning, hadn't left all those brain cells on Mount Igman, in order to lose to some stir-fry of green Americans.

The way the Yugoslav team came out of the locker room— "Like dogs that hadn't eaten for days," Alibegović remembered—the U.S. scarcely had a chance. The Americans were wary of Kukoč, for he had made 11 of 12 three-point shots in the teams' first meeting. But as the Yanks fussed over Kukoč on the perimeter, Divac and Radja had their way inside as Yugoslavia won 86–76.

A Spanish photographer captured the aftermath in hurriedly posed black and white: Divac, never one to stifle his emotions, keeling back in joy; Radja, more modulated in his happiness but glowing just the same, seemingly joined at Divac's hip, another shoot from the same plant; Kukoč, at the group's periphery, eyes narrowed in fatigue, too drained even to raise his arms fully in triumph; Djordjević, in the middle, his clenched fists and conqueror's glare seeming to issue the Americans a double-or-nothing challenge. Alibegović played sparingly in the final, so he looks fresh, fresher even than Pešić, who made prints of the photograph and sent one to each player as a holiday card. *Keep this picture,* the coach wrote on the back of each. *Never forget what we accomplished together.*

The innocence of that time abides with every one of them. Radja, a Croat, told me why: "You don't have no problems. You don't have no wife or kids, or car that's broke down, because you don't own one. No 'Oh why am I flying coach instead of first class?' because you ride the bus. You don't complain about anything because you're a kid and everything is fun, and you're on a winning team, and you kick butt. The only way we discussed ethnic groups was by making jokes about each other. Believe me, everybody was laughing. You wouldn't laugh now, but back then we were laughing."

"I spent the whole year playing basketball," said Kukoč, who grew up with Radja in Split. "The only friends I had were my club teammates and guys from the national team. Who could think about a war? No one."

"They used to come over to my place," said Djordjević, a Serb from Belgrade. "I used to go over to their place. That's not possible now because they're not coming to my country and I'm not going to theirs."

"We were Yugoslav," said Divac, also a Serb, who grew up 100 miles from Djordjević in Prijepolje. "Just like Americans might be from L.A., New York, Texas. Different accents, maybe. But not different."

The entire experience, said Alibegović, a Bosnian Muslim whose family lived in Slovenia, "was like first love. It stays with you for the rest of your life."

For Divac and Djordjević, Kukoč and Radja, the tapestry of those recollections would become brocaded with barbed wire. All four played in the 1996 Olympics in Atlanta, but for different sides—Divac and Djordjević for the Serb-dominated rump of Yugoslavia, Kukoč and Radja for an independent Croatia that had come to regard Serbia as its implacable enemy. Since the four last played together, for the Yugoslav senior national team that won the 1991 European Championships in Rome, more than 200,000 people had been killed and three million left homeless by the four-year conflict in the Balkans that pitted predominantly Orthodox Serbs against largely Roman Catholic Croats against the Muslims of Bosnia-Herzegovina.

Back in 1987 the Junior Worlds were held up for several days by heavy rains, which touched off mud slides that destroyed entire villages and killed more than 40 people. The citizens of Bormio nonetheless urged that the tournament proceed as planned, if only as a sign that life goes on. With their victory, the basketball prodigies from across the Adriatic seemed to represent genesis within apocalypse to the people of the Italian Alps.

And then, in what was Yugoslavia, apocalypse again. The ski jump on Mount Igman was turned to rubble. The resorts along the Adriatic were shuttered and shunned. And the boys who once mocked the wolves fraternized with one another at their peril.

For years there had been no surer way to win a title in international sports than to take a group of Yugoslavs and hand them a ball. Teams from the Balkans, whether composed of men or women, whether representing local clubs or the entire country, had outsized success in European, world, and Olympic competition. Whatever the team sport, whether soccer or volleyball, water polo or team handball, antebellum Yugoslavs seemed to know just how to integrate their disparate parts.

And if you coached basketball, oh the group you could gather. Coaches spoke frankly about the strengths each ethnic group brought to the national side. Croats from the Dalmatian coast are some of the tallest people in the world. Slovenes are Teutonic not just in appearance but in organizational skill, too. Montenegrins, flinty like mountain folk everywhere, are preternaturally large besides. Bosnians are consummate blenders given their history of assimilation; Macedonians, dervishes in their movements and thus perfect for the backcourt; Serbs, so up for a fight that over the centuries they had adopted the cry, "No war without the Serbs!"

After the World Junior Championship, Pešić became an enforcer in the service of the team's memory, with that black-and-white photograph the brass knuckles of his task. He spoke of a reunion game, for charity, perhaps against the Dream Team. But would the U.S. players be willing? he wondered in 1995, even before addressing the matter of whether his former players would agree. When he saw one of the Boys of Bormio, he would ask, Do you keep up with one another? You who are in America, do you get together? And, urgently: Do you still have that picture?

"When I look at that picture and think of the war, I feel so sad," Pešić said. He had won that European Cup back in 1979; in 1993, as coach of the German national team, he had won a European Championship. "But my greatest personal satisfaction was with the Yugoslav juniors in Bormio. That was the result of four years of living and working together. It will stay in my soul for all eternity.

"In sports, Yugoslav qualities include cooperation and a sense of togetherness. Unfortunately, the politicians in our country have learned very little from our athletes."

I found Vlade Divac when he was still playing for the Los Angeles Lakers, living in a gated neighborhood in Pacific Palisades with sweeping views over the cliffs to the ocean. That Divac made his way from Belgrade to Los Angeles and Magic Johnson's team was literally the happiest of occurrences, for he and Magic played the same way, with an expressive, lightfooted joy. Thus it was particularly hard for Divac to come to terms with how his oldest friendships had been so somberly reframed.

At the 1995 European Championships in Athens, organizers had lodged the teams from Croatia and Yugoslavia at the same hotel, but the two were assigned seating in the communal dining hall as far from each other as possible. Yet on the tournament's opening day, the first two teams to show up for lunch were Croatia and Yugoslavia. Before going up to fill their plates at the buffet, Divac remembered, "People were hesitating, wondering how everybody was going to react."

To Divac's relief, both Radja and Kukoč greeted him. The encounter was nonetheless too strained for Divac's taste. "We converse, but it's not the relationship that used to be," he said. "And that's not enough for me. For years we spent almost every day together. I deserve more from them than just 'Hello.'"

So desperate was Divac's need to talk with his old teammates that shortly after the war began in 1991, he called Alibegović, who was then playing at Oregon State, and asked him to make the drive from Corvallis up to Portland, where the Lakers were to play the Trail Blazers. Holed up with his former teammate in a hotel room, Divac brought up the war.

"Let's not talk about that," Alibegović said.

"Teo, we must talk," Divac replied. "I must know the truth: What do you think? I'm going to tell you what I think."

If a simple face-to-face meant so much to Divac, it may be because there was a former teammate to whom he wished he could still talk. In Buenos Aires in 1990, as Yugoslavia celebrated its 92–75 rout of the Soviet Union to win the World Championship, a fan ran out on the court waving a Croatian flag. Divac regarded this interloper as a vandal trying to cleave the team by politicizing a sacred moment, and he instinctively yanked the flag away. "I told the guy that Yugoslavia had won and to please leave," Divac said. "He told me my flag was bull-shit."

Divac and one of the Croats on that team in Buenos Aires, another budding NBA star named Dražen Petrović, had spoken on the phone almost every day after both came to the U.S. But in 1992, after the war began, Petrović suddenly stopped returning Divac's calls, and to others he cited the incident in Buenos Aires as the reason. Divac believed that Petrović, whose father was a Serb, froze him out because Petrović felt pressure to prove his Croat bona fides. Divac told himself that they would patch things up after the war ended. But Petrović was killed in a car accident in Germany in 1993 before the two could reconcile. "That was the most difficult thing for me," Divac said, "never having had a chance to talk."

A few weeks before my visit, Divac had pulled out what he thought was a videotape of an upcoming Lakers opponent and popped it into his VCR. But he soon realized he had mistakenly cued up Yugoslav television's broadcast of the 1991 European final, which had been played even as months of tensions in the Balkans were erupting into a shooting war. Something kept Divac seated until all of Yugoslavia's easy defeat of Italy spooled out. "This great team may be the best ever," a broadcaster intoned in Serbo-Croat as the game wound down. "And it has probably played its last game together." Deep in the comfort of his couch, Divac started to cry.

"To build one friendship, you need years and years," he said. "To break that friendship you need"—he snapped his fingers—"just a second. That's what happened to us. I have a nice life here—a great career, a wonderful marriage, wonderful children. As soon as I wake up and see the sun, I should be the happiest guy in the world. But I'm not. It's like my entire body's happy, except one part, which is hurt and dying."

During his first season in the NBA, while the war raged back home, you could see the labor in everything Toni Kukoč did. His basketball countenance had once been so ethereal that Kukoč opted out of Pešić's first weight-training exercises for fear his wraithlike 6'11" frame wouldn't hold up under the strain. Yet after joining the Chicago Bulls in 1993, he seemed to repudiate the style that had turned him into the finest young player in Europe. He bulked up, became sluggish, played tentatively. As a prodigy in Split, Kukoč had starred in his own highlight video, *Enjoy Like Me*, whose goofy title paid idiomatically impaired homage to teammate-to-be Michael Jordan and the *Come Fly with Me* video that sold hundreds of thousands of copies. *Enjoy Like Me* documented the essence of Kukoč's game, whether he was darting into the lane to shoot or pass, or setting up outside the arc the way he had in Bormio when he traced those 11 three-point parabolas over the American defense. "Easier than a layup," Kukoč told me in the Berto Center, the Bulls' training facility, as he recalled that day. "You just see that big, huge hole, and every ball you shoot is going in."

Crack through the shell into which Kukoč retracted and you could find an essential homebody, a player who back in the mid-1980s was always the most reluctant to take part in those late-night high jinks. His first coach in Chicago, Phil Jackson, would tease Kukoč about how he played better when a Bulls game was being broadcast back to Croatia and his mother might be watching. Indeed, on the day Jordan announced his first retirement, before Kukoč would play his maiden NBA game, the kid from Split puddled up in front of the entire team, for only the prospect of playing with the greatest of all time had been able to lure him from Europe.

He would get Jordan back. But as an expatriate, Kukoč lived a wary life. There was a story going around Chicago, which he didn't deny, that he once gave Bulls tickets to a couple he knew there— he a Croat, she a Serb—but asked that she not go, lest TV cameras panning the crowd catch a glimpse of her sitting in Kukoč's seats and his countrymen somehow hold him accountable.

He vividly recalled the beginning of the end, at the 1991 European Championships in Rome. Slovenia had declared its independence from the Yugoslav federation three days before the semifinals, and the Yugoslav army responded by attacking Ljubljana. On the afternoon of the semis, Kukoč's roommate, a guard from Slovenia named Juri Zdovc, received a fax from the Slovenian minister of sport: If Zdovc played that night, he would be considered a traitor to his people. With a wife and a child back home, Zdovc had no choice. He tearfully told his teammates good-bye. "I understood," Kukoč said. "It wasn't basketball anymore."

By September the war had spread to Croatia. The homes of some of Kukoč's relatives and friends were destroyed, and this man who loved domestic tranquillity in every sense gradually but ineluctably hardened. "It always gets down to asking how's your family, how's mine," he said of relations with his Muslim and Serbian ex-teammates. "And when you touch on families, you have to touch on the war, and when you touch on the war, you're on opposite sides. I know those guys aren't doing any-thing wrong—all of them, I know, are good guys. But it's war."

If Pešić really hoped to reunite his team, his toughest sell was going to be Kukoč, who didn't even know whether he still had

Pešić's picture. "Maybe it's back home," Kukoč told me. "It's not important. It was nice back then, but it's in the past. Now only the NBA counts. Too much has happened to say, 'Okay, let's go play.' Last summer in Croatia I visited hospitals to see the wounded. Once you see 19- and 20-year-old guys without arms, without legs, you don't think about basketball."

On the terrace of his apartment in Bologna, where he then played for Fortitudo, Sasha Djordjević ticked off the names of the NBA-players-to-be on the U.S. team in Bormio. When he reached that of Dwayne Schintzius, I let slip a snicker. Though he knew why I was chuckling—Schintzius's odd behavior and unfulfilled promise had made the seven-footer a cheap gag line among basketball people the world over—he reproached me. "Don't laugh," Djordjević said. "We kicked their ass. Two times. Usually American teams are pressing the others. *We* were pressing *them*."

To hear Djordjević talk, it seemed as if the events of the war had never encroached on the memories of his adolescence. "What I care about most are the friendships," he said. "Not making them. Making them is easy. Keeping them is the tough thing. Nowadays people may say, 'I know you, you play great,' and you don't know if they want to be your friend because you're a good person or because you're a good player. When you're 15, 16, 17 years old, the friendships you make are honest, innocent, pure.

"They"—he meant his Croat ex-teammates—"have problems being seen with us. They've told us. But I don't want to let stupid things ruin the best years of my life."

By 1992 the Yugoslav national team was made up only of Serbs and Montenegrins. During an exhibition tour of France that June, the players learned from watching CNN that they would be barred from the Barcelona Olympics as a result of UN sanctions against Belgrade. "It made us feel," Djordjević said, "like the word with four letters."

Perhaps the giddiness of returning to international competition, and doing so victoriously, accounted for the Yugoslavs' triumphalist behavior following their defeat of Lithuania in the 1995 European final in Athens. From its perch atop the medal stand, the entire Yugoslav team flashed the three-fingered salute used by Serb militants during the war. As the third-place Croats received their bronze medals, Divac and Djordjević applauded. But before the Yugoslavs could be presented with their golds, the Croats dismounted the stand and left the floor.

Up in the seats, too disgusted to watch, Pešić ushered his wife and daughter out of the arena. "I felt as if the entire world had gone mad," he would tell me. It had been four years since Yugoslavia's last European title—four years between one last noble stand together and this poisoned endgame.

Djordjević said he flashed the three fingers "not to be provocative. Just: That's Serbia, that's us, that's me—nothing else. It's my pride. The Croats, they had a lot of pressure on them. The proof is the way they walked out of the gym. I think someone told them to do that. They were not thinking with their heads. They were thinking with the heads of their politicians."

No, Dino Radja was saying, after a Boston Celtics practice in Waltham, Massachusetts. It was the players' decision—a decision made for them by the Serbian fans. "Croatian fans were saying only, 'Go Croatia,'" he said. "Serbian fans were insulting us, saying things about our mothers and fathers, about how they were going to kill us. You don't want to accept fans spitting on you and calling you names. We were advised to stay up there, but I didn't want to hear that no more.

"A lot worse things happen," said the man who as a teenager roomed with Djordjević. "Neighbors kill neighbors. So this is really a minor thing."

Croatian president Franjo Tudjman had joined the national team for dinner after Croatia won its silver medal in Barcelona in 1992, and there Radja and several other players asked him: When would the army take back the Krajina, the part of eastern Croatia then in the hands of rebel Serbs? Soon, Tudjman said—and that night he promised the players that they would be his guests for a traditional feast of lamb in Knin, the Krajina's capital, after its liberation. Three years later Croatian troops recaptured Knin with a sudden offensive. Radja caught up with Tudjman in the heady days following that victory, in the fortress commanding the city, where they shared their meal as promised.

Radja had a gentle enough disposition that he wore a tattoo with a church spire and a dolphin on his left shoulder. "I like the dolphin," he said. "It is a peaceful fish." But Radja's equipoise had been broken. "My country was attacked," he said. "My country was destroyed. A lot of kids have been killed, and a lot of people don't live together no more, don't have houses no more. You can't have the same relationship like before. You can't.

"I can't hate somebody because he's born on the other side of the river. And I don't think he should hate me because I'm born over here. But if he goes and agrees with all these things that happened, then I have to disagree with him. Unless he does that, I don't see why we shouldn't be friends."

But if you make a public display of that friendship?

"You're in trouble," Radja said. "Back home, you're in deep trouble."

If any member of that 1987 World Junior Championship team might be excused for holding a grudge, it would be Teo Alibegović. Twice during the 20th century numerous friends and members of his family had been slaughtered: once during World War II by radical Serb Chetniks, and again during the 1990s by Bosnian Serbs, or so witnesses say. Many Alibegović family members are officially listed as "missing."

Alibegović and his wife, Lejla, were married on Mount

Igman in the very hotel—a building destroyed during the Bosnian war—from which the Yugoslav juniors ran to the top of that infernal ski jump. An uncle, a general in the Yugoslav army, spent the war under house arrest in Belgrade for refusing to lead soldiers against his own people. Such is the fate of the Bosnian Muslim. "Serbs and Croats are fighting over our backs, and we're suffering the major loss," Alibegović told me in Berlin, where he was playing for Pešić at Alba. "They suffer, too. But we suffer the most."

Yet no one was more resolute about holding his old friends blameless. "We are lost lambs," he said of himself and his erstwhile teammates. "I still keep in touch with all of them. I still kiss them when I see them, same as before—shake hands and kiss." Once a child violinist so gifted that his mother made plans to send him off to a conservatory in Vienna, Alibegović struck me as the nomadic musician who recurred through this story, a kind of Muslim Fiddler on the Roof. I wanted to take the words of E. M. Forster—"If I had to choose between betraying my country and betraying my friend, I hope I should have the guts to betray my country"—and set them to his music.

Unlike his Serb and Croat ex-teammates, Alibegović had not gone to any recent Europeans, Worlds, or Olympics, because the country of which he had become a citizen, Slovenia, failed to qualify for them. But he watched all three events on TV. "What happened during the medal ceremony in Athens made me sick to my stomach," he said. "For three years the Serb players said they didn't want any part of politics, all they wanted was the right to play. And then, after they won, they showed their three fingers, their symbol of this war. The other thing that made me sick was the Croats' not being sportsmanlike enough to swallow it, to be proud and stand there with their bronze medals.

"Maybe my values are wrong. Maybe my father was wrong when he taught me that if you're going to be a sportsman, *be* a sportsman, not a politician. But you can't hate someone because he's some nationality or race. You can't hate all American guys because some American guy once slapped you. There's 250 million Americans. You can't hate them all."

Berlin is a kind of Rorschach test of cities, a place that's either the cradle of the ethnic hate to end all ethnic hate, or the home to a reunification improbable enough to give hope to the most far-fetched dreams of reconciliation. Like Pešić, Alibegović preferred to see that city as the latter. In Berlin the old coach and his longtime player clung to their twin hopes: the wisp of a possibility that the team might be brought together again, and a notion perhaps even more fanciful—that their deferred-dream team could beat a U.S. Dream Team composed of NBA stars.

Alibegović really believed in the latter prospect, and I heard him out. "They're an All-Star team; we know how each other breathes. They don't know how we play; we know how they play. They are individualists; we're very team-oriented. The American team, by names, is the better team. But under international rules it is not superior. Or if so, maybe by five percent."

Perhaps Alibegović so cherished his memories that he unwittingly empowered them to play tricks. In any case, the wolves weren't going to grant the plea of a lost lamb that such a game take place. While Tudjman and Radja toured the Krajina, Croatian forces were driving hundreds of thousands of Serb civilians from their homes, killing and plundering on a scale that led to indictments for war crimes. Only weeks before that, Bosnian Serb gunners laying siege to Sarajevo had celebrated Yugoslavia's victory in Athens by lighting up the night sky with tracer bullets, and General Ratko Mladić, the Bosnian Serb commander who would be indicted for genocide, hailed the Yugoslav players' "fighting spirit."

Military victories celebrated with basketball players. Basketball victories celebrated with gunfire. There is little difference.

I'd once remarked to Pešić how odd it seemed that people so adept at sharing a ball couldn't coexist. To underscore the point I began ticking off all the sports besides basketball in which multiethnic Yugoslav teams had won world or European titles.

"And chess," Pešić added.

"Chess? But chess isn't a team sport."

"Yes. But it too is a game of combinations."

At the time I hadn't given his remark much thought. But over the following years, after much more bad news and hateful propaganda from that part of the world, I'd mulled it over some more. I wondered whether Pešić's comment shouldn't have deterred me from idealizing the Yugoslav knack for the collective that I'd seen on the basketball court, and whether this Balkan gift for recognizing possibilities didn't cut both ways: You can calculate two and three moves ahead, to be sure, but the fantastical mind of the paranoid can also rewind and obsess over moves long since made. In the same way a ballplayer from the Balkans will seldom forgo a no-look pass or a dipsy-do shot for a more straightforward one, his nationalist counterpart will rarely offer a simple, benign explanation when a complex and sinister one will do. It was this atmosphere of compound mistrust, I realized, that would keep a reunion game from taking place, however much Pešić and Alibegović wished otherwise.

Alibegović had been insistent. "I guarantee you," he said. "Every one of us would love to play a game together. The only obstacle, I think, is the name. If we played under the name NBC, the name XYZ, the name Jerks—whatever—it might be possible. But under the name Yugoslavia it would be pretty difficult."

Talk of names and labels caused Alibegović to fall silent for a moment. Then he delivered himself of a thought: "You know, I never knew what nationality anyone was when we were playing with each other. And I bet you they never knew what I was.

"Well, now we know."

I caught up with Pešić at baggage claim. As we waited for our luggage, he reminisced about Bosna Sarajevo's European Cup and the scene at the airport in its aftermath. "It was Yugoslavia's first international basketball title ever," he said. "We came home with it on April 6, 1979."

He let that sink in.

"On April 6, 1941, the Nazis invaded Yugoslavia."

"On April 6, 1992, the war in Bosnia started."

In the Balkans, I was left to think, people certainly know their history.

We fetched our bags and made our way to the curb. Before we took our leave, Pešić introduced me to his friend Mirsad, who offered me a ride into town. I climbed into Mirsad's minibus and watched Pešić drive off. He was hunched over the steering wheel of a tiny rental car, trying to pick his way through a new, mine-free parking lot and onto a reconfigured access road. He tried what must have been an old exit, only to find it barricaded by peacekeeping troops. So he turned around and headed off to try another.

From where I sat I could only imagine what it must be like to be a Sarajevan of the heart, home and lost before you've so much as left the airport.

EIGHT

Bosnia

The Woman Who Sells Men

Snow began to fall as we drove into town. Mirsad tried to chat me up, but I wasn't much of a conversationalist. The cityscape out the window left me slackjawed. Pešić's old neighborhood was a stark honeycomb of roofless homes. Snowflakes puddled into divots gouged from the sidewalks by shrapnel. If an apartment building still stood, it looked like a huge dollhouse, with a cross-sectioned swath open to the elements and a lonely light burning in the odd room still habitable. Any patch of public space was spoken for, pressed into service as a cemetery.

Between 1992 and 1995, Sarajevo endured the longest siege in modern history. For 42 months Bosnian Serbs encircled and shelled the city, trying to partition by ethnicity one of the most stubbornly cosmopolitan places in the world. In 1991 and early 1992, as fighting flared first between Belgrade and Ljubljana and then Belgrade and Zagreb, war somehow spared Bosnia. This seemed to be an upset, given the republic's mix of Croats, Serbs, and Muslims, which made it ripe for the opportunists so determined to play on nationalist passions. In fact, a macabre joke was already making the rounds: Why is Bosnia quiet? Because Bosnia has advanced directly to the finals.

My room at the Holiday Inn looked out on the main boulevard paralleling the Miljacka River. The alpha and omega of the war lay before me. The 20 charred stories to the left contained the remains of the parliament building, outside of which, on that April 6 Pešić cited to me, 100,000 people had gathered to denounce the madness that politicians were about to impose on them. A 21-year-old woman from Croatia, in Sarajevo studying to be a doctor, took a sniper's bullet that day and so became the first of 10,615 of the city's residents to die—just about one fatality for every celebrant who, back in 1979, had greeted Pešić and his Bosna Sarajevo teammates at the airport. The last fatalities occurred not 75 yards to the right, at a spot in front of the state museum, where a Serb shell destroyed a streetcar shortly after the Dayton Accords had delivered a promise of peace.

No hotel but the Holiday Inn stayed open throughout the war. Its antebellum china was graced with the logo of the 1984 Winter Olympics, and it seemed disrespectful, given the intervening events, to park your 1998 self in the restaurant and sip coffee from an '84 cup. If you were quartered at the Holiday Inn during the siege, you did not want a room with a view, for a single rule obtained: If you could see a sniper on Mount Trebević, up where the bobsleds once ran, he could see you. After Sarajevo, I would never regard the name of the Holiday Inn frequent-traveler program, Priority Club, in the same light.

I had come to town for the Bosnian national team's European Championships qualifier against Lithuania, but the game still lay several days off. So the next night I went by Skenderija, the old Olympic figure skating venue, to watch Pešić's former club play an exhibition game against Split, the Croatian team for which Kukoč, Radja, and Micheal Ray Richardson once suited up.

Pešić filtered into the gym late and hung back from the crowd, watching from one of the concourses. Gradually people began to notice and approach him. A young coach who had made the drive from Tuzla, which had been swollen with refugees from some of the most remorseless ethnic cleansing of the war, addressed him deferentially. Another man, wiry and middle-aged, described how he had emigrated to the U.S. and landed a job teaching tennis in Dallas. As he proudly showed off a Texas driver's license, he explained that he could make this visit because of an American holiday called Thanksgiving.

This old friend called him Kari. Anyone named Svetislav is bound to pick up some sort of nickname, but just the same I asked Pešić if there was a story behind it. "Forty years ago—I was nine years old—I went to the movies," he said. "I liked the movie, and afterward I talked about it. My friends saw my face, saw that I was happy, and said, 'Harry! You look like Harry Belafonte!'"

Somewhere along the line Harry became Kari. As we spoke, we touched on all sorts of things that had happened somewhere along the line. "Many people say that Yugoslavia no longer exists," Pešić said. "Maybe. But I am Yugoslav." He sounded like the hardheaded child of an annulled marriage.

But in Sarajevo nomenclature was not to be deployed lightly. I had been in town only a day and a half when I learned a brief but important lesson in rhetorical custom. Though Sarajevo's population had a Muslim plurality before the war, many Serbs and Croats stayed to defend the city and the multiethnic ideal for which it stood. Indeed, the national team always included players of Serbian and Croatian descent; the Bosnian Basketball Federation had invited players from Croatian parts of Herzegovina and the Republika Srpska, entities provided for by the Dayton Accords, to national team tryouts for the current Eurobasket campaign, even though the bids were sure to be turned down. Thus I heard those who had besieged the city referred to again and again not as "the Serbs" but as "the aggressors." Several Sarajevans upbraided me for using the phrase "Bosnian Muslims." Would I, they asked, speak of "American Protestants"? Here in a city that still bristled with minarets and steeples and onion domes, a Bosnian Muslim was simply a Bosnian, as was a Serb, a Croat, or anyone who chose Sarajevo as his own.

Or her own. The next day I met a woman with whom I'd played phone tag during my stay in Bologna, where she now lived and worked as a player agent. A native of Sarajevo, she had returned to her hometown for the forthcoming Eurobasket qualifier, and she promised to show me around. Little did I know that I was about to meet the Mother Courage of Bosnian basketball.

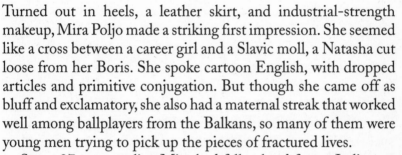

Turned out in heels, a leather skirt, and industrial-strength makeup, Mira Poljo made a striking first impression. She seemed like a cross between a career girl and a Slavic moll, a Natasha cut loose from her Boris. She spoke cartoon English, with dropped articles and primitive conjugation. But though she came off as bluff and exclamatory, she also had a maternal streak that worked well among ballplayers from the Balkans, so many of them were young men trying to pick up the pieces of fractured lives.

Some 27 years earlier, Mira had fallen hard for an Italian on a visit to Trieste. Within three months they were married, and she gave birth to a daughter before her 18th birthday. But the marriage soon foundered, and she moved to Gorizia, on the Slovenian border, where she opened a boutique. After spending most of the 1970s peddling designer fashions, Mira helped a Yugoslav star named Dražen Dalipagić clear up a contractual problem with a club team in nearby Udine. Pleased with how she had helped him, Dalipagić asked her to become his agent. She soon decamped to Bologna, hooking on with Luciano (Lucky) Capicchioni, an American-educated lawyer who had given up a picturesque job as San Marino's postmaster general to become the most powerful agent in Europe. To Capicchioni's stable she helped recruit Yugoslavs of all ethnic stripes, including Alibegović and Kukoč.

Shortly after arriving in Sarajevo, I'd spotted Mira's name in a headline in the local sports newspaper *Avaz Sport*. Mystified but intrigued, I clipped the story and showed it to her. "Headline mean 'Mira Poljo get two votes,'" she explained. The paper had conducted a poll to determine the most influential Bosnians in sports, and Mira had rated. "It call me 'The woman who sells men'!"

In fact, Mira did much more than sell men. During the war she had been a Bosnian ambassador without portfolio. She jaw-boned Italian companies into donating equipment and supplies to basketball players still trapped inside the country. She helped arrange for two dozen candidates for the national cadet team to be smuggled out and placed in high schools in Illinois, from which many would go on to American colleges. And she played a central role in delivering the Bosnian national team, against all odds, to the 1993 European Championships in Germany.

As the 1993 Eurobasket approached, three of Bosnia's stars already lived outside the Balkans, playing with club teams in Germany and Israel. But to field a national team Bosnia needed players like Samir Avdić, one of Pešić's 1987 World Junior Champions. And here was the problem: Avdić, a Muslim, had spent most of the previous year on the front lines, defending Sarajevo. In the early morning of April 1, with patches of late-winter snow still lingering on the ground, Avdić and six others—with nothing but the clothes on their back, the shoes on their feet, and small gym bags in tow—set out across a strip of no-man's-land by the airport. For two miles the players crawled, then ran, through a ditch and a stand of trees, before reaching the Bosnian-held town of Hrasnica. Then over Mount Igman and the adjacent Mount Bjelašnica, before descending at daybreak into the village of Pazarić, where a bus awaited to take them through Croatia to Italy.

They had been terribly lucky. In the Faustian bargain that kept the airport open, Serb troops agreed to let relief flights land as long as United Nations Protection Forces didn't permit civilians to flee. So every night the UN swung its searchlights across the tarmac, and Serb snipers opened fire as if squeezing off rounds at a booth on a carnival midway. On the night those seven ballplayers ran to freedom, nine other Bosnians were shot dead.

"Mira was our logistics center," Avdić would tell me. "Our mother, father, satellite phone, bank—everything." She helped arrange training sites and exhibition games for the team in Italy. The 80-foot-wide banner unfurled wherever the Bosnians played, with its fleur-de-lis heraldry and plea to STOP THE WAR, was stitched in the living room of her Bologna home. She appealed to Kukoč and Radja, who donated shoes, warmups, and money to the team's campaign. From their time together in Bormio and before, Kukoč remembered that Avdić wore his size. But he had no idea that Avdić, who stood 6'9", had bottomed out at 193 pounds the previous November—that hand-me-downs, even from the slope-shouldered Kukoč, now fit him like sackcloth.

During the first week of qualifying, Bosnia had faced Italy, whose players enjoyed a per diem of nearly $200. Though the Bosnians had no per diem at all, and most were emaciated from wartime living, they beat out the Italians and advanced to the final round. Their run ended with a loss to Croatia, when one of their best players, Mario Primorac, chose to sit out the game. Primorac's family had fled to Croatia, and he feared what might happen to them if he were seen trying to defeat Croatia's national team. "We win game and get to group of medalists if only we have Primorac," Mira told me.

Still, even as soldiers were trying to wipe it off the map, Bosnia had finished among Europe's final eight. To have finished at all was to defy being finished. And the team had stood for something in the process: Avdić, seven of his teammates, and coach Ibrahim Krehić were Muslims. Two other players were ethnic Croats. Their trainer—the man who dressed their wounds—was a Serb. If you have a national team, in at least some sense surely you have a nation. At the time, Avdić told me he was in Munich in the name of Munich, to remind the world that 1993 should resonate with both 1972 and 1938. "I must tell the world: Olympic City, Sarajevo, is not dead," he said, between fielding questions about a grenade wound the way another athlete might take a query about a sprained ankle. "Olympic City, Sarajevo, is alive. Bosnia-Herzegovina is a country of three peoples: Serbs, Croats, and Muslims. We can live together."

After the Eurobasket, most of the players on the team had no money, no home, and no prospects. Four of them followed

Mira to Bologna. For three months they lived with her, taking their meals and doing their laundry at the Casa Poljo while she worked her network of contacts. She found Avdić a gig with Málaga, a club team in Spain. The Turkish Basketball Federation offered basketball nationality to any Bosnian ballplayer aged 25 or under, providing refuge for a few more. Mira's halfway house slowly emptied.

She told me all this over a meal at the grill restaurant her sister ran near the caravanserai of Sarajevo's Turkish quarter. As remarkable as her tale was, it was no more so than its flip side—the story of how the game survived in the city during the war. Tomorrow, she promised, I'd hear testimony from those who rode out the siege. In a perverse way, the fighting had promoted basketball. "We now have national wheelchair team," she said. "Before war, we don't."

At the end of the evening I bade Mira good-bye. Spending so much time on the Continent, I'd begun to think of myself as a bit of a sophisticate, and I tried to take my leave Euro-style, with three kisses—right cheek, left cheek, right again. "No! Three is number used by aggressors!" Mira said, referring to the three-fingered Serb salute. "So never three! Two or four!"

The next day Mira and I drove out past the airport to Ilidža, site of the Hotel Oaza, a cluster of bungalows lodging the Bosnian nationals as they prepared for the game. Ilidža had been infested with Serb snipers the night Avdić and his teammates escaped over the airport tarmac. Now the suburb was resolutely Bosnian again, albeit running on little more than the economic fumes of international aid workers and UN bureaucrats. I took a table in the restaurant, and Mira sent over her men, one at a time, so I could hear their war stories.

First was Sabit Hadžić, a former Bosna Sarajevo teammate of Kari Pešić, who now coached the national team. He had spent the war in his home only a few miles from here in Hrasnica, which had been virtually encircled by Serb troops. Hrasnica lay on the far side of a tunnel, burrowed under the airport runway, that served as a filiform link between Sarajevo and the outside world. One day a shell landed in Hadžić's kitchen moments after he had left it for the living room.

When not helping defend his hometown or ferrying goods through the tunnel, Hadžić coached Hrasnica's basketball team. The regular Bosnian league season was canceled because of the fighting, but in and around Sarajevo, Tuzla, and Zenica, in gyms with bombed-out windows and no heat, metropolitan leagues played on. Sarajevans always seemed to know the sites and times of games, though Bosnian radio and *Oslobodjenje,* the daily that published throughout the war, never publicized them lest the venues become targets for Serb artillery. In fact, games were better attended during the war than they had been before or would be after. People desperately needed to see one another every week, if only to ascertain who was still alive.

For each game Hadžić and his players would troop the nine miles through the tunnel and into the city, then nine miles back. "Somehow in between we found the energy that first year to reach the final of our region," he told me. At season's end, winners from each city played off. "It is only 43 miles between Sarajevo and Zenica, but it took three days to make the trip because of roadblocks," he said. "If a team drove at night, it drove in a truck with no lights to avoid snipers."

Mira introduced me to Damir Mirković, a 21-year-old reserve guard on the national team. Only 16 when the war began, he was one of the young players she had helped smuggle out of the country early in the conflict. He spent two months with her in Bologna. "There was delicious food and beautiful girls," he told me. "In peacetime people dream of a life like that, and here I had it in war."

But there is a Bosnian proverb that goes, "A tree does not grow from the sky." Mirković's roots were in Sarajevo, and he wanted to go back, even if that meant returning to a regimen of rice soup for breakfast, rice pie for lunch, and boiled rice for dinner—and to a girlfriend who might be taken from him by the caprice of a bullet. Mira pleaded with him not to. "Why do you want to go back?" she asked him. "To be killed?"

"My parents asked me this, too," Mirković told me. "I couldn't explain."

He very nearly didn't make it back, when his bus was strafed by machine-gun fire as it traversed Mount Igman, short of the Hrasnica end of the tunnel. But once home, he resumed playing basketball. Most of his games and practices took place in a gym on a hillside, in the lee of sniper fire. But sometimes he had to go to Skenderija, and that meant crossing the river. At first he would run across the bridge and throw in a juke here, a jab step there, as if a sniper's bullet, like a defender, could be subdued with an open-court dodge. But in wartime another proverb had gained currency: "If you run, you hit the bullet. If you walk, the bullet hits you." Eventually he just put his head down, walked, and prayed.

"Each day I went, I knew I might never come back," he said. "Many guys on my team were wounded. Some were hurt in the leg and couldn't play. One was shot in the right hand, so he changed to the left and got to be pretty good. How can I call it? Crazy. But this was our life. In the morning you were alive. You never knew if you would still be alive in the evening. Many times I would step over dead people on my way to practice, and many times I was in big danger and didn't know it. But not once was I wounded. I was protected by a greater power than we can know."

Since the Dayton Accords, Mirković had come to regard his inability to abandon Sarajevo as a kind of grace. He had become a devout Muslim and adopted the name Abdul Karim. "I found myself here," he told me. "I finished school. I continued playing and became the top scorer in the league. I met many religious people who are wiser than me. I don't know how my life elsewhere would have proceeded."

Finally, Mira produced the team's captain. Avdić had been 20 years old in Bormio and 26 in Munich. Now he was a very old 31. When war broke out, he and his extended family lived in Grbavica, the neighborhood just across the river from the Holiday Inn. But within two weeks the Serbs had occupied Grbavica, and Avdić and 10 members of his family fled to the other side of the Miljacka, to his sister's apartment. From there he spent a year shuttling to and from his foxhole, and to and from basketball practice. "Eleven persons," he told me. "We were like a soccer team in her home—like luggage, lost and found. Now you look back on the reality of five years ago and wonder, Was it really possible that a single egg cost eight dollars? That like a pregnant woman you had one craving all the time—for an apple? You could see them growing on trees in the hills. Still, we were alive."

Avdić now played in Turkey for Tuborg Izmir, and only four days earlier his team had traveled to Banja Luka for a game. Now the capital of the Republika Srpska, Banja Luka was a place where Muslims spared by the cleansers were forced to wear white armbands during the war. The directorate of the club there, Borac Nektar, had ties to the SDS, one of the most militantly nationalist Serb political parties. Avdić may well have exchanged bullets with some of the same players with whom he swapped baskets. "We lost by four points," he told me. "It was difficult for me and another Bosnian guy on my team. The game was played fairly by the players and coaches, but the spectators said some personal things, some nationalist things."

As captain of Bosnia's national team, Avdić asked two Serbs with Borac Nektar if they would be interested in playing for their country. They said, "Now isn't the time."

"All my life I've been a Muslim living together with Catholics and Orthodox," Avdić said. "In Sarajevo, Christmas and Bairam were the same—you got out of school. Now I'm counting on the political people to solve this problem. Because if I can't go like before to Banja Luka, I am not free. Just like if you are from New York, and you can't go to St. Louis, you are not free."

Avdić went on in this vein, his remarks never betraying the spirit of Bormio. And then his comments took a twist. A year ago that very week the Bosnian nationals had played their first game in Sarajevo since the war. They defeated Croatia 74–67, and afterward 200,000 people poured into the streets to celebrate. Though individual Croats like Kukoč and Radja had provided the Bosnian team with generous support in 1993, Croatian troops launched a savage offensive in western Bosnia that year, trying to annex as much territory as possible while the Serbs kept the Bosnian army pinned down in the east and north. So Skenderija had been thick with chants and songs during the game, as fans denounced the Ustashe, the Croatian fascists who collaborated with the Nazis during World War II.

Avdić didn't believe he and his teammates were being asked simply to play basketball, and that bothered him. "People always think we owe some debt to them," he said. "They grab me as I go out on the floor and say, 'Oh, you have to win this for us!' But when I play I don't want to feel I must play for anyone but myself. The president of our federation says, 'Our national team is the only bright spot at this time.' That may be true, but it's a heavy obligation."

As someone who had done time both on the front lines and on the floor, Avdić was singularly qualified to assert that war and basketball couldn't be proxies for each other. "Yet tomorrow it will be the same thing again. Nine thousand people screaming, 'You must win!' For that, I feel pain."

I'd asked back in Springfield: To whom does the game belong? Surely it belonged first to a man like Samir Avdić, both player and minister of the game.

Tip-off at Skenderija was set for 6 P.M. At dusk I followed Damir Mirković's old route across the Miljacka, as the sarabande of the muezzin summoned the faithful to prayer. After five days here I'd stopped gawking. I now walked briskly through the late-November chill like a native Sarajevan, almost inured to the destruction around me. There were odd indications of hope, as chores of rehabilitation had been put up for international adoption—public transport to the Japanese, airport mine removal to the Swiss, a new national library to the Austrians. But they always seemed to be canceled out by other signs, like the bright yellow barrier across from the Holiday Inn, the one that still warned MINE!

After their remarkable showing in Munich in 1993, Bosnia's national team had struggled in the biannual European Championship competition. During qualifying for the 1995 Eurobasket, the government refused to let the team play a game against Yugoslavia because a Serb mortar attack in Tuzla had just killed more than 70 people, mostly children. In 1997 the Bosnians suffered a string of injuries and placed 15th. But the current campaign, for the right to advance to France in July, couldn't have been going better since that victory over Croatia a year earlier. Bosnia was leading its group with a 5-0 record, and it had already upset Lithuania in the teams' first meeting, in Vilnius the previous November.

On this night the Forest Brothers proved to be a much tougher opponent. Arvydas Sabonis, idled by the NBA lockout, had nothing better to do than drop several months' worth of pent-up energy on the home team. Next to the Lithuanians' huge center, the Bosnians played timorously, and Avdić was unable to launch anything but the occasional errant fallaway. Mirković showed confidence, but he played most of his minutes off the bench in the second half, when the game had long since been lost. Hadžić could do nothing to stay Lithuania's 87–57 victory. Mira sat next to me, screaming furiously at her feckless men.

Afterward I found Avdić as he made his way through Skenderija's smoke-shrouded bar toward the arena exit. He introduced me to his wife, Monika, who had escaped Sarajevo several months after him, and whom he wed in a ceremony at the Bosnian consulate in Bonn, with Mira as their "best man." He struck me as oddly relieved. "Sometimes you simply say 'Congratulations' to the better team," he said. Sometimes, I thought to add on his behalf, it's more important to survive than to prevail.

This evening's victor owed the sustenance of its very sense of nationhood to basketball. The loser, by contrast, wouldn't even have a national team if Yugoslavia hadn't disintegrated in spite of the best efforts of the game. Basketball wins some, I thought. Basketball loses some. And though it wasn't able to gratify every human wish, or bridge every human difference, the game at least gives those hoping to do so a means with which to try.

I made the short walk back over the river to meet Mira for dinner, her favorite meal. All week she had sounded the same cry every day—"Tonight we eat *Bosnian* food!"—and I'd come to respond in Pavlovian fashion. As we settled into a banquette, she ordered a dish called *bosanski lonac,* and announced that she was tucking into it as much for its symbolism as its flavor. A stew of assorted meats and vegetables, all the better for being a motley of tastes, *bosanski lonac* is Bosnia in a bowl.

Nothing about the game was worth discussing, so Mira quickly transported herself 325 miles across the sea. With her hands in full gesticulation and her voice lubricated with wine, she held forth on Bologna, *campanilismo,* and the Derby. She told of her friend Paolo, a Fortitudo fan who was asked, when a lottery jackpot hit $45 million, what he would do if he were to win. "I'd buy Virtus so I could put it in *bankruptcy!*" he had replied. And she laughed so hard as she began her next story that I didn't think she'd get through it.

"In Barcelona for EuroLeague final four last spring, 2,000 Virtus fans send postcards back to Bologna. All to [Fortitudo star] Carlton Myers. All with greetings, 'Sorry you are not here!'

"But here is real joke: They send all postcards *with no stamp!* So Myers must pay postage due *2,000 times!*"

The night went on like this, with Mira's adopted home standing in for that of her birth. For 25 years she had lived in that most blithe and luxuriant city, where people in opposing camps only made clever pantomime of war. But tonight in her cackle I could hear anger—fury that Yugoslavs hadn't had the sense to do the same thing.

WINTER

The American Game and Her Far-Flung Offspring

NINE

Peoria, Illinois
Crossover Dreamers

I did alight in the U.S. from time to time. I washed clothes. I paid bills. I told the doorman in my apartment building, "Guess who I am and win valuable prizes!" And after Thanksgiving I pledged to better understand the game close to home—where it had been and where it was going, to be sure, but also where it might be nudging a world that took its hoop cues from Michael Jordan's homeland. My fieldwork would include a Wednesday night run in which I'd faithfully participated for 15 years. Our ranks had thinned as a result of marriages and babies and moves to the suburbs, so an APB went out for fresh bodies. I found a conscript literally under my feet.

Johnny Suarez was the son of the superintendent of my building. I'd watched him grow up, passing through the lobby on his way to the Vanderbilt YMCA, which sits like an annex across East 47th Street. He'd usually be wearing his Allen Iverson T-shirt, the one with THE ANSWER emblazoned on the back. When the pay phone just off the gym rang, regulars knew to answer, "John's office. May I help you?" It was usually his mother, with a summons to dinner.

Johnny would run with anyone at the Y, and though he never played in high school and seemed to have topped out at 5'10", he became pretty good. Word of his game even reached Puerto

Rico, where his parents came from, and the coach at the Universidad Interamericana in Fajardo signed him to a basketball scholarship. But after one season Johnny had left school and come home to help his mother look after his father, Angelo, who was suffering from bone cancer. Housebound for much of each day, Johnny needed basketball more than ever, and I had no trouble roping him into our game.

One Wednesday evening, after we rode the subway up the West Side to the gym, I realized that this was going to be one of those deadbeat nights when we failed to muster a quorum. Two regulars who did show up left in disgust, and Johnny and I faced a choice: play one-on-one, or have the entire evening go to waste. We decided to play one-on-one. And that night, trying to defend someone half my age, I discovered the cynosure of basketball's next generation.

Johnny had a killer crossover dribble. He would take the ball and send it across his body in lullaby rhythm from hand to hand. He'd let it ride up high, larding it with spin with each pass. As he did this he'd stare me down—I even thought I could see a faint smile fissure out on his face—and, sure that I'd locked in on his eyes, give his head a toss, sometimes with and sometimes against the direction of his dribble. Eventually I'd reach for the ball as it crossed tantalizingly before me, and he'd lower his shoulder and be gone.

Once or twice with that first step to the basket Johnny would cross the ball in such a tautly spun rush that it would grip the floor and run, like water in a millrace, out of bounds. But usually he'd play me for the fool, and then (for we were playing make it, take it) he'd play me for the fool again. On those rare occasions when I'd get possession, I didn't do much more than back him down on the blocks and throw up a turnaround jumper—a geezer's recourse, we both tacitly understood. After an hour of this I was exhausted, but exhilarated, too.

James Naismith made no mention of the dribble in his original 13 rules. He stipulated only that there be no running with the ball, and that a player throw a pass from the same spot he received it. But the dribble—which is really a series of drops and retrievals—hewed to the spirit of the ban on carrying the ball, and the good doctor came to delight in what he called "one of the sweetest, prettiest plays in the whole bunch." He would have loved the crossover, I'm sure.

For Lloyd Hill, a character in Rick Telander's 1976 book *Heaven Is a Playground,* the dunk was so much a part of his sense of self that it touched off a fantasy. "I think I may put my bed out under that basket, sleep right there, and take a few jams when I get up in the morning," Hill said, referring to the main court in Brooklyn's Foster Park. But basketball had changed. Where the angels of *Heaven* once nicknamed their dunks with a train of modifiers, today kids spoke diabolically of "breaking ankles." Where once there was no more satisfying schoolyard moment than an ascent to the rim, now young hoopheads yearned to go by people. And the crossover was more democratic than the dunk: Only an elite cadre of athletes could get enough air to throw the ball down, but with work, anyone could cross it over. From time to time I picked up *Slam,* the self-described "in-your-face basketball magazine," whose back pages still carried ads for devices to improve your vertical leap by building up calf muscles ("Be a Skywalker!"). I resolved to watch that space. How soon before *Slam* would be cluttered with come-ons for blindfolds and quadriceps exercisers and other aids to developing dribbling legerdemain and a sudden first step? How soon before the self-improvement ads asked, "How Low Can You Go?"

I got Johnny to talk about the move during our subway ride back. He made clear that it wasn't something he just fooled with or fell into. His crossover was a work in constant progress. He watched the moves of others—at the Y, on the playgrounds of Manhattan and Puerto Rico, and of course on NBC and TNT and the *SportsCenter* highlight packages. Then he filtered what he saw through his imagination into something entirely his own. As he spoke about "my game," he struck me not so much as a grasping wanna-be, but as an artisanal practitioner, a craftsman, in a way no mere dunkmeister would.

"I might cross over three, four, five times, just to play with a guy before making my move," Johnny said. (So he *had* been smiling at me.) "Whether I go left or right depends on what he's showing me. Half of it is seeing what I can get him to do, then reacting. Okay, Michael Jordan was the best player in the NBA, easy. But I don't look up to his game. I look up to point guards. At the Y, they call me Baby Iverson."

Iverson's behind-the-back, do-si-do dribble in a Reebok commercial helped make a cult of the crossover. But Johnny's influences also included Tim Hardaway, who had developed his signature move, the UTEP Two-Step, at the University of Texas at El Paso. He spoke of the move Jordan had used to free himself for the buzzer-beating, title-winning dagger against Utah in Game 6 of the NBA Finals the previous June. He invoked Kobe Bryant's crossover, and Grant Hill's, and Stephon Marbury's. "I really like that little cuff move Stephon throws into it," Johnny said, demonstrating with a slalom around a pole in the aisle of the Broadway local as it rumbled downtown. He knew nothing of such ball-handling pioneers as Nate Archibald, Bob Cousy, Bob Davies, Marques Haynes, Pete Maravich, and Earl Monroe, all of whom grafted footwork to dribbling. But Johnny's ignorance of history didn't put me off, because he clearly wouldn't have begrudged others for taking *his* crossover and adapting it for their own use.

Indeed, the move is of a piece with hip-hop culture. There's the rat-tat-tat rhythm, the badinage and braggadocio, and the distinctly big-city yearning to break free of the crowd by making one's mark. The many homage-paying borrowings aren't much different from sampling in rap. As a dribbler and his defender faced each other one-on-one, they might throw the mother word at each other. But as in the old African-American street-corner game of swapped insults known as "the dozens," and the musical one-upmanship jazzmen call "cutting," the victim of a move didn't take anything personally. He simply went back into the lab to develop some new means of comeuppance. Each "mother" was a kind of mother of invention.

That Wednesday night I realized that something had hap-

pened at the grass roots. The American game had moved from
up around the rim to down around the ankles. To be down with
the crossover, I needed to head for the flyover. And so I prepared to make a pilgrimage to Ft. Sooy.

At the Macker nationals in Celebration, I'd met a broad-
chested black man, a coach and chaperone for a youth team
from Champaign, Illinois. His name was Verdell Jones Jr., and
he wore a T-shirt that read FT. SOOY.

You will not find Ft. Sooy in Rand McNally. I learned this
by asking Verdell Jones exactly where Ft. Sooy was. He
answered by pointing at each letter, left to right, across his
chest: *"For . . . the . . . sake . . . of . . . our . . . youth!"*

If Ft. Sooy, a foundation based in downstate Illinois, was a
sort of basketball Est, Verdell was a whole new Werner
Erhard—good cop and bad cop, Norman Vincent Peale and
Parson Weems rolled into one. He preached a message of optimism, discipline, and self-improvement, with hoops the means
to hook kids (with drills), challenge them (with competition),
and reward them (with an end-of-the-season blowout awards
banquet). T-shirts served as sartorial carrots for those who got
on the stick. Anyone who passed off for 15 assists in a game, for
instance, became a member in good standing of Ft. Sooy's Ugly
Dimes Club. Those who took care of business on and off the
court were mustered into Verdell's elite fraternity, Men of Des-
tiny.

To help keep kids on the straight path and a sense of purpose
in mind, Verdell constantly spouted homilies. In the first few
hours I spent in his company, I heard him say, "Young men don't
care how much you know until they know how much you care,"
and "If it's garbage in, it's garbage out," and "You know how you
eat an elephant? One bite at a time." In one unusually evangelical moment he told me, "Alexander the Great, Mother Teresa,
Gandhi, they *revolutionized* culture!" I couldn't remember the
exact context of this remark, but its point—that Ft. Sooy also

had the potential to transform—didn't escape me. The trick was to keep kids interested. "Challenge 'em while you make it fun, and kids'll rise to meet expectations," he said. "They say you can lead a horse to water, but you can't make it drink. Well, you *can* salt its oats to make it thirsty."

So far Ft. Sooy existed only in Champaign and Peoria, and Verdell's plans to start chapters in cities across the country seemed terribly ambitious. But if he could extend the concept half as well as he could extend a metaphor, I had no doubt that kids nationwide would soon be saying, "If it's to be, it's up to me!"

Verdell lived in Champaign, but he had grown up in Peoria, the city that Madison Avenue regards as emblematic of middle-American taste. Peoria is also the cradle of the crossover dribble. More guards with a handle have come out of Peoria than any other city of comparable size. Ballplayers with light hands and light feet may seem an odd export for a place that's home to the Caterpillar heavy equipment company, but as Verdell told me, "Every one of our kids wants to break ankles." Ft. Sooy was where they learned how.

When we met at the Champaign airport, Verdell didn't have to tell me that his day job was in sales. Right in front of baggage claim he began pantomiming his youngest son, Clayton. "Clayton was doing two-ball drills at three. Now he's five and he can speed dribble *and* go behind his back. Didn't even know he had it. Clayton got it from watching his older brother."

That would be Verdell III, who was nine. Verdell *père* told me how he once left his eldest son alone in a gym for 15 minutes while he went off to pick up his wife. "Came back and V says, 'Daddy! Look what I got!'" Young Verdell had taken a ball and hid it under the front of his loose-fitting T-shirt. He slapped at it from one side, so the ball worked its way 180 degrees around his midsection, even as it stayed under his shirt—in utero, as it were. Then he reached behind his back and whacked down at the ball, to deliver it through his legs, back to front, where he resumed dribbling.

Young Verdell's inspiration was Shaun Livingston, Papa

Verdell's godson, a seventh-grader at Peoria's Concordia Lutheran Middle School, whom the most voyeuristic recruiting magazines already ranked as the best prospect of his age in the country, though Shaun was still only 5'9" and 110 pounds. He was likely to attend Peoria's Manual High School, which had just finished an unprecedented run of four straight state titles under its coach, Wayne McClain. The star of those teams, Wayne's son, Sergio, was now a sophomore at Illinois. I began to see how the dribbler's art was passed—not from generation to generation, but virtually from grade to grade.

The next day, with his sons in tow, Verdell took me by the practice gym on the Illinois campus. In the locker room he introduced me to Sergio McClain, and so began my indoctrination in how they play in Peoria.

"After a while you get a rhythm with it, like a dance," Sergio explained. He was 6'4" and broad-shouldered—not the kind of player you'd imagine breaking down a defender off the dribble. "You go out in the parks to see if you can make people stupid with it. Gotta test it first, see, before you put it on the market. Then you break ankles. Wrap 'em in, juke 'em down, shake 'em up, spin 'em off." He laughed. "I call 'em bad habits. Just pick up all the bad habits and make 'em good.

"If you're a big man, people want to see you dunk. But big men today all want to be guards and handle the ball like a yo-yo. People are finding out, if you can be a triple-threat player—shoot, pass, *and* dribble—you've got a better chance to get to the league."

Sergio took a ball in his hands to demonstrate. "Now, you can bring the dribble up high, and if the defender draws up, you just go on by him with it. But if you have a real quick defender, you go low, like Jordan did a lot. His crossover kept a guy honest. Jordan sucked him in, the guy reached, then Mike lowered his shoulder and went to the hole. But if the defender stepped back, Mike had all the space he needed. He didn't go through with his move. He just stepped back and shot the J."

"So who invented the crossover?" I asked. "In Peoria, anyway?"

"Frank, I think. Frank makes up new moves every day."
Sergio turned to Clayton. "Who invented the catwalk, Clay?"
"Frankie!"

Frankie—Frank Williams—had been a teammate of Sergio's at
Peoria Manual on the last three of those four state title teams.
Then, as a 6'4" senior guard and the tallest player on the team,
Frank had led Manual in every statistical category, winning the
title of Mr. Basketball in Illinois. Now he and Sergio were
teammates again, though Frank would be sitting out his
freshman year with the Illini to get his grades up.

The Manual High Rams had ended every quarter the same
way, with Frank breaking ankles. Sergio's dad would call for a
clearout and signal a play. "No number," Wayne McClain later
told me. "We just called out 'Frank.' And you know what?
Sometimes when he put the ball on the floor the defender
would literally back up. Like he'd been hit with a *punch*."

Each summer Sergio and Frank played together in the Peoria
Macker. Scott McNeal had told me in Celebration that Peoria
was his favorite stop on the tour, and from his description I could
understand why. Fans ringed the court and filled an adjacent
parking deck, which served as a kind of bleachers. The local CBS
affiliate telecast the games live, with tart-tongued commentary
worthy of the town where Richard Pryor got his start. "Our first
year playing Top Men's, Frank was just *playing* with the guy
guarding him," Sergio said. "Three times Frank crossed him. The
first time was to get him going. The second, that's when the guy
started slipping. By the third it was over. He bit, and Frank sent
it between the guy's legs—twice. I mean, sent the ball through,
took it back, then sent it through *again*. The guy got mad and
tackled him after that. Said, 'Don't be embarassin' me like *that!*'"

Gus Macker himself had been there. "I saw it," Scott had
told me. "People were running out onto the court screaming, '*I
saw it!*' It was even better than the year before, when Howard
Nathan dribbled with his knees."

Only a few months before my visit, Sergio, Frank, and a couple of their Manual buddies had beaten a Macker team from Peoria Central that included A. J. Guyton, then a star guard at Indiana. As Sergio reminisced about that game, Verdell started chuckling. "Poor A.J.," he said. "Got a better medal at the Goodwill Games than he did at the Peoria Macker!"

We left the locker room for the Illini's subterranean practice gym. Out on the floor by himself stood Frank Williams. He had a face that could have fit anyone from 15 to 50. His hands were huge and his physique almost fatless. But his arms were his most astonishing feature. Each was a long rattail.

Frank began loping up the court with a ball, crossing it over, folding first his feet, then his shoulders, finally his head into each dribble. Verdell believed that the secret to Frank's crossover was its unpredictability (though when he cocked one leg up ever so slightly, you could be sure he was about to do something). Given the length of those arms, Frank could tele- graph his every twitch, and still no defender would be able to stop him.

He paused and sidled over to us. "I try to dance with the ball, like the ball is my girlfriend," he said. "You get the form down. Then you watch other guys and try to add a little something to it, so you can say, 'It's mine.' Feels good once you lay it on some- body. Like getting a dunk and an and-one."

The catwalk, Frank's latest invention, is three kinds of diffi- cult. It's a behind-the-back, through-the-legs crossover, which he demonstrated while walking a perfect line, like a runway model. As he dribbled, he would take a step with the foot on the same side of his body as the ball. The length of his arms and the size of his hands would allow him to wrap the ball around his midsection, then bounce it under that very leg, up into the same hand. Frank strung two, three, four of these preposter- ously slinky dance steps together, then opened his body up, the way a ballerina might strike a pose of the fourth position. When the Harlem Globetrotters staged a dribbling exhibition or Mar- ques Haynes launched into an all-court cadenza, their acts had a herky-jerky quality. But Frank's catwalk was so smooth, and he wrapped it up so gracefully, that I was convinced everything he had just done could have been performed on a balance beam.

Verdell pulled out a video camera. He needed to break down the catwalk at home, because no matter how many times he saw it here, he couldn't figure out exactly what Frank was doing. But he beamed like an impresario. Sergio only sounded like one.

"Now, for his next move, Frank draws you in with a rollback dribble," he said. "Then he goes behind his back with *the same hand*. Calls it the chicken fajita wrap. I mean, Frank makes up new moves every *day*."

Frank showed us the chicken fajita wrap. "I use it on guys who play real tight D—who cut you off one way," he said. "You get 'em going that way, then wrap the ball behind your back real fast. Gotta do it fast. Do it slow and it won't loosen you up."

As Frank repeated the chicken fajita wrap, Verdell dissolved into rapture. "Frank! You don't even realize what you *got!* Iverson and them, they start with their body the same place as the ball. You—you start with your body going *away* from the ball!"

As Frank left the Illini's practice gym for class, he disappeared through the door to a stairwell, then reappeared above us, literally on the catwalk overhanging the gym. Clayton spotted him from the floor. "Frankie, this is for you!" he yelled. He sent a strained shot just over the front of the rim.

Frank watched approvingly from overhead. "I'll take it!" he called out, then headed for the exit.

The next day Verdell and I drove to Peoria, so I could be taken to school.

I took English. I learned how to tell a yo-yo (the pendular dribbling of the ball, left to right with the same hand across the front of the body) from a rollback (much the same, only forward and backward with the same hand on one side of the body). I learned a stutter step (mambo with the feet, independent of the ball) from a butterfly (the fake that involves collapsing your knees inward). And I learned some of the rhetoric Peorians laid on their marks before breaking them down: "Gonna make you twist your ankle," and "Got me a mouse in the house," and (my favorite) "You reach, I teach."

I took phys ed, in the form of one of Wayne McClain's practices at Manual High. His players were drilled in the basics, dribbling right-handed and left-handed, doing two-ball and big-ball drills, even dribbling with special eyeglasses that precluded any sneak of a peek at the ball. They loved the crossover, Wayne said, because they had success with it, and they had success with it because they'd started doing it, as kids, at Ft. Sooy. "The only thing that concerns me," he said, "is that we have kids with killer crossovers who can't make a left-handed layup or a 10-foot jumper."

I went to middle school. In the halls of Concordia Lutheran I met Shaun Livingston, and learned two things about his precocious ability to dribble. One was that he had grown up without a hoop in the driveway, which led him to take a ball down to the basement and dribble like a fool. The other was that, as Shaun said, "Breaking a guy off the dribble, it just feels good."

"Better than a dunk?" I asked.

"I don't know. I haven't dunked yet."

More than anything else, I learned history. Of course, Frank Williams hadn't introduced the crossover to Peoria. Before him there was Howard Nathan, who lifted up one knee and threw in a little hop when he crossed over; and Brandun Hughes, who was a master of hesitation and keeping the ball low; and Tony Wysinger, who could cripple a guy with "the T-Wy," cuffing the ball close to his chest, then launching into a spin move with light body contact that levered him free.

A few names, like Nathan, Hughes, Wysinger, and Kenny Drummond, I recognized, for they had all played major-college ball, at DePaul, Michigan, Illinois, and North Carolina State, respectively. Others—Tom Campbell, Floyd (Chico) Taylor, Percy Baker, Johnny Washington, Tony Gower, G. G. Branscumb, Ivan Watson—I didn't recognize. But they were all part of an unbroken line, influences on and benchmarks for one another. You could trace the evolution of style through everyone still active in the city's parks, with subtle shadings distinguishing T-Wy from Nathan, and Nathan from Guyton, and Guyton from Frank, on down through Shaun Livingston and, eventually, Verdell III and little Clayton.

But one thing still nagged at me, and it was a geography question. Why Peoria of all places? Why not Chicago—or for that matter Rockford or Springfield or plain old Normal? I asked Verdell, and he stabbed at an answer. "The ballplayers here are talented, but they're disciplined, too. They work on fundamentals every day. You go up to Chicago, they have skills, they have talent, but they're out of control. You ever go into an abandoned home and turn on all the lights? That's how they play in Chicago. Like roaches, just scattered in all directions."

Verdell and I pulled up outside Proctor Recreation Center, a gemstone in Peoria's bleak South Side. Manual High culled from Proctor, which proudly kept up appearances even as its surroundings fell away. Two Proctor personalities took credit for the fine fettle of the place. Tom Gordon, the building's manager, was from the generation that still called pickup ball "sandlot." Younger and beefier, John Dill had been a defensive specialist at Manual before graduating in 1988, and he was now Proctor's custodian. As John launched into a disquisition on defending the crossover, and Tom occasionally jumped in, I felt as if I'd stumbled into one of those old Nike commercials, with George Gervin and Charles Barkley trading banter in a barbershop.

"With an evenhanded guy like G. G. Branscumb, had to watch the waist," John said. "Can't go nowhere without your waist. Now, guys with a hesitation crossover you'd best be careful with. They might hesitate and pull back, but they just might keep on going, too. Like Brandun Hughes. His crossover was *low*. But whatever you do, don't fall. 'Cause if you fall, you're not gonna hear the end of it."

Tom jumped in. "None of this can be taught, see. Basically basketball is watching and adding your own things. Coaches, they don't teach this stuff. They don't like it. Well, if you can do it, it's fine by them. But if you mess up even one time, even if you do it right 10 times, they get all upset."

In fact, I thought, coaches were becoming more indulgent of the crossover artist, and for a simple reason: Breaking ankles was now more tactically important. Through the 1990s, as the three-point shot developed into a greater offensive weapon, teams needed players who could penetrate with the dribble. Penetrators caused defenses to collapse, which allowed shooters to spot up for their three-pointers.

But this was a clinical explanation for the ascendancy of the crossover. It didn't speak to the move's romance. Why did Johnny Suarez devote countless hours to getting his down? Why did he and untold others put themselves in the thrall of a one-trick character like Allen Iverson, the Answer? Why were kids in Peoria and everywhere else dreaming their crossover dreams? That afternoon at Proctor Center, from Tom and John, I got an answer of sorts, and it came when I asked about the dunk.

"The dunk is nothing no more," Tom said.

"Unless," John interjected, "you dunk *over* somebody."

Tom uh-huhed his assent.

So it all came down to face, to saving it and losing it, that hoariest of playground transactions. With the crossover, a penetrating guard could still play to the crowd—could still show someone up—while taking care of the workaday tactical business of going up the gut of the defense. Sometimes a dunk is just a dunk. But there's no such thing as an uncontested, breakaway crossover dribble. The crossover is the bomb because it's always laid *on* somebody.

TEN

Eastern Kansas
Driving Mister John

The white Chevy Astro was tattooed with loudly painted basketballs and exclamations. As *Fun!* and *Respect!* and *Sportsmanship!* rang out like toots from a klaxon, heralding our progress up rural roads from the university town of Lawrence, Kansas, I had a chance to consider a feature of being back in the States. For a b-ball road trip, my journey thus far had been awfully pale. But back in America I was never far from Afro-America, as hardly any precinct of the domestic game goes untouched by race. And a visit to Ft. Sooy had only piqued my curiosity about the origins of basketball's blackness.

So here I sat, in a vehicle that was a rolling inversion of stereotypes: its honored passenger black, its driver white. In fact, the van's chauffeur—our James, as it were—was Ian Naismith, the grandson of basketball's inventor and the next best thing to the good doctor himself. Glib and blustery, with coloring and quick emotions that gave away his Scottish roots, Ian nonetheless had much of the Texan about him, having spent years in the oil patches near Corpus Christi and McAllen. On his pinky he wore a gold ring with the letter *N* described in diamond studs.

Ian carried 250 pounds, a few too many for a six-footer pushing 60, and early each day a stipple of sweat formed on his forehead, the result of a baffling condition that was causing his heart to sound out a double beat. Lately he had tried to take life easy, living in Chicago, from which the family's Naismith International Basketball Foundation spread the Gospel According to Gramps. But he couldn't, not with the game's commandments (*Fun! Respect! Sportsmanship!*) in a state of perpetual contravention as basketball evolved into more and more of a coach-choking, trash-talking, bottom-line business. So if a school principal or rec director felt kids needed a lesson in the doctrine of original intent, Ian would hop into this very van—the Naismith Fun Van—and tool into town. Ian called himself "the world's largest messenger boy," and he liked to say, "The Naismith family will not stand idly by and watch this great game be destroyed!" There was a timpani roll in the way he hit the phrase "idly by." "We'll be scratchin' and clawin' and screamin' before we let *that* happen."

NBA commissioner David Stern once suggested to him that Ian was "carrying the torch." Ian's reply was typical. "Hell, torch was layin' in the mud. I just picked the sumbitch up."

Wherever Ian carried that torch he sent a bio in advance, but never of himself. He always sent a summary of the life of his grandfather, who had died when Ian, the youngest child of Maude and James's youngest son, Jimmy—the infant whom Doc Naismith had marked up in that child development class—was only a year old. Then, when he hit town, Ian would get kids' attention with his answers to their questions.

A kid once asked his opinion of Latrell Sprewell, the NBA player who had wrapped both hands around his coach's windpipe.

"Where's your English teacher?" Ian replied. "Whoever it is isn't doin' a very good job. That's La-*trine* Sprewell. L-A-T-R-I-N-E."

Ian wasn't quite the pious character his grandfather was. He'd let slip a salty word or two, and he took the occasional drink. "Went into the Sports Page bar in Lawrence the other day," he'd told me that morning. "Ordered a martini. Tipped my head back and, right there above me, there's a picture of my grandfather. Lookin' right at me."

I had to ask. "Did you push your glass away and make a silent vow to his memory never to drink again?"

"No."

But Ian was abstemious about anything at odds with the spirit in which his grandfather invented the game. "The original rules are in a bank vault in Chicago," he said. "Was offered $5 million for them a year ago. But the family hasn't made a penny off the game. By today's standards, guess that makes us three generations of stupid."

Ian and I were bound for the Kansas town of Hiawatha, birthplace of our traveling companion, a man who sat in the backseat with a map on his lap. He had little outwardly in common with our driver. Wispy and aged, he wore a tie and a wine-colored Basketball Hall of Fame blazer, and spoke in a pinched, tinny voice. More, he had but one heartbeat, which sounded out a pulse so languid that he never drew a technical foul in 40 years of coaching.

At the same time, John McLendon was virtual kin to the Naismith family, for he had been Ian's grandfather's advisee and student for the final three years Doc Naismith taught at Kansas. The inventor of basketball was 71 when McLendon arrived in Lawrence in the fall of 1933. As a result of an act of the state legislature, the good doctor was still teaching phys ed and health, anatomy and kinesiology, and McLendon took virtually every one of his classes.

Whenever Ian met someone with living knowledge of his grandfather, he was no longer the world's largest messenger boy. He was the world's most eager student. "Tell me," he'd say. "What'd he walk like? What'd he talk like?"

Though McLendon was now 83, he recalled James Naismith in mesmerizing detail. As he spun out his stories, Ian listened raptly from the driver's seat.

When John McLendon was a sixth grader, his father moved the family from Hiawatha to Kansas City. It was there, after catching the gleam off the buffed hardwood of the gym at all-black Northeast Junior High, that John told his dad he was going to become a basketball coach. "My father decided to find out where the inventor was," John told us. "Imagine his surprise to learn that he was only 40 minutes away. Now *that* was providential placement."

John McLendon Sr., a mail clerk for the Rock Island railroad, looked into Doc Naismith's background. In the early 1930s public schools in Kansas were still largely segregated, and Linda Brown's lawsuit against the school board in nearby Topeka lay 20 years off. But a handful of Negro students had already matriculated at the university, and from what John Sr. could find out, Naismith was someone who would give his son a fair shake. So John Jr. marched into the phys ed department that fall to inform Doc Naismith that he, the inventor of basketball, was going to be his adviser.

"And who told you this?" Naismith asked.

"My father did," John replied.

"Well, fathers are always right. Have a seat and we'll see what we can do."

So began their relationship. "Ever seen *Gray's Anatomy*?" John asked us. "Know how big that is? We'd take ours out, and Doc would say, 'Today . . . the humerus.' And guys would start elbowing each other till one of us went, 'Uh, Doc Naismith, before you get started, do you think you could tell us about that day you invented the grand old game of basketball?' He'd close the book and say, 'Well, boys, it went like this. . . .'

"In phys ed class, he taught with his arms folded. Must be the only man in the world who ever taught gym with his arms folded. 'I'll give you a word picture,' he'd say.

"In kinesiology, he'd take us out to the highway. He'd fix us up in a car with blindfolds and earplugs and cushions, trying to block our vision and hearing and sense of feeling to test our kinesthetic sense—to see if we could maintain 35 miles an hour without any clues.

"In health, he was telling us that secondhand cigarette smoke could hurt you. Knew that even back in '34. We'd ask all sorts of questions and never did consider ourselves bold to do so, because he was open to just about everything. Basically told us, 'Keep your pants zipped.' But he shared that kind of stuff—facts of life. We thought we were really something, hearing about all that. We thought, 'Doc's all right.'

"In 1936, just after the Olympics where Jesse Owens did so well, someone asked him why the Negro was superior in track. There were all sorts of stories going around about extra-long heel bones giving Negroes more leverage, that the Negro thigh was like a horse's, that the Negro had a knack for short bursts of speed from running after game in Africa. And Doc Naismith said, 'It's not any measurable physical difference. It's all psychological, all in the minds of the competitors.'

"He told us to look at who ran in the last two Olympics. Eddie Tolan was stumpy in build. Jesse Owens was almost effeminate, with sloping shoulders. And Ralph Metcalfe looked like Atlas. 'And everyone finished a winner!' Doc said. 'So you see, it can't be in the physique. It must be in the mind. You have people who have been put down, so they practice longer, they have more incentive, because they want to demonstrate that they shouldn't be discriminated against.'

"A white student asked, 'When will we catch up?' And Doc said, 'The day everyone is treated equal. Then everyone will have an equal chance to be first.'"

I tried for a moment to imagine the racial climate in Kansas in the midst of the depression. Before the Civil War, clashes between pro-slavery and free-state factions led to what came to be called "bleeding Kansas," and by the 1930s the state was still a patchwork of attitudes on race. But Lawrence had been founded in 1854 by abolitionists from New England, and its main street was named for the state in which basketball was invented. With Massachusetts so prominent a part of his pedigree, Doc Naismith and his gently righteous progressivism must have fit in well with the sympathies prevailing in town. In any case, we know he went out of his way to help the school's only black phys ed major find teaching and coaching opportunities during McLendon's final two years on campus. Although

Lawrence Memorial High was integrated, it had to field a separate Negro basketball team if it hoped to play any kind of schedule. So Naismith arranged for his pupil to become its coach.

"First game I ever coached was against my alma mater, Kansas City Northeast," he told us. "My father won a box of El Productos betting on my team." A year later, McLendon coached Lawrence Memorial to the championship of the all-black Kansas-Missouri Athletic Conference.

McLendon's presence on campus forced Naismith to confront several racial dilemmas. McLendon showed up for Phog Allen's basketball tryouts each fall, and each fall he was cut after the first day. (Kansas didn't suit up its first black basketball player until 1951.) At the same time, the school had no objections to him stepping into the boxing ring. Naismith was so troubled that the university would permit a black man to participate in a gladiatorial sport, but bar him from a team one, that he moved to suspend the boxing program for the duration of McLendon's years on campus.

In the matter of the whites-only swimming pool, however, it was McLendon who forced the issue. "Swimming was required for all phys ed students, but I was told they'd give me an automatic A if I didn't take it. I told Doc Naismith that I wouldn't accept an automatic grade. Didn't tell him I could already swim well enough to be a lifeguard during summers back in Kansas City, either.

"So anyway, one day I just jumped into the pool. There were seven or eight students in it at the time, and they all got out. Then the attendant started draining the pool. I asked him, 'Are you draining the pool because it's Wednesday, or because I was in it?' He said, 'What do *you* think?' And I said, 'I think you're gonna have one heckuva water bill, because I'm gonna be in there every day.'"

Phog Allen, who then ran the phys ed department, said he banned black students from the pool because he feared the reaction of a white student would jeopardize their safety. But McLendon persuaded Allen to try an experiment: Open the pool to any student of any race for two weeks. If the fortnight passed without incident, Allen's fears would be unfounded and the pool could be thrown open unconditionally. Unbeknownst to Allen, McLendon had already told every black student on campus to steer clear of the pool during this probationary period. So there were no incidents, and the pool stayed open.

Naismith taught aquatics, and his contribution to McLendon's quiet insurrection was to remind his students that if they refused to swim they wouldn't pass his course—and that without aquatics they wouldn't get their phys ed degrees.

"Doc Naismith, he couldn't afford to get in the foreground," John said. "He just supported me. Told me, 'Whenever you run into a problem in life, see if you can turn it to your advantage.'"

Over an extraordinary career, McLendon would do that again and again. In 1937, at age 21, he took an assistant coaching job at all-black North Carolina College, rising to head coach three years later. Inside a barricaded gym in Durham in 1944, he coached in the first integrated game in the Jim Crow South, the "Secret Game" between NCC, which is now North Carolina Central University, and all-white Duke Navy Medical College. One Sunday morning, with what would have been a scandalized white citizenry of Durham at church, the Navy medics-to-be stole into the NCC gym with jackets pulled over their heads. They would leave 88–44 losers, but not until after a second game, in which the players picked up sides from among each other's ranks and went shirts and skins.

McLendon posted blazes along trails far beyond Kansas and North Carolina. He went on to be the first black coach to win a national collegiate title, leading Tennessee A&I, now Tennessee State, to NAIA championships in 1957, '58, and '59— the first time any college coach had won three national titles in a row. He was the first black man ever to coach in the pros, in 1962, with the Cleveland Pipers of the American Basketball League. At historically black Kentucky State, where he coached during the mid-sixties, he recruited that school's first white ballplayer. And when Cleveland State hired him in 1966, he became the first black coach at a predominantly white university. At the time of our road trip he was still living in Cleveland, where he taught African-American sports history at Cleveland State, a course he had put together after hearing a coed admit she didn't know who Jackie Robinson was.

For the rest of our ride, McLendon flitted from one entry on his C.V. to the next, dropping commentary as he went. "In 1954, when I was at Tennessee A&I, the NAIA invited us to its Christmas Invitational in Kansas City. I said we'd come if we could stay in the same hotel and eat at the same restaurants as all the other teams. Well, all but two maids at the Kansas Citian Hotel quit in protest. So we made those two women heroes. Hung up all our towels, made all our beds. They'd never seen it so clean.

"Our first game was against Illinois State. Their cheerleaders were chanting, 'We are the Redbirds! You are the Blackbirds!' Well, we beat 'em by 68 points and went on to win the tournament. The guy from the NAIA said to me afterward, 'You may not get 'em to love you. But they sure do respect you.'"

In Cleveland in 1962, at halftime of a Pipers game, the team's owner, a local businessman named George Steinbrenner, knocked on the locker room door to tell McLendon that one of his players had just been sold—to that night's opponent. "Steinbrenner wanted me to tell him right then, so the guy could suit up for the other team in the second half," McLendon said. "I told him no, and I got fired."

Taught by James Naismith; fired by George Steinbrenner. A 20th-century sporting life couldn't be more all-encompassing than that.

The late 19th century wasn't a particularly good time to be black in America. Between 1877 and 1881, amid quailing hopes for 40 acres and a mule and widespread fears that slavery would be reintroduced, more than 40,000 Negroes left the South during the Kansas Fever, lured to the Sunflower State by the millenarian promises of a black promoter named Benjamin

(Pap) Singleton. McLendon's ancestors had been among those "Exodusters," and a few distant relatives still lived in and around Hiawatha. When we reached the town, an hour north of Lawrence, they joined a local newspaper reporter and several employees at a reception in John's honor at Citizens State Bank and Trust. For an hour I listened to John banter with cousins and throw occasional sideglances at a table with a spread of basketball-shaped sugar cookies arrayed next to a punch bowl. He slipped a stack of them into the pocket of his Hall of Fame blazer before we returned to the van for the drive back.

Toward the end of his life, Ian's grandfather had supplemented his meager wages by preaching in towns even smaller than Hiawatha, places that couldn't afford a full-time pastor. People turned out for Doc Naismith's sermons because he touched on the travails of daily life in a demotic style, and they loved listening to the rolling Scottish-Canadian burr he never entirely lost—the way he hit the *r*'s in his favorite word of transition, "Furrrrtherrrrmore." Ian had retraced the circuit his grandfather rode, and thus knew many of the doglegs in the roads now taking us back to Lawrence, some of which weren't much more than glorified cowpaths. "One night my grandfather focused on the taillight of a Greyhound bus and it right near put him to sleep," he said. "Hypnotized him, anyway. Bus pulled to a stop and he whacked into it from behind."

The story got me worrying about Ian's performance at the wheel, what with the sweat on his brow and that extra heartbeat. But he and John had already settled into another topic—the question of how Doc Naismith and Phog Allen really felt about each other. "Doc Naismith was reconciled to coaching by the end," McLendon said. "Coaching put basketball in a competitive framework, which helped the game grow, and he saw that you could teach more to more people the farther the game spread.

"Of course, he and Doc Allen disagreed rather vehemently about a lot of things. They disagreed about the center jump after each score, the 10-second line at midcourt, and whether to raise the basket. But in his book *Better Basketball,* Doc Allen showed his respect. He knew Doc Naismith didn't like zone defense, so he called it 'a stratified transitional defensive system.' Not calling it a zone was his way of honoring Doc Naismith."

Ian pulled off the highway in the town of Holton and turned into a Quik-Stop. John was still listing badly to one side from all the cookies in one blazer pocket. He bought a can of Dr Pepper, dropped it into the other pocket, and, his equilibrium restored, hopped into the van with renewed vigor.

"I've had a great life," John said shortly before the rise of the campus came into view. "And it all followed from that day my father said, 'I've found out where the inventor is, and that's where you ought to be.'"

Allen Field House is the shrine to Phog Allen where the Kansas Jayhawks play. It sits off Naismith Drive, not far from Naismith Valley Park, and within an outlet pass of a dormitory called Naismith Hall. Roy Williams, the Kansas coach, makes a daily jog from his office adjoining the field house to the inventor's grave in the Naismith Memorial Gardens. Nowadays Lawrence is pretty good about commemorating its adopted son, but the town hasn't always been. During Ian's two years on campus as a student in the late 1950s, that street sign read "Nesmith Drive." "Got me a screwdriver and a ladder one day and took that thing down," Ian said. "Marched into the mayor's office and put it on his desk, rusty screws and all."

That snub fits in with the faintly melancholy quality of Doc Naismith's dotage. The marginalization of basketball's inventor in the Kansas phys ed department was an abiding disappointment in the Naismith household. But the good doctor didn't wallow in his lot. He remained an uncommonly robust 5'8" and 190 pounds even as he pushed through his seventies. Sometimes he walked on his hands in front of his students. He continued to coach the fencing team, though he would probably prefer to be remembered as its teacher, for this gently contrarian man—so devoted to learning that he earned medical and divinity degrees, yet never practiced medicine or held a pastorate—was in fact more resigned to coaching than reconciled to it. He faithfully attended all Jayhawks home basketball games, but he never cheered, and he considered wrestling, tumbling, and fencing to be superior entertainments.

This did not mean that the fate of the game failed to concern him. Basketball's great advantage would be that it was invented, and thus had a proprietor to see it through nearly its entire first half century. The game's rules weren't handed down like some sacred text, with each successive generation more intimidated than the last to amend them. Basketball allowed for all sorts of necessary tinkerings, from the formalization of the dribble and elimination of the center jump after a basket to the introduction of the shot clock and the three-pointer. Naismith sat on the rules committee from its very founding in 1898, and never stopped worrying about the health of his baby. You might say he was constantly marking it up, just as he had marked up the infant who became Ian's father.

During those late Lawrence days, Doc Naismith would typically go home for lunch. He and Maude would take the noon meal, and he would adjourn to the living room to recline on the davenport for a brief nap. So as neither to return late to campus nor to saddle his wife with the burden of waking him, he devised an ingenious alarm system. He would place a tin pan on the floor next to the davenport and lie down, prone, with his keys held loosely in his outstretched hand. Then he would drift off. When he heard the keys drop from his hand into the pan, he would awaken and, knowing he had been completely relaxed, head back to work.

James Naismith died on November 28, 1939. Three days later the citizens of Lawrence gathered at the First Presbyterian Church to pay their respects. "Men like him are so much needed in the world that it seems that the processes of human disintegration ought not to touch him," the minister said in his eulogy. "That he ought to be permitted to live on and on."

As we pulled back into Lawrence, I asked Ian a question. "Did you ever consider that your second heartbeat might be for someone else? That it might be, I don't know, for your grandfather, or for the game?"

He seemed startled by this. But the more he pondered it, the more he seemed to like its sound. "I tell you what," he said. "If that's what it is, I'll take it."

Ian swung the Fun Van into a parking space downtown and took the keys from the ignition. As our James returned them to his pocket and John and I hopped out, I thought I could hear the clink in the tin pan beside the davenport. Of course Doc Naismith didn't get up. He lay serenely on the eastern edge of town, having done all he could. It was his grandson who walked off toward Massachusetts Avenue, with the gait of a man who still had work to do.

ELEVEN

El Paso

The Bear in Winter

1998-99
UTEP
Miner Basketball
vs. Texas Southern, Dec. 17
MEDIA
Name: *Alex Wolff*
Affiliation: *Sports Illustrated*
One Game Only

Through the final third of the 20th century, three men hastened the passage of the American game from roundball to hoops. One, a white coach, did his most important work in the mid-sixties, delivering basketball from its unsatisfying status as an essentially Caucasian preoccupation. Another, a black player, came along just as that coach had made his great contribution, and spent two decades literally towering over the game as it became steadily more popular and nonwhite. The last had thoroughly reworked hoops by the end of the century. Seeming to belong to a race of his own, he all but made race moot.

To better understand what had become of Ian's grandfather's legacy, I decided to seek out each of this trinity: Don (the Bear) Haskins, Kareem Abdul-Jabbar, and Michael Jordan.

And so I left my chauffeur in Lawrence and drove a rental southwest through the sunwashed prairies of Kansas. Through Admire, through El Dorado, through Kismet. In Meade, a cop caught me doing 46 in a 35 mph zone and I discovered that "Greetings from Šarūnas" loses something in the translation. Just over the Oklahoma line, in the Panhandle hamlet of Hooker, a sign outside a baseball field read HOME OF THE HOOKER HORNY TOADS. I crashed for the night in Amarillo, with El Paso still a day's drive away.

The next morning, just beyond Lubbock, I came upon a town called Wolfforth and took it as a signposted lash personally urging me on my way. In New Mexico motel marquees tried to make FREE LOCAL CALLS seem like a bargain, though there couldn't have been more than a handful of phone customers for hundreds of miles. Somewhere in the fastness beyond Carlsbad Caverns, I hit seek on the radio. It cycled infinitely on.

"Wolfforth," I mumbled lamely to myself.

You have to make this trip by car to fully grasp the isolation in which Don Haskins spent his entire college coaching career. In 1966 he had pulled off a wondrous two-fer, winning an NCAA championship and revolutionizing college sports with a single victory, playing nobody but blacks to beat all-white Kentucky in the final. The game came to be known as basketball's *Brown* v. *Board of Education*, and it was the kind of achievement a more complacent character might have long since retired on. Yet Haskins had stayed in the same place for another three decades, and his teams at Texas Western College, now the University of Texas at El Paso, had lately fallen on hard times, failing to turn in a winning record for three years running. I wondered what it was like to look back at a career in which you had crested the highest summit imaginable at age 36, only to spend the next 32 years climbing knobs.

I was headed to El Paso for another reason. Before leaving Lawrence I'd swung by Doc Naismith's grave, and noticed an adjacent cenotaph honoring another basketball giant with connections to Kansas. A native of Halstead, Kansas, and a graduate of the university, Adolph Rupp also studied under James Naismith before settling in as coach at Kentucky. The plaque noted that he won 876 games over 41 years in Lexington, and that he was proud of his full-blooded German roots. It did not note that Rupp chose to field all-white teams until the very end of his career, or that he played the foil for Haskins in the 1966 title game.

Over the years the Bear had been lionized, and the Baron demonized, for their roles on that epic night. I had accepted these characterizations as handed down. But they somehow seemed too pat, too tidy, and I wanted to sort the history out for myself.

I reached El Paso just before tip-off of UTEP's game with Samford and took a seat with an unobstructed sight line to where the Bear sat on the home team's bench. His elbows rested against knees spread far apart. His forearms dangled down, and much of the rest of him—the ursine swell of his torso, the melancholy wattles, the oddly serene lacework of his clasped hands—seemed also to hang in the chasm between his legs. As the game played out before him, its ebbs and flows occasionally moved Haskins to hoist himself up by levering elbows on knees. Yet he did this with such effort that it was hard to believe that this was how he would have most enjoyed passing the days of his 68th year—watching as his team struggled to beat Samford, a mint-julep Princeton, in a third-full building bearing his name.

The Miners trailed at halftime, and four minutes remained when they finally minced out to a two-point lead and Haskins ordered them into a zone. Though Samford would not score again, for the game's final two defensive possessions the Bear did not watch. An assistant leaped up, waving, yelling instructions, while his boss lowered his head, closed his eyes, and fingered the bridge of his nose.

It would have been easy to conclude from this scene that the game had passed Haskins by. But though he no longer always looked, the Bear could still somehow see. If UTEP hadn't switched to that zone, Samford would have sustained its accustomed patterned style and very likely won. Game time still set Haskins alight with passion, and only his physical inability to spring up in the faces of referees had spared him several technicals earlier that season.

A small knot of reporters and cameramen assembled wordlessly around him in the locker room after the game. As

Haskins sat in a metal folding chair with his head down, studying the box score, I imagined the data behind a half dozen of the game's most critical moments transferring themselves osmotically from that page to his head. At long last he looked up to remark that his players were in the midst of a week's worth of final exams: "You take tests all day, you're not gonna play very good."

The alibi, his age, even the dishonorable halfheartedness of the crowd in the Don Haskins Center—all underscored what I'd feared. The Bear was in winter. Strict scholarship limits imposed with two rounds of NCAA probation had hamstrung his program virtually throughout the 1990s. At the time of my visit the Miners had failed even to qualify for the last two Western Athletic Conference tournaments. Little of this went remarked upon beyond El Paso, just as Haskins's more than 700 wins, with that one exception, had passed largely unnoticed, and just as his name had to be suggested six times before exhausted electors finally waved him into the Hall of Fame in 1997. A few months after that tardy honor, Utah coach Rick Majerus told me how much it pained him to see the way Haskins was going out. "He's still the fiercest competitor," said Majerus, who hooked up with Haskins several times a year in the WAC. "He just doesn't have the players anymore to implement what he wants to do."

Once upon a time he did, famously so. Although Haskins's college coach at Oklahoma A&M, Henry Iba, picked Kentucky to beat Texas Western in the 1966 title game, Haskins knew that a small, quick lineup would give his Miners their best chance against the team known as Rupp's Runts. He started 5'6" Willie Worsley in place of 6'8" Nevil (the Shadow) Shed, then watched his decision vindicated in the game's opening moments. Worsley and his 5'10" running mate, Bobby Joe Hill, pressured the Kentucky guards into turnovers, and twice in a row Hill sailed in for tone-setting conversions. On the Texas Western bench a bespectacled white reserve named Togo Railey fainted from the excitement, and the Miners eased to a 72–65 victory. Not everyone welcomed this; during the months following the game, Haskins received 40,000 pieces of hate mail and a dozen death threats. But to most of a generation that remembers them, the names of the players who unnerved Kentucky that night still resonate with a kind of forerunning cool. Not just Hill and Worsley and Shed, but Orsten (Little O) Artis and Willie (Scoops) Cager, David (Big Daddy) Lattin and Harry (Flo) Flournoy, became outriders of basketball's new wave.

Yet the Haskins I came upon was in failing health. At half-time of a game against New Mexico three years earlier he had suffered a heart attack in the locker room. A few weeks before my visit, at San Jose State, a bout with the flu had left him so weak that he remained seated the entire game. He was suffering from diabetes, an infected foot, and lingering problems from a freshly operated-upon left eye, on which he had had implant surgery before the season, and which accounted for his going to the bridge of his nose and missing those dying minutes against Samford—or so he'd later tell me.

Later, too, Haskins recalled things he still saw vividly in his mind's eye. He told me of a Mexican guy he watched in the early 1960s whacking golf balls out of a sandpile by a construction site in El Paso, a guy daft enough to say he would someday play the PGA Tour—someone who turned out to be Lee Trevino. He spoke of his coach at Oklahoma A&M, whom even peers in the profession were careful to address as Mr. Iba, and whom Haskins called "the finest defensive coach who ever walked." And he mentioned how, when he had once gone up to play Iowa State, where his former assistant Tim Floyd was coaching, he went hunting with Floyd before a game in which the officials granted the Miners precisely four free throws. "Got me more pheasant that trip than foul shots," he said.

He still talked that way, in that idiom, about such things. And though it might have sounded like some carnival act for media folks intrepid enough to make their way to the badlands of Baja New Mexico, it wasn't really, for hardly any writers came anymore, and there would have been no advantage to keeping such a shtick sharp.

But stories had their use. They were deflective. They led the listener to something else, somewhere else, someone else, ideally fixing the discussion in another time altogether—1949, say. Mr. Iba. Stillwater, Oklahoma. An A&M practice: "Back then it wasn't supposed to be fun, see. Over Christmas break he'd have us go nine to noon, two to five, seven to 10. And seven to 10 would be three one-hour scrimmages. No water. No sitting. One night by the end, the skin on the fat part of the ball of my foot had come off. Literally come off. School president was at that practice, and he asked me if I was tired when I came off the floor.

"'No, sir,' I told him.

"'Sure shouldn't be,' he says back. ''Cause you haven't done a damn thing all day.'"

Thus he wove more diverting scenes on the tapestry of his basketball life, so many distracting stitches that I could scarcely make out the fundamental fibers. That's the thing about sitting at Haskins's knee, which is to say at his jowls and gut and hands: I'd come to Rome to hear Caesar on Caesar. But Caesar wanted to play Gibbon, so I got story after story about Rome in which Caesar figured only glancingly.

"Funny, he holds Iba in such regard, to such legendary status," Majerus had told me. "Now he's there himself and doesn't even realize it. Everything east and west of him is wasteland. Everything south of him is a foreign country. North of him is Albuquerque, which has the [University of New Mexico and its notorious home court, the] Pit. If he wasn't in our league and wasn't in our time zone, he'd have been in the Hall of Fame 20 years ago."

Haskins became the Bear, but Iba called the kid from Enid, Oklahoma, something much less magisterial: Rope, for his taut physique, and for the hair surmounting it that seemed to be made of coir. In 1955, three years out of A&M, Haskins landed at the high school in Benjamin, a West Texas crossroads. "I went into coaching because I didn't know how to do anything else," he told me. "Being some guy in Peoria at a desk, punching a time clock—I *knew* I didn't want to do that. It was like I'd grabbed a lifeline and pulled myself out of the water."

It scarcely mattered that terra firma was strewn with tumbleweed, or that he and his bride, Mary, pulled up in front of what was to be their new home to find a rattlesnake coiled on the porch. By the time he reached El Paso six years later, the desert fit him fine. For a golden while Floyd sat at his elbow and enough talent flowed, including NBA crossover artist Tim Hardaway, for the Miners to win their 20 games a season. But matters remained relatively quiet for a quarter century after the Kentucky game, with no one paying Haskins and UTEP much mind. Then, at the end of the 1980s, the program attracted attention of the most unwelcome kind.

Haskins wasn't sure why NCAA investigators began crawling around town, but he had his suspicions. The day after the Samford game he shared them with me while a trainer attended to his infected foot and his players worked out amid his occasional interjections. Haskins believed the NCAA's interest could be traced to a day in 1988, when he took on as a volunteer assistant coach a man named Norm Ellenberger.

Ellenberger had presided over an epic scandal at New Mexico during the late 1970s, a motley of pay-for-play and academic fraud that left him essentially unemployable. Haskins competed against Ellenberger, yet during off-seasons he would go hunting with him and, high among the mesquite and pronghorn, man-to-man, broach the subject of his ways. "I told Norm exactly which of his guys were bought and paid for," Haskins said. "I'd say, 'This one is,' and he'd say, 'Yeah.' I'd say, 'That one, too,' and he'd say, 'How'd you know?' I told him it was obvious: The ones who talked back to him, cursed him out in the huddle, they wouldn't be doing that unless they had something on him. Give a player something, see, and you can't coach him anymore."

But it was just like Haskins to give Ellenberger another chance years later, when the former Lobo coach was down-and-out and desperate to get back into the game. And it was just like Haskins never to suspect that his act of charity might prick up the ears of the NCAA.

Haskins said he didn't regret having helped out an old rival. Indeed, he worried that telling me this story might embarrass Ellenberger. Though he said he never had anything to hide, he also wondered whether he had been a fool to be so cooperative with the NCAA's investigation. He freely admitted that he broke a rule (if not the code he lives by, which is something else entirely) when he shared some pumpkin pie and a cup of coffee with a recruit's grandmother at seven one morning, three hours earlier than permitted, because she had to go off to work. And he acknowledged that two of his assistants provided improper rides to players, which led the school to let them both go. But Haskins defied me to look at similar cases elsewhere and conclude that UTEP's punishment fit its crime. The entire episode, as people in West Texas say, smelled like a wet dog. And the program hadn't righted itself since.

To Haskins, the most mortifying thing about all this was that Mr. Iba, then still alive, might have thought that Rope wasn't doing right by the way he'd been taught. Why, Mr. Iba knew better than anyone that no coach worth his clipboard would consent to letting a player have him by the short-and-curlies. "If I'd have got caught in buying 'em cars or giving 'em money, I'd have quit then," Haskins told me. "But I've done my damnedest to do it the right way."

Some friends and followers believed that Haskins, owing to bad luck and a big heart, couldn't really afford to quit. "It's not to that point," he said. "Don't want it to seem like I'm on Skid Row." But he had supplemented his income by going out on weekends to call and shoot coyotes, then sell their pelts for $75 apiece. And he admitted to a number of financial misadventures, including a $22,500 investment in a failed scheme to grow lettuce. Others told me of Haskins, returning from a hunting trip, picking up a poor family whose car had broken down, then putting them up in a hotel until the garage had done its work; and of the $10 tip he'd invariably leave for a waitress in an undertrafficked coffee shop. Nothing, however, set Don and Mary further back every which way than the death in 1994 of the eldest of their four sons, Mark, after a long illness. Insurance covered most of Mark's medical care, but bills still gouged out a piece of the Haskinses' savings, which had included a $500,000 annuity arranged for Don in the late eighties by a circle of UTEP boosters. "I didn't take care of myself real well," he said. "Fifteen years ago I thought I was going to coach forever. Now I know better."

By my third day in town I knew exactly why Don Haskins still showed up at the Don Haskins Center every day. It wasn't because he didn't have enough money invested in the bank. It was because he had too much of himself invested in the program.

"Don't know what it was like where you grew up. . . . "

Haskins had launched into another story, one that threw light on his sympathy for the customerless waitress, for the family whose car broke down, for Norm Ellenberger. It illuminated what Floyd, who would go on to coach the Chicago Bulls, has called Haskins's "tremendous appreciation for people who have been through hard times." He was telling the tale of Herman Carr.

". . . But Enid was set on a town square. I lived on the east side, and like most towns of that era, blacks lived on the other side. Back then I played basketball daylight to dark. It was my sophomore year or so that I met Herman in Government Springs Park. I was supposedly one of the better players at my high school. He played for [all-black] Washington. He was about 6'2". We'd play, never more than the two of us, and it was always a battle."

Though 6'1", Haskins could dunk. He loved the game so much he spent his prom night shooting hoops in the gym while his classmates swanned with each other on the far side of a curtain. "Thought everybody was crazy but me," he said. But being called one of the best players in the state, fielding Mr. Iba's invitation to play at A&M, didn't mean quite so much when you knew there was someone just across town who might be better than you but wasn't permitted to show it. "Would have been nice to have played with Herman in high school. I remember just thinking how unfair it was that this guy couldn't play. Unfortunately, there wasn't a little more equality back then."

And that was the closest thing to a ringing social statement I was going to get from Don Haskins. "They made it a big deal after the Kentucky game," he said of his long-ago role as basketball's Earl Warren. "That particular night, believe me, I'm not thinking about that. We got home, and all of that was a total shock to me. The mail, it started a week or two later. Got about a year of it. 'Dear Niggerlover.' And every once in a while a letter from a black leader calling me an exploiter. *That* hurt a little bit. To say I went in there waving the flag, that's not true. I just played my best guys, like any coach would. There were three black players on the team when I arrived in El Paso. It's not like I started it."

Haskins's demurral would seem to dim his halo. What, then, about those horns of Rupp's? The exculpatory case goes like this: Kentucky reached the final by beating Duke, which was all-white, too (although the Blue Devils had signed a black player for the following season). If Duke had beaten Kentucky, *it* would have lost to Texas Western, and the Blue Devils would have been shown the back of history's hand. Besides, even if Rupp had wanted to recruit blacks, in the mid-1960s few schools in the Southeastern Conference would have agreed to play an integrated team. Where would that have left a founding member of the SEC like Kentucky?

In 1992 I received a letter from one of Rupp's granddaughters. It defended him as someone who had been misunderstood and unfairly maligned. Carlyle Farren Rupp described a quiet humanitarian, someone who donated his time and support to charities and youth groups, and she recalled going into Lexington's black neighborhood with him as a little girl to hand out tickets to kids for the Shrine Circus. Many who knew Rupp have stood up for him, pointing out that if the old coach didn't much like people, he liked change less—and that we shouldn't mistake a crotchety misanthrope for a racist.

On the other hand there's plenty of evidence for the prosecution. For more than three years before the Texas Western game, Rupp implacably resisted the efforts of Dr. John Oswald, Kentucky's president, to begin the integration of the basketball team. Longtime Kentucky assistant coach Harry Lancaster recalled his boss's reaction after Rupp first discussed the subject with Oswald: "That son of a bitch is ordering me to get some niggers in here. What am I going to do?"

Stories like these only multiplied after Rupp retired. In the late 1970s Rupp told Jere Longman, then a student journalist at LSU, that "the problem with the game today is that there are too many blacks." Referring to the American Basketball Association, he told agent Ron Grinker, "The trouble with the ABA is that there are too many nigger boys in it now." Years after the loss to Texas Western he was still slandering Haskins's players as "crooks" (in fact, none were); charging that one Miner had been recruited from prison (none had); and alleging that the school had been placed on probation right after its title (it hadn't been).

I'd brought up the subject of Rupp with John McLendon a few days earlier, after our van jag through eastern Kansas. "I never met the man," he told me. "People from Kentucky have written me over the years to ask if I had any personal knowledge of Rupp being a racist. I wrote back that I myself experienced none."

But McLendon did share a story related to him by William (Goody) Goodwin, who served as sports publicist at Kentucky State, one of the schools at which McLendon coached. Goodwin had a friend in Lexington who worked as a barbershop boy, a Jim Crow job that involved fetching newspapers, holding towels, and performing other servile tasks for a shop's white customers. Barbershop boys were expected otherwise to recede into the background. But this meant the walls had ears. And Goodwin's friend said that, on the eve of the season that ended with Texas Western's victory, Rupp addressed the issue of blacks playing for the Wildcats as he sat for a shave, his face hooded with white towels: "I'd like to win one more championship without niggers on my team."

Even if we give Rupp the benefit of every doubt, it's hard to avoid concluding, based on his words alone, that he was at least a bigot. What is bigotry anyway but a toxic brew of more benign human failings, such as stubbornness, superstition, begrudgery, and distrust, all of which, even his defenders agree, Rupp had in abundance?

On this subject I felt mislocated. I was in El Paso, after all, and judging Rupp was a chore best left to history. Haskins, however, I wanted another crack at.

There's this thing about stories: The Bear can tell them, but others can, too. Dan Wetzel, a writer for *Basketball Times,* had been through El Paso a year before me, and in advance of his arrival he tracked down two of Haskins's first black players. One, Andy Stoglin, the coach at Jackson State, told of a time during the 1962–63 season when Haskins called him into his office. "He said to me, 'I know you should start, but I can't start five black players.' He pulled out this drawer and dumped these letters out and said, 'Read these and tell me what you think.' He left me in the office for 30 minutes and I read some of them. The mail said, 'You're playing too many niggers.' All sorts of awful things like that. He told me not to tell the other players about it. I could tell the pain it was causing him."

Arkansas coach Nolan Richardson was also a Miner that season, one of the players who had helped Haskins unload his U-Haul when he arrived in town. Richardson remembered one game day when Coach Haskins told him much the same thing that Stoglin was told—that he wouldn't be starting that night. The coach added that he believed Richardson, a senior and an El Pasoan, could cope better than any of his black teammates with what Haskins made clear he regarded as an injustice. As

Richardson recalled it, "Right before game time he says, 'Richardson! Piss on 'em, you're starting. Piss on what they'll say.'"

Dan Wetzel had asked Haskins about the former players' stories. "I don't even remember," Haskins replied. "Nolan and Andy? I think they're dreaming. I don't remember getting hate mail back then. I don't know, I don't remember."

I asked him, too. Even read the accounts to him, so his memory might respond to the prod of detail. He was even more emphatic. "I don't recall this sack of letters," he said of Stoglin's story. "Andy said that?" And of Richardson's: "Don't remember that ever happening."

There was only one problem with Haskins's forgetfulness. He has a snare of a memory. He ticks off phone numbers on demand. He summons instantly details about people and places from his past. His former players said this: When he tells you he doesn't recall, don't believe it. He remembers everything.

That night I caught up with Dan Wetzel on the phone. "Both Nolan and Andy told me he'd deny it," he said. "But all that detail? I have no doubt they're both telling the truth, and that the Bear is trying to save El Paso's reputation. In those days El Paso was a racist town. Nolan had to cross the river to Juarez if he wanted to see a movie."

I'd driven west suspecting, even hoping, to discover that these two gigantic historical antagonists wouldn't diverge so sharply along Manichean lines—that Haskins would turn out to be less of a hero, if only so Rupp might look like less of a villain. And while Rupp may indeed have been no worse a man than many in his retrograde times—in the South during the 1960s, few figures in a position to do so moved to integrate college sports—Haskins cannot escape a judgment he may not care for. He was courageous long before that spring evening in 1966. And if he really was oblivious to the significance of what he did in that NCAA final, it was because he had already made his stand.

Exam period wasn't over yet, and UTEP had a new opponent with which to muddle through a game: Texas Southern, a historically black college in Houston that could no longer attract the best African-American players in the land because of what Haskins and Texas Western had done 32 years earlier. The crowd seemed veiled with the same indifference that had afflicted the team several nights before. *"Awwwwwright!"* said the man on the mike, with a kind of dutiful enthusiasm. "Time for some *noise!"* Only no one made much. With a late effort the Miners flicked TSU away, and afterward Haskins repaired to the locker room, huddled with the press, then headed out the tunnel to an RV parked in the lot outside the arena. He motioned to me to follow him.

If there were a Don Haskins Center true to its eponym, this would be it—a structure small and anonymous, with wheels attached so that, on a whim, it might take a man up into the hills for the day. Haskins called the place the Swamp Cooler. Its owner, a pediatric dentist named Hampton Briggs, and Bill Dickey, a urologist who served as the Miners' unofficial team physician, joined the coach there after many home games.

The scotch poured forth, more of the Bear's stories did, too, and together they flowed until the Swamp Cooler seemed buoyant, as if the parking lot were a high-desert arroyo quick with runoff after a storm. *There was that time David Lattin was getting a little chesty so we left him at home for the Utah State game and when we passed him hitchhiking on the highway we refused to pick him up but David made it to Logan anyhow and said we'd never have another problem with him and we didn't, and the pecan orchards outside La Mesilla which you oughta see in the springtime when they're green and the boughs arch out over the road, and be sure to stop by Chope's on Highway 28 on your way back but only between noon and 1:30 'cause they're closed the rest of the time, and I'll never vote for another Republican again not after what they've done to that guy though it's a mess of things he's making in Iraq says Doctor Dickey, who I was once out shooting whitewing with and . . .*

"Was pigeons, wasn't it?"

. . . No, you pecker checker, it was whitewing, and on the way back the air-conditioning in the truck broke down and this was the middle of the desert see and I didn't have the faintest what to do so I turned to Doctor Dickey and he just shrugged and said, "If it ain't bleedin', I can't fix it."

No great battles were fought in the Swamp Cooler. No society got integrated there, no son's illness got cured, no inquisitional bureaucracy was brought to heel. But neither could any shrapnel from the skirmishes of life pierce its steel and further wound a man who had chosen it as his bunker. Here was an audience that delighted in a particular past being recounted, just so, by this man who had but one abiding, overriding wish: to be regarded not as saint, not as sinner, but as just plain innocent.

The storyteller's stream ultimately eddied into another tale from the past, from when Haskins was a college sophomore. "Back then they held the All-College Tournament in Oklahoma City around Christmas, and it was one of the highlights of the season. Made all-tournament that year, and afterward Mr. Iba didn't play me for three straight games. Asked him about it years later. I said, 'Coach?'—he let me call him 'Coach' by then—'remember how I made all-tournament at the All-College and you didn't play me for three straight games?'

"He said he didn't recall. Which is a lie, because he remembered everything."

TWELVE

Whiteriver, Arizona

Shoots from the Sky

Basketball is a Native American game, you know."

I didn't know. Visits to Springfield and Almonte argued otherwise, and my last few stops suggested the game might be African-American. But that's what the man said, and who was I to dispute him? He was a published historian, a student of Native American culture, a man with basketball credentials as impressive as anyone's anywhere.

"I told the people at the Hall of Fame the same thing," Kareem Abdul-Jabbar said, leaning back in his chair to gauge my reaction. "They didn't know, either."

Professor Abdul-Jabbar went on, elaborating on points of history about which I'd only vaguely heard. In the 10th century B.C., the Mayan and Olmec people of the Yucatán apparently played something called *pok-ta-pok*. Using only their elbows, knees, shoulders, and hips, they tried to send some sort of spherical object through a stone ring affixed to a wall. The captain of the losing team had his heart cut out.

"The Aztecs played a game much like it in the 16th century," Kareem went on. That would have been *ollamalitzli*, another projectile/receptacle pastime, though pastime may not be the correct word given the fate awaiting the captain of the losers—decapitation. "The Aztecs settled as far north as

Sedona in Arizona," he said. "So that makes basketball a Native American game."

Kareem's assertion sounded plausible. Passing a ball through a hoop was now such a fundamental part of our lives, it hardly seemed possible that people could have done without it until barely a century ago. But I was struck most by the expansiveness of the man seated across from me in the Chief Alchesay Activity Center, on the White Mountain Apache Reservation in eastern Arizona. As we spoke in the arena's training room, I recalled how the training room at the Forum in Los Angeles, a refuge off-limits to all but players and staff, had been Kareem's favorite place to hide out from the press during his years with the Lakers. Yet here I'd shown up virtually unannounced and he was playing the host, expounding with animation on history, Apache culture, and the state of the game.

Kareem was in Whiteriver, a down-at-the-heels crossroads that serves as the reservation's administrative seat, to spend a season as a volunteer assistant coach at Alchesay High School. He had come at his own initiative and expense, as much in desperation as a spirit of philanthropy, after failing to hook on as a paid assistant in the league over which he had so recently lorded. It seemed to me terribly sad that a master of the game, a captain of championship teams, someone who clearly loved basketball and wanted to serve it by giving something back, could find no team willing to put him on its payroll.

But a kind of misfortune had tracked Kareem for much of his adult life. In 1973 a family of Hanafi Muslims, the orthodox sect to which he belongs, was murdered in a townhouse he owned in Washington, D.C. A decade later a fire destroyed his Bel Air home, including thousands of his beloved jazz albums. A soured relationship with an agent ended with Kareem losing millions in investments. Migraine headaches sometimes left him bedridden. For years he seemed to gunnysack every slight and frustration, and on two occasions he snapped on the court, each time throwing a punch that left him with a broken hand.

The recent death of his part-Cherokee mother, Cora Alcindor, together with his inability to find a coaching job, had led him to take stock of his life and himself. He had paid a visit to Whiteriver in the mid-1990s while researching a book on the Buffalo Soldiers, the all-black cavalry regiment stationed at Fort Apache during the Civil War, and Native American history fascinated him. So he had returned to the White Mountains, to learn and to teach, and there I'd gone to find him, because of where he was as much as who he was.

The drive from El Paso had taken up all of the previous day. Through much of it—first over desolate llano, then along switchback roads rising through rangeland carpeted with spruce, finally in my room at the Hon-Dah Resort and Casino (*hon-dah* is Apache for "be my guest")—I'd wondered how forthcoming Kareem would be. His seven feet two inches acted as a beacon from afar even as they became terribly intimidating up close. When he smiled he looked capable of being your best friend, but he didn't smile much. He was a man who clearly had something to say and thus drew people to him, but whose standoffishness often left them feeling turned away.

Nevertheless, no matter how remote a pose Kareem struck or how summarily he made clear his distaste for talking, I always believed it was worth making the approach. I covered the NBA Finals during the 1984–85 season, when Kareem, then 38, captained the Lakers to a title with such grit and grace that he was named both playoff MVP and *Sports Illustrated*'s Sportsman of the Year. Only once did I sense that a question of mine had really reached him: in the locker room before a playoff game, when he kindled to the subject of Robert B. Parker's Spenser novels. That lone success hatched my suspicion that only by avoiding the subject of Kareem could one get through to him. Here, as he spoke easily on topics far from his private self, I felt that hunch being confirmed.

To reach the Activity Center, I'd waited out rusting pickup trucks that turned languidly off the main highway, onto dirt driveways ramping up to shotgun dwellings. Besides abundant flora and fauna, basketball was the reservation's most vital sign of life. Kids on "the res," their imaginations fired by the Alchesay Falcons' 1993 state title, played constantly, in school gyms or one of several youth centers built to interrupt cycles of poverty and alcoholism. Kareem was trying to channel their energy and enthusiasm for the game in new directions. "Most kids around the world learn from highlight films of Michael Jordan, and these are no different," he told me. "They've embraced a lot of bad habits and found a comfort zone in them. The biggest problem we have is these guys think the game is all about speed and agility, and size if you've got it. If they had their way, basketball wouldn't be more than a track meet. I'm trying to show them that efficiency and smarts are part of the game, too."

Just as Native American language and culture were in peril, so were the principles of orthodox post play. To pass along the rudiments of the drop step, of fronting the post, perhaps even of his signature move, the skyhook, would be to act in accordance with the values of the Apache people, who revere their elders and handed-down ways. Kareem was a stranger here— Shoots from the Sky, in the manner of Dances with Wolves. But he regarded himself as a kindred preservationist spirit. "It's scary how the stuff I know is dying out," he said. "Kids aren't learning how to play with their back to the basket. That's how Americans used to dominate the world, by knowing how to use size and position.

"Growing up in New York, I was fortunate. Because I was so tall, in sixth grade I was told, 'You're playing the pivot.' So I'd go down to Madison Square Garden and watch centers like Bill Russell and study what they did. And I played CYO ball. On a team I had structure and coaching and playoffs at the end of the season. There was a student at Manhattan College, a guy named George, a volunteer who taught me the drop step, how to box out, how to front the post—the basics."

The phenomenon he was describing—vanishing basketball knowledge amid burgeoning basketball interest—threw that much more responsibility on teachers, including volunteers like George then and himself now. Here in Whiteriver, even though the game wasn't rewarding him as it had during his years as a pro, it paid him back just the same. "To see the light go on in

their heads when they understand that their way isn't necessarily the best way, that they have more to learn, it's very grati-
fying. For the longest time I tried to get them to shoot layups
with their weak hand and they resisted. Then we lost a couple
of games because we missed layups. That's when they understood."

Kareem went on in this vein and then, suddenly, caught me
unawares. He began talking about the subject I didn't dare bring
up. He began talking, confessionally, about himself.

"As an NBA player, I was in such a position of serious
responsibility, and trying to live up to standards I set, that I put
a lot of pressure on myself. I accepted the challenge every year.
I had fame and money. But all of that certainly had a negative
influence on my life. Today I have no relationship with my
eldest daughter because I wasn't there when she was growing
up, and she resents that. After my career was over I found out
that I'd been resented by my teammates, too. I found out that
fans thought I was strange, and that owners didn't see me as a
poster boy of a person. I wasn't aware of any of this at the time."

I didn't know what to say. I hadn't expected our conversation
to take this turn, so I wasn't prepared to prod him to reveal
another layer of himself, although surely here lay an explanation
for why the game's greatest scorer was paying the steepest of
entry-level dues.

Soon Kareem had wended the conversation back to his high
schoolers. By leaving the moment hanging, I'd let it slip away.

I had reached Whiteriver just in time for Alchesay High's
annual holiday tournament. More than 5,000 people filled the
Activity Center that night, as the PA announcer welcomed the
Falcons' opponent, San Carlos High, "our neighbors and relatives" from the San Carlos Apache Reservation across the Black
River to the south. This game would be for a national championship of sorts—for supremacy of the Apache nation.

As the game began, I recalled what Coach Kareem had told

me about each of the team's post players. Brennen Butterfield, a senior starter, seemed to have the best basketball instincts, but at 6'3" he was the team's smallest big man. Willie Zagotah, a limp-limbed 6'4", wore his teacher's old number, 33. At 6'6" and 230 pounds, Ivan Lampkin was the Falcons' biggest player, but he was also the most self-conscious. "Ivan's athletic but a little timid," Kareem told me. "I spent three weeks just trying to get him to attempt a layup with his weak hand in practice."

The Falcons wound up winning 75–66, because their guards took care of the ball well enough to protect a lead. But later Kareem elaborated on his frustrations. "They care too much about face. In their culture, losing face is just not cool. Which means they're afraid to try something if they think they might fail. Take Ivan. He's not a good ball handler, but we need him to be one as an outlet against the press. It's all I can do to get him to turn and face the backcourt and make himself available.

"The other thing about Apache culture is that you don't talk unless you absolutely have to. Everybody is a warrior unto himself. So even if a guy sees a teammate who's about to have the ball stolen away, he won't yell to warn him. Even if a guy's lost his man on defense and needs help, he won't call to get it. They won't even talk when they're trying to defend the pick-and-roll. The other night one of our guys got clocked because another didn't tell him a pick was coming."

In Kareem's dilemma I found a delectable irony. Fourteen years ago I'd tried to get the most emotionally opaque player in the game to speak. Now the ultimate Warrior unto Himself was spending a season struggling to get these kids to do the same thing.

Growing up, the realization that I could shoot a basketball provided a comfort I could count on. I had no brothers ready to callous me to the bump and grind of the game as it's played in close quarters, and only in high school did I really begin to appreciate the welter of possible combinations that come with team play. Thus I never really stopped spending those hours alone in the driveway, becalmed by that single act. The groove of my stroke was a refuge into which I could burrow.

Even today, those basketball beginnings are apparent to anyone who watches me play, in the same way you could study a midwestern shooter of the fifties and, from the trajectory of his shot, reconstruct the architecture of the barn in which he played while growing up. Never big or strong or aggressive enough to bogart my way inside, I've always known I can step back and bring replicable shooting technique to bear. Given a choice, that's what I'll do—step back, and back and back if need be, before I'll take the ball to the hole. I once regarded this faith in my shot as a virtue. But I'd long since come to recognize it as a flaw that paralyzed my game, putting me at the mercy of any defender perceptive enough to figure me out. I wish I'd had a Jack McMahon in my youth, someone to hector me with "only good things happen when you go to the hole."

What I saw of the Apache lands touched off these ruminations. With scarcely 13,000 people scattered over 2.6 million acres, the White Mountain Reservation was shooting country. Here a ball could be launched in unspoiled air. Nothing but the trumpet of an elk could distract someone locked in on the rim. Everywhere there was room to take another step back.

The late coach and referee Charley Eckman once said there were only two great plays: *South Pacific* and put the ball in the basket. *South Pacific* closed on Broadway nearly a half century ago, and from all available evidence the final curtain was coming down on putting the ball in the basket, at least in the U.S. I didn't know if this was due to the diversionary appeal of a jiggy-widdit skill like the crossover, or the scaled-back attention spans of kids enamored of it. But from my travels thus far I knew that if America were to continue to be curator of the sport it birthed and popularized, it would have to do so without being the best in the world at basketball's most essential act. During the 1995 World Junior Championships, a U.S. team featuring Stephon Marbury and Vince Carter won only half its games, finishing seventh in a 16-team field. Most ominously, 18- and 19-year-olds from six

countries—Australia, China, Croatia, Greece, and such terri-
fying basketball powers as South Korea and Venezuela—all fared
better than their American peers in every shooting category,
from two-pointers to three-pointers to free throws. The coach of
that team, Oklahoma's Kelvin Sampson, returned to the States a
shaken man. "Overseas they play basketball in its simplest form,"
he said. "Their game is about making jump shots. They penetrate
and kick it out to the open man. Our players do a great job of
slashing to the basket and making plays, but then we're into
degree-of-difficulty basketball."

That's why Kareem's preservationism struck me as so important. No one in history had put the ball in the basket more often
than he. Usually he did so by unfurling the skyhook, the shot
his coach with the Lakers, Pat Riley, called "the most awesome
weapon in the history of any sport." It seemed curious that a
man so tall should have shot a hook at all, much less one
involving so much arc and complexity. Where the jump hook
consists essentially of two parts, the skyhook involves perhaps a
dozen discrete movements run seamlessly together. Certainly a
seven-footer didn't need all of the shot's arc simply to protect
the ball from a leaping defender; the skyhook, Kareem told me,
had never once been cleanly blocked.

But a man's shot is like DNA, an infallible marker of who he
is, and the skyhook fit Kareem perfectly. It was a kind of out-
of-body projection, at one with his devotion to such recondite
or non-Western subjects as jazz and Islam. To shoot a parabolic
shot is an act of faith; to shoot one on a line is an act of will.
Those who devote enough time to their shot learn to reconcile
faith and will, finding the midpoint that coaches call the
optimal arc. But Kareem did something confounding with the
skyhook. He released the ball from a point so far beyond himself, and he traced with it such a majestic path, that the skyhook
appeared to be an absolute subjugation of the will to faith. At
the same time, the shot was so well-practiced that, whenever
Kareem swung into one, the ball had his will tattooed all over
it. For who but the most stubbornly willful person could have
mastered the damned thing?

He was fully aware of its singularity. "Everybody wants to see the ball as they let it go, to have it on-line from the start," Kareem said. "They find it awkward not to do that. But the hook won't let you see the ball as you release it. It requires tri-angulation. And rhythm, touch, and repetition."

He laughed. "In high school I was no good in math. I once did a public service announcement with Jaime Escalante, the teacher portrayed in *Stand and Deliver*, and mentioned to him that I'd barely passed elementary algebra. He said, 'What are you talking about? The skyhook proves you're a trigonometric genius! Your ability to calculate height, trajectory, ballistics—it's incredible!'

"Of course, I couldn't go into math class and shoot the hook for an A."

In fact, the skyhook began in a moment of serendipity. "I shot it in the first game I ever got into. I still remember: There was a long rebound beyond the free-throw line. It was a miracle that I even got to it, but I got to it. I went up and into this hook shot. I just did it—didn't even think about it. And I missed. But I *just* missed. My coach saw it and said, 'That's good! Keep doing that!' "

I thought of the kid Doc Naismith saw in the gym who "just liked to see if he could make a basket every time he threw the ball." Then I asked Kareem if he had tried to teach the skyhook to any of the Falcons.

"Nobody's ready," he said. "I'm still trying to get Ivan, Brennen, and Willie to make 10 layups in a row with each hand. Ivan's the one who could learn it the quickest, because he's athletic and has a good shooting touch. But he's also the most tentative and afraid to fail."

Before Alchesay and Holbrook High tipped off in the tour-nament final the following night, a seven-year-old in a green suit sang "The Star-Spangled Banner" in Apache. Then Brennen, the post player with the most adventurous spirit, stepped forward for the Falcons. In the opening moments he potted a jumper, blocked a shot, and, with a barked shout, even alerted a teammate to a Holbrook screen. Just before the first-quarter buzzer he sank a fadeaway along the baseline, show-casing the kind of footwork that only comes from hours spent in a gym—and the guidance of a good coach.

The Falcons' guards became careless with the ball late in the game, but Alchesay squeezed out a 47–45 victory just the same. Brennen was voted the tournament's MVP. Afterward I asked him what he had learned from his new coach. He ticked off a list of things, including how to make eye contact with teammates.

Kareem had been clever. If they wouldn't talk to each other, they could always send ocular smoke signals.

"Has he taught you how to shoot the skyhook yet?" I asked.

"No," Brennen said. "But I hope he does."

Weeks after my visit to Whiteriver, I came across a passage in James Naismith's *Basketball: Its Origins and Development*. In it he wrote how, within a few years of the game's invention, a physician introduced basketball to the Sioux. Out on the South Dakota prairie, this doctor cut saplings for poles and bent willow branches into hoops, then watched with gratification as members of the tribe took avidly to the game.

Doc Naismith recounted this, then added: "I have talked to several coaches of Indian teams, and . . . one coach told me that he had several good players who would not take part in the sport for fear of ridicule, and that some of the boys felt it inexcusable to make a mistake. They would not run this chance before a group of people."

I faxed the page to Kareem, with a note remarking how little had changed over a century. Though I never heard back, I felt as if I were continuing a conversation begun in the Arizona high country. He knew he had wisdom to share with others, and at long last, in his own groping, earnest, surprisingly traditionalist, and sometimes fitful way, he seemed even to be enjoying their company. As much as the kids at Alchesay were getting out of Coach Kareem, he was getting out of them. At home in the salon of the game, prodding kids to speak up, he was finding his voice, too.

Surely the last in my trinity of 20th-century American basketeers also had something to say. Unfortunately, I was going to have a hard time hearing him.

THIRTEEN

Boone, North Carolina

Mayberry Friends

What Kareem had been to me during the mid-1980s, Michael Jordan became by the end of the nineties: basketball's unknowable, unreachable Untouchable. This wasn't because Jordan shared Abdul-Jabbar's aloofness, but because of my affiliation with *Sports Illustrated*.

In 1994, after Jordan embarked on a midlife career change, our top editor was astonished to discover that the freshly retired Chicago Bulls star wasn't as good at baseball as he had been at basketball. To trumpet this news, he ordered up a cover story—delicately billed BAG IT, MICHAEL!—that charged Jordan and the Chicago White Sox with "embarrassing" baseball. At the time this screed appeared, baseball was hardly capable of embarrassment. The game had no commissioner, no star with a measurable Q-rating, and labor ills so thoroughly metastasized that they made the NBA lockout look like a touch of the flu. The article failed to take into account the belief in sport for sport's sake that we had long advocated in our pages. Instead, Jordan's willingness to take on a new challenge was played as a cynical publicity stunt at best, and a character flaw at worst.

Everyone on our staff did penance for that oafish story. Competitiveness and pride accounted almost as much as talent for Jordan's greatness, and to score a point and sheath his ego he vowed never to speak to us again. He kept that vow even after resuming his basketball career. Thus I'd long been resigned to approaching Jordan at one degree of separation. But this enforced distance would disguise a blessing. It forced me to view him through the eyes of his old friend, former teammate and roommate, and, I was to discover, original prod.

As the crow flies, perhaps even as Jordan does, there's less distance between Raleigh and New York than between North Carolina's Outer Banks and the hollows abutting the Tennessee line. Jordan's hometown, the Atlantic coastal port of Wilmington, stakes out one of those geographic poles. The Great Smokies gateway of Asheville, home of Buzz Peterson, marks the other. The NBA lockout had just ended when my flight alighted between the two, where the land ramps up from the sea. This was the Piedmont, seat of the state's high-tech industries and largest universities, including the Chapel Hill campus where Jordan and Peterson first met as high school seniors-to-be during the summer of 1980, at North Carolina coach Dean Smith's basketball camp. They would return to spend three seasons together on Smith's Tar Heel team.

I rented a car and headed west for Boone, where Peterson was now in his third season as coach at Appalachian State University. I arrived to find the town veiled by a freezing fog, and Peterson in circumstances drastically different from those Dean Smith once enjoyed: a cramped office on the second floor of something prosaically called Varsity Gym. Nappy carpeting lay underfoot, and scuffed-up filing cabinets lined walls covered with suburban rec-room paneling. But Buzz himself had an incandescence that trumped this ambient drabness, and he drawled with a welcoming ease.

With the lockout now over, the Bulls, the league, and fans everywhere awaited word from Jordan. Would he return, or would he let the jumper he dropped on Utah to win that NBA title stand as his last act? For days he had been incommunicado, keeping the counsel of no one but some caddie on a golf course in the Bahamas.

Buzz sat at his desk, waving a sheaf of pink while-you-were-out slips handed to him by a secretary moments ago. "It's every sports-talk radio jock in the country, all wanting to know about Michael." Such was the burden of being best friend to the most famous athlete in the world—a burden I thought nothing of adding to.

"Well, what's he going to do?"

"I don't know. But I do know how he'll go about making up his mind. He's one of the best people I've ever seen at making a big decision. He'll be absolutely businesslike. If he doesn't think the pieces are in place to win another title, he won't stay. But he's got a heart like everybody else, and he doesn't want to be the one who kills the team. Physically, he'd like to come back. And it wouldn't be as demanding mentally, because the season will only be 50 games and you can always get fired up for the playoffs. On the other hand, why not go out on such a good note?

"I spend $79 a month for DirecTV to watch him play. It's only $69 if you sign up for the Early-Bird Special. So I told him to hurry up and make up his mind so I can save the 10 bucks."

"What did he say to that?"

"He told me to shut up."

In 1996, New York Knicks coach Jeff Van Gundy made a remark that got under Jordan's famously thin skin. He suggested that Jordan befriended opposing players off the court in the hope that they'd go soft on him come game time.

The comment infuriated Jordan not because it implied that he needed to con his way to an advantage. Everyone in the NBA hunted down and seized any psychological edge he could. Rather, Jordan was offended that Van Gundy would impugn his notion of friendship. And Peterson was someone with whom he had upheld that ideal, dating back to when he didn't have to wonder, as Sasha Djordjević had put it, if people wanted to befriend you "because you're a good person or because you're a good player."

Jordan had been an awkward adolescent, with jangling limbs and rattling insecurities—"goony" by his own description. Fearing he might not be marriageable, he took home ec classes at Wilmington's Laney High in case he might someday have to do his own cooking and sewing. As unlikely as it seems in retrospect, Jordan would not be named the state's finest schoolboy athlete the following season, or even its basketball player of the year; Peterson would win both awards as a senior at Asheville High.

Yet at basketball camp in Chapel Hill the state's two finest players—one black, middle-class, and from the state's lowcountry; the other white, well-to-do, and from its highlands—quickly fell in together. They shared a suite in which Buzz roomed with a high school teammate of Michael, and Michael paired up with a high school teammate of Buzz. Later that summer, at Five-Star, the competition camp staged as much for the benefit of leering college recruiters as the players themselves, they grew even closer, making a pact to play together for Dean Smith. After Jordan made an early commitment to North Carolina that November, he reminded Peterson of their agreement, and every few weeks thereafter he called to hold him to their pledge, never so insistently as after Buzz gave a nonbinding oral commitment to Kentucky.

The following April, after superb senior seasons, Buzz and Michael both flew to Wichita for the McDonald's High School All-America Game. In the spring of 1981 the game showcased an unusually talented high school class that included such NBA Dream Teamers–to–be as Jordan, Patrick Ewing, and Chris Mullin. Organizers put the players up at a hotel with an indoor pool. One day, during a game of tag around that pool, a player named Adrian Branch sent Jordan into the deep end with a shove. Jordan wasn't a swimmer, and from where Peterson stood he could see panic flash across Jordan's face as he flailed in the water. "People were kind of laughing," Buzz told me. "And Michael does not like to be embarrassed. I helped him out of the pool and told him, 'We don't need to be playing this game anyway,' and we left."

That same month, Peterson overcame his infatuation with Kentucky and signed with Carolina—but not particularly out of loyalty to Jordan. The Tar Heels had no incumbent upper-classmen at Peterson's position on the wing, and Buzz liked his chances against the competition. "Kentucky had Jim Master. Maryland had Greg Manning. Virginia had Rick Carlisle. But at Carolina the only guy I'd have to beat out was this freshman." Buzz shook his head as he told me this. "And I'm a coach now, trying to judge talent."

In preseason drills during the fall of their freshman year, Peterson beat Jordan in the 40-yard dash, and Jordan's vertical jump measured only an inch higher. But after Buzz suffered a stress fracture in his foot and missed the first several games, Michael opened the season as the Tar Heels' starting small for-ward. Within a year Buzz could no longer beat him in the 40. Peterson began to realize that his roommate was a preternatural talent, next to whom he was fated to be a role player. "That's when I made the decision," Buzz told me, "that I wasn't going to let it affect our friendship."

Gradually the contours of that friendship began to emerge. Jordan detested losing, whether the game was one-on-one, five-on-five, Ping-Pong, pool, or cards. Peterson was accommo-dating and guileless; that drawl highlighted vowels as broadly open as his manner. During a freshman year visit to the Peter-sons' in Asheville, the two were playing crazy eights with Buzz's mother, and Buzz couldn't believe it: "My roommate was trying to cheat my own mom!" Even the room they shared became an arena, with the thermostat the joystick on a kind of electronic game. The mountain boy liked the room cool. The kid from the coast liked it warm. Jordan would sneak out of bed and turn the heat up; Peterson would wait until his roommate was asleep and dial it back down. Last one to drift off got his way, and that was usually Buzz, who one morning awoke to find Jordan in a swaddle of blankets.

No longer rivals for the same spot on the court, they felt free to become much closer off it. They stocked their refrigerator with NuGrape, borrowed each other's cars, even consolidated their laundry for Michael's sister Roslyn to do. It was Buzz who figured out the surest way to shut Michael down: drive him out to Red Lobster, fill him with a huge dinner, then watch him fall asleep. It was Michael who steered Buzz toward courses in geography, which both would decide to major in, and would eventually provide coach Peterson with an easy laugh at Rotary luncheons when he divulged the average salary of a geography grad from Chapel Hill.

Every August, Buzz's father and grandfather would take him shopping to replenish his wardrobe before he headed off to Chapel Hill to begin a new school year. Buzz and Michael had roughly the same shoe size, and Michael would frequently dip into Buzz's closet. But Jordan's feet were slightly wider, and at the time of my visit, Buzz said, he still sometimes pulled out a pair of shoes only to realize he needed to wear sweat socks under his dress socks to fill out the leather, for it would still be stretched from Michael having worn the pair years ago. Buzz would get his revenge later, when on every visit to Chicago he raided Michael's closet for a few pairs of Nikes.

At the beginning of Peterson's sophomore year, the Tar Heel coaches asked him to room with an incoming freshman, a laconic kid from a small town near Asheville. Brad Daugherty was only 16, and the staff hoped Buzz could help ease his transition to college life. Jordan nonetheless shared a suite with Peterson and Daugherty, and it was that season, during a home game against Virginia, that the basketball paths of Buzz and Michael diverged for good. Just before the end of the first half, taking a charge, Peterson tore the medial collateral ligament in his right knee. Medics trundled him out of the Dean Smith Center and into a campus police cruiser, which rushed him through driving rain to the university's medical center. As he was wheeled into the emergency room for X-rays, he pleaded with the nurses to let him watch the rest of the game on TV.

From his bed Peterson saw Jordan rally the Tar Heels from 16 points behind, then win the game by fleecing the Cavaliers' Rick Carlisle of the ball and sailing in for a dunk. In the postgame television interview he addressed Buzz through the camera. "I miss you, buddy," Jordan said. "I wish you were here."

Before Carolina's next game, in a kind of half-mast tribute to his convalescing teammate, Jordan took a sweatband and pulled it midway up his left forearm. Though Peterson would return the following season, he was never the same player, and in some ways not the same person. And so it was symbolic that Jordan wore a sweatband in the same place for the rest of his career. Whenever Buzz saw kids on the playground wearing their sweatbands just so, he thought to himself: If only they knew.

By the following season, Jordan's last at Chapel Hill, the injury had crippled Peterson's psyche as well as his knee. Dissatisfied with his role and playing time, he retreated into self-pity. When an aunt fell fatally ill during the season, he suddenly left campus, telling no one but Jordan, now his roommate again, where he was going. The Tar Heel coaches were worried enough to alert the state police. Buzz had left his room a mess, but when he returned three days later he found everything tidied up—every sweater neatly folded, every shirt cleaned and ironed.

That spring it would be Jordan's turn to be restless. Three years earlier he had guilt-tripped Buzz into keeping his promise to join him at Carolina. Buzz believed that they'd agreed to a four-year hitch, and here he tried to make that argument. But Jordan was no longer someone who had to fall back on skills from some high school home ec class. He was likely to be among the first several picks in the NBA draft, and even Dean Smith was urging him to go pro. Buzz learned firsthand that, when faced with a big decision, Jordan is "absolutely businesslike."

Peterson came back to captain the Tar Heels his senior year. After graduation he played in Belgium for half a season, worked briefly as a bird dog for a high school scouting service, then hooked on as an assistant at Appalachian State before taking similar positions at East Tennessee State, North Carolina State, and Vanderbilt. Buzz and Michael sustained their friendship throughout these peregrinations, though it remained tinged with Jordan's competitiveness. Growing up, Peterson had idolized Kyle Macy, the veteran guard who was still with the Bulls when Jordan joined the team. What, Buzz wanted to know, is my idol like?

"Get another idol," Michael replied.

"I never knew if Michael wanted me to have another friend," Buzz told me. "I don't know if it was jealousy exactly, but he can be very possessive of some things." Several years after college, as Buzz made plans to marry his fiancée, Jan Maney, he asked Jordan to be in the wedding party. "He told me yes, but only if he could be best man. I explained to him that my dad was going to be best man. He could accept that. But that's Michael. Whatever it is he's doing, he wants to be the best."

While at Vanderbilt, Peterson interviewed for head coaching jobs at Murray State and East Tennessee State. He failed to land either one, though Jordan had called the athletic director at each school on his behalf. Then, in 1996, the top job in Boone came open. Shortly after Peterson applied for it, Jordan called him to ask for the name and number of the Appalachian State athletic director.

Hardly a day of Peterson's life passed without his relationship with Jordan coming up somehow. Buzz had once told Michael this, gratefully, emphasizing that in almost every instance their association surfaced in a positive light. But here he asked his friend to cool his competitive jets. "I've already struck out twice with your help," he told him. "I think I can handle this one on my own."

As he sat in his office, Buzz added a postscript to the account of his and Michael's years together in Chapel Hill. One spring day during the early 1990s, in the midst of the playoffs, Peterson flew to Chicago to pay his old friend a visit. Together they spent an off-day playing golf, just the two of them, and out on the course Buzz made a confession. Just because I'm your friend, he said, doesn't mean I can't this once make like a fan and tell you I think what you've accomplished is just mind-boggling.

Jordan had a confession of his own. "Buzz, you helped make me what I am. When you came out of high school, you were it. When I left Wilmington I had one goal, and every day freshman year I told myself the same thing: 'I have to be better than Buzz.'"

"Well, I sure wish you'd told me that then," Buzz replied. "So I could have said, 'I have to be better than Michael.'"

Peterson recounted this and added, "I feel I'm a pretty driven person. But being the best basketball player I could be wasn't as important to me after my injury as it was before. Now I look back and ask myself why I was like that, and I wish I could have that opportunity one more time. I know I'd handle it better. Michael always said, 'Fear of failure will lead you to despair.' And if you played with him, you knew he wasn't a bit afraid of failure."

In fact, Michael ultimately did challenge Buzz. He accused him of having used his injury as a crutch. As a result Peterson came to regard coaching as a second chance granted by the grace of the game, and made sure to approach the profession with as much Jordanian resolve as he could. "Buzz, your time is coming," Jordan said after each of Peterson's failed attempts to land a head coaching job. "You've got to step out on a limb and go for it."

As a head coach, Buzz was clear now, safe in a field in which he wouldn't have to compete with or be compared to his friend. Coaching was something Michael freely admitted he could never do. Basketball couldn't be played to Jordan's standards by anyone other than Jordan—standards a coach Mike would surely demand, as any former teammate could testify.

Only a few months before my visit, Buzz had faced his latest test in defining his relationship with his old friend. Following the Bulls' sixth title, Phil Jackson announced that he was quitting as the team's coach, and the Chicago general manager, Jerry Krause, appointed Don Haskins's old assistant, Tim Floyd, to replace him. But Krause was eager not to antagonize Jordan, who had already expressed wariness about playing for anyone other than Jackson. Suddenly Peterson, whom Floyd had gotten to know from the recruiting trail and social events for Nike-affiliated coaches, became useful to the Bulls—as a backchannel to their superstar, and perhaps even as an assistant coach who might lure Jordan back for one more season.

"When Tim got the Bulls job, I let Michael know that Tim's a good guy," Buzz told me. "But Michael's a grown man and a hardheaded person. I wasn't going to influence him in any way. Michael told me to tell the Bulls not to hire me based on what he might or might not decide to do."

Peterson was never formally offered a job. But he was asked what kind of interest he would have in a position involving advance scouting and breaking down video. And Bulls owner Jerry Reinsdorf indicated to Jordan that Jordan could more or less name Buzz's salary. The entire episode left Buzz feeling uneasy. He shared his misgivings with Floyd. "My whole life I've been known as Michael's boy," he told him.

"Well, I've always been known as Jerry's boy," Floyd replied, referring to Krause, who had spent several years courting him.

Buzz laughed at that. But after watching Jordan go through much of his life wondering if people wanted him around simply because he was Michael Jordan, Buzz didn't want to wonder if people wanted *him* around simply because he was Michael Jordan's friend. He told Floyd and the Bulls he wasn't interested.

"Glad I was a geography major, what with all the moves we've had," Buzz was saying as we left his office for practice. "At least I kept the same latitude. Boone, Johnson City, Raleigh, Nashville, then Boone again."

Since Buzz's arrival, Appalachian State had made a habit of finishing near the top of the Southern Conference. Every one of the Mountaineers but two came from in-state, and all were in the thrall not only of Jordan, whose name came up within the first few minutes of virtually every recruiting call Buzz made, but of Peterson's own associations with the Carolina papacy. If Boone was to be the only place he'd leave his mark, he could be perfectly happy. Still, Buzz sometimes sounded like a man ready to follow Jordan's advice and venture out on that limb. Athletic directors at bigger schools called every spring with offers of jobs paying much more money.

As the team went through full-court drills, Varsity Gym reverberated with shoebeats. The report of a shout came as often from a player as a coach. The Mountaineers' star was Marshall Phillips, a 23-year-old forward who never played high school ball, but found his way to the mountains with the help of a midnight basketball league in Atlanta in which he had showcased his skills. "Figured if Coach played with Michael, he'd know a little," Phillips told me after practice. "And when I first met him, he had on a ring about the size of Texas." Phillips was referring to one of the Bulls championship rings that showed up in the Petersons' mail, Buzz said, "every year, like Christmas gifts."

Peterson then introduced me to one of his assistants, Lavell Hall, a scholarly looking black man with glasses. "Lavell has every *Andy Griffith Show* on tape," he said. "He has an alarm clock shaped like a basketball in his office, and every morning at 11:05 it goes off and he watches that day's episode on TBS. I'll take Lavell's tapes on the road with me. If we're gonna play East Carolina that week, I might take four ECU tapes and an *Andy Griffith*. Watching Andy and Barney and Gomer and the guys, it picks me up."

Andy Griffith, Hall said, "is a good wholesome show about friendship. Harks back to a time when people genuinely cared about one another and treated each other right. There's one episode, 'The Cave Rescue,' where Andy and Helen get caught in a cave and Barney organizes this huge rescue effort. Well, Andy and Helen get out of the cave on their own, but when they see the way Barney's moved heaven and earth, they go back in just so Barney can have the satisfaction of savin' 'em—so Barney looks like the hero. There are a lot of life skills lessons in the show, things that Buzz and I try to emphasize when we go into a home."

I pictured Mayberry—like Mt. Airy, the Piedmont town where the real-life Andy Griffith grew up and on which Mayberry is based—sitting between the coast and the mountains. I imagined the temperature: warm enough for Michael and cool enough for Buzz. The place seemed to get just right both the piebald union between these two friends, and the small-town atmosphere surrounding this throwback team.

Buzz and I left the gym and headed for his house. To get there we had to negotiate a serpentine ascent on the edge of town. Buzz drove a Nissan Pathfinder, in which lies a story.

When Buzz first told Michael that he and Jan were building a house, he mentioned in passing that it sat on the top of a steep hill. "You're gonna need a four-wheel-drive to get up there," Jordan had said, and Peterson didn't think anything of the remark. A few months later he returned from a recruiting trip to find a message to call the Watauga County sheriff's office. The last time a North Carolina sheriff had been looking for him was 1984, when Buzz went missing, the Tar Heels' coaching staff panicked, and Michael made like a maid. This time Buzz feared that one of his players had gotten in trouble. "Come to find out, that rascal had delivered this Pathfinder for me and the sheriff's office was holding the keys," Buzz said. "I called him right away, of course. Told him, 'What, no insurance? No gas card?' But can you believe that?"

We entered the Petersons' house through a cluttered garage. Their three kids pinballed around the living room while a man on a big-screen TV spoke gravely about the aftermath of the NBA labor settlement. "The one remaining mystery surrounds Michael Jordan's plans, but he can't be found to divulge them. In the meantime the Bulls await word, hoping he's coming back."

"No way he's coming back," Jan Peterson said from over the Formica of the kitchen counter. "That's off the record," she added, turning quickly to me.

I thought I saw Buzz wince at his wife's disclosure. For an

instant I wondered if what he'd told me earlier—perhaps even that tale about busting Jordan's chops over the DirecTV Early-Bird Special—was only a ruse to keep my curiosity at bay. But if Buzz had indeed been less than candid with me, I didn't mind playing the fool. For in that moment I was reminded of exactly whom Jordan had found in Chapel Hill, besides a yardstick, inspiration, foil, buddy, and reliable source for shoes. He had found a friend so loyal he could be trusted to keep the most closely held secret, a Gomer who would mature into an Andy—a man who knew how to let someone else be the hero.

Yet that hero was no small-town Barney. He was an international icon, someone who could, as much as anyone at the end of the century, shed light on other parts of the world. Leaving the country for the first time in weeks, I stowed him in my luggage. I'd seen much of America. Surely he'd come in handy as I went in search of America abroad.

FOURTEEN

Ireland

To Build a Gym

I met Niall O'Riordan the day I arrived in Cork. He was an official with Neptune Basketball Club, a Corkonian "born, bred, and buttered," as they say in this city on Ireland's southwest coast. Moments after he walked into the lobby of the Metropole Hotel, we fell quickly into the kind of conversation that in Ireland follows from simply being and gathering, with or without a pint or two.

For all its beguilements, Niall's homeland would make less of an impression on me than my own country had apparently made on him. On a recent visit to New York he had gone to Madison Square Garden to watch the Knicks. The experience left him transformed. "The game wasn't till eight, but I got there at six and didn't leave till 11," he told me. "Just drank up the whole experience. First off, it was totally sold out, with a queue a mile long just for returns. The spectacle was amazing— the cheerladies, the franchise shops selling kit and all, everyone buying popcorn and Cokes and burgers and chips. Just big, big, big. And so professionally done."

Buildings for basketball, where players could play and fans could watch, didn't strike me as so remarkable. Like roads and bridges, they were standard infrastructure in every part of the world I'd visited so far. But listening to Niall rhapsodize about what he'd seen in New York, I realized that I wasn't in a typical basketball place. I was in Ireland, where the story of the game is an epic quest for shelter.

At the time of my visit, Ireland was riding the tide of membership in the European Community. Its economy had surged past easy stereotypes of urban squalor and rural backwardness. One-fourth of the Irish now lived in cities abustle with prosperity, and people under 25, who made up nearly half the population, no longer reflexively emigrated when they came of age. Any place becoming younger and more urbanized is likely to be receptive to hoops, and while basketball hadn't yet become part of the contours of everyday Irish life, young people played and followed the game in unprecedented numbers.

But when Niall O'Riordan and his buddies took up basketball after World War II, they didn't have the luxury of playing on what the city of Cork would provide for the Harlem Globetrotters' visit during the 1960s: a wooden floor overlying a football pitch. Instead they rode their bikes 15 miles to the macadam behind a rural school, playing until the Gaelic football they'd brought went flat. Eventually they talked a blacksmith into welding a hoop, which they bolted to the gable end of a friend's house, and they could play a game without sandwiching around it a couple of cycling events. Still they'd have to cope with what are known in Cork as "soft days." As Niall said, "We have the best climate in the world but for the weather. We like to say that if you can see the mountains it's a sign of rain, and if you can't, it's raining. November to the end of March, it's cold, dank, dark, and miserable. We can tell when summer's coming. The rain gets warmer."

So if they are to play with any kind of regularity, Irish devotees of basketball must do so indoors. And to play indoors, over the years they'd crossed the threshold of every structure imaginable. If they were lucky, players could take refuge in a parochial hall, and so, in addition to the Ten Commandments drummed into every schoolchild, Gaelic basketballers obeyed an eleventh: Thou shalt thank the nuns for the use of the hall. But just as often they played in military barracks, where the boots of drilling soldiers left the floor textured like sandpaper, so a stumble led to what a friend of Niall's called "instant acupuncture"; or in slick-floored dance halls, forgiving each other's traveling violations so long as offenders came to a sliding stop with both feet steady; or in tiny theaters like the one in the western coastal village of Ennistymon, where action flowed around a post in the middle of the court and, besides suffering the indignity of being picked off by an architectural feature, players had to listen to a custodian bark, "Leave the fookin' hall as ye found it!"

Because of the expense of erecting them, Ireland has long suffered from a dearth of spacious indoor buildings. For one stretch during the 1960s, the mecca of Irish basketball was a psychiatric hospital just north of Dublin called St. Ita's Portrane, whose cafeteria was believed to be the most expansive roofed space in the Republic. The patients at St. Ita's weren't considered dangerous, and social workers believed interaction between the certifiably addled and the merely hoop crazy to be healthy for all concerned. So several times a week after dinner the tables were pushed back and a couple of baskets wheeled in. As the patients lined the walls to watch, cackling at players wiping out on sausage patties and clumps of peas that had missed their mark, the basketball regulars began to wonder if their hosts weren't intentionally seeding the floor with land mines to enliven the postprandial entertainment. One evening, before the final of the Irish championship, the man charged with producing the program used a crude ditto machine whose ink drum missed the occasional sheet, and that evening mistakenly distributed a blank page to one St. Ita's spectator. The inmate indignantly thrust it back, saying, "I'm not *that* fookin' mad!"

Facilities in Cork had once been even more primitive. "We played our first indoor matches in the band room of the Michael Collins Barracks at two poles stuck in the ground," Niall told me. "Our referee was a wee fellow, maybe five feet five, name of Tossie Bruton. Tossie did his job without the luxury of a watch. The barracks are on a hill overlooking the city, and Tossie would look out the door of the band room at the clockface of the Shandon steeple a mile away. Tossie had no choice, really. He would start the match with a glance at the clock outside, then open the door for a look when it seemed like it might be halftime. Sometimes the fog had rolled in, but Tossie had an imagination you might call fertile. If the team he fancied was behind when the match should be over, well, he might arrange for a few more minutes of play. Who was to know better? Tossie was the lad with the whistle. All-powerful. Om-nee-*poe*-tent."

The Collins Barracks still stood, but they had been eclipsed by a venue altogether more remarkable. My guidebook, published in London, described Cork as having "a reputation for clannish behaviour amongst its businessmen." Niall told me a story that exposed this assertion as rank British understatement—a tale that could have been lifted from the works of Roddy Doyle.

Niall was a partner in an accounting firm with an old basketball buddy named Liam McGinn. During the early 1980s, Niall and Liam began making the rounds of Cork's business community, tapping friends and touching clients, asking not for mere spondulicks (that's local dialect for money), or even a tosser (a term for a little more money), but for a stocking (lots of money). The perfectly daft plan of these two gligeens (or goms, mebses, mugs, stumers—all Corkisms for "fools") was to build from scratch a basketball hall for dear old Neptune.

As they canvassed commercial Cork, the partners at McGinn, O'Riordan, and Co. had an advantage. If you couldn't trust your accountants, whom could you trust? "We squeezed everybody," Niall said. "We begged and borrowed. We didn't steal—in the end everybody got paid—but some had to wait longer than others. We collected about $40,000 from jumble sales, draws, and morning coffees. We bused ladies in from five counties for bingo, and on a good night took in $3,500. The stadium cost us about $770,000, so of course there was a wee gap. But with a lot of financial maneuvering we worked it out. We weren't white-haired when we started out. We're both white-haired now."

I set out on a stroll through the bedraggled North Side, where Niall had grown up. Unemployment still ran to 70 percent in this quarter of Cork, which the Celtic economic joyride had somehow bypassed. I mounted a hill, doglegged past the old Butter Exchange, then passed the late Tossie Bruton's timepiece, the Tower of Shandon, before continuing down a long lane. At its end, in a gully to my right, sat Neptune Stadium.

It was an unprepossessing box, styled in early Quonset, with siding of corrugated steel. It made the typical American collegiate arena look like a palace, and Madison Square Garden beyond fathoming. But once inside I softened my judgment. Neptune Stadium had a roof high enough to permit the launching of an actual jump shot, lights with enough candlepower to let a player follow the ball's progress, even a bank of bleacher seats. Weekly bingo helped pay for heat, electricity, and the salary of a full-time caretaker. "On any night there'll be a hundred kids in there running around," Niall had told me. "The game kept me on the straight and narrow, and we wanted to give something back to basketball for what basketball gave to us. It'll be there for the next generation. It'll stand as a monument."

Neptune Stadium's opening in January 1985 touched off a basketball boom in Cork. Neptune's archrival, Blue Demons, continued to play in a dingy parochial hall up the hill. But both clubs signed up two Americans each, and for a stretch during the late 1980s their rivalry flourished, with Neptune filling every one of the stadium's 2,500 seats. "When we started, we never knew what dunking was," Niall said. "Something with biscuits, we guessed, but in any case alien to us. The Americans would come out dunking, and we'd just sit there, gobsmacked."

In the early 1990s, with financial pressures squeezing its clubs, the Irish Basketball Association passed a rule limiting each roster to one American, and fans began to drift away. But just before then Neptune briefly transited one of FIBA's cup competitions, and that season the club rated a mention in newspapers across Europe for an episode that could have happened nowhere else. A game had been scheduled between Neptune and a German team for a Tuesday in Cork. The home team cabled FIBA its regrets: It was obliged to reschedule, because Neptune Stadium wasn't available for basketball on Tuesday night. Tuesday night was Bingo Night.

Something about the Irish resists the imposition of limits. "An Irishman's heart," George Bernard Shaw wrote, "is nothing but his imagination." This is the story of the peculiar hold another basketball arena had on the Irish-American imagination, and how heartstrings pulled purse strings.

Dreams of a single home for Irish basketball date back at least to the late 1950s, when a Dublin priest, Joseph Horan, launched a buy-a-brick fund-raising drive for a new building. Father Horan went so far as to pick out a plot of land. But a convent stood next to the site he preferred, and his plans collapsed when the nuns objected to the prospect of rowdy young athletes congregating next door. There matters stood until 1971, when Father Horan dedicated $35,000 he had inherited following the death of a great-uncle—a philandering great-uncle, he scrupulously disclosed—to building a parochial hall in his home parish of Inchicore. The priest got what he paid for: dark and cramped Oblate Hall, around which Irish basketball centered until the early 1980s. That's when two auspicious events converged. The Irish Basketball Association established yet another committee to study the feasibility of building a national basketball arena. And the Irish met someone who lifted their eyes toward a more distant horizon, an Irish-American named Dan Doyle.

In 1981 Doyle had just quit as coach at Trinity College in Hartford, Connecticut, to devote time to his autistic son and various sports-related projects. Someone tipped off IBA chief executive Noel Keating that Doyle would be laying over in Dublin en route to Prague for a clinic, and Doyle was astonished to hear his name paged at the airport. Sure that some emergency had struck back home, he walked briskly to the information booth in the main arrivals hall. That's when he spotted a man pacing back and forth with a sign. In any other country that sign would have read MR. DOYLE. But this was Ireland, so it bore an impish, freehand rendering of a basketball.

Soon Doyle found himself in a car, headed downtown for a meeting with Keating. Over a few pints in a pub, the two laid plans for the Irish-American Sports Foundation, to be chartered with the goal of finally building that arena. Back in the States, Doyle followed up a lead on a wealthy Irish-American with a weakness for all things Gaelic. His prospective donor had grown up in northern New Jersey, where he played high school baseball with future NBA coach and broadcaster Hubie Brown. He worked his way through Cornell selling sandwiches to undergraduates, then went on to become such a successful businessman that he established a foundation to underwrite a portfolio of causes. Each gift came with only one proviso: that the giver remain anonymous.

Doyle first met this reclusive philanthropist at a hotel in Dublin. The two took a cab to Father Horan's Oblate Hall, to watch the finals of Ireland's prestigious Roy Curtis International Tournament. The building may have been the pride of Inchicore, but it left Doyle's guest unimpressed. And the scene at the end of the game left him enchanted: Following Neptune's overtime defeat of Killester of Dublin, the Cork coach tearfully rushed into the stands to embrace his wife, not five feet from where these two American visitors sat.

Doyle and his mark met in New York City two weeks later.

"What do you need?"

Doyle had no clue whether to ask for spondulicks, or a tosser, or a stocking. He swallowed hard and took a stab at a figure.

"$150,000?"

"We can do that."

A month later Doyle stumbled upon a chart in *USA Today* listing America's 20 wealthiest people. There among the top five was his seatmate at Oblate Hall. Charles Feeney had amassed a fortune worth $3.5 billion from a chain of duty-free shops. Eventually, as a result of papers filed in 1997 when he sold his share of the business, the identities of his causes became public. Feeney had written cashier's checks worth hundreds of millions of dollars to support hospitals, universities, and scores of other worthy institutions, while himself making do with off-the-rack clothes and public transportation. Among Noel Keating and the other grandees of Irish basketball—gob-smacked, as they might say, by their good fortune and not knowing whom to thank—Feeney came to be known simply as the Man With No Name.

Doyle then set his sights on another Stateside sugar daddy, only one who was Feeney's opposite in every apparent respect but ethnicity. Garrulous and showy, Edward T. Hanley had been a bartender on Chicago's West Side before rising up the ranks of the Hotel Employees and Restaurant Employees International (HERE) to become president of the 400,000-member union. Over a quarter century, Hanley had settled into a humorously luxurious lifestyle. He drove a $63,000 Cadillac. He owned a summer house on a private island in Wisconsin. He used a union-owned jet to shuttle from his home outside Chicago to Washington, site of the union's headquarters, and to Palm Springs, where he kept yet another home and the union maintained a local. Even as HERE's membership shrank and its finances slid into debt, the union's board, packed with Hanley's relatives and cronies, authorized raises and added employees, many of them also Hanley family and friends.

In 1984, called before a Senate committee investigating organized crime, Hanley fielded 36 questions, and 36 times took the Fifth. A year later the President's Commission on Organized Crime alleged that HERE was a union in the grip of the mob. The government would spend years trying to pin down those ties and fail to do so. But with its fuzzy budgeting, loose management, and fungible job categories, HERE smelled enough like a kleptocracy that, in a 1998 settlement with the feds, the union agreed to a range of reforms, including Ed Hanley's retirement—although the boss would still collect a $310,000 annual pension as long as he lived.

Doyle knew that Irish-American organizations played

Hanley's ties to the Auld Sod for all they could. When an outfit like the James Joyce Society called, he could be counted on to give, even if *Ulysses* was unlikely to grace his nightstand. But Doyle quickly sensed that a gym in Ireland struck a particular chord. Hanley told Doyle that he wanted to throw a huge party in Chicago to attract attention to the cause—a gesture that Doyle realized he and Keating should support, as part of "the cultivation process." Hanley could get local dignitaries to attend, including Mayor Richard Daley. But the evening had to have cachet. He asked Doyle to deliver the Irish ambassador.

The event was set for the fall of 1986. Over that summer, with Keating's help, Doyle was able to get a commitment from Irish ambassador Padraic MacKernan to fly in from Washington. But in July, *Reader's Digest* ran an exposé on union corruption. Millions from the HERE treasury had been diverted to mobsters and associates, the story charged. The party still lay several months off. If the ambassador sees this story, Doyle thought, we're toast.

Doyle decided to gamble that the article would escape the attention of the Irish foreign office. At three o'clock on the afternoon of the great fete, having not yet heard a discouraging word, he went by the ambassador's hotel suite. One of the envoy's aides greeted him somber-faced at the door. "We have a problem," he said. That's when Doyle realized his luck had expired.

The ambassador had indeed seen the *Reader's Digest* story. A compromise was struck: MacKernan would attend the party. He would make some general remarks. But under no circumstances would he be seen, much less photographed, with Edward T. Hanley.

That night the main ballroom of the Chicago Hilton looked like a gymnasium floor during a well-run basketball practice. Every time Hanley made a move toward the ambassador, MacKernan's minder would pivot smartly in the opposite direction, leading His Excellency away. Every time a photographer captured the union boss and the Irish envoy together in his viewfinder, this subaltern set a perfect screen. If Hanley was aware of any of this obstructionist choreography, it didn't dull his desire to move from cultivation to harvest. He told Doyle that all he needed was a sign of good faith from the Irish government, in the form of a substantial gift, and his own donation would follow.

Enter a second figure with a dodgy reputation. Irish Prime Minister Charlie Haughey was a well-rounded political operator, a composite of Bill Clinton, Yasir Arafat, and Ferdinand Marcos. He was a married man carrying on an affair with a married woman. He had been implicated in, then acquitted of, running guns for the IRA. In 1999 he would be indicted for obstructing an investigation into why he had received almost $2 million from an Irish department-store mogul. As the Irish-American Sports Foundation trolled for funds, Haughey was still indulging Hanleyesque tastes, including an $18 million retrofitting of a government building he wanted to occupy. But this simply meant that no dream was too grandiose for Haughey to wrap his imagination around. Or so Doyle hoped. With an introduction from Christopher Dodd, the senator from Connecticut, Doyle and two lieutenants booked a meeting in Dublin with the man known as the Teflon Taoiseach.

"And what can I do for you gentlemen?" Haughey asked.

"We need a big gift from you if we're going to get a big gift from an Irish-American."

"How much do you need?"

"A million dollars."

Haughey picked up the phone and called his minister of sport, Frank Fahey. "Frank, I'm here in my office with three *very close friends* from the U.S. . . . ." He cupped his hand over the receiver and stage-whispered, "What are your names?

". . . —And Mr. Doyle, Mr. Blaney, and Mr. Moriarty need a million pounds," he continued. "I don't care where you get it. Just get it!"

The Taoiseach hung up, then turned to his visitors—they had asked only for a million dollars, not a million pounds—and shot them a wink. Thanks to Haughey and his successors, Albert Reynolds and Garret FitzGerald, Doyle and his associates were able to go back to Hanley for the funds needed to complete the building.

In the end, the Irish government gave a total of $1.6 million. County Dublin donated 10 acres of land. Irish citizens and the IBA rank and file contributed $200,000. The Man With No Name ultimately gave $250,000. And the Hotel Employees and Restaurant Employees International handed over $350,000 in the name of Edward T. Hanley, in extravagant gratitude for his many years of faithful service to the union—which is to say that hundreds of thousands of dollars deducted from the paychecks of Filipina chambermaids and South Side busboys would make it possible for Irish kids to shoot hoops into the next century.

Some of the men who made the arena a reality, like Haughey and Hanley, were scoundrels. Feeney was something closer to a saint. All, I thought, were mad—that fookin' mad.

In February 1993, almost a dozen years after the transatlantic campaign to build it began, more than 3,000 people showed up for the arena's dedication. Among them was Ed Hanley, who came with entourage in tow. HERE paid for the boss and 34 of his friends and associates to fly over and celebrate with a banquet costing $19,000. When kids at the festivities discovered that Hanley was from Chicago, they naturally wondered if he knew Michael Jordan. There was no one in Chicago whom Hanley didn't know, so he took names and addresses and promised to send off packages as soon as he returned to the States. Sure enough, 20 Jordan-autographed T-shirts arrived in Dublin a short time later. If you pay a visit to the Irish National Basketball Arena, hard by the ring road on the southern fringe of the capital, you may well see an urchin playing in one, his face too small for his smile.

In accordance with his wishes, Charles Feeney's name is nowhere on or in the building. Ed Hanley's, by contrast, graces the plaque over the doors that open on to the floor of Edward T. Hanley Hall. But the building itself is dedicated to no one. "National Basketball Arena" struck me as awfully prosaic, especially given the imagination of the people responsible for it. So I asked a Dubliner why the name had been left at that.

"It's nothing more than this," he said. "We want Irish kids to be able to say they've played in the NBA."

Doubling back from my visit to Cork's Neptune Stadium, I had paused at St. Anne's Church. The Shandon steeple surmounting it has a deck with fetching views of the city, and a belfry in which tourists can punch out the melody of their choice. The guide on duty collected my three-pound fee to go up. "Ask me anything," the man said. "I know *everything*."

Time seemed to be a malleable concept in Cork. No two public clockfaces I'd seen read the same—not the one outside a bank by the River Lee, not the one by a jewelry store downtown, not any of the faces of the Tower of Shandon. So I asked him about that.

"Aye," he said. "The clock here's affectionately known as the Four-Faced Liar. But only I can tell you why! The Roman numerals on her face are made of gilded wood. The gilt on 'em's of different thicknesses. So the hands catch. If all the clocks showed the same time, see, we'd need only one clock."

With his creative timekeeping, that old ref Tossie Bruton had only been conforming to local custom. I summitted Shandon precisely at noon, and the carillon from the belfry chased me right back down, to the relative shelter of the plummy voice of my new friend.

The guide's name was Declan Kelly. He was easing into his fifties and dressed for a soft day. The Blarney Stone wasn't six miles from this spot, and Kelly hadn't just kissed it, but given the thing a hickey. He flitted from subject to subject, holding forth on religion and history and, upon hearing the purpose of my visit, basketball. He touched on the Chicago Bulls, on the game's vogue in Cork during the late 1980s, even on those civic leaders Niall and Liam. "Gangsters," he called the accountants who built Neptune Stadium. "Wouldn't trust 'em from here to there. But we owe 'em a huge debt."

Declan Kelly, it turned out, had a son—"He's Declan, too;

keeps things simple"—and Declan Jr. had been a basketball player. A guard, wiry and quick, he had come to the game in those heady years just after the stadium opened. Father and son would go watch Neptune together, arriving two hours early to be sure to secure a seat for themselves. Gradually young Declan got hooked, and got good, too—good enough to represent the tricolor, first on the national cadet team, then as captain of Ireland's juniors.

"Sixteen, my boy was, when he played for the national juniors in Scotland," said Declan the dad. "We were destroying Scotland in the second half when Declan stole the ball and drove for a layup. He was fouled and made the free throw. Scotland threw the ball in and Declan intercepted, and he scored and was fouled again, for three more points. He intercepted and scored *again*, and made the free throw once more—that's nine points altogether. And wouldn't you know? Again he intercepted, and again he scored a layup. This time they chose not to foul him. Came to their senses. But 11 points my boy scored— 11 points in three seconds off the clock! The coach took him out after that, and the crowd gave him a standing ovation."

Just as I was thinking that Declan Sr. sure liked to talk, especially about basketball, he said, "Let me tell you why I don't like to talk about basketball."

His mood darkened. "A high school in Connecticut offered my boy a chance to come play. He had his bag packed. And then some schools administrator raised an objection. A short time later a college in the States offered him a scholarship for four years worth $100,000. And a few days before the deadline the college withdrew that offer. Those two things crushed my boy. Just crushed him. He was never the same after that.

"Declan had been a *talent*, I tell you. The best young player we've had in Cork. I really believe he would have made it to the NBA." He did not mean the arena. "And remember, this isn't just a father talking. This is the man who knows everything."

Declan Sr.'s eyes were moist as he recounted how his son had made his way to America just the same, only without his dream. The younger Declan lived in Boston now, painting houses for a living. "He watches the Patriots. Plays some golf. But he's never played basketball again."

"Never?"

"Would you?"

Well, yes, I thought. One of basketball's mystical powers is its hold even on those—especially on those—whose dreams it dashes most brutally. The game will beat someone down, but out of dependency or stubbornness the vanquished can rarely just walk away. Why else do players everywhere, at every level, finish practice with a half-court shot or two? Why do coaches order intentional fouls in the final seconds of long-lost games? Why was that movie called *Hoop Dreams*? For the same reason, I thought, that so many Irish of Declan Sr.'s generation and before chose to leave their homeland: out of a conviction that something better lies in store if only you get one more shot.

Indeed, I'd soon be meeting a man who had changed his very faith for a chance to play more ball. But here I chose not to take Papa Kelly on. His question, like so much about him, was rhetorical. He had a script to follow and a point to make. And, it turned out, another subject to broach.

"Big press conference today," he said suddenly. "Michael's going to announce his retirement." A beat, and his eyes came alight again. "Told me himself."

This really was the man who knows everything. Buzz Peterson's wife was off the hook.

FIFTEEN

Israel

The Long Arm of the Law of Return

The Israeli papers brimmed with accounts of Michael Jordan's abdication. Both he and the Bulls would be starting anew. And fresh starts were something to which my new surroundings are particularly well suited.

Tel Aviv is younger than many of its residents, with beach-fronts for cleansing, nightclubs for forgetting, and an ambient Middle Eastern hurly-burly ideal for slipping undisturbed into a future of one's own devising. At Ben-Gurion International Airport a baggage carousel off-loaded a flight from Siberia. Another crop of Russian Jewish émigrés was no doubt being processed elsewhere in the airport, experiencing a first brush with the country whose very mission is to welcome their kind.

Within two years of its founding in 1948, Israel passed the Law of Return, which grants citizenship to any Jew requesting it. The law served to quickly populate a barren nation-in-progress, but it also underscored the basic tenet of the Zionist state: To be an Israeli you need be nothing more than a member of the tribe of Israel, even if you began life as, say, an American, as had a friend of a friend I decided to look up.

Steve Kaplan had grown up in South Jersey. He played at Rutgers during the late 1960s and early 1970s, then headed for Israel, figuring he'd prolong his career by a few years before returning home to get on with his life. Instead he stayed. He played on the national team, served in the army, even spent four months on a kibbutz, picking oranges, milking cows, keeping his beard trim enough so a gas mask would fit over it. During 14 seasons in Tel Aviv with Hapoel Ramat Gan, Kap met his wife, Irit, and they went on to have two kids. Since easing into a job as director of logistics for a chemical company, he told me, "Not a day goes by without basketball coming up in some way."

A few months after my visit, the daily newspaper *Ma'ariv* would choose the finest ballplayers in Israeli history, and Kap made the short list of six. But he was alone among the honorees in never having played for Israel's most storied basketball club. No team—not Žalgiris Kaunas, not Red Army Moscow, not even Bill Russell's Boston Celtics—has ever lorded over its competition the way Maccabi Tel Aviv has dominated Israeli basketball. Over the 45-year history of the national league, Maccabi had won 39 titles, including 23 in a row between 1970 and 1992. The club had won another 29 Israeli Cups, including all four finals in which Maccabi ran up against Kap and Ramat Gan.

I went by the Kaplans' apartment on a Thursday night. As I took a seat in their living room, joining Steve, Irit, and their son Tom for the telecast of Maccabi's EuroLeague game against Pallacanestro Varese, Kap couldn't entirely suppress his feelings about his old nemesis. Still, with as much dispassion as possible, he tried to explain how Maccabi had helped create Israel's identity during the 1970s and 1980s, when it reached six European Cup finals and won two, in 1977 and 1981.

Every Thursday the Sabbath would come a day early. The streets of Tel Aviv would empty at sundown, and restaurants and cinemas would go quiet. If Maccabi was playing on the road, Israel's lone TV station would carry the game live; if the club was at home, Israeli defense minister Moshe Dayan would be sure to shake the hands of players on both teams before tip-off. Most Israelis understood a curfewed existence, for if they couldn't remember life under the British Mandate, they had lived through the Six-Day War or the Yom Kippur War. But this was different. This was voluntary curfew. The hostility of its Arab neighbors forced Israel to join FIBA's European zone, and Maccabi competed in European Cup play essentially as an Israeli national team. In a country where two people are said to produce three opinions, Maccabi became a rare point of unanimity—a team that Israelis and Jews throughout the diaspora counted on to win one for the *kippah*.

"We're a small enough country that we're a kind of community," Kap told me. "And that was a period when the nation's identity was still developing. Likud came to power around then [in 1978], and suddenly we weren't a one-party state anymore. It was okay to step out a little bit, to flaunt your wealth and strut your stuff. And there we were, succeeding in basketball on the international stage. The newness of it all made everyone giddy. It was like this full flowering, and a lot of people still identify with that period—how we were associated with something besides war and all the other things that were going on."

A few of those Maccabi stars were repatriated Americans, such as former Illinois guard Tal Brody. Others, like Mickey Berkowitz, were homegrown Israelis. As its ambitions grew, the club added mercenaries like Aulcie Perry, a 6'10" American who became first an icon and then a generic. People would come up to Kaplan on the street and, recognizing him as a ballplayer, say, "Aulcie Perry!"

"Only time in my life I've been mistaken for a black guy," Kap said.

Maccabi still inspired such a following that Steve's own son openly pulled for the team that haunted his father. But on this night Maccabi wound up losing in overtime, and Kap allowed himself a moment's gloating. He offered Tom sarcastic consolation, then drove me back to my hotel.

As we crossed Tel Aviv's main boulevard, Dizengoff Street, Kap gestured at a billboard commanding the intersection. It featured the head and torso of a huge black man in a basketball jersey, with a ball cocked over his head—a ferocious image, leavened only by a few lines of Hebrew and the logo of a fast-food chain.

"That's Aulcie Perry," Kap said. "After he retired he got into some trouble with the law. Said he was innocent. Of course, guys always say they're innocent. He now runs a Burger Ranch franchise a few blocks from here. Every morning I take this route to work—down Frishman, left on Dizengoff—and every morning I see him. He always has that look on his face, ready to dunk. Even after all these years, I can't escape him."

Late the next morning I made my way back to downtown Tel Aviv. Dizengoff Street had long been quick with bustle, but the ambiance was seedier now, and it attracted hustle, too—though gracious rows of margosa trees still hemmed both its sides.

I ducked inside the Burger Ranch franchise at No. 99. The place had a vaulted ceiling and walls festooned with black-and-white poster prints of its proprietor, in a Maccabi jersey with the number 8 and a sponsor's name gracing its back.

There isn't a burger joint in the world where clerks don't ask for your order before you're ready.

"No, thanks. But is Mr. Perry in?"

The clerk indicated a set of stairs to the side. I followed them to find, talking on a cell phone, the man depicted on that bill-board and all over these walls. Perry was fleshier now, not at all ferocious, but so tall that his head nearly scraped the ceiling. In Israel, he told me, Burger Ranch didn't serve cheeseburgers out of respect for religious sensibilities, but the Tel Aviv rabbinate refused to certify his outlet as kosher because it stayed open on the Sabbath. "This isn't Jerusalem," he said. "Tel Aviv is a 24-hour city."

I asked if he had a moment to talk, but he begged off. He was a busy man. Tonight he'd be coaching a youth wheelchair team. Now he was rushing off for a meeting of the local merchants' association, which was trying to gussy up the neighborhood. He slipped me his card. I said I'd be back in touch.

He walked me to the door, and we stood together below one of the margosa trees. Perry scowled at the berries that had fallen from its branches to the sidewalk, where pedestrians ground them underfoot. "They're a pain," he said. "People track the red dye into the restaurant. And when it rains, they give off some foul kind of odor."

I wouldn't fully piece together Aulcie Perry's story until I returned to New York. But from speaking with Kap and others, and from another session with Perry himself, I was able to make out its basic shape. Perry had graduated from Newark's West Side High and a small, historically black college in Florida, Bethune-Cookman, before hooking on with the Virginia Squires of the old ABA in the fall of 1974. That season the Squires were so comically bad that management decided to get rid of every player but two. Perry was among those cut, and he spent the rest of the season in the semipro Eastern League, the forerunner of the CBA. The New York Knicks invited him to camp the following fall, but the Knicks had just traded for Spencer Haywood and their frontcourt was full, so Perry found himself back in an Allentown Jets uniform. By the summer of 1976, Perry was 25 and broke, with no apparent prospects. He thought he'd play overseas for a season before making another pass at the NBA, but he had no idea where.

That summer a Maccabi scout saw Perry play in the Rucker League in Harlem. Maccabi had never advanced beyond the second round of European Cup play, and the club was determined to find a foreigner to carry it further. Perry's game was fluid and sweet, but for all his skills he spread only 215 pounds over those six feet 10 inches. So Maccabi also scouted out a seven-footer named Floyd Allen, who was wider and bulkier. With the team booked to play in a preseason tournament in Belgium, the Maccabi coach, Ralph Klein, decided to try out both.

Within several days Allen proved to be the more effective individual player. But something about Perry's manner, and the way teammates responded to him on the floor, impressed players and management alike. One afternoon, as the team met in the hotel dining room over coffee, a waitress brought out a plate of cake. Perry took one piece and passed it on. Allen grabbed a handful. If he's going to take all the cake, Klein thought, he'll probably want to take all the shots, too.

Maccabi signed Perry for $6,000 a month, and quickly the team began to function like a kibbutz. As their new American dedicated himself to rebounding, blocking shots, and scoring only when the chance arose, Maccabi's other players followed his lead, playing with more and more selflessness and sharply defined purpose. Perry couldn't recall ever before even sharing the court with a Jew, other than the odd rival in high school. Here, he thought, it's not as if we're on the same team; it's as if we belong to the same family. And Tel Aviv wasn't at all what he expected. It was full of nightlife and English-language cinemas and Mediterranean sophistication, not dowdy women in headscarves and mumbling men in sidecurls.

Perry went on to lead Maccabi to the most extraordinary season in its remarkable history. The Soviet government, which then refused to recognize the Jewish state, denied Maccabi permission to travel to Russia for a European Cup game against Red Army Moscow. So FIBA ordered the two teams to play on a neutral court in the tiny Belgian town of Virton. There Maccabi beat the Muscovites, and more than 100,000 people massed to greet the team upon its return to Ben-Gurion Airport. In the aftermath, in ragged Hebrew that betrayed his American upbringing, Tal Brody spoke words that would frame the meaning of that game for millions of Israelis: "We're on the map, and we're staying on the map, not only in basketball, but in everything."

Several months later Maccabi beat Varese by a point for its first European Cup title. Perry had been the only significant addition from the previous season, the one new ingredient that brought out all the other flavors in the casserole. Shimon Mizrahi, the canny lawyer who serves as Maccabi's chairman, called him in to give him a raise.

Perry was stunned. "But I have a contract," he said.

"We think you deserve more."

What so endeared Perry to the Maccabi family also projected beyond it. Israelis sensed his guilelessness. The team would eventually bring in former NBA and U.S. college stars with more impressive pedigrees—Ken Barlow, Kevin Magee, Mike Mitchell—but never again would the club find a more harmonious fit, on the court, in the locker room, and with the fans. Four years after that victory over Varese, with Perry still feathering jumpers as soft as his bountiful Afro, Maccabi would beat Virtus Bologna to win its second European Cup.

Perry became the Jordan of his time and place. He hawked refrigerators on TV. He fielded congratulatory hugs from Prime Minister Menachem Begin. He bought a spacious apartment in the northern end of the city. And he began squiring around town a statuesque supermodel named Tami Ben-Ami. The two became icons of Israel's coming out into the society of nations, and the papers chronicled their every move. Exhibitions didn't really open, and movies didn't really premiere, without these two ambassadors of the new Israel. Dizengoff Street was then lined with cafés and nightclubs, and Aulcie and Tami could be found canoodling in a banquette or wriggling on a dance floor late into the night.

Yet Perry capitalized only fitfully on his fame. He opened a restaurant and a sporting goods store, and signed a few endorsement contracts, but he lacked a cold business sense. People sometimes took advantage. If Perry knew a customer who walked into his restaurant, the patron's kids would soon be noshing on ice cream, compliments of the proprietor. Even Ben-Ami seemed to have the better of him. One year, with Maccabi playing in a tournament in the Netherlands and Tami booked for a modeling gig in Amsterdam over the same dates, Aulcie prevailed on the driver of the team bus to swing by her hotel. As it happened, Tami's cab from the airport pulled up just as the Maccabi bus did, and teammates watched with amazement as Aulcie turned into the world's tallest bellhop, bounding out of the bus and ushering his lady and her valises safely out of the rain, through the lobby, and up to her room. His obliging nature, her diva's delight in his attentions—no scene better captured their personalities than that.

Only one thing restrained Israel's embrace of the Maccabi
star. Every week Perry suited up for European Cup competition. But when Maccabi played twice a week in the Israeli
league, he had to sit in civvies and watch. Only Israeli citizens
could play in the national league, and the only practicable way
to become an Israeli citizen was to become a Jew.

For two seasons Perry had ascended splendidly for the land.
Over the summer of 1978, with Maccabi's encouragement, he
decided to make aliyah—to ascend to the land.

In the late 19th century Theodor Herzl, the Viennese journalist
considered the father of Zionism, asked the British to cede part
of the Sinai for the establishment of a Jewish state. The Brits
offered Uganda instead. Herzl passed, and that was as close as
the paths of Zionists on the one hand and black Africans and
their descendants on the other were fated to come for nearly a
century. Then "the basketball rabbis" got busy.

By 1982 more than half the starters in the Israeli league
would be Americans, many of them so-called snip-'n'-dunk
converts who had become Jews with little more than circumcision and immersion in a ritual bath. The circumstances of some
of those spiritual transformations—one involved payments to a
synagogue in Milwaukee; another followed from a civil wedding in Cyprus between an American import and an Israeli
grandmother—caused Israel's National Religious Party, which
is affiliated with the Orthodox rabbinate that must sign off on
all conversions, to raise holy hell. (Of course, the NRP's own
team, Elitzur Netanya, was then fielding so many converted
Americans that Israelis called it "the Orthodox Globetrotters.")

All the chicanery would come to an end in 1986, when the
Israeli Basketball Federation enacted a rule requiring a three-
year grace period before any new immigrant could play in the
league. But at the end of the 1977–78 season, when Aulcie

Perry went back to visit his Baptist parents in New Jersey, the escalating number of basketball conversions hadn't yet become an epidemic. Perry insisted on the sincerity of his desire. The warmth of the people, he said at the time, "the way we can go anywhere, north to south, and it's a holiday everywhere we go, told me I want to be here for life."

Late that spring Perry walked into Orthodox synagogues in New York City, introducing himself and explaining what he wanted to do. His visits started to follow a familiar pattern. A rabbi would hear him out and then wordlessly leave the room. Maybe he had to go to the bathroom, Perry would think. A few minutes would pass, then 10 minutes, then 30, and finally Perry would realize: He isn't coming back. Ultimately, with Maccabi's help, he found a rabbi willing to take him on. Sunday through Thursday, from May through September, he schlepped out to Brooklyn, to an Orthodox synagogue on Ocean Parkway.

Judaism is not an evangelical faith. It holds that a rabbi should wait for a potential convert to knock three times, to be sure the petitioner really wants to become a Jew. A passage in the Talmud pointedly questions the motives of anyone who wishes to join a people so "scorned, oppressed, humiliated and made to suffer." At the same time, Abraham, the patriarch of the Jews, was himself a convert, and the Torah enjoins the Jewish people 36 different times to welcome the stranger. Perry was eager to be welcomed. Raised a Baptist, he had been frustrated at being told the same thing whenever he questioned what came from the pulpit or Scripture: "You must have faith." Judaism seemed more accommodating of his inquisitive spirit. The more Perry studied, the more questions he had, and if his teacher, a Rabbi Rabinowitz, couldn't supply an answer, he'd say, "I'll get back to you on that." Perry liked this. The Torah has 613 commandments; the Talmud, 63 books. Rabbi Rabinowitz always got back to him with something.

However much basketball figured in Perry's motivation for converting, he put in a summer of diligence. In September he sat before Tiferet Israel, a religious court of three rabbis, and for more than an hour fielded their questions about theology and

tradition. Though he had already been circumcised, he under-
went the *hatafat dam brit*, in which a drop of blood is removed
from the penis to signify the covenant between Abraham and
God. He was immersed in the *mikveh*, the ritual bath symbol-
izing the cleansing of the unclean. He held the Torah and read
a pledge of loyalty: "Of my own free will, I choose to enter the
eternal Covenant between God and the people of Israel and
become a Jew." Mizrahi, who had flown over to represent Maccabi at the ceremony, watched as Aulcie Perry was pronounced
Elisha Ben-Avraham, proselyte of righteousness. Elisha was a
miracle-working prophet who, even if he had never led Maccabi
past Red Army Moscow and to a European Cup, once brought
a dead child back to life; Ben-Avraham, son of Abraham, stood
for what all Jews consider themselves to be—descendants of the
first Jew, who was asked to kill his own son, Isaac, to prove his
faith.

When Elisha Ben-Avraham returned to Tel Aviv, several
conservative politicians challenged the legitimacy of his conversion. Apparently, Tiferet Israel was notorious for certifying conversions that failed to hold up under scrutiny. The political
party affiliated with one ultra-Orthodox sect even threatened to
pull out of Begin's governing coalition if the interior ministry
approved Perry's citizenship. But over two years Aulcie had
built up a huge reserve of goodwill with the Israeli people, and
here it carried the day. Jewish law holds few wrongs graver than
causing blood to rush to a man's face by embarrassing him in
public. The commentators and vox populi sounded in Perry's
defense. Whatever the track record of Rabbi Rabinowitz, most
Israelis objected to the second-guessing of a personal decision
by someone who had done so much for the country.

Able now to play in every one of Maccabi's games, Perry
lived the life of a man pleased to be starting anew. He kept
kosher. He studied Hebrew at an *ulpan*, a language school for
immigrants like himself. In time he would serve in the military.
When the team left the country to play in the European Cup,
he, too, felt the sting of anti-Semitic taunts from fans and
learned to find motivation in them. During road games in the

Israeli league, fans of Maccabi's rivals weren't all that different
from the wiseguys at Madison Square Garden in the sarcastic
way they'd shout an ancient Jewish proverb when a player lined
up a foul shot: "The whole world is a narrow bridge! The main
thing is not to be afraid!"

If left right there, Perry's transit would have been remarkable
enough. But there was an elision in his story, and it threw a different light on all that came before and would come after. Perry
would teeter on that bridge, and he would fall.

In December 1982, as Maccabi went through warmups before
a home game against Real Madrid, Shimon Mizrahi fell into a
panic. Aulcie Perry was nowhere to be found. The game began
and ended without him, and later the club issued a statement
saying its star had been home with the flu. But in March, Perry
was charged with buying heroin in Tel Aviv's Arab Quarter, and
in retrospect drug problems seemed to explain his absence that
night. Perry pleaded guilty in May and was fined $150,000,
given a three-month suspended sentence, and ordered to
undergo counseling.

Perry was now 32. He had played seven seasons in Israel. He
could still shoot a milk-and-honey jump shot and be counted
on to take one piece of cake and pass the rest. But he was no
longer Maccabi's reliable anchor. He would retire two years
later, and over the following summer begin traveling widely
through the Middle East and the Indian subcontinent. He told
people he was working with an import-export business called
Best Carpets, Inc., and he flashed a business card bearing an
address in the Empire State Building.

On September 15, 1985, Aulcie and a cousin from New
Jersey, Kenny Johnson, met in Amsterdam. From there they
flew together to Turkey, and then to Pakistan, where they spent
six days. In Islamabad, Pakistani police spotted them meeting
with suspected drug traffickers and tipped off officials of the
Drug Enforcement Administration at the U.S. embassy. The

DEA alerted Dutch authorities that two black Americans, one roughly six feet and the other about a foot taller, had boarded a PIA flight to Amsterdam's Schiphol Airport on September 24 and were believed to be carrying contraband. Perry and Johnson spent two days in Amsterdam, then boarded KLM Flight 643 for New York, where customs agents lay in wait.

From where he stood that day, at the bottom of the escalator leading to the customs area at Kennedy Airport, inspector Thomas Falanga spotted two passengers matching descriptions he had been given. The shorter man came first, carrying a large portable stereo. The taller one lagged a dozen or so passengers behind. By Falanga's lights, his marks were conforming to the standard MO of drug smugglers. The man in the lead was the "mule" who carried the goods. The tall man, Falanga figured, was the "shotgun," the mule's director of logistics and patron, who bankrolls the mule's expenses and monitors his progress. A shotgun never carries contraband, and he usually waits until his mule has cleared customs before walking through himself, always courteous, cooperative, and clean.

Falanga cut through the immigration area to an inspection station in Kenny Johnson's path. He picked up Johnson's stereo and thought it felt unusually heavy. He tried to dismantle it with a screwdriver but couldn't, for the screws had been stripped. He took the stereo to a back room, where an X-ray machine revealed foreign objects inside. As Johnson looked on, Falanga used a hammer to crack open the stereo. He found nine plastic bags filled with what a lab would determine was three pounds of heroin, 89 percent pure, with a street value of more than a million dollars.

Johnson said he had bought a stereo in Turkey and given it to a flight attendant upon boarding in Amsterdam. She must have given him back "a different radio." Falanga read Johnson his rights and placed him under arrest.

Even as he intercepted Johnson, Falanga was bird-dogging Perry, throwing glances at him over by the baggage claim. Other inspectors detained and questioned Perry, but a search of his bags revealed little more than his personal effects, a rug, a few scarves, and a tea set. He was released on the advice of a U.S. attorney.

Perry must have been mortified to watch his cousin Kenny being led to an examination room. But he soon returned to Europe, unaware that the DEA would spend the next several months developing a case against him. Investigators got hold of Johnson's and Perry's plane tickets to Amsterdam and Islamabad, both of which had been paid for with cash. They found registration forms from a hotel in Islamabad, indicating that Perry and Johnson had shared a room there. They interviewed a desk clerk at a motel near Schiphol, where Perry and Johnson had spent a night en route to Pakistan, and she identified Perry as the man who had emptied a safe-deposit box full of cash into a gym bag on the morning the two checked out.

In January, the U.S. government issued a warrant for Perry's arrest. Two weeks later Dutch police seized him at a hotel across from Amsterdam's Central Station. They confiscated $14,000 in cash, along with a business card for Best Carpets, which indicated a nonworking New York City phone number and an address in the Empire State Building that came up cold. For nine months Perry successfully staved off extradition. But in November 1986, with all recourse exhausted, he was indicted on three counts of heroin trafficking and returned to the U.S. for trial.

Upon returning from Tel Aviv, I would hole up in the federal courthouse in Brooklyn with the case file from *United States* v. *Aulcie Perry*. At first I suspected that Kenny Johnson had roped his cousin into an international drug-smuggling scheme. The trial record showed that Johnson failed to report even $5,000 in income during the previous tax year, and he already had a rap sheet for conspiracy, drug possession, and theft. Surely he knew, as Tami Ben-Ami, patrons of Perry's Tel Aviv restaurant, and Maccabi's players and coaches all knew, that Aulcie was eager to please and fit in. Perry had been no big star in the U.S. before suddenly blossoming in the Promised Land. Perhaps, sensing basketball slipping away, he was an easy recruit for anyone who could help him sustain his lifestyle, or at least bankroll a drug habit.

But the government pressed an altogether different case. The trip to the Netherlands, Turkey, and Pakistan had been Johnson's first abroad. Perry, by contrast, was a sophisticated world traveler, a man of means, someone who had been to Pakistan at least once before. As the prosecutor would ask the jury, "Who goes on vacation to Pakistan with a gym bag full of money?"

Perry's fate turned on the testimony of a KLM flight attendant named Ingrid Ruys. Almost four months after authorities at JFK had let him go, she picked Perry out of a photo spread shown to her by a DEA agent in Holland. An encounter she had with Perry on Flight 643 that day still stuck in her head. As the crew prepared the cabin for departure, Ruys wanted to move two business-class passengers to adjacent seats in the last row of the section—seats she believed to be empty. But she found that one of the seats she had in mind was already occupied by a tall black man. The purser had upgraded him from coach after he complained that he needed more leg room.

She noticed something else. She noticed that the man in seat 16A was looking down at a portable stereo in his lap. And the way he looked at it led Ingrid Ruys to believe he might play it. "Please don't play your radio," she said, explaining that the operation of electronic equipment can interfere with the aircraft's navigational system.

"I won't play it," the passenger promised.

To depict Perry as having enlisted his down-and-out cousin as a mule, the prosecution highlighted the phony address and telephone for Perry's import-export "business." It cited the evidence of hotel rooms and plane tickets paid for with fistfuls of cash. And it rested on the testimony of Ingrid Ruys. "Take a look at Aulcie Perry," the DA said in his summation. "Take a good look at him, all six feet 10 of him. Does he look like a man who's easy to forget, a man you're going to mistake for someone else? I submit that he doesn't."

The state returned again and again to the same thing. Asked how he was able to keep track of Perry at the baggage carousel even as he was examining Kenny Johnson's baggage, customs inspector Falanga said, "He seemed to be the tallest man on the flight." Another customs inspector had searched Perry's bags, and she said, "I remember large sneakers in his luggage." Ingrid Ruys recalled her first impression: "He had a very nice face. He looked very gentle, and he was rather big."

Few people failed to remark on Aulcie Perry's size. In Israel people not only recognized him everywhere he went, but also, as Steve Kaplan knew firsthand, places he didn't go. He certainly wasn't going to escape notice at a casbah in Pakistan, or in a photo spread in Holland, or in a courtroom in Brooklyn. The only person unaware of Aulcie Perry's recognizability, it seemed, was Perry himself.

On February 23, 1987, jurors deliberated only three hours before convicting him on all three counts. That May he was sentenced to 10 years in prison.

Perry's arrest and trial had been a cause célèbre in Israel. After one newspaper published his address, so many letters poured into his cell that he felt the resentment of prison officials. The federal government grades penitentiaries as it does hurricanes, one through five; Perry spent his first year of incarceration at a grade-two facility in Sandstone, Minnesota. Nonetheless, Shimon Mizrahi twice traveled to the U.S., and only once could he get in to see him. Perry spent much of his first year unsuccessfully trying to win a new trial, pounding out appeals in stilted legalese on a manual typewriter. Some of those letters, still moldering in the case file, have an aching poignancy.

For years two and three he was transferred to the grade-one Club Fed in Allenwood, Pennsylvania, where he shared quarters with doctors, lawyers, Wall Street financiers, and other white-collar criminals. Every day he devoted himself to several Old Testament psalms, and sometimes fellow inmate Ivan Boesky joined him for Jewish services. Finally he landed in Goldsboro, North Carolina, at Seymour Johnson Air Force Base, detailed to the kitchen of the officers' mess. The squadrons at Seymour

Johnson specialized in desert warfare, and it was strangely familiar for this former member of the Israeli Defense Forces to watch Israeli pilots passing through, to be trained in how to fly F-15s.

By April 1990 Perry had won parole. But because of an unauthorized trip he took outside North Carolina, he was ruled in violation of the terms of his release and returned to prison for 15 months. Finally, in January 1992, he was set free for good. Whereupon Maccabi Tel Aviv came back into his life.

There's a program on Israeli TV, modeled after *This Is Your Life*, in which a celebrity encounters a parade of characters from his past. That spring, while Perry was living in a halfway house, the program was scheduled to feature Shamluk Maharovsky, the Maccabi fixture and fixer whose duties included keeping stars like Aulcie Perry out of trouble. The U.S. Department of State declined to issue Perry a passport so he could travel to Tel Aviv for the show. But Perry still held Israeli citizenship, and somehow Mizrahi persuaded the Israeli consulate in Washington to open its passport office on the Sabbath so Perry could steal back into the country, just in time for Shamluk's TV special.

When Perry appeared on the screen, everyone in the studio, certainly Maharovsky himself, assumed that he was on some satellite hookup from the States. Then he emerged from backstage and draped his arms around his old friend, to a starburst of applause and emotion.

Israel's first prime minister, David Ben-Gurion, once uttered something that struck me as a companion to George Bernard Shaw's comment equating the Irish heart to the imagination. "In Israel," Ben-Gurion said, "in order to be a realist, you must believe in miracles." That night, reality set in. Shimon Mizrahi, witness to the *hatafat dam brit* and *mikveh* that ushered Elisha Ben-Avraham into the tribe of Israel, had brought Aulcie Perry home again. Back in the late 1970s, Steve Kaplan had been one of the people to regard Perry's conversion cynically, as just one more Maccabi power play. But even Kap was moved by what Maccabi had done on Aulcie's behalf. "It was an incredible act of loyalty by those guys," he told me. "I really think they saved his life."

Perry moved into the apartment he had bought during his playing days and to which he still held title. Tami Ben-Ami, who had gone on to bear a child by an Israeli doctor, was terminally ill with cancer, but Aulcie was able to visit her bedside one last time. His conversational Hebrew would come back, though when I met him Aulcie still read at a second-grade level and wanted to return to an *ulpan* to improve. A Tel Aviv banker and Maccabi supporter had set him up in business with Burger Ranch. His biggest joy was coaching his wheelchair team. "They've put me in a chair," he would say. "I'm learning, but I must have fallen a hundred times."

Perry told others what he would eventually tell me. "No question about it. I'm here for the rest of my life."

Before leaving Tel Aviv, I made one last pass along Dizengoff Street to see its tallest merchant. To speak with him is to see instantly how Aulcie Perry connected with the Israeli people, and why they had willed and welcomed him home. It wasn't just his warmth in greeting someone who had walked cold into his life—the whole be-kind-to-a-stranger-for-you-were-once-a-stranger-in-Egypt thing. It was his willingness to make eye contact, to field questions about subjects either painful or personal (or, in the case of circumcision, both), and to speak frankly of his failings.

"I knew people would remember me," he said. "I mean, we'd represented the country in tournaments all over the world. But when I came back it was like I was still playing. That boost was something I really needed after some sad years. Back here, I've discovered a lot about the virtues of working hard. As an athlete I worked very hard. And after my playing days were over, I had to transfer that somehow from the court. It's not that I didn't want to. I just didn't know how. So I did things I wasn't proud of.

"I believe that everything happens for a reason and that no sin will go unpunished. So it's not just that 10 years of my life disappeared. I could very well not be here. Everything that happened was God's way of giving me a sufficient smack to wake me up. I don't know if a small smack would have done the job."

He drew a Diet Coke from the tap and handed it to me, and for an instant I wondered if he was still the softhearted businessman. But before that notion could take root, he brushed it aside.

"I think more now. I think a lot more. I was very open, very naive. I wouldn't say my experiences hardened me, but I look at everything from a lot of different angles now and question things I didn't question before. I also know what I want from life, from having seen what I don't want. I got a *big* picture of what I don't want."

Kap and Mizrahi agreed. He was more guarded and less trusting. In short, he was more like the members of the tribe he had returned to, a people who had been "scorned, oppressed, humiliated and made to suffer," and who ration out their joy knowing that they'll need plenty to unleash the day the messiah comes.

But here was the most Jewish thing about him: For all his protestations of innocence at the time of his arrest, for all the vigor with which he fought the charges against him in a secular courtroom, Perry sat across from me in this all-but-kosher burger joint acknowledging what he had done. Atonement sits at the heart of the faith. Where some religions ask adherents to pray for God's forgiveness, Judaism puts as much emphasis on self-reparation, crediting everyone with the ability to sort out the errant path from the righteous one and follow the latter. The Hebrew word for repentance, *teshuvah*, literally means "returning." There may be misery, even shame, in befouling God's expectations, but there's also joy in coming home to his good graces. Choose *teshuvah*, said Isaiah, and "though your sins are like scarlet, they shall be like snow; though they are red like crimson, they shall become like wool." Muscular Christianity may have given rise to basketball, but Judaism is a pretty sinewy faith, too. Brought down by the long arm of the law, Perry had been resurrected by the long arm of the Law of Return.

As I left, I realized that I'd tracked margosa berries into Aulcie's restaurant. Those infernal berries. I would leave it to the man behind me to make his small plot of land like snow, like wool.

SIXTEEN

The Philippines
Madness and Mimicry

BOARDING PASS 登機証

NAME 姓名
WOLFF / ALEXANDER

FROM 出發地
HONG KONG

TO 目的地
MANILA

FLIGHT 班機
CX903

DATE 日期
27 JAN99

DEP. TIME
起飛時間
1625

GATE 登機門
3

BOARDING 登機時間
1545

CLASS 艙等
U

SEAT 座號
46K

SMOKE
吸煙區
NO

SEQ. NO. 序號
181

CATHAY PACIFIC

Wherever I found basketball, I found America. If it wasn't American jurisprudence in Israel, it was American expectations in Poland or American largesse in Ireland. Yet in all these places I also found Israelis and Poles and Irish eager to fit the game with a frame of their own. And then, in Manila, I encountered a people not satisfied with merely adapting the American model, but determined to replicate its every detail. Everyone in the Philippines—players, coaches, executives, sportswriters, fans—pointed proudly to the exactness of the facsimile.

During the Spanish-American War, after defeating the Spanish fleet at Manila Bay, Commodore George Dewey sent an urgent cable to Washington: "Have captured the Philippines. What shall we do with them?" President McKinley's exact response is lost among the loose balls of history. But soon enough America made clear what it would do with the only foreign country the U.S. directly ruled during the 20th century: accustom it to Doc Naismith's invention. Springfieldites introduced basketball in their Y's, Jesuits taught the game in their schools, and GIs shared the fine points with Filipino cooks and houseboys in pickup games on army bases.

One hundred years later, basketball still came expressed in an American idiom. You could order a Fastbreak Value Meal at any franchised Jollibee, the Filipino McDonald's. An army jeep elongated into a jitney provided mass transport, and every other "jeepney" I saw was detailed with some totem of the NBA, whether a Jordan jumpman silhouette, a poster of Hakeem Olajuwon or Kobe Bryant, or the logo of the Lakers or Rockets or Bulls. On the news I caught a clip of a guerrilla with the Moro Islamic Liberation Front, the rebels fighting for independence in the south, and he wore a knockoff Bulls cap, yellow logo on a field of green. The previous June, on the day the government had set aside for a nationwide voter registration drive, two of every three TV sets in the country had been tuned to Game 5 of the NBA Finals between the Bulls and the Jazz. Authorities took one look at the turnout and quickly scheduled an additional voter registration day.

In truth, Filipinos devour virtually every other American pop cultural export, too, from music to movies to beauty pageantry, and this makes for a country at once Asian and not Asian at all. China, Korea, and Japan all have ancient cultures and contemplative traditions. The Philippines, by contrast, is the only predominantly Christian country in Asia, and the one nation in the Pacific Rim starkly shaped by a colonial past—a place where the navel gazing is done by patrons of the strip clubs in Ermita, Manila's tourist district. If Korea is the Land of the Morning Calm and China is the Middle Kingdom, the Philippines is the continent's nation on the edge, figuratively as much as literally: the Land of the Midnight Rush.

With its hundreds of dialects and more than 1,000 islands, the country is so geographically and linguistically unwieldy that a borrowed cultural identity has its uses. Next to the Spaniards, who for 300 years enforced cultural apartheid and barred Filipinos from holding positions of power, Uncle Sam was regarded as a liberator. Why else would Filipinos actually celebrate, in 1998, the 100th anniversary of their independence, even though the U.S. occupied the islands for almost half of the 20th century? When I met Joey Concepción III, the owner of Pop Cola, a team in the professional Philippine Basketball Association (he was wearing jeans and a polo shirt in the executive suite, but this was a Friday, so I put his attire down to yet another imported Americanism), he said, "I'm not sure it's a good thing or not, but if you were to ask Filipinos if they'd like to be the 51st state, they'd probably say yes."

An old saw about the Philippines is meant to summarize the result of those three and a half centuries of foreign occupation. It's said that the country reflects "300 years in the convent and 50 years in Hollywood." Given that the U.S. granted full sovereignty in 1946, the very year the NBA was founded, we could add, "and 50 in the thrall of 'Fan-tas-tic!'" As the PBA's commissioner, Emilio (Jun) Bernardino, told me, "No other sport even comes close to basketball in popularity, and I think it's because of the American influence. It's funny, because as a people we don't have height. But we have creativity. We like action. We want to see surprises. We're not deliberate in anything we do."

The PBA rulebook is cribbed almost bylaw-for-bylaw from the NBA's. Unlike teams in national leagues in virtually every other member country of FIBA, Filipinos have 24 seconds to shoot, can't play zone, and observe the same foul-lane markings and three-point lines as the NBA. "It's so much a miniature NBA that guys'll see a move on TV and the next morning be trying it out," said Ron Jacobs, who began a legendary coaching career in the Philippines after Loyola Marymount fired him in 1980. "Even back in the 1980s, everything here was one-on-one, NBA-style. Anything American they see that works, they're trying. It drives me nuts."

I met Jacobs, as well as Bernardino, Concepción, and other wise men of Filipino basketball, in the company of Joaquin (Quinito) Henson, a Manileño who agreed to show me around. A columnist for the *Philippine Star*, Quinito was in his early forties, with a courtly mien and beatific face. He counted Jim Henson, the Muppeteer, as a distant relative, and was something of a multimedia phenomenon himself. Like many Filipino sportswriters, he laced his writing with nicknames —Captain Lionheart, the Flying A, the Tower of Power, the Executioner, Golden Boy—that seemed to have been lifted from the 1940s, and evoked another local sporting passion, boxing. He doubled as the television voice of the PBA, and he and his color man, a Sri Lankan émigré and old buddy of Ferdinand Marcos named Ronnie Nathanielsz, broadcast in Taglish, a hybrid of the English preferred by Manila's elite and the indigenous Tagalog language understood throughout most of the country.

Each morning Quinito and his driver picked me up at the Hyatt in an air-conditioned Honda CR-V. We'd pull out past the squatters who sat close enough to the hotel's motor entrance to exchange pleasantries with the doormen. A sign in the window of one jeepney read AMERICA'S LEAST WANTED, and the more I saw of Manila, the more this seemed to capture the city and a heartbreakingly large number of its Yankee wanna-be residents. I'd never seen such concentrated, supine poverty. One of every five residents of metro Manila is a squatter, and many live not even in shacks but in lean-tos or tents or under slats of plywood crutched against trees along roadsides. Most squatters had abandoned the provinces, believing that the city held out a better life. I could only imagine the circumstances they were leaving behind.

But destitution wasn't the most immediately daunting thing about Manila. A plea stenciled on one highway overpass— OBSERVE TRAFFIC DISCIPLINE—went unheeded. Drivers routinely nosed out into traffic and cut one another off, compounding gridlock with a blithe air, while barefoot children dodged bumpers and pressed beseechingly against the windows of cars. If Filipinos played ball at all the way they drove, the PBA commissioner's wish to highlight creativity, action, and surprises was surely granted many times over.

Amid this squalor and chaos, basketball thrived. Even for the very poor, the PBA was a diversion available nearly year-round on a communal TV in one of the city's neighborhoods, or *barangay*s. For the lucky few favored with talent, the game was a way to get rich. Quinito guessed that 85 percent of the Filipinos in the PBA had used basketball to lift themselves from the poverty afflicting roughly half the population. Every Filipino male, rich and poor alike, seemed to spend his free time testing his skill at the game. "Take a random American fan out of the stands for one of those halftime shooting promotions, and there's a better than even chance he'll throw up some ugly shot," Tim Cone, the American who served as the Filipino national coach, told me. "Whereas in the Philippines, 80 percent of the people know exactly what to do with a basketball."

Except for an aircraft carrier, I couldn't think of another place where every spare scrap of horizontal space is dedicated to so uniform and specific a purpose. On rooftops, on road shoulders, in alleyways, on the tiled floors of half-destroyed abandoned buildings, Manileños will basketball courts into existence with their imaginations. For baskets they lash together the handles from two buckets, or fashion a skirt from rubber matting. Often they launch mini-basketballs at goals barely the circumference of the ball. In any random game one player might be in sneakers, another in flip-flops, and the rest barefoot, all of them heedless of the random incursions of toddlers, washerwomen, chickens, and traffic.

We passed a narrow street completely blocked by a stanchion thrown up by some kids. "When they come across that, what do the police do?" I asked.

Quinito laughed. "Referee!"

Filipinos so love the game, he explained, that the PBA operated 11 months of the year, in three stages called—and here was a rare departure from NBA nomenclature—conferences. In the first conference a team could field only Filipinos and, lately, "Fil-Ams," Americans of Filipino ancestry. This all-Filipino conference was the most prestigious and keenly followed phase of the PBA season. The average Filipino stands 5'5" and the typical PBA Filipino only six feet and change, so the first conference featured lots of running, shooting, and low-to-the-ground jostling. The second stage, known formally as the Commissioner's Cup and informally as the "big" conference, permitted imports as tall as 6'8"—a ceiling that gave Filipinos a chance of guarding them. But it was the third conference, the Governors' Cup, that lent the PBA its distinctiveness. Ringers were allowed, but couldn't be taller than 6'4". In a sport forever marked by a quest for height, here were the vertical equivalents of all those stories I'd heard about wrestlers trying to make weight. Players shaved their heads to shed an eighth of an inch. They ran two hours through the Manila heat to lose enough water to shrink the body another quarter inch. They breathed deeply and exhaled to contract the spinal column three-quarters of an inch. "I have the conversation with agents in the States all the time," Ron Jacobs told me. "I'll ask how tall a guy is. They'll say, 'He's 6'6"!' I'll explain that he's of no use if he's taller than 6'4". And suddenly he's 6'3½" in his bare feet." And so Sylvester Gray, the 6'4" former star at Memphis, was one of a passel of no-necked frontcourt players who had earned a good third-conference PBA living, while Anthony Frederick, the former forward at Pepperdine, flew over, topped out at 6'7", and was put on the first plane home.

Quinito had arranged for me a schedule like the PBA's, with virtually no breaks. As we pinballed around Manila I tried, like a hostage seeking to understand his captors, to make peace with the traffic. Spotting a bumper sticker reading PBA, PA RIN! I asked Quinito what it meant.

"It means, 'Still, the PBA!' Many fans beyond the capital are frustrated that Manila is home to all nine PBA franchises. So a TV conglomerate has founded a rival league called the Metropolitan Basketball Association to bring the game to other parts of the islands. Instead of naming each team after a sponsor, the MBA is trying to capitalize on local identity and pride. They're naming clubs things like the Pasig Pirates and the Cebu Gems and offering huge sums to induce PBA stars to jump. They've changed the rules, too. A team gets only 23 seconds to shoot and eight seconds to bring the ball into the forecourt. And during the final two minutes, a team in the bonus has the option of shooting one unobstructed three-pointer instead of two free throws."

Here was one thing that could get Filipinos to abandon the American model: a chance to feed their appetite for more creativity, action, surprises.

I wondered if Filipinos so loved to be in the thrall of anything American that they weren't willing to step forward as themselves. The national team placed fifth at the 1936 Olympics and third at the 1954 World Championships, and both remain the best finishes ever by an Asian country. But the Philippines hadn't qualified for the Olympics since 1972, and at the most recent Asian Games, in Bangkok, it had won only a bronze. National leagues throughout the world limit foreigners, to encourage native talent to grow and bloom, and the PBA banned imports entirely from one of its conferences. So what accounted for Filipinos being so basketball nuts within their borders, and so feckless beyond them?

Size didn't explain it. Koreans and Japanese weren't big, and they fared no worse than Filipinos in international play, usually better. More likely, the problem lay in an NBA-conditioned penchant for one-on-one play and obedience to that trinity of creativity, action, and surprises. Koreans and Japanese didn't have the individual basketball aptitude of Filipinos, but when mustered into teams they ran sophisticated patterns and prospered. The PBA's dominance posed an additional obstacle. Those three conferences sucked up virtually the entire year, leaving little time for a national team to train and cohere. A few weeks of practice before a FIBA competition wasn't enough to adjust to the longer shot clock, shorter three-pointer, changing defenses, and trapezoidal lanes. Sponsors who paid huge salaries to the PBA's top players had no interest in lending out their stars, even for the greater glory of the country. Fans, so many of them poor in their own right, hardly expected a player to donate his time and risk an injury. Over the years Amando Doronila, a columnist for the *Manila Chronicle*, has mused repeatedly on the unshakable Filipino attraction to basketball, even as that tropism always seemed to lead to disappointment: "Perhaps we relish to play the role of martyrs and punish ourselves in being disadvantaged. This is perhaps a manifestation of a colonial [past]. . . . Filipinos love to improvise. They hate the tedium of long, sustained training and discipline. They like to do things ad hoc, waiting for fast breaks, and . . . basketball expresses our distaste for long, methodical, and thorough preparation."

This all rang true. But I'd had enough cultural analysis, and likewise wearied of the practice gyms and office suites where I'd heard again and again that more than 30 NBA first-round picks had played in the PBA. I wanted to see an example of how Filipino basketball was distinct from the American game, not similar to it. And so one afternoon I slipped out of my hotel on foot, determined not to stop walking until I found one.

Behind the Hyatt, modern Manila quickly dissolved into the *barangays* of Pasay City. One alley doglegged into the next, and all were apparently trafficable, though cars couldn't have passed two abreast. For the length of my walk I saw what I'd come to expect in backstreet Manila: plywood hutches canted one against another; barefoot kids with ready smiles; the occasional fighting cock tethered to a utility pole; everywhere, outdoor altars of homemade hoops.

And then, where Villanueva Street met Sanchez Street, I came upon the smallest basketball arena I'd ever seen, and in its own way the grandest. Here the carriageway was squeezed by two stucco walls scarcely 15 feet from each other. On one wall someone had painted the frozen dribbler of the NBA logo, alongside the words NBA IN VILLA SAN; on the other, a metal brace fastened in place a backboard and hoop. There was a scoreboard; a bulletin board, with a roof to shield it from the elements; even lights and a loudspeaker, both wired to an electricity source in a house that loomed over a free-throw line almost flush with one wall.

A slight man stood on the roof of a minibus parked right under the hoop. He was absorbed in tightening a bolt on the brace of the backboard. Dennis Villanueva lived in the house that electrified the lights and loudspeaker. He had installed the court in 1995 for the same reason Doc Naismith had invented the game in the first place—in the hope that basketball could keep young males, in Dennis's case a preadolescent son, occupied. Here he staged a series of tournaments, and a PBA player who lived in the *barangay* donated trophies for the winners. Dennis translated for me the two injunctions in Tagalog inscribed below the basket: DON'T HANG ON RIM and PLEASE STOP PLAY FOR PASSING TRAFFIC.

The first thing a mayor of a *barangay* did after gaining power was to build a basketball court. The second was to requisition a cache of trophies to give away. But even in the Philippines, politicians sometimes pandered to interests unrelated to hoops, and that's apparently what had happened in Villa San. Eight years earlier the neighborhood had a full court in a public park. Then some taipan bought up the park, leveled it, and built a bus terminal. Dennis had drawn up a petition of protest and circulated it from house to house and shanty to shanty: The buses were noisy, especially in the evening, and besides, a bus terminal had no business in a residential neighborhood. "But this businessman had so much money and the officials are so corrupt," Dennis told me. "I ran for *barangay* office last election. I lost because my mother has cancer and I couldn't campaign."

I asked him whether streetball didn't create a lot of noise in the evening, too.

"I just park the minivan under the basket around 10 each night. The noise dies right down."

The bulletin board was an open-air archive of all that Dennis had accomplished. The NBA in Villa San staged three tournaments, over two school vacations and the September fiesta. Dennis fervently hoped that St. Raphael, patron saint of both the *barangay* and of rain, would arbitrate his twin obligations so the games could be squeezed in. The next tournament lay a month off, and I'd caught Dennis on the minibus roof, reattaching the basket assembly. He had just painted the rim. But more than that—and this was enough to make the heart catch—he had laundered the net.

The place of the game in the Philippines finally became clear to me at the corner of Villanueva and Sanchez Streets. Yet Villa San also became a kind of window through which I could now regard someone I hadn't met. He was the great legend of the Filipino game. People spoke his name reverently in places like this, and it was in just such a slum that he got his start. When I mentioned his name to Quinito or a few of the panjandrums of the PBA, they reacted with discernible disapproval. But if he was Mephisto to some and a messiah to others, no one disputed his status as a Methuselah.

If Robert Jaworski's origins are clouded, it may be because so few people are still around to recall them. He was born in 1946, the year the Philippines gained its sovereignty, and he was still listed as an active PBA player at 53. In interviews over the years he had confirmed that his father was a GI from Brooklyn—no surprise, for any influential cultural force in the Philippines almost has to have an American pedigree.

Filipino fans were certain they could see an explanation for Jaworski's longevity in the way he played. Over a career of 34 years, Bobby (a.k.a. Sonny or the Big J) never gave up, just as he hadn't let an impoverished childhood stay him from success. Though he stood only 6'1", he routinely outdueled players, imported and Filipino alike, who were bigger, faster, and stronger. As recently as 1995, at age 49, he had led Ginebra, a team sponsored by a gin distillery, with 5.8 assists a game. As Ginebra's 50-year-old player/coach he had led the team to the Commissioner's Cup. He had even lasted long enough to play alongside his own son, Robert Jr.

In Filipino cockfighting, a loser has a ready-made consolation prize, the *talunan,* or "loser's repast"—the meal he makes of his beaten bird. Jaworski always played like a man who would rather go hungry than tuck into a *talunan.* "The thing is, he's not that good," Ron Jacobs told me. "He can't jump, and he's not real tall or fast. But if the game's on the line, he'll take the shot. And he'll make the shot. I remember them talking about him retiring in the early eighties. Well, here we are in the late nineties, and here he is."

Every Christmas, gifts and food showed up at hospitals around the country, courtesy of Jaworski. In the 1970s, when a company began selling Big J underwear in packaging that bore his likeness, Jaworski sued to stop it, but scores of small businesses have used his nickname over the years—in Manila there was a Big J Taxi, a Big J Hamburger, and a Big J Sari-Sari Store, a sari-sari store being a sort of homespun 7-Eleven—and he has left them alone. During the fiesta season, towns and departments celebrated the feasts of their patron saints by staging basketball tournaments like Dennis Villanueva's, and Jaworski tried to visit even the smallest ones. He'd spend hours signing autographs, never turning anyone away. "To me, an autograph is meaningless," he'd say. "But to someone willing to stand in line for an hour to get it, it must mean something."

In return, Filipinos showed him a devotion illustrated by a story told me by Ronnie Nathanielsz, Quinito's TV sidekick. "In the town of San Mateo, in Rizal, the dying wish of a man with cancer was to meet Bobby. This man wrote me a letter saying he died a little more each time Jaworski's team lost a game. Before one game I showed the letter to Bobby and told him he had to make a visit. Well, they lost that game, and Bobby felt guilty. He said, 'How can I go see him? He probably died some more today because of me.' But he agreed to go. The guy was 73, with a plastic tube running down his throat. He could barely stand up. But he climbed out of bed and wouldn't let Bobby leave. Three months later I got a letter with a picture of this man in a playground in San Mateo. He was shooting baskets, wearing Bobby's jersey. And that man lived another year, a beautiful year, before he died.

"You know those processionals on feast days? I've seen people touch Bobby as if he were a religious figure himself. Actually take a handkerchief and daub his body with it to soak up his perspiration. Because Bobby, he'll fight to the death with everything he has. Or even something else."

With that last comment Ronnie was alluding to the nadir of the Big J's career. During the second half of a game in 1971, Jaworski had left the bench to assault a referee. He knocked him to the floor with one punch and kicked him. As a result Jaworski was banned from Filipino basketball for life. His team's sponsor disbanded the club and refused ever to be involved in the game again. But a year later Jaworski was reinstated, and soon he was back in the good graces of most fans. Indeed, having bottomed out and clawed back to the top seemed only to enhance his mystique. Several years before my visit he had been elected to the Senate.

But neither that second career nor his age had dimmed his desire to play. He was now a free agent, and the fledgling MBA had offered him his own TV show, even ownership of a franchise in the league, if he made the jump. The PBA was just as determined to keep him. Any team of Jaworski's would draw, regardless of its record. Perhaps it would draw even better with a lousy one, for Filipino fans so adore an underdog.

I saw a chance to meet the Big J at a huge banquet that Tanduay, the rum company, was throwing to celebrate its return to sponsorship of a PBA team. Quinito was able to score an extra ticket. There was only one problem: The affair was formal, a stipulation that Filipinos take seriously, and I had nothing but rumpled slacks and polos in my vagabond's bag. Quinito came up with a solution. He suggested I wear a *barong tagalog*.

You may recognize the *barong tagalog* as the generously tailored shirt in which Ferdinand Marcos always looked more unruffled than he should have back in the early 1980s, when he and Imelda were bungling their way out of power. Though the *barong* is made from cloth spun from the fibers of pineapple leaves, and it's always worn untucked, Quinito assured me that there's no occasion too formal for it. So I bought one off the rack in the hotel gift shop for $15 and lit out for the Century Park Sheraton in Manila's moneyed Makati district.

Tsismis is a marvelous Tagalog borrowing from the Spanish, a sibilant bit of onomatopoeia that means "gossip," and the *tsismis* coursing through the ballroom that night was that Bobby Jaworski would be introduced as Tanduay's new signee. Word was that he'd play a few games for the publicity value, then gracefully slide into a role as an endorser and consultant.

The *tsismis* put the deal at 15 million pesos—roughly $390,000. During the cocktail hour I found Joey Concepción, the mogul from Pop Cola, and he thought this was a steal for Tanduay, which competes in Ginebra's product category: "Jaworski is saying, 'I'm going from gin to rum! C'mon and follow me!' You can't beat a message like that."

But as the program played out it became clear that, if a deal had been struck, it wasn't going to be announced here. Instead the evening was turned over to music, conviviality, and reminiscence. A Tanduay old-timer told of the night his mother came out of the stands with an umbrella to whack away at the man who had fouled her boy. Soon others joined him on stage to sing what they'd sung on team buses back in the fifties. Throughout, even as photographers made repeated passes by his table at the front of the room, Jaworski sat quietly in a navy blue suit.

He looked the way middle-aged men are supposed to look— thin on top, a little thick in the middle, not someone who'd be flattered by a basketball uniform. But he didn't resemble a fifty-something senator, either—he didn't look like, say, Phil Gramm. He had Filipino coloring and what might be described as a Polish-American physique, in the Bronko Nagurski sense. The emcee favored him with an extravagant introduction, but of all the people honored he received the least enthusiastic applause. These were well-heeled Manileños, not Jaworski's public. Many in the audience didn't believe he should have been here at all, for he had played only one month for a team called YCO, Tanduay's forerunner, long ago. Besides, hadn't he once left the bench to lay out a referee?

But the more the swells sneered at Jaworski, the more the poor lionized him. As the program wound down, the wait staff and kitchen crew spilled out into the ballroom to surround his table, petitioning for an autograph or a posed picture. "Compress!" a busboy with a camera commanded, as his colleagues leaned in on Jaworski's flanks. "It's *cheese* time!" As the band launched into uniquely Filipino recessional music—"We Are the Champions," "Boogie Wonderland," and the theme from

The Good, the Bad and the Ugly—Jaworski signed banquet programs, autograph books, even drink doilies, always being sure to ask to whom he should dedicate each signature. I slipped into this scrum to catch a glimpse of one of these scribblings: "May greater success and happiness be always yours. Sincerely, Bobby Jaworski."

If I was going to get a chance to speak with the Big J, it wouldn't be here, not in this crush—certainly not given his priority, which was to please his public. But the night hadn't been a complete waste, for I'd learned two things. I'd learned how hard Jaworski worked to please his fans. And I'd learned that it's possible to pass for formal in a compostible bowling shirt.

The next morning the phone rang in my hotel room. Ronnie had come through. He had passed along my request, and Bobby Jaworski was willing to meet with me.

Over a bowl of pasta in the Hyatt coffee shop, he spoke haltingly, warily, but courteously. He mentioned a bill he had introduced in the Senate to restructure the sports bureaucracy in the Philippines. He confirmed that he was "in discussions" with Tanduay and intended to keep playing. And he described the most extreme example of how his fans venerated him.

Filipinos dedicate the Christmas harvest festival to Santo Niño, the Christ child. A believer will bathe an icon of the Santo Niño, then dress him as a soldier or a farmer. "I don't really want to talk about this, because all of us have to believe that there is only one God," Jaworski said. "But for me, certainly the most embarrassing is the time someone put the Santo Niño in my uniform. About this I feel bad. I like to reserve religious things for God. Some things are not even for imagining."

He took a call on his cell phone, then lingered over the autograph requests of three young men in *barong tagalog*s who had spotted him. After they left, he turned back to me. "You know," he said, "you have probably heard many beautiful stories about me. But I want you to know another story." And here he launched into an account of how he came to coldcock that referee.

"In 1971 I was captain of the national team that placed second in the Asian Championships and qualified for the Munich Olympics. A short time later my team had a usual Filipino league game, and in the third quarter I fouled out. Not only that, five or six players on my team already had four fouls. A teammate of mine drove to the basket and was bumped as he made a layup. The referee annulled the shot and called a charging foul. On the next possession, the player on the other team—the same player who had just bumped my teammate— drove to the hoop and did the same thing. Only this time the referee counted the shot and added a free throw."

Just like an American politician, I thought. Divulge the worst about yourself, but spin it.

"Seeing this, my body went into possession. I got up from the bench and hit the referee with one punch. Yes, I was wrong. I'll admit that. They suspended me for life. But that year they also suspended 36 players for game-fixing, and two months later reinstated them all in time for the Olympics, but still left me in the cold.

"I was suspended on the 19th of December. On the morning of the 20th I was out running. A taxi driver saw me and asked, 'What the hell are you running for? You're banned for life!' I kept running. I crossed the street and passed another man. He said, 'Why'd you punch that ref? You should have *killed* him!'

"There was one word that kept me going. The word 'hope.' You have to keep that word burning all the time. That's why they love me. I think I give them hope. My life, you know, it could really be a movie."

A Hollywood movie, of course. About a controversial, bootstrapping, fabulously wealthy celebrity athlete and sometime actor turned populist politician—in other words, a composite of the menagerie that would crowd onto the soundstage of American third-party politics shortly after my return to the U.S.: Beatty, Buchanan, Trump, Ventura. Especially Ventura. Bobby Jaworski and Jesse Ventura scanned the same. Both had ethnic surnames and given names that couldn't be more all-American. Their nicknames were virtually interchangeable. Jesse (the Big J) Ventura, Bobby (the Body) Jaworski: Both played their personas for all they were worth, and by sheer force of personality had transmuted what might have been a disqualifying notoriety into a virtue.

At each overseas stop I'd exerted myself to look for signs of the States in the game as I found it. Sometimes those signs were well-hidden. More often they lurked near the surface. But in the Philippines, in basketball and beyond, I found a country that was parodically American—so American, in fact, that it could anticipate America.

SEVENTEEN

China

Qiao Dan, Celestial Citizen

O ne day toward the end of his life, James Naismith found a letter in the mail from China. The correspondent, an American named M. V. Ambros, had traveled that country by train and rickshaw and seen hoops everywhere he went. Even the humblest game drew a clutch of soldiers, coolies, and peasants, all keen to follow the action. "You can just feel what the game means to them," Ambros wrote. "It will be a real pleasure for you to travel through the Orient to see how much basketball is played. It cannot be described or pictured; it cannot be told; it must be seen."

The inventor never made it to Asia. But I could have written much the same thing on my postcards home from the Philippines. And I left for Beijing wondering if basketball in China still held out scenes to defy description.

I was going just as the Chinese prepared to celebrate the Year of the Rabbit—the Year of Doc Naismith's Track Coach's Favorite Training Meal. I could regard this either as an omen of a visit fated to descend into Elmer Fuddian farce, or as an auspicious sign, as most Chinese would. Auspicion is a well-respected variable in everyday Chinese life. For example, certain colors carry promising associations. Red is one such color, which I thought might explain one of the mysteries impelling my visit—why Jordan and the Bulls had been as popular here as anywhere on earth. But the most immediately encouraging portent appeared on my Cathay Pacific flight from Manila. The airline and its flight attendants were in the midst of a nasty labor dispute, and the cabin crew was threatening the ultimate sanction in the Asian service economy: to withhold its smiles. The stewardesses nonetheless beamed all the way to Hong Kong, and soon after connecting to Beijing, I found myself in the lobby of my hotel, illuminated by the similarly incandescent Xu Jicheng.

Xu was China's Quinito equivalent. He stood 6'4", which made him huge by Chinese standards, and wore almost exactly what I did: a denim shirt, khaki slacks, and size 13 Rockports. Those feet helped account for his nickname, Big Xu. That's how he was known to the nine million countrymen who watched him host China Central Television's *Basketball Park* twice a week. "A lot of fans don't know my real name," Xu told me. But when NBA stars David Robinson and Joe Smith came though China on a Nike promotional tour, seven- and eight-year-old kids ignored them to get Big Xu's autograph.

Xu still worked for the Xinhua News Agency, for which he volunteered to cover the NBA shortly after the 1988 Olympics in Seoul. "Some of my colleagues laughed at me. 'Who knows that NBA?' they said. 'Too complicated! Too far away!'" But Deng Xiaopeng had just signaled China's plunge into the free market with his pronouncement that "It doesn't matter if the cat is black or white as long as it catches mice." And if sport and global capitalism were about to collide in his country, Xu decided, he wanted to rubberneck at the scene. The Dream Team made its debut in Barcelona four years later, and with the ensuing vogue of Jordan and "the Red Oxen," Xu looked like a prophet.

China was still a market cluttered with the knocked-off and jerryrigged. In the back of a cab I came across an abandoned sweater with a label reading "Alvin Klein." A T.G.I. Friday's–style bistro featured a facade of candy-cane striping and billed itself as "Saturday's." Ersatz Air Jordans filled market stalls just steps from my hotel. Yet Chinese youth already had a sophisticated brand consciousness. A legit pair of Air Jordans, as opposed to fakes costing one-tenth as much, ran about $100, close to a month's salary. The knockoffs looked pretty persuasive to me, but Xu told me a high school kid could tell the difference at a glance. "Nike may sell a lot of Air Jordans," he said. "But they can't sell their basketball jerseys here. From watching our broadcasts all the kids know that Champion makes the NBA's jerseys.

"In the old days there were three luxury items: a watch, a bicycle, and a sewing machine. Now it's a house, a car, and a computer. A TV is hardly special anymore. A third of the families in Beijing own two. And even if some people still think in the old ways, they're learning quickly. Ask the commissioner of the Chinese Basketball Association how he envisions the future, and he'll say he wants to be the Chinese David Stern."

Before Deng's démarche, basketball had occupied one out-of-the-way corridor in the labyrinthine Chinese sports bureaucracy. A "basketball section" reported to a "department for ball sports," which was subservient to a "state sports committee." But everything changed in 1997, when each sport was left to make its own way administratively and financially. Cleveland-based International Management Group stepped in to run the CBA and manage one of the teams, the Liaoning Hunters. The shackles hadn't come off completely; the basketball federation insisted on keeping the People's Liberation Army entry stocked with half of the national team, and thus the August 1st Rockets so dominated the CBA that they would lose only two games during the season of my visit. The federation wanted to avoid the Filipinization of the national team by keeping its nucleus intact. And it wanted to acknowledge the importance of both the army in Mao Zedong's revolution and the August 1st team in the country's basketball history. But Beijing now expected every other team to find its own sponsors, set its own budget, pay its own free agents, and win without state support.

Likewise, the government-run provincial sports schools, in which every elite player in China once learned the game, no longer enjoyed a monopoly. Big Xu himself had emerged from one of these hoop collectives. Unusually tall even by the standards of his home province of Shandong, Xu had been plucked as a 12-year-old and told he was going to study basketball. "I didn't really like basketball," he said. "Even if I had, I couldn't have gone to the sports school if I hadn't been tall. The Communist Party and the government arranged everything for you, from the day you were born until the day you died."

Xu enrolled just the same. The strain of playing eight hours a day led to chronic knee problems. Still, at 16 he was promoted to the army youth team, and though he began to enjoy the game more, he suffered a bad ankle injury. That's when his parents stepped in. They were both professors who had suffered during the purges of the intelligentsia during the Cultural Revolution. With academic life respectable again, they wanted their son to follow their path. Xu's bum ankle provided a pretext for him to leave the army team and begin studies at Shandong University, which eventually led him to Xinhua and CCTV.

Versed in English, business, and hoops, Xu could both see the future into which China was hurtling and limn its outline for others. For three years now, Chinese professors of management had brought him into their classes to lecture on the NBA as a marketing phenomenon. "I begin my talk by breaking down the abbreviation," Xu told me. "'N' stands for 'national'—the market. Of course 'B' is at the center, because 'basketball' is the product. 'A,' 'association,' indicates organization. Market, product, organization. It's all right there in the name."

Except that "N" no longer defined the market. "I first met David Stern in 1997, at the NBA Finals in Salt Lake City," Xu said. "I told him that China could be his second-biggest market after the U.S. You know what he told me? He said, 'It should be the *first*.'"

Xu and I left the hotel by cab. Cars in Beijing moved within a black ectoplasm of bicycles all traveling, as if roped together, at the same speed. Our pokey trip in this cordon seemed at odds with the boundary-breaking place we were headed. The Song Xiaobo Basketball School was an example of the free market's impact on the game—the first private basketball academy in China and one of three such schools now in the city.

Song, who starred for China's bronze-medal-winning

women's team at the 1984 Olympics in Los Angeles, didn't own her own building. She rented out a gym at a teacher's college. But two things distinguished her academy from the provincial sports school where Xu got his start. One, it was completely private: founded by Song, owned by Song, run by Song. Two, in a country where the concept of celebrity was still something of a novelty, her name was on the door.

We pulled up to the gym as classes were changing. Boys and girls filed in and out, each carrying a basketball in a net slung over a shoulder, the way English schoolchildren tote their books. Inside, light filtered weakly through a scrim of upper windows, and hortatory banners hung from one wall. A stocky man in a sweat suit, perhaps 6'4" and not quite 50, was leading a class of 40 preadolescents through the basics of the layup. The children were there because they wanted to be, not because of some mandate from Big Brother, infatuated with an overactive pituitary gland. They paid 10 to 15 yuan, about two dollars, for a dozen two-hour classes. To sort out which parents had made the biggest sacrifice to send a child here, Xu urged me to look at the children's feet. "The shoes," he said, "tell the family."

After a while the teacher ordered the class to run laps and sidled over to where we stood. He introduced himself as Huang Pinjie. Before joining the faculty at Song's school he had coached in Indonesia, and prior to that spent the Cultural Revolution in the backcourt of the Chinese national team.

Basketball flourished during that benighted period of China's history, when Red Guards roamed the land, stamping out with sometimes whimsical ruthlessness anything suspected of being intellectual or foreign. The game might have been implicated as the latter, but at the time of the founding of the army in 1927, basketball was already the most popular pastime among the troops. Still, I could scarcely comprehend the straitjacketed lives Huang and his teammates must have lived until the terror ended in 1976. "They checked what music we listened to," Huang said. "We could not fall in love or have kids too soon. If we traded T-shirts with a player on another national team, we had to wear the shirt inside out. If a foreigner approached us, we had to assume a position like this." He turned his back, bowed exaggeratedly, and showed us his clasped hands as if they were shackled.

"All of that you could bear," he went on. "But the hardest thing was, no one was allowed to be a star." If anyone played too well, the coaching staff would call an emergency team meeting. These were like the "struggle meetings" chaired by Red Guards, at which brigades of students denounced their peers and elders. Teammates cut down anyone with the counterrevolutionary cheek to score too many points or otherwise stand out from the group. If you dared to exhibit "the unhealthy American imperialist sport style of seeking headlines," you would experience metaphorically what Jordan did after a raid on Buzz Peterson's closet: You would be "forced into shoes smaller than your feet," as the Chinese say.

Though Huang is remembered vaguely as a mainstay of the national team, no records document exactly how he contributed—how many points he scored or rebounds he grabbed or baskets he passed off for. Indeed, until a year before my visit, the CBA didn't even keep individual statistics.

Xu and I stepped from the Song Xiaobo Basketball School into the meager light of a winter afternoon. "Now I think we're finally realizing that the world is changing," he told me. "But in the history of Chinese basketball it's very hard to identify the top players of each age—who our Mikan was, our Big O, our Magic and Bird. People know, of course. People have their own eyes. As we say, 'People's eyes are clear.' But you must understand, I had no hero growing up. I couldn't, because today's hero could easily be tomorrow's goat."

The next morning I stumbled out of my hotel room, over a copy of the official *China Daily* ("Sino–St. Lucian relations are progressing satisfactorily, says Chinese Premier Zhu Rongji"), and onto a plane to Shanghai, where the Ao Shen Eagles, one of the CBA's two Beijing-based teams, were to take on the hometown Sharks.

Both teams emblematized the trend toward privatization, but

in sharply divergent ways. A communications firm, Oriental Broadcasting Corp., owned the Sharks, whose 7'5" star, Yao Ming, would be playing his first game after a month spent rehabilitating a broken foot. Yao was a local treasure, the 18-year-old son of two former national team players, a 6'10" father and a 6'4" mother. He had averaged 17 points, 14 rebounds, and four blocks a game as the Sharks opened the season with three wins in a row. But then a Beijing Duck landed on his foot, and during his four-week absence the team went 2-5. The previous summer Nike had sent Yao to Santa Barbara, to Michael Jordan Flight Camp, and he had dropped a couple of three-pointers on the camp director during one evening scrimmage. "We want him right now," Jordan had said. "I'm calling Jerry Krause." The comment quickly made its way back to China, where even there it's known that Jordan so despised Krause, the Bulls' general manager, that he avoided any opportunity to speak with him. Millions of Chinese instantly knew that Yao must have made quite an impression.

With a record of 5-4, Ao Shen stood barely ahead of Shanghai in the CBA standings, but the Eagles didn't have nearly as good an alibi for their middling start. The team's owner, a Taiwanese-American real estate and medical-equipment magnate named Winston Li, wasn't going to let the Eagles' won-lost record suffer for his yuan-lost record, so he had brought in such ex-NBA players as Greg (Cadillac) Anderson, Acie Earl, and Stacey King. Word had it that three Ao Shen players each made a million yuan a year, cash, or more than $100,000—this in a country where a university professor typically earned an eighth of that. But no one knew this or anything else for sure because Li never spoke to the press, and his players were too afraid of him to do so themselves. Li didn't believe he was getting his money's worth: The Eagles had lost by a point to August 1st, and by two points to the Liaoning Hunters, after Ma Jian, Ao Shen's captain and a former forward at Utah, committed a foul in the game's dying seconds.

Sprawling in dimensions and pulsating in feel, Shanghai leaves the visitor with an impression of two things: people and the structures that house them. Nowhere else did the Chinese better make the case that they will always have a place in international basketball, if only because of their numbers. In China, the old line goes, when they tell you you're one in a million, there are a thousand more just like you. Moreover, Shanghai's bustle proved that even decades of central planning hadn't suppressed the mercantile instincts of the people. For several seasons during the 1980s, the Chinese league featured a splendid example of market incentives. Believing that its players weren't likely to be the tallest or the strongest in international play, the basketball federation decided to encourage the development of better outside shooting by altering the rules to award four points, not three, for a successful shot from beyond the arc.

I'd brought along an interpreter, Huang Yong, and we were Shanghaied, after a fashion, as soon as we emerged from the cab outside Luwan Stadium. A knot of five young men in leather jackets—Shanghai Sharks in the *West Side Story* sense—surrounded us and began pressing tickets in our faces. From one tout we bought a pair for 20 yuan, or about three bucks, each. Afterward Huang explained that we'd just had a quintessential Shanghai experience: The tickets had been given away as part of a sponsor's promotion, and for the guy in the leather jacket those 20 yuan were all clear profit. As Huang said, "Shanghai people like to make money, in large amounts or small."

The arena was modern but unheated. The cheerleaders wore sweatpants and ski sweaters and, like rhythmic gymnasts, waved sticks with ribbons attached. "Cheerleading, with Chinese characteristics!" Huang said approvingly, underscoring one of many stark differences between Shanghai and Manila. As the players went through their pregame layup lines, they wore knit wool caps that gave "warmups" a whole new meaning.

We tried to find a spot close to the front-row railing, but every seat had been given away, sold, or scalped. Huang and I were about to retreat to the upper bleachers when a westerner—the only other Occidental I could see who wasn't affiliated with one of the teams—waved from the floor.

"Are you friends of Xu Jicheng?" he called out.

Big Xu, bless him, had phoned ahead to alert someone of our arrival. The man fixed us up with a couple of floor passes. I soon realized I'd just experienced the global reach of Nike.

Terry Rhoads was an old China hand. He had come over in the afterglow of the Barcelona Olympics as one of hundreds of missionaries of the swoosh who fanned out along the Pacific Rim. Nike had retrenched drastically after the Asian monetary crisis of the late 1990s, closing its 350-person office in Hong Kong and cutting back its staff in the People's Republic to Rhoads and a handful of others. Nonetheless, he did not have the look of a daunted man, and Yao Ming's return occasioned his appearance tonight.

To expand its share of the market, Nike was desperately trying to develop a Chinese basketball hero. All Rhoads needed was someone who could get to the NBA and stick, and Yao was their most promising candidate. Nike had already locked him up as an endorser. The sport-utility vehicle he drove had been purchased with $50,000 of the company's money. But Rhoads still ran up against daily frustration. If some hidebound bureaucrat in the basketball federation wasn't keeping a kid from traveling to camps or colleges in the U.S., reluctant fans were resisting Nike's attempts to work its marketing mumbo-jumbo with a spokesman other than Jordan. "Right now the average Chinese won't accept one of his countrymen as a hero," Rhoads told me. "If we tried to highlight a Chinese player in an ad, the fans here would say, 'C'mon, he doesn't *deserve* a Nike ad! You're trying to pull one over on us!' The NBA just suffocates Chinese basketball."

He pointed out Yao Ming's parents, huge figures standing against one wall. "That's where China's one-child policy comes back to haunt us. If Mr. and Mrs. Yao had had five, there'd be an NBA franchise in Shanghai right now."

Yao was still a bony teenager, and through the game's first 30 minutes even the 6'9" Jevon Crudup, a former star at Missouri, muscled him out of the lane with ease. But after Ao Shen's lead crested at 75–55, Shanghai began to find its rhythm and came back. The Sharks somehow scored three baskets in one 12-second stretch to nudge the game into overtime.

For the entire extra period the crowd stood, urging Yao Ming and his teammates on. Blocking shots and sinking critical free throws, Yao seemed to stand taller with each tick of the clock. Winston Li wasn't in the building; he was watching on TV at Ao

Shen's hotel, unwilling to appear with his team in public, lest it lose and he lose face. Perhaps it was best that, with the game running long, CCTV cut away to previously scheduled programming. That way Li didn't have to watch Ao Shen, once up by 20, lose 100–95.

I waded into the raucous crowd in the corridor outside the Sharks' locker room. Mama and Papa Yao towered above the scrum as Bill Duffy, the American player agent, maneuvered toward them with congratulations. Yao Ming wouldn't be going anywhere without the blessing of the federation, and the mayor of Shanghai, a big fan, would surely have a say in his future, too. But Terry Rhoads floated exultantly above this crush. He wheeled, met my eyes, and shouted over the hubbub, "When Nike sent me over here, they told me not to come back until I'd signed an NBA player. I've waited *five years*. Tonight was the night. *This* is the *guy!*"

No one took Ao Shen's loss harder than Ma Jian. As the Eagles' highest-paid and highest-profile Chinese player, Ma already felt acute responsibility. But on this night he was personally implicated by a careless foul on a Shanghai player who was in the midst of sinking a three-pointer, which led to a four-point play during the Sharks' comeback. Huang and I had been in touch with Ma in Beijing, and he had promised to meet us after the game. But none of us had counted on so dispiriting a loss.

We nonetheless took a cab to Ao Shen's hotel and phoned Ma from the lobby. He had just emerged from a bitter team meeting. Winston Li had lit into his players, telling them they didn't deserve to eat, much less be paid. Though Ma would be taking a huge risk being seen with us, he invited us up.

I stowed my notebook as we stole up the elevator. Ma met us in the hallway, then made sure Li didn't see us duck into his room. Slowly at first, then more rapidly as he warmed to an exercise that must have had therapeutic value, Ma sat on the lip of his bed and let his frustrations tumble out.

Ma was 29 now, a forward with rugged dimensions that

belied a thoughtful, sometimes rueful manner. In 1993 he had become the first Chinese to play U.S. college ball at the elite level. At first the basketball federation tried to keep him from leaving, arguing that the country had sunk too much into making him a player not to reap the result. Then, grudgingly, the federation let him go, but ruled that he could never again play for the national team.

Ma spent six years in the States, never impressing his coach at Utah, Rick Majerus, enough to get more than occasional playing time. He married an American, bought a house, had a son, and believed his Chinese career was over. But then the pace of change back home quickened, and in 1994, before the World Championships in Toronto, Ma petitioned for a spot with the Chinese nationals. Though the coach wanted him on the team, the federation said no. Two years later, in advance of the Atlanta Olympics, Ma called one sports official after another, desperately trying to win reinstatement, again with no success.

Winston Li didn't care about any of this. He just wanted to assemble a championship team, the cost be damned. Meanwhile, with a family in Salt Lake to support, Ma found Li's offer too good to pass up. But there was something Faustian in the circumstances of the man sitting before me. If a loss peeved Li, he simply wouldn't pay his players. In Poland, Pekaes's failure to do so had incited the players to revolt; here, nonpayment was a cudgel that management wielded with impunity. "We haven't been paid for two months," Ma said. "But I know his personality. If we win, he'll pay us double."

A year earlier, after the Dallas Mavericks had offered to make him the first Asian ever to be signed to an NBA contract, Ma tried to leave Ao Shen. "But Winston Li told me, 'If you go to Dallas, you'll never come back to China.'" He didn't doubt that Li had the power to back up his threat. "It's *guanxi*," Ma said, using the word that indicates politics, connections, influence—the levers of power in Chinese life.

The next morning I spotted Ma at the airport, waiting in the departure lounge for the same flight I was taking back to Beijing. I didn't approach him, for Li was pacing the hall in his brown leather jacket. But Ma took a seat near me, close enough that I could see in his bloodshot eyes that he hadn't slept. Figuring small talk was best, I asked if the team flew first class.

Ma threw me a you're-shittin'-me look. "Last night after the game he threatened to send us back by *train*."

The anonymity of the terminal must have given him a momentary sense of security. Or maybe he believed I still didn't understand his plight. For whatever reason, he shared with me one last confidence. "Look," he went on. "A while ago I scored five points in a game I played with a shoulder injury. Li thought I was game-fixing. He came up to me afterward and asked if I wanted to live or die. I told him I was hurt—that he could investigate me, and if he found any evidence he was free to break my legs. If he saw you talking to me right now, he'd probably think you were with another team, trying to steal me away. He trusts *nobody*. Winston Li wants me to be his forever."

Black cat, white cat—to Ma Jian, Deng's feline formulation didn't speak to a future with limitless vistas, but a sinister present from which he couldn't wriggle free. Even if the black cat of the state no longer forced players into literally shrinking from foreigners, the bureaucracy could still indenture or exile them. Meanwhile, a plutocratic white cat controlled Ma and his teammates like a despot. Perhaps over time Chinese basketball would cross-breed into some sort of tabby. But right now, spited by the Communist mandarins, manipulated by a ruthless taipan, Ma couldn't win for losing.

I had grown accustomed to the slightly odd way the Chinese rendered and pronounced Michael Jordan's surname. They called him Qiao Dan, and at first I wrote this off to the vagaries of people exploring a foreign tongue. Surely Big Xu could hear the way I mangled his name, mispronouncing Xu as "shoe" rather than the more correct "tsu." But upon my return to Beijing, Xu explained how the Chinese name for Jordan is far from accidental.

In Mandarin, *qiao*— 乔 —means "skillful," "ingenious," and "clever." It has connotations of honor and honesty. *Dan*— 丹 —is a term from medicine suggesting miraculous power. But *dan* also indicates the verb "to shoulder or carry"—to take upon oneself. And *dan* signifies the color red, with its associations of action, celebration, and authority, in addition to the esteemed Oxen for which Qiao Dan played.* Thus the Chinese could essentially sound out Jordan's English surname while conveying in their own tongue the attributes they associated with him.

Perhaps this delicious crosslinguistic coincidence helped account for China's insatiable desire to chow down on Qiao Dan. At the time of his retirement he had been as ubiquitous as that wart on Mao's chin. No American but Thomas Edison exceeded his recognizability. In villages during seasonal festivals, kids imitated Qiao Dan instead of playing traditional ceremonial games. In Jiangxi province, a factory famous for ceramic teapots turned out Qiao Dan figurines. When he announced his retirement, one Chinese newspaper likened the news to a death, and another suggested a new career: striding onto battlefields in his jersey so combatants would lay down their arms.

"There are more Michael fans here than in the U.S.," Xu told me. "But you'll notice people never talk about his statistics, only his spirit and technique. Girls cried the morning they learned of his retirement. Some parents and journalists have criticized Nike because the company makes so much profit on Air Jordans, but most people don't mind paying the money because they like Michael so much."

I asked Big Xu if anyone could fill the big shoes of Ingenious Red, the Mighty Miracle Worker.

"Chinese fans don't like Shaq or Rodman. They think Shaq is too big and Rodman is too immodest. Chinese fans like players who share the characteristics of the Chinese people—who are quick and fit and humble, and do great things without boasting about them. So when Shaq or Rodman comes on TV, a Chinese parent will say, 'Come now, it's time to go to bed.'"

"So I guess Allen Iverson isn't very popular, either."

"A lot of high school students like him because he's not very tall and plays a clever style. But he never passes the ball. And some Chinese people don't think he should dribble so high—that it's against the rules."

---

* Red was so beloved in Mao's China that, during the Cultural Revolution, an edict went out that traffic go on red and stop on green. Only after a rash of fatalities did Beijing rescind the order.

"Grant Hill is pretty humble. What about him?"

Xu shook his head. "Chinese people say Grant Hill lacks the quality of a king. A star must have the regal quality of an emperor. He must behave as if everything is under his control, as if he's unwilling to obey anyone else or have anyone overtake him. And his team must be at the top. In Chinese history, over 3,000 years, every emperor had his dynasty."

Years ago the Chinese prostrated themselves before their emperor. An emperor wasn't human. He was the "son of heaven"—a celestial envoy on earth. Qiao Dan's appeal to modern Chinese, by contrast, was that he was indisputably human even as he did celestial things. And he emerged at a turning point in Chinese history. At the very time Jordan was shucking the role of prodigious scorer on a mediocre team to mount the throne of the Chicago dynasty, Deng was proclaiming a new China. A people never before permitted even to count a ballplayer's baskets, let alone idolize someone other than Mao, found in Jordan a man for whom their turn to the West had created a craving. Qiao Dan was a human being to exalt to the heavens.

On my last full day in Beijing, Xu invited me to the CCTV studios, where he was anchoring an episode of *Basketball Park* devoted entirely to Qiao Dan. In one segment I would share with Xu several of Buzz's stories from Chapel Hill. Then three young Qiao Dan acolytes, culled from local colleges, were to discuss the object of their veneration.

Before we began taping I had a chance to meet them. Each was 21, serious, and tack-sharp. One, a law student, was simply a fan; another, who studied broadcasting and played point guard for his school team, watched Qiao Dan as he would an instructional video, to improve his game. Both were bemused by American ignorance of the Chinese passion for Jordan. "There was an American professor lecturing in Guangzhou," the broadcasting student told me. "The first day he asked the students if they knew who Qiao Dan was. One student said, 'Do *you* know what Qiao

Dan's *wingspan* is?' Of course the student had to tell him the answer. The professor was shocked."

But it was a female sociology student who soon captured my attention, and subdued even her fellow panelists into silence. Zhang Silai was slight and short, with a braided ponytail that didn't quit until her coccyx. She spoke in impassioned bursts. She kept a journal in which she recorded her feelings about Qiao Dan, and shared with us an excerpt from one entry: "I went out to buy a newspaper. Two birds flew toward a setting sun. I had a strong feeling that one might be Qiao Dan. But I was so far behind this bird. . . ."

As producers prepared the set, we decanted tea from huge thermoses and listened to Zhang describe her infatuation. "I read once that in high school Qiao Dan fell in love with a girl named Angela. He would save a seat for her on the school bus. But she never realized his feelings for her. Angela might regret this today. But if I had been Angela, *I* would have realized. People say that no one in high school would have known that someday he'd be a star. But *I* would have known! Why do you have eyes? You have eyes to know people!

"Sometimes my mother says to me, 'If you love Qiao Dan like this, who will you marry?' And I say, 'I will marry someone like Qiao Dan!' In 50 years, his technical skill may be surpassed. But his spirit will never be surpassed."

I asked Zhang if she hoped someday to meet Qiao Dan.

"No," she said quickly. "I want to keep him as a dream. If I meet him he would no longer be a fantasy. He would be a reality, and he may not match the fantasy."

"Do you think he has human flaws? Did you know he likes to gamble, for instance?"

"Gambling is very normal. Every Chinese plays mah-jongg, and that's a kind of gambling. A game of basketball is a kind of gambling, too."

"If you could say something to him, what might it be?"

At that, Zhang said she didn't really like the movie *Titanic*, nor did she much care for Celine Dion. But the words fit, she said, and soon—in English—she was singing: *My heart will go on. . . .*

And then Zhang seemed to swap her schoolgirl's persona for a maternal one. She pointed out something I didn't know, and might make a promising plot point for a sequel to *Space Jam*. "Qiao Dan was born in 1963, the Year of the Rabbit. The year coming up is also the Year of the Rabbit. The year of your birth is called your life year, and a person is very vulnerable during his life year. Qiao Dan should be very careful. He should wear a very thin red belt around his waist for protection. I would like to give him this belt, to protect him."

Mao famously said that "woman holds up half the sky." Listening to Zhang over green tea in the green room, I thought, Yes: So Qiao Dan might fly through it.

The morning I left Beijing, I picked up the copy of *China Daily* outside the door of my room. The lead on the top story was familiar: "China is pleased relations with St. Lucia have progressed smoothly since the nations forged diplomatic ties in 1977, said Chinese President Jiang Zemin."

Four days had passed in this souped-up country of 1.25 billion and counting, and to believe the official accounts, nothing new was going on. But just as Doc Naismith's correspondent had urged, I'd come to see for myself, and seen otherwise.

Yet inspection tours can only take you so far. There's an unseen game, too, that knows no political boundaries. It exists in the vaulted space of basketball's temples, in the supple imaginations of players, in the subtle synergies of collections of teammates, in the mystical relationship between ball and basket. It's older, larger, more resistant to understanding than the territory I'd tracked so far. But that didn't make it any less worth exploring.

SPRING

The
Game
Within

EIGHTEEN

Philadelphia

Quaker Meeting House

It sounds proverbial: "I'd hurry back from China to see a game between Princeton and Penn." But I would, and I did. The Tigers or Quakers had won every Ivy League men's basketball title but two since 1969. In light of that history, and the league's policy of giving its NCAA bid to the regular-season champion, a fan could scarcely afford to miss the teams' two meetings. One game would be at Jadwin Gym in Princeton. The other would take place at the St. Peter's of basketball, the destination of any pilgrim in search of the spiritual essence of the game—the Palestra in Philadelphia.

In my experience cathedrals have a single main entrance, in the front. So too with the Palestra, which I'd yet to visit without feeling such churchly emotions as humility, reverence, and a sense of homecoming and community. This may seem odd in someone whose Princeton ties go back to preschool. I can't imagine North Carolina bluebloods getting the warm-and-fuzzies over Duke's Cameron Indoor Stadium, or followers of the Knicks or Sixers or Lakers doing anything but cursing the old Boston Garden and its meddlesome leprechauns. My affection for the Palestra had always been a bit of a mystery to me, too. And so on a late-winter Tuesday that hinted at March—six hours before Princeton and Penn, unbeaten and tied for first, were to play each other—I emerged from a cab at 33rd and Walnut, determined to solve it.

For hosting more fans at more games involving more schools over more seasons than any other college gym, a building might get a little chesty. But the Palestra has a tweedy look and a tenured ease, like some red-brick-and-sandstone Mr. Chips. It fits snugly, rightfully, on the Penn campus, both with its name, thought up by a classics professor at the time of the building's dedication in 1927, and its location, just steps from the math and physics lab and the school gym.

"The gym?" you may ask. "Isn't the Palestra itself the gym?" I'd wondered the same thing. It turns out the ancient Greeks had gymnasia, in which athletes trained, and attached to them *palaistra,* rectangular courtyards where those skills, once perfected, were publicly displayed. And so an umbilical corridor joined the Palestra to Hutchinson Gymnasium. It was all just as the Greeks had it, except for the roof, a sop to the Philadelphia winters. A brace of 10 arched steel trusses raised the ceiling high, and a row of skylights on one side supplied southern exposure. Until Penn sank several million dollars into renovations during the late 1980s and early '90s, that ceiling looked like something an old locomotive might have stopped under. Now, painted a light blue, it pulled your eyes up and gave you pause.

For years the Palestra served as a kind of Quaker meeting house, where Philly's five major colleges—the Big Five—gathered to play one another. No arena has taken in so many disparate schools as regular tenants: Villanova of the Main Line, Augustinian, faintly snooty, so stolid that it had had but four coaches in 64 years; La Salle, the working-class, Christian Brothers school, whose longtime coach, the rough-edged Speedy Morris, was a caricature of its constituency; St. Joseph's, with the educational mission of the Jesuits embodied in its line of teacher-coaches, from Jack Ramsay, a Ph.D., through Jim Lynam, a calculus professor, to John Griffin, an M.B.A.; sprawling, egalitarian Temple, once with a Jewish coach, now with a black one; and private Penn, munificent landlord to the other four, the sporting fellow who took regular beatings before turning the tables gloriously in the 1970s, and winning the City Series every now and again since.

Through the 1950s and 1960s the typical Palestra parishioner was a young fan, usually raised and schooled Catholic. Bannerball was among the games he played. "Rollouts" were scrolls of shelving paper, unfurled slowly in the stands, that bore messages of Bolognese puckishness, usually laced with three-way puns and references to pop culture and the day's headlines: HAWKS BANK ON MCFARLAND TO CHASE MANHATTAN, or NIXON IS A QUAKER. The best could have been appended right to the box scores: A—9,208; Technicals—None; Rollouts—PENN HAS HOT DOG STARTERS AND WEANS AND FRANKS ON BENCH; HAWKS ARE SO VAIN THEY PROBABLY THINK THIS ROLLOUT'S ABOUT THEM. Rollouts had their sublime moments, as during one Villanova–St. Joe's jihad when, as the Wildcats' student section chanted, "The Hawk is dead," the St. Joe's side rolled out what seemed like a dozen banners, all reading THE HAWK WILL NEVER DIE. But then crude rollouts began to appear. Shortly after WHAT'S THE DIFFERENCE BETWEEN CHRIS FORD AND A DEAD BABY? A DEAD BABY DOESN'T SUCK, the Big Five athletic directors insisted on approving each before any could be brought into the building. The ritual soon died.

But there was much more to the texture of a Saturday night at the Palestra during the early sixties. You tried to sit up high, for the higher you sat, the hipper you were. You tried to sneak in, too—whether by using the indentations of the mortar between the bricks on the east facade as a crude stepladder to a transom window, or by slipping through a door left open by fans exiting after the first game of a doubleheader. (The piddling cost—three bucks for two games—has surely caused some of those sneaks to blush retrospectively.) You sported a blue beret if you fancied Villanova, for that's what Wally Jones, the Wildcats' star guard of that era, had gotten everyone on the team to wear. ("We're 'Cats with hats," he said, like some beat poet.) You threw a glance up at the broadcast booth at Les Keiter, the voice of the Big Five, who opened each of his telecasts sounding much like local teen impresario Dick Clark—"We're here in Panicsville, U.S.A., the Palestra in Philadelphia!"—and by the end might say, "The arithmetic reads 62 to 60, and if the Hawks don't come down the maplewood floor and tickle the twine, it'll be good night, Irene!" Even leaving the Palestra had a fashion to it: You gave your ticket stub away to someone who wanted to see the second game, then bought a soft pretzel from one of the vendors lining Walnut Street and walked the few blocks through the chill to 30th Street Station.

As a basketball plant, the Palestra was peerless. Until those renovations, the basket stanchions rose primevally from the floor. The floorboards ran widthwise, lending the court as distinctive a look as the old parquet gave Boston Garden. In those days before collapsible rims, the baskets were notoriously firm and granted nothing cheap, but shooters forgave the Palestra that, for every other circumstance was ideal. Jeff Hall, a kid from the mountains of eastern Kentucky, came into the building with Louisville in 1984 and marveled at how "you could almost reach out and touch the basket."

Until the early 1990s, a mysterious door under the north stands led to the Historical Archaeology Lab of Penn's University Museum. There, unbeknownst to the good burghers of Panicsville overhead, heaps of chips of china and fragments of flower pots sat for graduate students to clean, tag, and catalog. "*Sure* you've got to 'study a few relics,'" I could imagine a crotchety usher saying. "You buy a ticket just like everybody else." So archaeology grad students avoided working on game nights. But on other occasions, with the Palestra at rest, they could hear the creaking of the joists when the heat went down, and the clanking of the pipes when it went up again—noises that kept them company.

Perhaps those apprentice archaeologists came across the remains of some of the highly ranked teams interred over the years beneath the famous floor: Western Kentucky, with Jim McDaniels and Clarence Glover, upset by La Salle in 1971; Wichita State, with Nate Bowman and Dave Stallworth, upset by St. Joe's in 1964; Bowling Green, with Nate Thurmond and

Howard Komives, also upset by the Hawks, in 1962. It was preposterous that West Catholic High should have beaten Wilt Chamberlain and Overbrook High for the 1953 city title, yet after practicing all week with someone standing on a card table under the basket, the Burrs did so, at the Palestra.

Over the years, asking Philadelphians to account for these miracles on 33rd Street, I'd heard many theories. Some people pointed to the great rollers of noise and energy sent back and forth by 9,000 people sitting elbow to elbow, in four banks, in so intimate a space. (The Palestra didn't have a capacity so much as a lawful occupancy.) Those who had spent the most time in the building credited ghosts, risen from the 19th-century potter's field on which the place was built. But I'd always been partial to the theory that the upsets were karmic payback to the home fans, who generously applauded visitors who played well and, arriving early to watch warmups, counted in an audible whisper in 1965 as Bill Bradley dropped in practice shot after practice shot—26 straight, legend had it.

At its height the Palestra was as much a think tank for coaches as a player's proving ground. Ramsay, Lynam, Chuck Daly, Mike Fratello, Harry Litwack, Jack McCloskey, Jack McKinney, Al Severance, Paul Westhead, and Dick Harter all advanced to the NBA, the Hall of Fame, or both. One night in the early 1970s, with his La Salle team trailing Duquesne by 24 points and the Dukes holding the ball, Westhead sent two defenders ahead to the opposite foul line and ordered the Explorers into a three-man zone. The idea—to make it impossible for Duquesne *not* to shoot—worked so smartly that La Salle wound up losing by only two. No wonder Ramsay, the coach's coach, always said that winning the City Series meant more to him than winning a national title ever could.

The coaches remained collegial. They applied gentle peer pressure on one another to excel, but in gentlemanly fashion. To be sure, something festered between Harter, the Penn coach, and Jack Kraft after the Quakers' infamous 32–30 stallball upset of Villanova in 1969. But things like that had a way of getting smoothed over, either at Cavanaugh's Tavern after the game, or at the regular Herb Good press luncheons. And if coaches insisted on holding grudges, the decency of the players carried the day. After Villanova paid off Kraft's IOU two years later, embarrassing Penn 90–47 in an NCAA tournament game in Raleigh, the two teams happened to take the same flight home. When a teenager in a Villanova T-shirt began taunting Penn's Corky Calhoun at the baggage claim in Philly, it was Howard Porter, the Wildcats' star, who chased him off.

Alas, by the late eighties all this brotherly love had evaporated. One by one, three of the Big Five abandoned the building. Only St. Joseph's still brought an occasional home game into the old barn on the Penn campus, albeit less and less frequently. The Big Five disintegrated mostly, as Les Keiter might have put it, because of how the arithmetic read. When they first took up with one another, the schools agreed to split the take and share expenses, knowing they were generating interest greater than the sum of their individual followings. But in those days most colleges were independents. Soon the Big East and Atlantic 10 had gained footholds up and down the East Coast, wherever the demographics looked good. With its need to appeal to the broadest audience possible, television made a City Series seem quaintly parochial. There was simply no place for the Palestra in the spreadsheets on the desk of Big East founder Dave Gavitt, who said, "The Palestra and the old Garden were two places kids always looked forward to playing. Now kids look forward to playing in the Carrier Dome. All things change."

Still, it didn't seem right to bid Irene good night.

I filed through the front doors and past the exposed steam radiators in the outer corridors—the same radiators to which, spurious legend had it, Dick Harter dispatched players who had committed turnovers in practice, with orders to sear the offending hand. I gazed up at the portraits of old teams that hung by the thread of picture wire, yet were never stolen. I nodded at the plaque, the gift of a Penn alumnus, that reads TO WIN THE GAME IS GREAT/TO PLAY THE GAME IS GREATER/BUT TO LOVE THE GAME IS GREATEST OF ALL.

I followed a ramp down to the floor. There I found Curtis Brown, Penn's equipment manager, who wasn't at all fazed that some stranger had stumbled in off the street to explore the Palestra. "Happens all the time," said Brown, who was in his early thirties. "This is home for a lot of people. They say, 'My parents took me here years ago. Can I have a ball and take a shot?'"

A floret of keys hung from his neck, and I realized that Brown held the ultimate key to the gym. "If I had to pull out the key to the Palestra, it would be . . . "—he fingered the end of his lanyard—" . . . *this* one.

"You know, this place would rather not have elevators and corporate boxes. The Penn kids don't get scholarships. Every fan stands in line to buy a ticket. It's just a place to watch the game. Temple has its new building, the Apollo, but it isn't really the college *try,* if you know what I mean."

Brown introduced me to the Palestra's custodian, Dan Harrell, a 55-year-old former football coach at West Catholic High. Harrell had kept the place clean for six years, but he'd been a regular for 40. He still associated the Palestra with illicit glimpses of his youth: It was here that he first saw female cheerleaders; here that a favorite usher waved him in with a wink.

Harrell arrived each weekday morning at five, and as he worked the cryptogram in that morning's *Philadelphia Inquirer,* he listened to the ghosts. "They're good ghosts, though," he told me. "If I peek out of my office, they'll stop their chattering. I'll yell good morning to 'em and they don't bother me. They say ghosts are between heaven and reality. If that's true, this is definitely where they wanna be."

A young man was toeing the floor in street shoes. "Hey!" Harrell yelled. "You don't wanna be doing that! That's a venial sin!"

The kid looked up. "I don't wanna be doing that," he said in an obedient monotone, then slinked off.

Finally, Brown and Harrell made sure I met Tony Crosson. As the Palestra's electrician, Crosson was responsible for the building's veins and arteries. And a story he told left me believing the Palestra has a heart.

One afternoon at the turn of the decade, a few hours before La Salle and St. Joe's were to tip off in a Big Five game, Crosson placed a call to the main power station on the Penn campus. From all the information he could gather and a few calculations he made, Crosson concluded that there wouldn't be enough electricity that night to sustain the building's many needs. So he made a painful decision. He ordered that no popcorn be popped.

Now the Palestra's aroma has an almost ineffable quality. It smells something like popcorn, yes, only laced with sweat, pizza, hot-dog steam, pretzel salt, stale tobacco smoke, wood, and all the different brands of disinfectant used over the years—"like a circus," former Penn coach Tom Schneider once told me, taking as good a stab at a simile as any. Well, La Salle blew St. Joe's off the floor that popcornless night, in a game not nearly as good as it should have been. But the next evening, with the popcorn poppers running, and aromas once again wafting through the building in just the right proportions, Penn and Villanova played a magnificent game that the Quakers won by a point.

To judge by Crosson's tale, the Palestra was involved in every game it hosted. The building put college kids on notice to heed the words of that plaque in the lobby. Then it let the ghosts serve as handmaidens, to see that its will be done.

Forty minutes before tip-off the Penn student section was already full. Undergraduates flipped double-barrel birds at the Princeton players during warmups. They waved placards at the Tigers' co-captain that read BRIAN EARL LIKES THE BACKDOOR and EARL IS A GIRL. They wore PUCK YOU, FRINCETON T-shirts and chanted an unspoonerized version of the same message.

All their invective hardly seemed necessary. After Earl threw in a three-point shot to open the game, Penn scored 29 points in a row. Twenty-nine points, uninterrupted. I couldn't remember the last time I'd sat through anything like it. The Quakers scored inside and out, off set plays and in transition, willfully, whimsically, almost ridiculously. Meanwhile Princeton seemed determined to commit every known offense against the game, and invent a few more. The Tigers played matador defense, and committed shot-clock violations, and once (this I'd never seen before) hit a teammate in the back with an inbounds pass. Leading this pathetic parade was Chris Young, the Tigers' freshman center, who, when not throwing away outlet passes, was having his shots blocked in the low post (quite an achievement when you're 6'10"), or allowing himself to be stripped of the ball entirely. He missed all four of the three-pointers he took, including one that wasn't a mere airball, but an airball wide, as if it had come off the toe of a placekicker with the yips.

When the Quakers' lead crested at 29–3, the Penn students launched into their lustiest G-rated cheer of the night: *You have!* (beat, beat) *Three points!* They called for Penn coach Fran Dunphy to send in the end-of-the-bench freshman who served as the Quakers' human victory cigar. After Young sank a foul shot to bring Princeton up to 29–4, they gave him a sarcastic standing ovation.

At halftime the scoreboard read 33–9. Over 19 consecutive possessions, Princeton had failed to score a basket. On the regional cable network carrying the game, the announcers called the result "a football score." Along press row, writers began to rap out their stories, secure that they could soon hit send. "It makes me nervous to have such a big lead so early," I heard a Penn fan behind me confide to his date. But elsewhere in the Palestra, hubris carried the day. The ghosts don't like hubris, I thought, any more than they could have approved of all the profanity in the cathedral. But surely the ghosts had already adjourned to Cavanaugh's, disgusted at this sorry excuse for a game.

I disengaged my elbows from those of my rowmates and left

the east stand for the men's room. The Palestra provides only two such facilities for each sex, so every one is jammed at halftime with a queue folded intestinally over on itself. I watched as a liver-spotted Princeton alum, class of thirty-something, wearing a hearing aid and a tie festooned with tigers, minced his way toward a urinal. A young Penn fan in line looked at him pitifully and said, "Hang in there, old guy."

By the time I got back to my seat, the second half had begun. Princeton's position had deteriorated further. The Tigers now trailed 40–13 with 15 minutes to play. The game was a farce, a travesty unworthy of the hallowed Palestra.

"The hallowed Palestra," I'd later discover, is an anagram for "What?! O hell. Drat. *Please.*"

Disgusted, I let my mind wander. I thought back to more satisfying nights spent in the building, when a toothless gnome of a man would spend timeouts prancing around that maplewood floor in a kind of mummer's strut, with one basketball wedged under an arm and what looked to be another stashed under his suitcoat. Exactly how Bernie Schiffran came to be called YoYo wasn't clear. It may have been for the "Yo!" with which he greeted people, as if he were Rocky Balboa, or for the way he moved, as if being unspooled and gathered up on a string. But ushers never asked to see his ticket, and fans always shared a piece of their pretzels, and coaches made sure to let him follow them to Cavanaugh's, where he'd deliver malaprop-laced monologues about "cape-city crowds" and "Frank Scenario of Hobobroken." In accordance with the fraternal spirit then still alive in the Big Five, those same coaches made YoYo their ward. His shirt was a gift from Ramsay, his pants came from Litwack, his suitcoat was handed down from McCloskey. After last call, YoYo usually found a bed amid the newsprint rolls by the loading dock behind the *Bulletin* building at 30th and Walnut.

There would come a day when college basketball was different, and most of the Palestra's tenants left to pursue money and vainglory. And there would come a day when someone like YoYo was called homeless. But on a winter's night at the Palestra not so very long ago, no one called him that.

I was stirred from my reverie by the strangest thing.

Princeton had begun to score. Every shot denied the Tigers in the first half seemed to be granted to them now. Playing in a frenzy of opportunism, they hopped into a full-court press after each basket and began a turnabout that Penn couldn't begin to make sense of. From 40–13 the score went to 40–19, and 42–28, and 42–36. Earl found open three-pointers, as did his fellow co-captain, Gabe Lewullis; and a Princeton substitute with a blustery style, Mason Rocca, came off the bench to seize every rebound within range. A Penn guard with the burdensome name of Michael Jordan sank a leaner in the lane as he was fouled, and he followed this up with a free throw, to push the Quakers back out to a 45–36 lead with slightly more than six minutes to play. Earl nonetheless sank another three. And then the game offered up an extraordinary reversal of individual fortune.

For the first six minutes of the second half, Chris Young had continued to play listlessly enough that Bill Carmody, the Princeton coach, sat him down. But Carmody sent Young back into the game with 8:25 remaining, and within a couple of minutes, the crowd's whipping boy suddenly found himself. Here, from notes I never thought I'd have reason to consult, is my best attempt at reconstructing what happened: Young sank a short jumper in the lane after Earl found him with a pass (4:40). He fearlessly eyed and let fly his fifth three-point shot of the game, only this time, at long last, he sent it whispering through the net—and permitted himself a little pump of the fist in relieved celebration (3:55). After Earl slipped along the baseline for an unchallenged scoop shot, Princeton lay within a point, 49–48, with three minutes still to play. Jordan missed a hurried jumper. Rocca rebounded the ball. And Princeton came downcourt hunting for an unimaginable lead.

When he took an entry pass on the right block, Young wheeled into a move as old as the Palestra itself. He swayed his shoulders right, then left, then right again, before sweeping a right-handed hook into the air. The ball kicked off the rim, came back down for one more bounce, then fell through the net. Scarcely two minutes remained. Young, nothing-for-eight in the first half, had tossed in seven critical points over three decisive minutes.

A few seconds later Young went to the bench with his fifth foul. But he knew by then his work was done. As he would later say, "I could see in the other guys' eyes that we weren't gonna lose." Both teams missed field goals and free throws after Young fouled out, and the very last chance was Penn's. But the Quakers' best shooter, Matt Langel, left a leaning 12-footer short and Lewullis back-tapped the rebound. Earl came down with the ball as the Palestra's horn consecrated the result: Princeton 50, Penn 49.

This had been a game not of ebbs and flows, but of two great tidal surges. Princeton had answered 0–29 with 37–9, in part by committing only one turnover in the entire second half. There had been bigger comebacks in college history. But no team had ever faced making up so large a percentage of its scoring—27 points constituted 54 percent of Princeton's point production for the evening—and done so. I thought of that old guy in the men's room. He sure hung in there.

Young had scored the game's final points with that quailing hook more than two minutes before the buzzer. But of course he had also won the game with his free throw in the first half, the one that brought Princeton to within 23—the very point for which the Penn students, now silent in disbelief or screaming for Fran Dunphy's scalp, had mocked him for making.

There's another anagram for "the hallowed Palestra." It's "Plethora; death as well."

For all his merits, Pete Carril probably would not have guided Princeton to this victory. He would have taken his team's first half far too personally and spent the break grinding his players into the locker-room floor. Nonetheless, for an epigraph to this game, I could think only of Carril and a comment he had made after a victory long ago: "I believe Shakespeare said it best. One half does not a whole game make."

I returned to the Palestra around 11 the next morning. The place was still. There wasn't a lumen of artificial light anywhere, only diffuse rays of sun filtering through the skylights. You could stand on the floor and yell something—say, "Ring-tailed howitzer!"—and hear each syllable as it got passed among the building's nether reaches, like basketballs afly in an acoustic weave.

Six hours earlier Dan Harrell had greeted the ghosts, then slipped into his office to fold back to the cryptogram in his copy of the *Inquirer*. (The morning's headline read SWALLOW THE LEADER.) Soon after I found him, he set a boom box on the scorer's table and tuned it to a classical station. The chords of a toccata began to fill the vault of space.

Curtis Brown, still in shock, could barely speak. Harrell had been less thrown by the events of the night before because he had witnessed so much over the years, but to see Penn players still sobbing 30 minutes after the buzzer left him shaken, too. "I was the last guy to see Fran before he left," Harrell said. "He was devastated."

I'd come back because Jack Scheuer, the 66-year-old Philly-based correspondent for the Associated Press, organized a noontime pickup game for journalists every Wednesday. No one was sure whether Jack did this as a favor to his sportswriter colleagues or so he could continue to call himself the all-time leading scorer in Palestra history. But the game had gone on for 25 years, usually in accordance with the hierarchy of values spelled out on that plaque in the lobby.

We writers were still a little hungover with astonishment, too, but we did our best to play three-on-three in a spirit worthy of the building—that is, with lots of cutting and screening, and no pantywaist make it, take it. Between games I chewed over the previous evening with my teammates, Dick of the *Daily News* and Neil of Comcast SportsNet.

We noted how no one had left early, despite the rout, if only because fans at a sold-out Palestra are shoehorned so snugly into their seats that they're captives of whatever might play out before them. We speculated on what Dunphy could have done to stem what Gary Walters, the Princeton athletic director, would call "a riptide that was dragging them out and carrying us in." And we wondered what it was like to be one of those Penn students who, sequestered in an economics midterm until 8:15 that evening, didn't show up until early in the second half. To catch a glimpse of 40–13 on the scoreboard, and then witness what followed—the applicable economics term would be "dynamic scoring."

"You know," Neil finally said, "I just have this feeling. I've got a hunch that Penn is going to win the league."

I would recall Neil's words three nights later, after Princeton lost to Yale—the team standing last of more than 300 Division I schools in the computer rankings, and a 66–33 loser to the Tigers several weeks earlier. The result returned Penn to a tie for first place. A week after that, Princeton lost again, this time to Harvard, the one Ivy team never to win the league title. Princeton had somehow let its victory transmute into hubris, and for that the Palestra ghosts, basketball's proctors, had rapped the Tigers hard on the knuckles. The Quakers took a one-game lead in the league standings, a lead they wouldn't relinquish. "I felt like Bill Buckner," Dunphy would later say, citing the goat of the 1986 World Series. "Only I got another chance."

Neil had no way of knowing that any of this would happen. He only knew the Palestra and the game, and the knack the former had for regulating the latter. Perhaps his insight came from the way he spent his lunch hour once a week. In any case, he had one thing to add before joining Dick and me as we trudged toward the showers. "Just think," Neil said. "In the old days, last night's game would have been only half of a double-header."

NINETEEN

Brazil

Women of the Laughing Blood

B asketball came to Brazil in 1896, when a Presbyterian missionary shared the game with a group of men at McKenzie College in São Paulo. Then, suddenly, it disappeared. Here's how Doc Naismith explained this brief transit: "The team took up the game readily and was well on the way to becoming adept at the sport. One day, as the coach was working with the boys, he accidentally left [an American newspaper] on his desk, and in this paper was a picture of a girls' basketball team. Some of the team saw the picture and immediately refused to play any game that was meant for girls."

For the longest time I'd wondered why so many men hold women's basketball in such disdain. To be sure, very few women dunk. (This has something to do with the contours of their bodies, a feature about which men have rarely otherwise been known to complain.) Yet by the 1990s women's hoops had markedly improved. Women could create their own shots, break a press, even run an offense that no longer terminated in what looked like a bout of tournament Twister. Besides, even if they rarely threw it down, I knew from my stopover in Peoria that most of us had gotten over a juvenile obsession with the dunk. In fact, the WNBA was an instant hit in part because the guys suffered in the comparison. Fans had wearied of the shifty loyalties of NBA athletes and owners. At the Atlanta Olympics, kids and their parents watched the Dream Team men whine about hotel room service while their distaff counterparts literally turned cartwheels upon winning the gold. When I first mentioned the WNBA to my mother, she thought I was talking about a radio station. Yes, I said to myself: a 50,000-watt, clear-channel, more-platter, less-chatter alternative to the same old thing millions of people had unthinkingly punched up for years.

My ears still rang with a comment I'd heard at the Palestra from Curtis the equipment manager, and it seemed to get women's hoops just right: "The college *try*, if you know what I mean." And so, after months of taking the measure of the game on Mars, I decided to venture to Venus—to explore basketball as filtered through the female imagination. I would make tracks for the very place where women's hoops had been dismissed a century earlier. But first I read up on one more point of history. In 1895 Clara Baer, a female phys ed instructor at Newcomb College in New Orleans, asked Doc Naismith to send her a copy of the rules of his new game. With his reply Naismith enclosed a diagram indicating where players might ideally be positioned. Baer misread this, thinking his notations meant that each contestant was confined to a certain spot on the floor. So she developed the six-to-a-side, three-on-offense, three-on-defense women's rules that would predominate for 75 years, and could still be found in pockets of Illinois, Iowa, and Oklahoma at the end of the 20th century. Even after the misunderstanding was pointed out to her, Baer stood by her circumscribed version of the game so, as she put it, "a delicate girl, unaccustomed to exercise, and for the most part averse to it, would become interested in spite of herself."

The schism in the rules would come too late to placate the macho sensibilities of the men at São Paulo's McKenzie College. Eventually women in South America's most populous country would develop a basketball style unmatched in the world. But at the turn of the century Brazilian women busied themselves preparing meals and raising children, not practicing sports, and thus failed to embrace this game that their male countrymen believed to be meant for them. And so basketball in Brazil died aborning.

At bottom, basketball comes down to two choreographic essentials: lots of lateral movements and a few bold vertical ones. Players spend all sorts of time and energy moving here and there, trying to find an opportunity to spring upward, either to release a jump shot or to scale the goal for a layup or dunk or rebound. Virtually everywhere in the world, it's this up and down that makes addicts of fans and players, and makes film at 11.

In Brazil I found an exception. Brazil was the motherland of lateral movement. Daily life was shot full of it: hips swaying on sidewalks, kids converging on soccer balls, cars careening through streets. Each year Brazil's roads are the scene of more fatalities than those in the U.S. even as they're plied by one-tenth the traffic, and motorways serve as a staging ground for displaying yet another national trait: a predisposition to improvise. Brazilians have a word, *jeito*, to indicate a resourceful cleverness, and everywhere *jeito* rules. The favelas, the shantytowns housing Brazil's urban poor, are to the jerrybuilt what Celebration, Florida, is to the slavishly planned.

No developing country is better positioned to join the ranks of the developed than Brazil. It's blessed with plentiful natural resources and suffers neither earthquakes nor hurricanes. Brazilians create their own disasters, usually economic ones. Nowhere can you find a greater disparity between the richest and poorest 20 percent of a population; the day before I arrived, the Brazilian real hit a record low against the dollar. But what was a crisis except another opportunity for someone accomplished at *jeito* to devise some way to wriggle out of a fix? Each morning outside the window of my São Paulo hotel, a truck rumbled up the rua Augusta, its flatbed freighted with steel canisters of propane gas. The driver cried *"Gaz! Gaz!"* over a light calliope rendering of Beethoven's "Für Elise." In Brazil, even something as workaday as a utilities delivery came in the trappings of *carnaval*.

Improvisatory, rhythmic, full of sinuous movements, basketball seems perfectly adapted to the Brazilian character. But after those male students at McKenzie College gave in to their insecurities, the game disappeared completely for five years. For more than half a century thereafter, Brazilian women were virtually invisible, too. As recently as 1962 they couldn't exercise such elementary rights as enter into a contract, drive a car, or leave the country, without the consent of a father or husband. Even on the cusp of the 21st century, men charged with crimes of passion against women could mount an honor defense and know that the odds favored exoneration.

Just the same, machismo didn't cow women in Brazil the way it did females in some other Latin American countries. At dedicated police stations in many cities, victims could file reports of domestic violence. São Paulo elected a woman as its mayor in 1988. Indeed, women carried themselves with an all-hung-out ease that would never fly in countries with a beauty-queen culture, like the Philippines. In Brazil women called their hindquarters their *poupança*—their "savings." And while this wasn't much different from women elsewhere who might refer to their "assets," Brazilian women had a way of making clear that their savings sat in an account to which they alone held title.

Much of this comfort with their bodies and confidence in themselves was the product of the samba culture and the role women have long played in it. Samba grew out of *candomblé*, the slave religion that the ancestors of today's Afro-Brazilians took with them across the passage. The Portuguese slave traders tried to ban its practice, but nothing could suppress the dancing and drumming at the heart of the faith. After slavery was finally abolished in Brazil in 1888, freed female slaves set up *candomblé* temples, and the music and movement soon leached into mainstream culture. The descendants of these women became pillars of the samba schools that thrived in the favelas. Seamstresses and choreographers, musicians and dancers, they galvanized the country each February during *carnaval*. Every samba school recruited a celebrity for its annual parade into the Sambadrome in Rio, and a samba school would be delighted to land as its grand marshal one of the two giants of Brazilian women's basketball.

By the 1980s, the women's game in Brazil had rallied from its inauspicious beginnings to produce a Bird and a Magic of its own. Because of these two, and because of the success they brought Brazil in international competition, women's hoops was now every bit as popular as men's, drawing comparable crowds and TV ratings. It was simply understood: The two— Hortência and Paula—couldn't play for the same team in the national league, for if they did there would be no competition. Hortência had retired after the 1996 Olympics, and Paula's career was winding down. But during the season before my visit their rivalry had still thrived, as the team Hortência served as general manager, Fluminense, beat Paula's team, BCN Osasco, in the final of the playoffs.

At *carnaval,* the samba rhythm never stops. A samba school's rhythm section, the *bateria,* must lay down and hold a beat for hours at a time. Drum straps routinely leave bloody abrasions on a percussionist's shoulders. Until she gave up the game for good at age 37, Hortência had played like a *percussionista*. At 5'8" and 132 pounds, she wasn't particularly tall or strong, but she moved ceaselessly without the ball. Always up on her toes, her ponytail flapping behind, she had a knack for searching out gaps in the defense and angles to the hoop, like John Havlicek in his prime. As one of her coaches said upon Hortência's retirement, "If I could, I would put her in a refrigerator to preserve her forever."

The *cuica* is a percussive squeak thrown in over the *bateria*'s backbeat—a kind of sonic juke. The *cuica* marked Paula's game. She too was 5'8", but she didn't move as Hortência did. Rather, Paula shook and jittered, trying to insinuate herself past a defender, either to find a path to the basket or to whip or wrap a pass to a teammate. She had just turned 37, but she could still command a game from her spot in the backcourt. When a

WNBA All-Star team featuring Lisa Leslie and Sheryl Swoopes had recently stopped off in São Paulo, Paula led Osasco from 17 points behind to win.

Hortência and Paula, *percussionista* and *cuicista*, embodied and defined Brazilian women's basketball—*carnaval* below the rim.

To leave São Paulo by car is to suspect that you'll never leave São Paulo. The cab ride to the suburb of Santo André took almost an hour, and we passed stand after stand of Brazil's urban weed, the *apartmentus altius*. I was bound for the Ginásio Pedro dell'Antonia, the home arena of Arcor Santo André, whose star, Janeth, also played for the Brazilian national team, as well as for the WNBA champion Houston Comets. Arcor stood atop the standings at 4-0, level with its opponent that evening, Hortência's Paraná Basquete Clube.

Brazil was in such economic chaos that, only a few weeks earlier, no one knew whether there would even be a women's league season. Hortência had been placing two dozen calls a day, trying to line up a sponsor for her defending champions after her patron at Fluminense bailed out. But in typically Brazilian fashion, everything was cobbled together just in time for opening night. The government of the southern state of Paraná finally signed on to underwrite Hortência's team for four years. In return, she agreed to lead an initiative to teach the fundamentals of the game to 3,000 local boys and girls.

Hortência was born Hortência Maria de Fátima Marcari in 1959 to parents who worked as subsistence farmers. Unlike the Philippines, Brazil isn't blessed with a basket around every corner, and shortly after she began to play, at age 13, Hortência nearly quit because she couldn't afford the bus fare to practice. But through an "adopt-an-athlete" program set up by the local government she received assistance from a bicycle factory, and quickly hinted at such promise that by age 15 she won a place on the national team.

Two years after that, Tennessee coach Pat Summitt tried to lure her to Knoxville. Hortência chose to sign to play professionally instead, and soon she was making $5,000 a month. In 1987 she actually scored 124 points in a game. But like Brazilian ballplayers of both sexes, she cared little for defense, and in 1988 she let her guard down even for the Brazilian edition of *Playboy*. That appearance and others, plus royalties from a Hortência doll, helped push her annual income into the six figures. It seemed that every year she led the league in scoring and the national team to some international honor—reminders that *hortência* is Portuguese for a perennial, the flowering hydrangea. "I feel sorry for any man who falls in love with me," she said in the mid-1980s, at the peak of her career. "I'm not ready for long relationships." But a few years later she married José Victor Oliva, a São Paulo club owner and restaurateur known locally as "King of the Night." She was the most celebrated and accomplished female athlete in Brazil, and Pelé was José's best man at the wedding.

Hortência's valedictory was to have been the 1994 Women's World Championships in Australia. There she averaged more than 27 points a game during Brazil's march to the gold medal, which included a 110–107 defeat of the favored Americans in the semifinals. Then she retired, and in late 1995 had a son, João Victor, by cesarean section. But in the spring of 1996, only four months after her son's birth, she stunned and delighted the country by rejoining the team for one last stand, at the Atlanta Olympics, where she helped lead Brazil to a silver. Now she had moved into the front office with no regrets.

I recognized Hortência the moment I stepped into the *ginásio*. She stood by her team on one sideline, turned out entirely in black: scoop-neck tricot, slacks, open-toed platform heels. Her ensemble threw a fall of bottle-blond hair and cantilevered cheekbones in brilliant relief. When she moved, the stickstrokes of the *bateria* still seemed to sound with every step.

As soon as the game began I could tell I was in an entirely new province of the country of basketball. Play featured none of the grinding on the blocks that marked the WNBA. The action raced and flowed as the two male referees, overweight and out of shape, strained to keep up. For all the movement, there was very little contact, only penetration and passing, dervishing and shooting. A televised soccer game accounted for the late arrival of the crowd, but by the middle of the first half a knot of Arcor rowdies, all male, had gathered in the stands. They seemed to be there for no purpose but to haze Hortência. They launched into a lewd chant that went something like, *Bada bada bing! Bada bada boo! Hor-tên-ci-a! Hor-tên-ci-a! Fuck! Fuck! You!*

Hortência gave no sign that she heard a word. She scowled at calls. She floated down to the end of the bench to offer advice to a young player. Equal parts corporate woman and mother hen, she appeared as dedicated to her players as she had been to wheeling and dealing to assemble them. "If the only sponsor she could find was in the Amazon," a writer along press row told me, "she'd move her team to the Amazon."

The two teams were uncommonly well-matched, and neither could open a gap on the other. Midway through the second half a player hit the floor and left behind a skid mark of sweat. A mop patrol rushed out at the next dead ball, touching off a scene I'd never witnessed at a men's game: a star player from each side—Janeth and Paraná's Marta, who played center on the national team—acting as forewomen, making sure the custodial staff didn't miss a spot.

With the score tied at 65 and the game in its final seconds, Paraná's two frontcourt stars, Marta and Vicki Bullett, the WNBA veteran and former center at Maryland, each took a hammering under the basket, to no call. Hortência appealed in vain to the scorer's table, but the game moved into overtime.

Janeth had been the most effective player on the floor all night, and several minutes into the extra period, with the game tied at 69, she and Arcor took charge. She stripped the Paraná point guard of the ball and sailed in for a layup. After a front-the-post pirouette that led to another steal, she came upcourt, stared down a defender on the left wing, then spun along the baseline for another layup. The game turned on those two plays, and Arcor went on to win easily, 84–72.

I found Janeth afterward in a tunnel under the stands. She was a short-waisted collection of long and supple limbs—built, more than any other Brazilian woman ballplayer I'd seen, to explore vertical space. She spoke English honed during two years as a seasonal laborer for the Comets.

"I like basketball because normally you don't know what you're going to do," she said. "You just do what comes into your mind."

Her spin along the baseline during the overtime, I suggested, was an NBA move. She laughed. "Well, it was at least a WNBA move. But to me, you know, basketball has just one language."

I hurried off to find Hortência before she could leave the floor, and came across her by the bench. Her eyes still flared with an intensity that left me to imagine what it would have been like to face her in her prime.

"I'm not happy," she said. "I think my team is better even though we lost tonight. The problem is 'the laughing blood.'"

The laughing blood, Hortência explained, is an insouciance that somehow keeps a loss from mattering too much. But the phrase also fit everything I'd seen of Brazilian women's basketball so far. It fit the movement. It fit the creativity. It fit the blithe spirit that caused hips to sway to the *bateria* of the dribble, or a move to begin with the jab step of the *cuica*—the attitude that conditioned the body, as Janeth had said, to "just do what comes into your mind."

I awoke the next day to sheets of rain. These were "the waters of March" made famous by bossa nova crooner Tom Jobim. I made my way to the headquarters of the city's leading newspaper, *Folha de São Paulo,* and rode the elevator to the belvedere terrace. There I strained to hear my hosts—Melk Filho, *Folha*'s sports editor, and basketball reporter Luis Curro—over the rain as it pelted a drumbeat of its own on the sunroof over our heads.

"Brazilians are different," Melk was saying. "We appreciate sport as a magical activity, and we like to see a beautiful game.

It's just a cultural characteristic. Hortência and Paula play this way—very offensive oriented, very acrobatic. But because they play to entertain people, not for victory, they don't necessarily win."

Sometimes the laughing blood ran serious, as it had in the spring of 1994, when the Brazilian women won that world title in Australia. At the time, the country was looking ahead to soccer's World Cup, and the basketball final aired live at four in the morning, while most Brazilians slept. But after fans had a chance to appraise what Hortência, Paula, and Janeth had accomplished, the popularity of the women's game reached its crest.

Brazilian women excelled at soccer and volleyball, too. But soccer was still regarded as a male preserve. "A father gives a soccer ball to his son and a basketball to his daughter," Luis said. As for volleyball, Melk added, "Basketball is much more natural to Brazilians. Volleyball is mathematical, with sharp angles and set plays. In basketball, every play is different from the one before, and you can see Brazil in this. It's natural for Brazilian players to be creative. When they are young, the peer pressure is not to be effective or strong or even intelligent—only creative. You have to succeed, yes. You have to earn money. But *you* define the way you do it. You have a personal style."

Undergirding this cult of personal style was the *apelido*, or "handle." Rosters at the games I went to listed the *apelido* right alongside the *nome*. The *apelido* was what made Pelé Pelé, rather than Edson Arantes do Nascimento; the president of the Brazilian Basketball Confederation, Gerasime Bozikis, simply Grego, or the Greek; and the finest male basketball player in Brazilian history, Oscar Schmidt, Oscar, plain and simple. These mononyms conferred a cartoon-character recognizability on whoever went by them, which in turn made for easy entrée into the popular culture. Brazilians had such a propensity for personification that they referred to jogging as "Cooper," after an American running guru who, though unknown to me, apparently popularized the activity in their country.

And so the fascination with two people, Hortência and Paula, sustained women's basketball in Brazil. "There's too much chaos in the economy for teams to remain stable," Melk said. "Sponsors and cities change all the time, so fans don't relate to teams. They can't. So they relate to players." But women's basketball was at great risk if new personalities failed to emerge to replace Hortência and Paula. And doubts nagged over who would. Paula had a teammate with BCN Osasco, a guard named Claudinha, who shot a reliable three-pointer and, if she seized a step's advantage, always seemed to get to the basket. She also had a great alternate *apelido*: Furacão, the Hurricane. But though she was 24, she hadn't yet penetrated the public's imagination. Janeth had more of a following, but she hadn't joined the ranks of Hortência and Paula, and she was already 30. As I'd seen during the over-time in Santo André, she was as likely to score in ruthless, WNBA fashion as with the flamboyance the Brazilian public insisted upon. Fans watched the WNBA telecasts from the States, baffled and angry that the Houston coach, Van Chan-cellor, wouldn't let Janeth play a beautiful game. She had been the leading scorer at the 1994 Worlds, and—imagine!—the Comets used her as a defensive specialist.

The great obstacle facing the Brazilian national team during the age of Hortência and Paula, my hosts explained, was an aversion to defense. Defense isn't liberated movement. It's pre-scribed movement, dictated by the initiative of the woman you're marking, and the Brazilian women resisted playing it. Only under a coach named Maria Helena Cardoso, who had studied in the U.S., did the Brazilian women prove that they could play defense. They won the gold in the 1991 Pan Amer-ican Games in Havana, defeating the host Cubans after Car-doso pulled off the equivalent of teaching fish to ski.

Shortly before the 1994 Worlds, the Brazilian confederation replaced Cardoso with a man named Miguel Angelo Luz. Luz was less a basketball technician than a sort of psychological medicine man, retained to address the team's new problem: the relationship between its two stars. Their rivalry, stoked by the domestic *campeonato*, would persist even after Hortência and Paula joined each other on the national team. Hortência was the diva who would meddle in the selection process; Paula, who had fielded an identical invitation from *Playboy* and pointedly told the magazine no, cultivated an image of her own. She could be headstrong and contrarian, not the kind of clone of themselves that most coaches prefer at point guard. As Luis put it, "Paula wouldn't pass to Hortência. And Hortência wouldn't pass to anybody."

Somehow, Luz cajoled Hortência and Paula into sharing the ball. In Australia, the ball moved so well that Brazil shot 65 percent in its semifinal defeat of the Americans. Devotees of *futebol* would be loath to admit it, but the women's world title in the spring of 1994 foreshadowed how the Brazilian men would win their soccer World Cup several months later: by scaling back everyone's individual freedom just enough so the team could cohere.

My hosts and I took the elevator down from the terrace. I wondered how those chauvinists at McKenzie College in 1896 would have reacted if told that, a century later, a team of Brazilian sportswomen playing a "girls' game" would give Brazil's greatest male heroes an athletic object lesson. And I bade Melk and Luis good-bye.

"In a few minutes," Luis said, "you'll see cars floating in the streets."

I thought he was joking. But *paulistanos* live on what's essentially a slab of concrete with little parkland. When it rains, the city center becomes a huge catchbasin. We were in the midst of a storm so biblical, I'd learn from that night's news, that even then 60 cars and buses were being trapped in a highway tunnel, where two people lost their lives. I stepped from the lobby of the *Folha* building onto the sidewalk to find water moving everywhere: in lateral torrents in the street; in vertical lashes from the sky.

Either the São Paulo suburb of Osasco had been spared the worst of the downpour, or not even a flood could cancel a game involving both Hortência and Paula. That evening's matchup between Paraná and BCN Osasco went off as scheduled.

I arrived at the Ginásio Geodesico to find every member of the Osasco team turned out in a synthetic unitard uniform. Paula—officially, Maria Paula Gonçalves da Silva—made as distinct a first impression as Hortência had. Her mononym graced her back. She wore a white headband embroidered with "Magic Paula" in blue script. The ensemble made her look like a very serious aerobics instructor.

She intended to play only one more season after this, but from what I could tell she was far from the end of her career. Despite the lingering effects of a shoulder injury, which limited her to 31 minutes of play, Paula scored 23 points. She sank half of the six three-point shots she took, and all but two of her nine two-pointers, while adding five rebounds and an equal number of assists. She showed the exuberance of someone 20 years younger, unfettering her emotions after each successful three by throwing up both hands and turning herself about. At times she played literally with one-handed nonchalance. Once she retrieved a rebound and, in one seamless motion, hurled an outlet pass downcourt to a teammate for a layup. Twice she drove the lane and scored without using her off hand. I was watching someone play guard the way Willie Mays played centerfield.

Like the teams I'd seen two nights earlier, Osasco roamed far from Clara Baer's misreading of Doc Naismith's rules. Paula and Co. built a lead by fast-breaking on offense and pressing on defense; Paraná could do nothing right, but its errors, too, were ones of haste. Marta, the 6'3" center whose size should have kept her in the low post, launched hurried three-pointers early in several possessions, and midway through the first half the home team led by 20. Soon the Osasco fans were serenading Hortência with the same obscene cheer I'd heard in Santo André, only here many more spectators joined in, little girls included. On the floor and in the stands, women's basketball in Brazil was a thoroughly uncorseted game.

After Osasco's 97–71 victory, the mononymous matriarchs

crossed and quickly shook hands, acknowledging each other just as Melk and Luis told me they would—only as much as they had to.

At the very first collegiate women's game, at Smith College in Northampton, Massachusetts, in 1893, men weren't allowed to watch because the contestants wore bloomers. When I found Paula on the floor, she was in the midst of peeling off her unitard. Under one basket, wearing the Lycra sports bra and bicycle shorts that made up the foundation of her habillement, she invited me to pose my questions.

I did not ask Paula whether she loved the game, for what I'd seen tonight made the answer clear. But I wondered exactly what about the game she loved. She answered as she played, in exclamatory bursts. "The show! I love the show! And to assist! And the three-point shot!"

If she regarded herself as a role model, it was for all humanity. "The sex of the person does not matter. You have to believe in your own power to *do!*"

Suddenly we were interrupted by a nearby commotion. Perhaps a dozen fans were straining over a railing, imploring Paula to come over to sign autographs. Most were female teenyboppers, but a few young men in their twenties were sprinkled among them, including a scruffy guy with a week's worth of growth on his jowls and a cigarette hanging from his lips.

Paula obliged each, but her attentions only touched off more squeals. Soon her fans broke into a chant that I couldn't make out, but which they carried on with great lust and delight. It broke into six sharp syllables, followed by two beats of "Oooh! Aaah!"—*Bah! Ba-ba-ba Bah! Bah! Oooh! Aaah!* They rocked and swayed and clapped their hands. Then, suddenly, they swung around, all of them, and assumed a deep crouch. Never losing eye contact with the object of their affection, still chanting their chant, they began grinding their rear ends slowly, lasciviously, regarding Paula from over their shoulders, grinning all the while.

They had met her curtain call with a booty call. Paula smiled fleetingly and turned quickly away. I asked her what they were saying.

"They say, 'Paula is my love.'"

To my mild surprise, she said this sheepishly. But then I noticed the most extraordinary thing. Paula was blushing. Apparently, even in Brazil, there are limits to where some will let their imaginations take them.

I soon left these Dionysian goddesses for a sort of hardcourt Apollo, the most cerebral of ballplayers, a man who had devoted his life after basketball to government—to the notion that we can't just do what comes into our minds.

TWENTY

Des Moines

Unguarded Moments

On Grafton Street in Dublin, I'd spotted a mini-hoop mounted on a busker's guitar case so passersby could slam-dunk their spare change. In Beijing I'd found *Slam* stocked at the state-run Friendship Store. Across the Rio Grande from El Paso, I'd stumbled across a Mexican betting parlor where I could get down 10 bucks on a Princeton game. Each told me something about basketball's reach and touch. But so in its own way did a presidential candidate's garment bag, slumped against the doorway of a hotel coffee shop in Des Moines.

Bill Bradley was never someone we would have to elect president. He was simply going to ascend to the White House— just materialize there one day to throw a hoop up on the tennis court by the South Lawn and start running the country. Or that's what I'd believed, from almost as far back as that night my parents sent me to bed before Princeton took on Michigan and Cazzie Russell. Bradley had made himself an All-America by practicing for hours at a time, shooting with weights in his shoes and dribbling with blinkers on his eyes, and surely that was the kind of industry and dedication we wanted our leaders to have. Surely, too, the way his New York Knicks teams won their NBA championships—cohesively, always mindful of a greater goal—was the way we wanted our country to function.

Like others in a cohort of mostly white males born in the 1950s, I was raised on that myth. In 1971 I sent Bradley, care of the Knicks, an 8-by-10 glossy photo with a fan letter asking him to sign it. Today it would be unthinkable to expect a professional athlete to reply. But of course the photo came back, "To Alex, best wishes." Why wouldn't it? Considerateness was part of Bradley's portfolio of virtues, along with a determination to work hard, in school and on his game. Sure, he had natural talent and intuitive gifts, one of which was enshrined in the title of the book based on that *New Yorker* profile of him at Princeton, which became John McPhee's *A Sense of Where You Are*. But he was also "driven to excel by some deep, unsurveyed urge," as he put it in his political memoir, *Time Present, Time Past*. Over the years, comparing notes with generational peers, I was astonished at how many also regarded Bradley as the lodestar of their youth. Follow his lead and we too could become college players, All-Americas, Rhodes Scholars, Olympic gold medalists, NBA champions, U.S. senators— presidents, even. After that signed photo showed up in the mail, I worked harder in school, harder on my game.

"In 25 years or so our Presidents are going to have to be better than ever," a sportswriter wrote while Bradley was still in college. "It's nice to know that Bill Bradley will be available." Well, a quarter century passed, and in 1988 Bradley, by then representing New Jersey in the Senate, chose not to make himself available. Four years later he declined again. But finally he was mounting a long-shot bid to wrest the Democratic nomination from Vice President Al Gore. So after more than six months of plying the basketball road, I hit the campaign trail.

I left behind the waters of March for March Madness, arriving in Des Moines the morning after Iowa had lost to Connecticut in the NCAA tournament. The pages of the *Des Moines Register* were hung with crepe. But if you cracked open the paper, you could find early reports on the Iowa caucuses, which lay eight months off. Bradley was in town for a range of political events, including a round of flesh-pressing at the boys' state high school tournament.

It was odd to see Bradley embracing the game again. Upon first arriving in Washington he had shunned it. He was determined to establish his legislative bona fides, and the only basketball in his office was cut in half and used as a planter. "I don't want to end up as just Old Satin Shorts Bradley," he had said as an undergraduate. (It was the early sixties; people talked that way then.) He worked hard to make sure he didn't.

But his presidential campaign was as much made for ESPN as for C-SPAN. He referred to his exploratory committee as "training camp" and told gatherings that he was taking his shot now because "I'm at the top of my game." Phil Jackson, a teammate with the Knicks, was sharing with Bradley's field staff his "team circle" philosophy of organization. The candidate, who had positioned himself as a sort of b-ball William Bennett by writing a book of hoop homilies called *Values of the Game*, was now counting on the value of the game. "Basketball is like a language," he liked to say. "Not just words, but a deep, common experience many American men and women have had. It's not that different from the military, where there's also a high degree of cooperation and camaraderie."

Bradley also liked to tell of advice he heeded as a young player, a sentiment that evoked both Horatio Alger and John Calvin, and called to mind the Ahab-and-the-whale relationship between Magic and Larry: "If you're not practicing, remember: Somebody, somewhere is practicing. And if you two meet, given roughly equal ability, he's going to win."

Bradley had heard this as a 14-year-old basketball camper from St. Louis Hawks star (Easy) Ed Macauley. I'd been exactly the same age when Bradley's autographed photo showed up in the mail. By then I already knew Macauley's words, for I'd read them in *A Sense of Where You Are*. But the appearance of that photo only amplified their effect.

The Des Moines skyline has a blocky sameness that's relieved only by the swaybacked roof of Veterans Memorial Auditorium.

Stepping inside, I entered a scene that could have been yanked whole from Bradley's senior year at Crystal City (Missouri) High nearly four decades ago: stands full of people shaped by the generous bottomland of the Mississippi River basin; backboards of fan-shaped glass, just like those in the Crystal City gym; a state title game that would remain in doubt until the buzzer.

In the 1961 Missouri state tournament, Crystal City had lost the final by a point to University High of St. Louis. Here, with Bradley watching from alongside Iowa governor Tom Vilsack, Newell-Fonda High beat Des Moines Christian on a three-pointer slung through the net with a second to play. Bradley left his seat and headed not for the winners' locker room but for the losers'. At its threshold he found a senior from Des Moines Christian named Jon Moore.

The dozen points Moore had scored in the fourth quarter hadn't been enough. He had the damp hair and skewed clothes of someone who had showered and dressed hastily, and his eyes were edged in pink. "I know exactly how you feel," Bradley told him. "I was disappointed when we lost in the Final Four in college, too. It made winning an Olympic gold medal and an NBA title that much sweeter. Remember, this is just one stop along the road."

Moore was inconsolable. But of the many politicians who claim to "feel your pain," I couldn't imagine one having done so with more credibility.

Following Bradley around for the rest of that evening and the following day, I was struck by his ease in motion. He had made his reputation as a Knick with constant movement. He wrote an NBA road book called *Life on the Run*. He opened his political memoir by declaring, "I have always preferred moving to sitting still." As a senator he once made three round-trips between his home state and Washington in a single day. There's one verb central to electoral politics, and none was better suited to this candidate, running for president.

The next morning I watched him pass through the lobby of the Fort Des Moines Hotel, and that's where he flung his gar-

ment bag on the floor outside the coffee shop and ducked inside
to grab breakfast. What kind of person left baggage unattended
outside a restaurant in a big-city hotel? A trusting one, probably. An independent one, certainly. And an unencumbered
one, whose baggage, literally and metaphorically, didn't amount
to much.

We set out in a couple of vans for a roundelay of appearances.
At each gathering he'd say much the same thing: "I grew up in
a town of 3,492 people. There were 96 in my high school class
and one stoplight in town." He knew it was time to run one
morning when he "looked in the mirror." Again and again, he
invited people to "Tell me your stories."

In Indianola, a half hour south of Des Moines, a long strip
of fast-food franchises dissolved quickly into fallow cornfields.
A man at a Country Kitchen took Bradley up on the offer to
share his story. "Not too many years back, *I* looked in the
mirror," he said. "Decided to run for school board. Wound up
getting the fewest votes of anyone, ever."

The room broke out in laughter.

"That reminds me of a story about Adlai Stevenson,"
Bradley said, launching into a tale about the famously idealistic
and unsuccessful Democratic presidential candidate. "A woman
ran up to him and said, 'Mr. Stevenson, you have the votes of all
the thinking people of this country!'

"'That's nice,' he replied. 'But I need a majority.'"

When he met with these small groups, Bradley's damn-the-
charisma style must have reminded older voters that his surname was perilously close to "Adlai." "I don't know" stood in
just fine for an answer. For someone legendary for his periph-
eral vision, he had a remarkably focused gaze. He advanced
ambitious proposals, and his wonkish message found a stylistic
match in his loping gait, sloping shoulders, and hands that were
as likely to be found stuffed in his pockets as searching out
others to clasp. For now he had only a scatter of staff and no
Secret Service agents in tow—in other words, many unguarded
moments.

Most political handlers live in fear of what their candidate might say in an unguarded moment. But Bradley was trying to invert the conventional wisdom and make it work for him in the unmediated political environment of a state like Iowa, where candidates tried to sell themselves to voters at retail. He was trying to prove anew what old opponents had learned the hard way: Leave him in an unguarded moment and he'll make you pay.

If the campaign could remain nothing but a succession of these intimate encounters, how could Bradley fail to win? Like most good ballplayers, he was an ensemblist who played best in a small group. But there came a time in presidential politics when, no matter how hard you worked to spring yourself free, no matter how many cuts you made and how many screens were set on your behalf, the cameras and the crowds double-teamed you.

A basketball team is like most human communities. It requires that freedom and responsibility be traded off in turn. If government and the game held out any lessons for each other, Bradley seemed as likely as anyone to know. After all, he credited basketball with influencing his approach to public life. The game had exposed him to every part of the country and every segment of the electorate. It had sent him overseas. It had informed his thinking about race relations. Even if his beliefs couldn't be traced to his time spent in the NBA, many resonated with the teamwork people associated with that era, when the Knicks were hailed as utopians in underwear. Perhaps because of the way young men like me had put him on a pedestal, he had spent time ruminating on how we choose and idolize our heroes and leaders. He believed we too often anointed them for the wrong reasons, and then expected too much of them—often to avoid accepting responsibility ourselves.

It's odd that Bradley is from Crystal City, a town that took its name from an old plate glass factory, because he could be notoriously opaque in interviews. In fact, he struck me as less a window than a mirror, often throwing questions back at those who posed them. It's a tactic surely learned in the locker room, where questions can be inane and invasive. But in a couple of brief opportunities—in a van between campaign stops and in a hotel restaurant—I tried to tease a few answers from him just the same. I asked him if there were any way basketball could provide a template for society.

Society, Bradley believes, is a three-legged stool. Individuals and government make up two of those legs, and a healthy tension exists between them—between rights and freedom on the one hand, and order and obligations on the other. But society wobbles without a strong third leg. Bradley calls this leg "civil society," and he includes in it community-based, nongovernmental institutions—everything from churches and synagogues to schools, PTAs, Little Leagues, and Boys and Girls Clubs. Through these third-leg institutions, citizens practice not government but governance. They give to one another without expecting anything in return. But civil society embodies a happy paradox, because citizens active in it in fact reap all sorts of returns. The model might be applied to basketball, Bradley told me, "If we think of a team as society." You subjugate your own interests to those of the team to win games and, eventually, championships. The pass you make may seem momentarily unselfish. But how unselfish is it, really, if it leads to a basket that winds up putting a championship ring on your own finger?

Bradley likes to quote a social philosopher he admires, a Canadian named John Ralston Saul: "Individual rights are a protection from society. But for those rights to have any meaning requires one to fulfill his or her obligation to society." To me he emphasized the prepositions: "*from* society" and "*to* society." Consider a basketball team. A coach couldn't call every play from the sidelines, nor could players hope to reach their potential as a band of freelancers. So a coach (government) and his players (individuals) negotiated the sharing of power to best serve their common goal—winning (the hoops equivalent of peace and prosperity).

But sometimes even basketball needed that third leg. Bradley liked to point out how Phil Jackson handled the aftermath of a Chicago Bulls playoff game in 1994, in which Scottie Pippen had refused Jackson's orders to enter the lineup in the game's decisive moments. Acting quickly, wisely, and firmly—presidentially, you might say—the coach walked into the locker room and told his players he imagined they had something to say to Pippen. And he left. The broadside Pippen received from his teammates that day was much more effective than anything Jackson could have said, and Pippen apologized. This wasn't an example of a coach governing a team, but of a coach letting a team practice governance. And evidence that the game has its own civil ethic.

Bradley liked to ride another political hobbyhorse with ramifications for hoops. Again and again through American history, politicians have fixed on something to demonize and urge people to unite against. Always, the pols promised good times ahead if only this one last enemy—gold-standard advocates, Communists, big business, Catholics—were subdued. "[We] can scurry around looking for the enemy, foreign or domestic," Bradley writes in his memoir, "Or [we] can improve what we have by moving toward a more mature polity."

Macauley's exhortations channeled through Bradley's photo couldn't hector me into becoming good enough to play for Princeton. But two decades later I'd been thrilled to watch the team at Bradley's alma mater put into practice a kind of basketball version of this "more mature polity." Princeton hadn't so much played its opponents during the 1997–98 season. The Tigers had simply played the game.

I would soon leave the Bradley campaign to return to Asia. But I couldn't quickly chase from my head the image of that unattended garment bag.

Bradley had grown up an only child. As a 12-year-old he made a diagram of what his bomb shelter would look like—where he'd put his cot, his favorite books, his favorite foods, his basketball. Whether slipping into the high school gym to shoot alone the morning after a loss, or outstripping his Princeton teammates with his bountiful ability, Bradley had an apartness to him that persisted even after he joined the NBA. Loneliness was his companion on the road, and no white player in the league seemed quite so white. I remember thumbing through a yearbook from Philadelphia's Charles Baker League, where Bradley played over one summer, and coming across a page that seemed to underscore how oddly this small-town midwestern banker's son fit into a largely black world: One picture featured a point guard in full dervish. Another showed a power forward bogarting under the boards. Beneath them, in a tiny photo at the bottom of the page, was the future senator from New Jersey, his shoulders draped with a towel, and a caption that read, "Bill Bradley, on the bench."

Basketball rewards another lopsided ratio besides that one I'd come across in Brazil, of many lateral movements to a few vertical ones. This other ratio held the formula for Bradley's success: huge swaths of time spent alone, honing one's dribble and shot, so one could better serve, and integrate oneself into, the group come game time. Bradley had taken this basketball style—dogged, solitary preparation followed by surgical execution—and transferred it whole to electoral politics. And electoral politics wasn't very welcoming of it. The people and the punditocracy seemed to want their pols to be garrulous go-alongs who answered even those inane and invasive questions. In the end, nuanced responses borne of thoughtful preparation mattered far less than the quick-cutting sound bite and the here and now, the latest tracking polls and attack ads, the last pumped hand and slapped back. His plodding earnestness made Bradley admirable, and left so many members of my generation believing he would simply ascend. It was also, I thought, what would make him so hard to elect, even if the country of basketball would be pleased to swear him in as its chief executive.

In a fanciful moment I imagined Bradley convening his cabinet: a secretary of rebounding instead of labor; a secretary of passing instead of transportation; a secretary of *dee*-fense instead of defense. But the skill Bradley had mastered in his peculiarly Naismithian way, the shot, didn't submit to technocratic assignment. As I'd learned from Kareem in Whiteriver, it was too non-Western, too personal. Of course, that exoticism only heightened its allure. So with basketball's essential act on my mind I headed for the Far East, in search of answers to the game's lingering mysteries.

TWENTY-ONE

Japan

A Journey of a Thousand Miles, Begun with a Single Shot

Basketball is the most fleshly of games. It's played in close quarters by twisting, writhing people in skimpy clothing. With its projectile and receptacles, its successive buildups and climaxes, it's an awful lot like you-know-what.

But basketball also has a spiritual dimension beyond its Protestant missionary beginnings and the Calvinism Bill Bradley brought to it. Someone who has reeled off a string of baskets will say, "I was unconscious," as if he were following the Zen injunction to be mindful while suspending thought. As the ball makes its way hoopward there's something holistic in how it simultaneously spins backward and moves forward. When a shot finds its mark, yang (the ball—active, hot, light, heavenly, positive, male) and yin (the basket—receptive, cold, dark, earthly, negative, female) become one. A great master, once asked the most important word in Zen, could have been Marv Albert in his reply: "Yes!"

Zen Buddhists believe the world is in constant flux, and that human beings should therefore keep themselves open to the natural flow of life—should be prepared "to follow an arrow around a tree," as the koan goes. This may explain why a self-described Zen Christian, Bradley's buddy Phil Jackson, was uniquely equipped to coach that most crooked arrow of all,

Dennis Rodman. And it invites us to think of a basketball court as a glade of trees full of airborne arrows. Is it coincidence that Zen teachings tell us we should suppress the ego to achieve enlightenment, just as good teammates must? Or that so many basketball descriptives seem to be lifted from Heian texts, whether they're similes ("like snow on a bamboo leaf," former Laker coach Paul Westhead's phrase for the jump shot of one of his players, Jamaal Wilkes) or nicknames ("the Prince of Mid-Air," the handle of NBA journeyman Lloyd Free until he gave in to an insuperable ego and changed his name to World)? I'd read that the less force involved in launching a shot, the greater variety of arcs the basket is likely to accommodate. In addition to being a very welcome circumstance, this is also a classically Zen one. Imagine an act whose most artful practice is also its most effortless.

Back in the 1980s, curious about the relevance of Eastern thought to the game, I picked up a slim volume at a bookshop off London's Charing Cross Road. The copy on the jacket of *Enlightenment through the Art of Basketball* introduced the author as a former ballplayer from Osaka, someone who was "on the verge of international honours when he abandoned the competitive sport to devote himself to the practice of private basketball. Hirohide Ogawa's art of basketball is so completely clear and full of insight that the need to play basketball is superseded."

I liked to play. Frankly, sometimes I needed to, and I wasn't really interested in learning how to quash the urge. But I bought the book just the same, for Hirohide Ogawa seemed to be an interesting cat. He carried a basketball net around with him in public, and had a ready rejoinder when asked why: "The monk carries his belongings in an empty rice bowl. I carry mine in an empty net." During festivals he would make his way down to the sea, where he'd bury a hoop in the sand. "After the ebb tide retreats, the flow tide scores," he explained. "If even the ocean can understand the rules of basketball, and play diligently without failure or excuses, why cannot we, who have the inestimable advantage of a ball?"

Over the years of dipping into *Enlightenment*, I'd grown

grateful for Ogawa's Socratic interlocutor, one S. Yanagi of Sapporo, a pupil who had faithfully recorded the riddles and aphorisms of the master as he spun them out. Ogawa's pronouncements were fresh, wise, sometimes impish. He likened the net to haiku: Both were empty at each end. He tossed off aperçus like, "The player is the object with which the ball occasionally permits itself to play." And he issued this dismissal of competitive basketball: "To live at the expense of another is the habit of a beast of prey. Do not imitate the tiger unless you wish to be hunted in your turn."

Basketball now covered a huge swath of geographic ground. Why wouldn't it cover just as much spiritual territory? If there were a chance that the ultimate truth about a game sprung from the mind of a Presbyterian preacher rested with a Zen master on the other side of the globe, I would go to Japan, to take my place at his knee.

There was only one problem. No one at the Japanese Basketball Association had heard of Hirohide Ogawa. There seemed to be no Mr. Yanagi, either, in Sapporo or anywhere else, at least not with any standing in the Japanese basketball community. I contacted the NBA's Tokyo branch office. Nothing. I got in touch with Terry Rhoads's counterpart at Nike Japan. Nothing again. Every time I recited the title of Ogawa's book, I felt a little more self-conscious. No one was so impolite as to tell me I was nuts. But I had an increasing sense of my own ridiculousness.

Desperate, on the eve of my departure for Japan I made one last pass at the elusive wise man. I placed a call to his British publisher. A man answered in crisp Oxbridgese.

"Hi, is this Oleander Press?"

"Speaking."

"Yes, I'd like to find someone who can tell me about a book called *Enlightenment through the Art of Basketball*."

"Speaking."

"Would there be any way I might be put in touch with the book's author?"

The voice never lost its snappy tenor: "Speaking."

Suddenly everything became clear—why *Enlightenment* used malaprop Anglicisms like "touch judge" for referee and "the penalty spot" for the free-throw line; why no one in Japan had heard of this putative onetime candidate for its national team.

"Private basketball" indeed. Apparently, the book's need to have an author had been superseded. I thanked the man for contributing to my enlightenment and hung up.

I had been on the business end of the perfect Zen joke. I felt like Joshu, the eighth-century novice who, upon asking his master how best to pursue the truth, was told, "If you move toward it, it moves away."

I went ahead with my trip anyway. In Japan I had expected to see pebblegrain leather in the raked gravel of a Zen garden; to see a finger roll in the open palm of a supplicant making an offering in a shrine; to see parquet in the crosshatch of tatami mats lining the floor of a room. Instead, despite all my best efforts, I found myself lost in a bamboozling new country.

I quickly became the goggle-eyed mess that Tokyo can make of the first-time visitor. If the good folks who bring you The Sharper Image catalog were to design a theme park, this would be it. I had never seen so much gadgetry and celerity concentrated in one place. The public phones had modular ISDN jacks. A restaurant charged not by how much you ate, but how long you occupied a table. On the platform for boarding the *shinkansen,* the bullet train, seeing the markings that told embarking passengers exactly where to queue up, I marveled at how it was possible to titrate the flow of daily life to the last drop.

Such was my first sweeping gloss on the place. But within several days exceptions began to appear. I would turn a corner and find myself thrown suddenly from the chaotic into the contemplative. There'd be a garden. A shrine. Cherry trees, a pool, gravel. It was as if, after 40 minutes of running and pressing in a packed arena, I was suddenly lining up a free throw in an empty gym.

It took me a while to find my balance, but once I did, I decided to look up a woman named Sumiyo Iida. She agreed to meet me one morning at Tokyo Station, and together we took the commuter train to Kita-Urawa, a bedroom community an hour outside the city.

Sumiyo was in her early thirties, slight, shy, quick with a giggle. A medallion of the Virgin Mary hung from her neck and cartoon amulets dangled from her cell phone. Friends called her Pipi, after the sound of the whistle she always seemed to be blowing a number of years back when she served as manager of Nippon Express, a team in Japan's top women's league.

We took a cab from the Kita-Urawa station along narrow lanes fringed with hedges. After 10 minutes we came upon a half-moon driveway. A church. Madonna statuary, a crucifix, the welcome of a hunchbacked friar.

Pipi had no light to shed on Zen and basketball. But she had been witness to a remarkable spiritual journey just the same, one in which basketball figured, but which ultimately left the game humbled. To tell the story of that journey, however, I should rewind—rewind back to the States.

When Shelly Pennefather was of this world, a basketball leaving her hands traced a path with a righteousness all its own. In 1986, trying to win attention for her shot, sports publicity officials at Villanova dressed Pennefather in a white tuxedo and posed her alongside a limousine in front of a theater marquee bearing her name. The stunt probably helped her win the Wade Trophy that season as the women's college player of the year, but her ability to shoot a basketball hardly required hype. Pennefather starred professionally for Pipi's Nippon Express team between 1987 and 1991, and if she had chosen to return for a fifth season she stood to earn $200,000, a sum that would have made her the most lavishly paid women's player in the world.

Her shot was a gift that induced wonder, prompted delight, sometimes touched off tears. Her brother Dick, a former player at Providence, once cajoled Shelly into tagging along for one of his men's league rec games. Down by a dozen at the half to a team that included six Division I collegians, little sister came off the bench to sink six three-pointers and lead Dick's team to victory. When Pennefather went to Las Vegas to accept the Wade, her hosts gave her $100 to spend on amusements at Circus Circus, so she cleaned out every basketball arcade game in the place and headed straight for the Strip, where she plied kids with the stuffed animals she'd just won. In one game during her senior season, she found Providence's best defender draped all over her. Still she made shot after shot, notwithstanding the long arms of her opponent, who finally took a seat on the bench, buried her head in a towel, and cried.

Curious about the legend of this woman and her shot, I'd reached a man named Don DiCarlo, who supervised the athletic facilities at Villanova. Over the years DiCarlo had studied the shots of countless Wildcats, male and female, and this is what he told me: "If my life depended on one 15-footer, I'd want Shelly to take it."

Backspin is like prayer, beseeching the goal to take mercy on its spherical supplicant. Pennefather was born with a double-jointed wrist that dropped lower than most, allowing her to lard up every shot she took with extra rotation. Her father, Mike, an air force colonel trained as a physicist, nurtured her gift. *Bear-claw with those fingers, babe, and keep that elbow in.* Most shooting coaches believe you should sight your shot from the side of your head, so as not to obscure your view of the hoop. Not Colonel Mike. *Point of release from that sweet spot, right above your eyes.* You finger the ball as a believer does a bead on a rosary. You shoot with faith.

Then one day in 1988, in a gym not far from where Pipi and I stood, Pennefather brought her hands together for one shot that transformed her life, altered the lives of her friends and family, and may be touching untold others in ways we can't fully fathom. From her fingers it came: the shot that led her to become Sister Rose Marie of the Queen of Angels, a cloistered Poor Clare nun.

The Colettine Poor Clares are one of the most austere orders in the Catholic Church. They owe their founding to Clare Favarone di Offreduccio, an 18-year-old Assisian who first heard St. Francis preach in 1212. He and his message so moved her that she abandoned her wealthy family to establish a community of "poor ladies" devoted to prayer and penance under the most limpid circumstances.

The cord that girds the habit of a Poor Clare is knotted four times, once for each of the vows she takes: poverty, chastity, obedience, and enclosure. A Poor Clare never sleeps more than four hours at a time, never eats more than one full meal a day, never sees friends or family more than twice a year and then only through a screen. She may not use telephones, TVs, or radios or avail herself of books, magazines, or newspapers, save religious ones; while she may read letters and look at pictures, she keeps neither, for that would violate her pledge to possess nothing. Her waking hours are governed by the Divine Office, a centuries-old liturgy of prayers, hymns, and chants, each tailored to a particular time of day. She sleeps fully garbed on a bed of straw and goes barefoot except when entering the courtyard of the cloister, where she may wear rustic sandals.

Unless a medical emergency befalls her, she will not leave the monastery (which in Sister Rose's case sits at the end of a cul-de-sac in suburban Alexandria, Virginia) until she utters her final words, which every Poor Clare hopes will be the same as her patroness: "Oh my God, I thank you for having created me." To be called to a life of sacrifice, to abjure worldly things, is the greatest blessing a Catholic can receive, and all that she forsakes serves to focus her heart, mind, and soul on God.

Where Doc Naismith's missionaries took basketball without, Sister Rose chose to bury the game somewhere deep inside herself. She would never again send a ball splashing into the net.

Yet only to those unversed in the catechism was this a waste. "The skills a girl may have acquired in the process of being educated . . . will be almost unfailingly put to good use in the cloister," writes Mother Mary Francis, P.C.C., in *A Right to Be Merry,* an account of life in a Poor Clare monastery. "If occasionally they are not, then they can be used in the most perfect sense of all: for a sacrifice."

When members of the Pennefather family come by the Poor Clare monastery every few weeks for Mass, they can see Sister Rose for several fleeting seconds as she takes communion at the Dutch door that separates the nuns' choir from the public chapel. For the rest of the day she is in complete enclosure. Because Sister Rose stands more than six feet and members of her family are similarly tall, the sisters have raised the barrier separating the chapel from the choir with several panels of frosted Plexiglas—panels known within the cloister as the Pennefather Clouds.

On June 6, 1997, just before the NBA launched the women's league that would have been pleased to lavish on Shelly Pennefather more wealth and fame, Sister Rose came to the Dutch door, where family and friends, sitting in the packed chapel, could see her. She had spent six years cloistered as a novice; now her petition was simple: "I ask that I may be joined in solemn vows as a spouse of Christ."

As her parents knelt beside Father John Hardon, an octogenarian priest who was once Mother Teresa's personal confessor, Sister Rose accepted a crown of thorns for her head and a band etched with a likeness of her Divine Bridegroom for her finger. Then, for only the second time since she entered the enclosure, members of her family were allowed to come to the altar and fix her with a hug. When she celebrates her vows in 22 years, they will be permitted another.

As at any wedding, well-wishers formed a postnuptial receiving line. The remembrance card Sister Rose slipped under the screen to everyone who came by included this passage from St. Paul: "But those things I used to consider gain I have now reappraised as loss in the light of Christ. . . . For his sake I have forfeited everything; I have accounted all else rubbish so that Christ may be my wealth and I may be in him."

What Sister Rose Marie consigned to the trash, her old friends wanted all the world to see. They weren't surprised that Shelly took the habit. At Villanova she would slip into the chapel every day for Mass. During her sophomore year she gave everyone on the team a scapular, the sacramental medallion worn around the neck to spare its wearer eternal fire. Only Shelly wore one during games, and every now and then she would catch a finger on its cord while launching a shot and come running back downcourt wearing a grin. Lisa Angelotti-Gedaka, one of her teammates, remembered, "We'd be like, 'You have to have an excuse, Shell, for the one time you miss all game.'"

They figured she would either marry a guy whose company she kept during those summers back from Japan, or become a nun. But a cloistered nun? That seemed at odds with all they knew of their teammate: the irresistible laugh; the gift for service that led her to start a basketball camp for girls and become a student teacher of math while in college; the self-deprecating sense of humor and soft-touch spirituality that left the crowd at the Big East banquet in tears each spring when Shelly inevitably picked up an award as something-or-other-of-the-year. Someone else could cut herself off from the world and pray round the clock; let Shell do what she was suited for, what God surely meant for her to do—teach and coach kids.

Her friends struggled with her choice. Upon hearing the plans of the teammate who had taught her how to box step and knew every line from *Casablanca*, Kathy Miller said, "I cried for a week." Angelotti-Gedaka broke down, too: "She said she'd been 'called.' I said, 'Well, did you have to answer the phone?'"

Their bewilderment was natural, but it betrayed a misunderstanding of how a contemplative community works. "You really can't do the cloister thing unless you're a healthy person," Father

John Stack, Villanova's dean of students, told me. "If you bring your problems with you, they'll just become problems for the community. Her decision was confounding to her friends because she was so well-adjusted and so much fun to be around. If they saw her as some weirdo, they wouldn't care if she went into a convent."

Indeed, without a sense of humor, writes Mother Mary Francis, "the enclosure can easily become a spiritual hothouse where every trifle marks a crisis, and pettiness grows into a cult. . . . A group of dour females with their jaws set grimly for 'perfection' and their nerves forever in a jangle would turn the cloister into a psychopathic ward."

Sister Rose's first letters conveyed a get-a-load-of-this giddiness at her new life. One dispatch told of the wheat biscuit, nuts, grapefruit, and few slices of cheese making up her first meal. *Hors d'oeuvres!* she thought, before realizing that no more food was forthcoming. Then came appeals to friends to pray for her, and an admission that she did indeed wonder what was passing her by. But several years in, her letters began to give off a calm, always overlaid with the lightness that friends recognized as her quintessence. Gradually her old teammates came to accept her claims of happiness, and each made do with the occasional letter, the rare visit, and memories caught in amber.

Former Villanova teammate Lynn Tighe remembered the time she brought to the dorm four huge bottles of Coke—two regular and, for her roommate, two diet. Soon Tighe discovered the two bottles of regular Coke were gone and asked Shelly what had become of them. "I decided," Pennefather said, "I'd start my diet tomorrow."

Kathy Miller kept a newspaper clipping with a picture taken after the game in which Pennefather scored her 2,000th point. Shelly had thrust the ball into Miller's hands and hid in the back of the group. The paper misidentified Miller, a walk-on, as the star.

Lisa Angelotti-Gedaka clung to the memory of a long conversation she and Pennefather had one night about sin, and how the very next day, in theology class, the instructor asked which of the seven deadlies was the deadliest. Never one to participate in class, here Angelotti-Gedaka shot up her hand and shouted out the answer—*"Pride!"*—before sprinting to the dorm to tell her friend how she had scored on a sweet Pennefather feed.

"She never made you feel she was better than you were," Karen Hargadon-Daly, another former teammate, told me. "But let's face reality. She was better than you were."

But not perfect. Having grown up in a strict home without TV, Pennefather went off to college eager to compensate. At Villanova she watched every old movie she could on Tighe's little set. One evening Tighe came back to the room exhausted and ready for bed, only to find Pennefather in her upper bunk, engrossed in some black-and-white classic.

"Shell, turn it off," she said.

"Just a few more minutes."

"I'm going to bed," said Tighe, collapsing into her bunk below.

"Okay, Lynn," Pennefather said a while later. "Movie's over. You can get the lights and the TV."

"No thanks, Shell. You can turn 'em off."

"That's okay, Lynn."

Lights and TV burned through the night before Tighe finally turned them off the next day, after Pennefather had left for class.

"Obedience is the hardest vow they take," Dick Pennefather explained to me. "Because pride is the toughest thing to overcome."

The contract with the Nippon Express team for the 1987–88 season, her first in Japan, called for Shelly to receive a handsome incentive bonus. But in a fashion both Japanese and Pennefatherian, the bonus wasn't to be paid for any individual accomplishment. In keeping with the Japanese concept of *wa*, or togetherness, Pennefather would collect an additional $25,000 only if the team won a certain number of games. She made a vow: If she earned the bonus, she would donate a month of her time the following summer to the Missionaries of Charity, Mother Teresa's order of nuns who work with the poorest of the poor. So it was that she sank a shot at the buzzer to win a game that put her on the path to the convent. A journey of a thousand miles began with a single shot.

Pennefather returned from Japan in the spring of 1988 determined to make good on her promise. Mother Teresa's nuns didn't ordinarily accept offers of help from civilians who happened by. So, as she went up and down the East Coast knocking on doors, Pennefather couldn't get a Missionary of Charity to take her seriously. "You could see the humor of God in this," Dick told me. "Here she had made her vow, and God was testing her ability to honor it."

Finally she found a community in Norristown, Pennsylvania, willing to let her work in its soup kitchen. She began overnighting at the convent, sometimes for weeks at a time, living something close to a life of poverty. When the abbess in Norristown fell ill, Mother Teresa herself paid a visit to the hospital. Seeing Pennefather bedside, she said, "It'll take a big sari to handle you!"

For two years Pennefather alternated a season in Japan with an off-season among the Missionaries of Charity. The money she was making for playing a game she loved was "insane," she told people at the time: "If I turned it down, I would seem ungrateful." Yet the circumstances in which she lived overseas plunged her deeper into her faith. Nippon Express sprinkled 14 games over a five-month season and devoted only a couple of hours a day to practice. Try as she did to fill out the hours—attending Mass daily, studying Japanese, teaching English to kids in her apartment complex—Saitama prefecture was a virtual cloister of its own.

During her off-season trips back to Virginia, where her family had settled in 1988, Pennefather befriended another likely postulant named Patricia Melody. The two would meet one morning a week at a Shoney's to talk of the stirrings each felt within. Melody suggested Pennefather get in touch with her spiritual adviser, Hardon, the Jesuit associate of Mother Teresa. Soon Pennefather had a reading list, and during her final season in Japan she took an Ignatian retreat, modeled after the teachings of St. Ignatius of Loyola: While leading the league in scoring, she forswore TV, movies, radio, and all idle exchange, pledging every spare hour to reading, meditating, and pondering the question of what God wanted for her. That year, too, she cracked open Mother Mary Francis's *A Right to Be Merry,* a gift from her sister Jean. Halfway into it she broke down and placed one of her now frequent calls to Hardon. He counseled her to pull back, to resist letting emotion rule any decision. But back in the U.S., Shelly's mother showed her a newspaper clipping about the Poor Clares in Alexandria, a short drive from her parents' new home in Manassas.

As stark as the life of a Poor Clare was, she had glimpsed a life even more dauntingly sacrificial in Norristown. So, early in the spring of 1991, she rang the bell at the Poor Clare monastery and said she was interested in joining. The Poor Clares get this all the time—another young woman having a bad day. Nevertheless, the portress asked who had sent her.

"Father John Hardon," she answered.

"It was as if someone asked you, 'Who says you can play basketball?'" Mike Pennefather told me before his death from cancer in June 1998. "And you could answer, 'John Wooden.'"

Her addition would make the community a group of 15, but nothing else about the place suggested basketball. "If ever there were someone who could give up the game, it would be Shelly, because it came so easily to her," Dick said. Yet for someone who used to nap on the office couch of her coach at Villanova, Harry Perretta, until an hour before tip-off, and who in the dining hall would load up on chocolate pudding first lest she run out of room for dessert, to make do with drastically smaller amounts of sleep and food—her two favorite things, according to everyone close to her—would be unimaginably tougher.

Pennefather's friend Patricia Melody went on to become Sister Maria Anna, a Franciscan nun and schoolteacher in New Jersey. I met her at Sister Rose's final vows, and she told me that during those talks at Shoney's the two had speculated on what each's cross to bear might be. "Shelly used to say hers would be a marshmallow. 'If I'm hungry, I can eat it,' she'd say. 'If I'm tired, I can sleep on it.' The life she chose is no marshmallow."

In the weeks before entering the monastery, Pennefather invited her friends to pick through her closets. She gave her brothers and her coach money with which to make down payments on houses. For family and friends she underwrote a spree of horseback riding, clothes shopping, and amusement-park visits, interspersed with forays to fancy restaurants in Georgetown. This time she really would be starting her diet tomorrow.

On June 8, 1991, Pennefather passed into the enclosure. She swapped a world that had dressed her in a white tux for one that would wrap her in the postulant's brown jumper. That Las Vegas hotel suite she enjoyed during Wade Trophy week, with its mirrored ceiling and bedside Jacuzzi, gave way to a cell without mirrors in which the simplest cold-water ablution is a luxury. Already she had given most of her trophies to her old high school, peeling away the engraved nameplates so they could be awarded anew; now all the baubles of her career would indeed be accounted rubbish.

A rationalist could find much that might have impelled this journey from a 20th-century world back to a 13th-century one. Pennefather had uprooted and adapted herself seven times by her senior year of high school. She was accustomed to the cocoon and rigors of base life; at every post there were both basketball and the rosary that her mother, Mary Jane, made sure the family said together every night. ("I taught 'em how to play," Mike told me. "My wife taught 'em how to pray.") To play for a Japanese sports club was to serve the company sponsoring it. At Nippon Express home games, employees dutifully filled the stands and sang the company anthem. Shelly already knew a hierarchical, patriarchal, and conformist life from the military and the church.

There's a geisha creed called "the five hearts," and she comported herself in accordance with it. A geisha has an obedient heart, to say, "Yes." She has an apologetic heart, to say, "I'm sorry." She has a modest heart, to credit others for any accomplishments. She has a voluntary heart, to say, "I will do it." And she has an appreciative heart, to say, "Thank you." At the end of each season the best way to get Shelly to return wasn't to sweeten her contract. "We would simply say, 'Shelly, we need you,'" Pipi would tell me. "And she would come back."

Shelly had always wanted to play the role that the star wasn't permitted to play. She wanted to be a cog in some larger scheme, to recede by spilling beyond herself. Surely that's one reason a vocation as one of 18,000 Poor Clares worldwide, all saying the Divine Office in their respective time zones, lured and comforted her.

Yet in the end, her friends always returned to something Pennefather told them shortly before she went into the monastery. For a long time she had wondered, and sometimes despaired, why more young Catholics didn't choose a life in the church. "Now I realize that a vocation isn't something you choose," she said. "A vocation is something you're called to do."

Show, don't tell: It is the solemn vow of the expository process. As the Poor Clare's vocation turns on penance and prayer, so the writer's does on this. That's why I wrote Sister Rose Marie, asking permission to quote from letters she had sent friends over the years: . . . *so readers could be shown, through your words, the gradually ascending arc of your spirituality since you joined the Poor Clares and the joy that abides in the cloister.*

But "show, don't tell" is a profane inversion to the cloistered religious. To them, there is faith in the telling, in the Gospels; to them, the show—not just the revelation of their physical selves, but all that is gaudy and worldly—only distracts, and ultimately passes from the earth. So Sister Rose chose to keep her voice to herself. In a reply numinous with the quiet of the cloister, she declined my request. My letter had reached her just as she was to go into retreat in advance of her solemn vows. Cells of pride still dwelled within her, she said, and she regarded my petition as a last temptation to seek the approbation of the world. She hoped her decision wouldn't be disappointing or inconvenient, but to participate would be to compromise the spirit of the vow of enclosure. That's why I've told her story without her consecrated voice.

But there is a felicity in that, for Shelly Pennefather lived the lay chapter of her life in the same spirit that Sister Rose sat out the pages of this book. She lived it ducking behind others at photo sessions, and giving away her basketball winnings, and shooting only because God had blessed her with a gift for doing so. Though the Italian word for Clare, *chiara*, means "bright," best that this Poor Clare be refracted through her teammates. Best that she be seen in the light of opponents who cried when she beat them, and cried when she accepted prizes for beating them, and still dissolve when recounting both. Best, too, that she be illuminated by a Japanese woman who sheds tears over a distance so vast that no amount of longing can bridge it.

A breeze fruited with jasmine buffeted us as we stood outside Kita-Urawa's Church of the Sacred Heart. I followed Pipi to our left, where we poked our heads into a small chapel with an austere interior of stained glass, wooden benches, and unpadded knee rests.

From the chapel we walked past a 7-Eleven, apartment blocks fronted with banks of vending machines, and a Royal Host coffee shop, a sort of Nipponese Shoney's. Young mothers holding parasols pushed strollers. Here was a Let's Kiosk; just beyond it a stadium housed Let's Urawa, the local soccer team. The land of *wa* had a national grammatical case, and it was the first-person plural.

After 15 minutes we arrived at the Nippon Express athletic complex. Except for Fridays, when she wouldn't eat meat, Shelly had taken every meal here, where her teammates were obliged to live. The church and the athletic complex staked out the poles of her world. Over four seasons, virtually every day, she shuttled to one or the other from her small apartment, which sat almost exactly in between.

The caretaker of the complex, an elderly woman, greeted Pipi excitedly and invited us in. She scurried off to fetch slippers, and we soon padded into a common area. There Pipi began paging through scrapbooks. A picture showed Shelly on skis, towering over her teammates. A magazine story about her modest initial contract ran under the indelicate headline BIG THIGHS, SMALL CHANGE. Another photo caught Shelly with her head swathed in a bandage. "She went swimming and banged her head on the bottom of a pool," Pipi said, smiling at the memory. "We had to fold her up to fit her into the ambulance."

Shelly's predecessor had been a former star at Long Beach State named Janet Davis. One day Davis simply vanished—just left a note that she was going out for a bite to eat and never came back. (Apparently, a boyfriend beckoned back home.) As a result, Pipi felt a responsibility to make Shelly feel as welcome as possible, to do anything to keep the new girl from running off. After practice, she'd tag along when Shelly went out for a late-night snack. On the road, she'd drive her to Mass. Over time, curious about what went on in these sanctuaries, she began to follow Shelly inside. "I found churches to be peaceful places," Pipi said. "I go every Sunday now, and Shelly is the reason. I want to understand the catechism. I don't know if I can commit to the Catholic Church for a lifetime. But I do want to study."

Taking a closer look at the medallion around Pipi's neck, I recognized the Guadalupe virgin, the patroness of the Alexandria monastery.

"There was so much I liked about Shelly. When she asked me out to eat, I was happy. When she didn't want to go out, I was unhappy. It was almost like having a lover."

After that last season in Japan, when Shelly signed up for a team that others couldn't just join, Pipi didn't quite know how to handle it. The mother abbess permitted her to visit shortly after Shelly entered the convent, but Pipi felt pressure and confusion during her allotted two hours. She laid her hand upon the screen and sobbed. Still, she tried to visit the U.S. at least once a year, and every December 12—both the feast day of Our Lady of Guadalupe and Sister Rose's birthday—she sent roses to the monastery. She even took a job that required a lengthy posting in Canada, primarily to be closer to her friend. But her next few visits also left her in tears.

The Pennefathers supported Pipi as best they could. They put her up and took her with them to Mass. Mary Jane Pennefather explained that even she found joy in the turn Shelly's life had taken, for her daughter was now closer to God. On the morning Sister Rose vowed to remain cloistered for the rest of her life, the Pennefathers sat with Pipi, comforting her as she watched from inside the monastery's chapel.

Sister Rose also tried to help. She found a book in Japanese about the order and sent it to her friend. And she got in touch with a community of Poor Clares in Kiryū, several hours north of Tokyo, to ask if they might help Pipi understand a cloistered community. The sisters invited her to their hilltop convent. Life there wasn't as strict as in Alexandria; ants had eaten away much of the screen through which the nuns spoke to their lay visitors. For two days the sisters took Pipi in, comforting and counseling her and giving her a bed. "It was very, very quiet," Pipi told me. "Especially at night. Even though it was pitch-dark, I felt very protected."

The sisters provided some solace. "They told me that God opens the door for people to meet people. That God had a mission for Shelly in Japan, and part of that mission was to find me. Still, I was sad, because there was a wall I couldn't breach."

Why did women on opposite sides of the globe dissolve at the thought of physical separation from Shelly Pennefather? As Pipi and I took the train back to Tokyo the question intrigued me almost as much as why someone would choose to renounce the world.

Pipi walked me back to my hotel, where we lingered in the lobby. "This is a day of happy memories for me," she said. "To see you and to talk of those days, it is a celebration of Sister Rose Marie."

Pipi began to break down, and I gave her a hug before she could flee back out to the street.

"If you see Sister Rose Marie, please, will you say hi?"

I promised to do so.

Back in my room I picked up *The Lady and the Monk,* Pico Iyer's delicately lined explication of Japan. In it he makes this point: Sometimes their sensibility can be so potently romantic that the Japanese wind up preferring the idea of something—its memory or promise—to the thing itself. This phenomenon, Iyer notes, finds expression in the language, where the Japanese characters for "love" and "grief" sound exactly the same. But I'd come across a third emotion that dwells at the intersection of those homonyms: longing. A loving grief, a grieving love—I tried to imagine how much more intensely felt both love and grief would be if the object of one's affection, like Lady Pipi's monk, were to withdraw from the world.

Meeting up with Pipi had illuminated both Shelly Pennefather and the country that helped spur her journey. But in Japan I'd misconnected, too. I'd found no basketball Zen master. So in my search for hoop truth there could be no intermediary. It was time to head for the hills, not far from where Buddha himself was born more than 25 centuries earlier. It was time to go to the Dragon Kingdom of Bhutan.

TWENTY-TWO

Bhutan

Gross National Hoopiness

This chapter was supposed to be called "The King and I." It was supposed to be an account of how I arrived in Bhutan, beelined for the palace, bowed extravagantly in the throne room, and challenged His Royal Majesty, the fourth Druk Gyalpo, King of the Thunder Dragon People, to a game of one-on-one.

Bhutanese citizens routinely approach King Jigme Singye Wangchuck with grievances and petitions. I figured my request qualified as the latter. To nonnationals like me His Majesty was normally as remote and inaccessible as the Himalayan country he ruled, which as recently as the 1960s could be entered only on horseback or foot. Still, I felt sure he'd make an exception in the name of the game dear to us both.

We actually made a pretty good match. The king was 43, barely a year my senior. He stood only 5'9", but a well-packed upper body made up for my advantage of several inches. In regular pickup games with the Royal Bodyguards he was famous for coming off screens and letting fly a well-practiced three-point shot, although for our summit meeting the bodyguards would simply be spectators.

Some 300 years before King Jigme's birth, a lama prophesied that he would bring the Dragon People unprecedented prosperity and contentment. Though only a teenager when he mounted the throne, His Majesty had proven the lama correct over a quarter century of rule. Under a domestic policy he called "gross national happiness," King Jigme extended the average life span of Bhutan's citizens by 20 years, brought English-language education to the most isolated valleys, and kept the country from going the way of nearby Nepal, which was plagued by manky backpackers and chaotic growth. To further the king's goals, the government banned or restricted such emblems of modern life as satellite TV, logging, and tourism. An Indian diplomat once remarked that "few countries have mastered so precisely the delicate art of hastening slowly."

There was, however, one notable breach in the walls the king threw up to keep the world out. He imported almost indiscriminately anything to do with hoops. His aide-de-camp monitored shortwave radio broadcasts to keep His Majesty briefed on the latest from the NBA. Several times a week staff at Bhutan's mission to the United Nations gathered the sports sections of the *New York Times,* along with magazines and videotapes, and dispatched them to the palace by diplomatic pouch. Through most of the 1970s and 1980s, every day at three in the afternoon a crowd of Bhutanese and a few bewildered tourists had gathered at the one outdoor court in Thimphu, the capital, to watch His Majesty's daily pickup game. In 1979 the king even brought over and put up a tall Californian to enliven the action.

The Royal Bodyguards had essentially two duties during those royal runs. One was to set majestic picks. The other was to keep tourists from taking pictures of the king, who played in Pro-Keds and the traditional Bhutanese robe called a *gho,* only with the garment's upper half folded down to leave his arms free. But late in 1990, Nepali separatists launched a rebellion over laws designed to preserve Bhutanese cultural identity, including a requirement that all men wear *gho* in public. As the rebels began to make violent incursions from their bases in the south, security became too much of a problem, and the king hadn't played in public since.

But we didn't have to play in downtown Thimphu. Indeed, where we played would be entirely up to His Majesty. Perhaps he'd prefer the private court adjacent to Samtenling Palace, the modest, two-bedroom log cabin, nestled in a grove of pines just north of town, where he and the bodyguards now played. Or maybe he'd choose the gym at the Bhutan Olympic Committee Sports Complex, with its parquet of imported Indian teak, the first wooden floor in the kingdom, which was being laid even as I arrived.

I'd have my own dilemmas, of course, mostly pertaining to protocol. The particular sect of Tantric Mahayana Buddhism practiced in Bhutan regards the Druk Gyalpo as a deity. Mere mortals are supposed to avert their eyes in his presence. This would complicate the task of defending His Majesty and pretty much rule out upbraiding him if he were to bring any weak stuff. But these were all minor details. I was sure we could work them out, the King and I.

As it was, I arrived at a tipping point in Bhutanese history. Only days after my visit, the country would celebrate the silver jubilee of King Jigme's enthronement with all sorts of pomp and ceremony. It would broadcast its first TV transmission, dedicate its first Internet server, even add an epic digit to every phone number. But as the Druk Air BAe 146 launched into a series of steep turns on approach to Paro Airport, I felt myself being borne not into the future but into the past. Out the window, all but touchable on the hillsides and in the valley below, I could see prayer flags and small Buddhist shrines called *chorten*s, and *dzong*s, the fortresses that serve the Bhutanese as religious and administrative centers—things whose very names conjured up a world entirely unfamiliar to me, preserved against all odds.

Waiting to pull my bags from the baggage carousel, I spotted a spherical piece of freshly off-loaded cargo, shrink-wrapped and hung with a VIP luggage tag. It was a basketball with the Spalding trademark. The name on the tag—H.R.H. Dasho Jigyel Ugyen Wangchuck—belonged to one of the king's sons.

Just beyond customs a young man in a *gho* held a sign bearing my name. With his broad manner, he reminded me instantly of Big Xu. And he went by the most felicitous name a guide could have: Sherub, the Dzongkha word for "knowledge." Sherub led me out to the curb, stowed my bags in the van, and introduced me to our driver. Before we embarked on the serpentine, three-hour drive to Thimphu, I caught another auspicious sign: a Boston Celtics cap, lying on the front seat.

A few years earlier, Sherub explained, after he showed a

tourist from Boston around Bhutan, she invited him to visit the U.S. Her neighbor held Celtics season tickets and took him to see them play. "I learned all the history of the Celtics," Sherub said. "I know well this logo man with his walking stick and basketball. I know the colors, too. Green stands for peace. White stands for purity."

I'd lucked into a guide who knew basketball *and* dynasties.

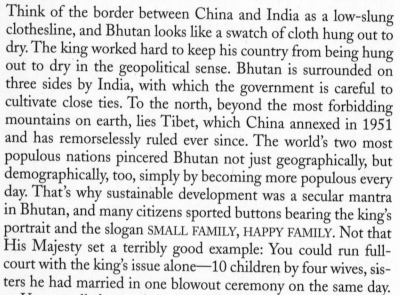

Think of the border between China and India as a low-slung clothesline, and Bhutan looks like a swatch of cloth hung out to dry. The king worked hard to keep his country from being hung out to dry in the geopolitical sense. Bhutan is surrounded on three sides by India, with which the government is careful to cultivate close ties. To the north, beyond the most forbidding mountains on earth, lies Tibet, which China annexed in 1951 and has remorselessly ruled ever since. The world's two most populous nations pincered Bhutan not just geographically, but demographically, too, simply by becoming more populous every day. That's why sustainable development was a secular mantra in Bhutan, and many citizens sported buttons bearing the king's portrait and the slogan SMALL FAMILY, HAPPY FAMILY. Not that His Majesty set a terribly good example: You could run full-court with the king's issue alone—10 children by four wives, sisters he had married in one blowout ceremony on the same day.

Uncontrolled growth had grave implications for an ecology in which nature bowed to no rules. Here the cranes had black necks; the sheep, blue fleece; the rhododendrons, the dimensions of trees. Bhutan was a living museum of all that seemed to be vanishing from the globe I'd been traversing. It wasn't just that this was a sober monarchy in a world drunk on democracy. Wildlife sanctuaries harbored the abominable snowmen known in these parts as yetis. Public buildings pinned down the limbs of giant spirits that would otherwise haunt a peaceful valley. Parents left crib-dead infants in the mountains so vultures might carry the deceased to reincarnation at a promising onward station. Thus had life been since the eighth century, when a Tibetan holy man flew to a mountain aerie on the back of a tigress, bringing Tantric Mahayana Buddhism with him. The Bhutanese regard that aerial voyager, the Guru Rimpoché, as the second incarnation of Buddha. Life is a way to pass the time as they await the third.

Here Shelly Pennefather's choice would be unexceptional. As recently as the early 1990s, every family was still expected to send at least one son to a monastery. In a land of such widespread and public piety, each flutter of a prayer flag and each turn of a prayer wheel constituted one petition of the verse gracing it. That was why prayer flags flew on mountaintops and from bridges, where the wind whipped, and why the faithful erected prayer wheels in small chortens over mountain streams from which entreaties went out to the gods as a paddle-wheel mills grain. Fold into this output the incantations of monks, and the murmurings of the elderly, who fingered beads and wristed handheld gewgaws while circumambulating shrines, and Bhutan surely issued forth as many prayers per capita as any country in the world.

To enjoy this sacred place, tourists like me paid a tariff of $230 a day, a price designed to keep things as they were. It also meant I shouldn't dawdle in arranging my audience with the king. The meter was running.

The next afternoon Sherub and I took up positions in the terraced bleacher seats of Changlimithang Stadium, overlooking the outdoor court where the king had played before the Nepali insurrection. This would be consecrated ground in Bhutan even if it weren't once the site of the royal run. Here in 1885, in a battle that could have been lifted from a Hollywood epic, the current king's great-grandfather Ugyen Wangchuck defeated his one remaining rival to end the last of a series of civil wars. The victory consolidated the power of the House of Wangchuck and launched the monarchy from which King Jigme derived his mandate. The battlefield now encompassed a basketball court, a soccer pitch, and an archery range, as well as a fringe of outbuildings all gussied up for the silver jubilee. A concrete wall, festooned with the eight auspicious symbols of Tantric Buddhism, set off the court from the soccer field. In the hills a bristle of prayer flagpoles commanded an outcropping of rock. In the middle distance the Thimphu River wandered aimlessly through a glen of trees nursed by the floodplain. Just below us a knot of kids launched shots with a similar lack of purpose at a pair of humpbacked basket stanchions painted light blue. Dry and desultory, the day featured all the things with which my time in Bhutan would come to mark itself. I felt like an extra on a kind of custom-built set at the top of the world.

"When the king played here, how did people guard him?" I asked.

"Quite uneasily," Sherub said. "But His Majesty really does prefer that defense be played against him. That is after all what it should be in a game. There is no king in a game."

Suddenly two figures materialized to our right. Each wore a *gho*. A slightly chubby boy of about 14 cradled a basketball; behind him a man held a walkie-talkie.

"That's the prince!" Sherub stage-whispered. This was Dasho Jigme Dorje Wangchuck, one of His Majesty's five sons. Soon he was down on the court, joining the scrum dribbling around and shooting hoops.

Minutes later two more figures appeared, this time through a doorway in the retaining wall girdling the court. "Another prince!" Sherub said. This was the very same Dasho Jigyel whose new Spalding I had seen describing loops at the baggage claim the previous day. He trailed behind him a valet, who carried a gym bag and a pair of basketball shoes.

Dasho Jigyel quickly fell in with the others. He sent a ball between his legs—no easy feat, as it had to clear the hem of his *gho*. Then he segued into a reverse left-handed layup that didn't quite find its mark but made clear that he had rummaged through his dad's videotape collection.

Presently another adolescent in a *gho* came walking toward us. Sherub, seeing him well enough in advance, was able to leap to his feet in deference. Dasho Khamsum Singye Wangchuck reached the embankment at the end of the bleachers. Then he shot a quick look around, slid on his rear end down to the court, hopped to his feet at the bottom, and smartly brushed his backside clean before joining the crowd.

Soon every recruitable specimen of His Majesty's male off-spring lay before us, going full. Only two princes were missing: the crown prince, Jigme Gesan Namgyal Wangchuck, who was finishing up the school year at Harvard; and Dasho Ugyen Jigme Wangchuck, the most recent addition to the royal family, who, all of three, was probably teething on a Fisher-Price backboard back at the palace. No one, least of all the princes, made much effort to get back on defense. Every touch of the ball constituted an opportunity to assault the basket, and in that sense the scene could have been set in a schoolyard anywhere in the world.

Soon a trim man in a sweat suit appeared through the door of the retaining wall. He wore glasses, a baseball cap, and a severe expression. Sherub led me down to the court and introduced me to Karma Lam Dorji, who pumped my hand crisply and welcomed me in slightly stilted English.

"*Sports Illustrated!*" It took several months for them to do so, he explained, but copies eventually filtered down from the palace and into his hands. "Do you know this Jack McCallum?" He was referring to a colleague of mine who covered the NBA. "His stories about the playoffs are so good, I think—I think it is almost better to read his descriptions than to be there oneself."

Karma Lam was Bhutan's only certified referee, only trained coach, and only employee of the basketball federation. He was busy supervising installation of the parquet at the Olympic Complex, and making preparations for the Silver Jubilee Cup basketball tournament, which lay several days off and was to inaugurate the floor. But he agreed to meet that evening for dinner. "We really have to think about food and health and education before we can think about basketball," he said. "We've had so many difficulties in Bhutan, the game should have vanished long ago. But the game is the most popular one among the kids, despite our having only one qualified coach in the kingdom, that being myself. Basketball here can only get better. It's not just a game, you know. Here, now, it's passion and fashion."

I'd now met the one commoner who completely embodied the sport in Bhutan. I had no idea how close he was to the king. But if he was on the routing list for the contents of His Majesty's airlifted hoop care packages, perhaps he could route me to the palace whence all that stuff came.

As I made my way back to the hotel by way of town, I could see everywhere evidence of how the king's passion had touched the people. At a video store, the stock of NBA tapes was completely checked out. If you heard a *thump thump thump*, it was as likely to be a kid pounding a ball into the dusty streets as an artisan in some doorless atelier hammering metal into a dragon or a raven.

Just after I crossed the bridge over the river, I came upon a boy on the roadside. He stood below a small apple tree a few paces ahead of me. No more than six years old, wrapped in a *gho*, he was picking small rocks off the pavement and hurling them at the upper branches of the tree, trying, so far in vain, to knock an apple free.

A couple of passing soldiers laughed. I wasn't sure if they were amused at the boy's stubborn futility or at me, for by now I'd stopped to watch, enraptured. But I knew this: Very little separated this boy from Colin Smith, my young playmate at the Naismith homestead. There was indeed something about "goal-throwing." Apple in a tree could be every bit as engrossing as duck on a rock.

A few hours later Karma Lam fetched me at my hotel and spun me back into town, where we met Sherub at a restaurant steps from Changlimithang Stadium. Sherub fearlessly tucked into a portion of *ema datsi,* a runny cheese sauce laced with incendiary chilies. I devoured a plate of tepid Indian food and Karma Lam's story.

He had grown up in one of Thimphu's well-to-do families in the thrall of the game. Like many of the sons of Bhutan's elite, he was sent off to India to boarding school, where he continued to play. Classmates teased him about his passion, making him the foil of practical jokes. One morning he awakened to find basketballs stuffed under the covers of his bed. At college in Delhi the gentle hazing continued. While he napped obliviously in his dorm room one afternoon, friends picked up his bedframe and carried it out to the basketball court.

Karma Lam's education allowed him to return home to a relatively well-paying position, a desk job with a firm that leased heavy machinery. He would sneak out regularly for those 3 P.M. royal pickup games, where he usually found himself matched up against the king. But he hated his job—hated it, he realized, because it had nothing to do with basketball. So in 1988, to the mortification of his family, he quit to devote himself to coaching, officiating, and organizing tournaments full-time, even though this was no way to make a living in an economy only a generation removed from virtual serfdom. For seven years he lived with and off his parents. He tried to land a job in the civil service, with no success, as the regime was determined to keep the bureaucracy lean. Finally, in 1995, he told me, "I had to try the back door."

By this, Karma Lam really meant the front door—the front door of the palace. He exercised the right of every Bhutanese citizen. He contacted the office of the royal chamberlain at the Tashichhodzong, the seat of the monarchy, and asked for an audience with the figure whose words, as the Dzongkha saying goes, "weigh heavier than the hills and are more precious than gold." He handed over a dossier: yellowing clippings of his exploits as a player in Delhi; letters of commendation; accounts of teams coached and tournaments organized; a statement proposing where he would take Bhutanese basketball if only His Majesty were to grant him the authority.

Two days later Karma Lam learned that he had received a dual appointment. He would serve both the Bhutan Olympic Committee on its office staff and Bhutanese basketball in every imaginable capacity, from national coach and federation general secretary to chef de mission and sweeper of the court. He would collect a standard civil servant's wage, barely $100 a month. But he would be his country's first and only basketball pro.

"Were you nervous when you went in to see the king?" I asked.

"To tell you honestly? To be really, really frank? I wasn't. I believed my request had a good chance of making an impression on His Majesty. He's not an old-fashioned king. He's really very open-minded. Often after we played against His Majesty, if we'd given him a good fight, he would give us pocket money and tell us to go have a meal in town. And he would always give the money to me.

"Also, during the time I was looking for a job, I volunteered to teach basketball in the mornings at Yangchenphu High School here in Thimphu. One of my students was the crown prince. After many years of trying and failing, Yangchenphu finally won the national high school tournament. We all went out to celebrate afterward, the whole team, but the crown prince ran straight to the palace to tell his father. As a thank-you for coaching his son, His Majesty sent me a watch."

But surely Karma Lam stuck in the king's mind for another reason. Bhutan holds an annual national club championship, and a dozen years earlier Karma Lam and a group of his friends had reached the final. "We played His Majesty and the Royal Bodyguards. Until then, no team could come close to beating them. His Majesty never takes twos, you know. Only threes, it seems. The big guys—the bodyguards—would give His Majesty double screens on the baseline, and His Majesty would come around them, again and again, making threes.

"But this time it was a good game, really close. I clearly remember, I must have scored as many as he did. He would take two threes, and we'd have to score three twos to keep up. But on this day we did. We lost, but only by a point. Afterward we were lined up, the dozen of us, for the ceremony where they gave His Majesty the MVP award. And His Majesty walked over and gave it to me, you know? A crystal decanter. I have it at home. So I thought he might remember me.

"After some time, of course, we didn't fear him. But we always respected him. It's traditional not to play too aggressively against members of the royal family. Really, you want them to win."

The conversation stilled for a bit. Karma Lam then pulled his head up from his food to pose something of me. "Do you suppose that Michael Jordan has any idea that in the most remote part of the Himalayas, in the Kingdom of Bhutan, there are people who know who he is—people who care what he does?"

It was a wondrous question to contemplate.

During dessert Karma Lam's cell phone rang. He carried on in English, affixing the deferential, interrogatory *la*—Dzongkha for "pardon"—to the end of every sentence: "Yes, yes, we have the trophies ordered, *la*? . . . Sponsors are all arranged for, *la*? . . . No worries, no, we will have the floor finished, I am sure of it, *la*?"

He hung up. "That was an officer at the palace, His Majesty's aide-de-camp. He's asking for details about the Silver Jubilee Cup. When you stage a basketball tournament in Bhutan, you must satisfy all the VVIPs. Orders come from the top, you know."

Clearly, His Majesty owed Karma Lam no favors, and Karma Lam owed the king nothing less than the turn in his life. The man across from me at dinner may have been a repository of everything pertaining to Bhutanese basketball. But he was not the man to plead for my audience.

In the fall of 1979, when Karma Lam Dorji was still an adolescent discovering the joys of the game, Steve Nycum was 28, freshly married, and settled into a workaday job as a technician with an oil-drilling equipment firm in Southern California. Nycum had already put his six feet nine inches to good basketball use. He had cycled through every level of the game short of American professional ball, ultimately (or so it seemed at the time) playing for a club team in Holland. But that September he heard that an outfit based in Long Island, People-to-People Sports, had just fielded an unusual request. The Druk Gyalpo, then 24, wondered if an American might be willing to billet himself in Thimphu for a year as basketball courtier to the king. Nycum gave notice, he and his wife packed their bags, and they arrived in Thimphu with orders from a People-to-People executive to "keep the king happy."

Nycum's duties turned out to be few. He spent a few hours a week teaching basketball at local high schools and coaching teams representing the Royal Bhutanese Army and the Royal Bodyguards. Otherwise, he was expected only to show up at Changlimithang Stadium for the royal run every afternoon the king was in town. In return he received gross national hospitality: a salary; the services of a driver, a cook, and a valet; lodging in a five-bedroom home in the prestigious Motithang quarter of Thimphu; and the occasional invitation to the palace to watch NBA videotapes.

The king decided that the daily games would be most competitive if he and Nycum played for opposing teams. To counteract His Majesty and the bodyguards, Steve's team invariably included the king's first cousin, Paljor (Benji) Dorji. Strong, stocky, deft at the point, Benji was Bhutan's chief justice, and thus went by the nickname C.J. But he proudly told anyone who asked that the initials also stood for "court jester." The king counted on his cousin's wisecracking manner to lighten the mood of a game forever shrouded by the opposing players' knowledge that they were defending and scoring on a deity in the Tantric Mahayana Buddhist faith.

Through that winter, Benji and Steve's team won about as often as the king's did. One afternoon Nycum watched as Migay, the 6'4", 230-pound bodyguard who played center on the king's team, chased down a loose ball. His Majesty also drew a bead on it, and as the two tumbled to the asphalt in pursuit, a royal elbow found the upper regions of Migay's chest. His Majesty popped right up, unscathed, ready to continue play. But the blow struck Migay with such force and accuracy that he had to be airlifted to Calcutta, where he was treated for cracked ribs and a dislocated sternum.

"He's very competitive," Nycum wrote his parents soon after arriving in Thimphu. "He acts like a king is supposed to act. Fits my image perfectly." At the same time, if a referee failed to whistle a foul that His Majesty knew he had committed, the king was known to denounce the ref for negligence. And he expected to be defended vigorously in turn. That spring, when the government permitted a rare visit of a delegation of international journalists, the king invited them all to the three o'clock run. "They don't believe I really play and get fouled," the king grumbled to his American ringer before the game. Nycum never actually coached His Majesty, for to do so would have been unacceptable. But if the king asked a question, he would field it as best he could. By the spring Steve and Benji rarely beat His Majesty and the Royal Bodyguards.

The young monarch was only in his early twenties, but he already had an acute wariness of foreign influence. During his stay Nycum received a letter from a group of Americans in Kathmandu who had heard of his posting in Thimphu and wanted to visit Bhutan to challenge His Majesty's team. He shared the letter with the king, who issued nothing but a curt laugh. Nycum knew His Majesty well enough to know he'd love the challenge of playing against the Americans. But he also knew of King Jigme's feelings about incursions from the wider world. His Majesty liked to import foreign ballplayers one at a time and not have them invite themselves.

Now 20 years older, the king was surely that much more set in his ways. The implications for my mission weren't good.

A remnant of the old three o'clock game survived, and Karma Lam invited Sherub and me to play in it. The men's competition in the Silver Jubilee Cup lay a week off, and though the crown prince hadn't quite finished up the semester at Harvard, the remainder of his team was mustering at Changlimithang, eager for some shakedown action. The team called itself Pawos, after the Dzongkha word for a brave, victorious warrior. In addition to Bhutan's future king, Pawos included two of Benji (C.J.) Dorji's sons, both of whom resembled their Yorkshire-born mother in stature. Benjo, the eldest, was chatty and powerfully built. His youngest brother, Toby, a strapping and diffident post player, was being groomed as aide-de-camp to the crown prince. He dunked several times as we warmed up, and Karma Lam told me Toby was one of the first in the kingdom to throw it down.

Karma Lam and I were among the players who would provide Pawos's opposition. Karma Lam wasn't more than 5'7", but a decade of office work, officiating, and coaching had left his skills undulled. He juked and probed with the ball, and I could easily imagine him giving His Majesty a game. As the tallest player on our team, I was left to flash the post on offense and anchor the back of a very passive 2-3 zone. My teammates fell back into that alignment so reflexively that I wondered if the Bhutanese had solved the dilemma of defending the king simply by never playing man-to-man.

The game was full of mannered showboating and extravagant courtesies. Players threw no-look touch passes and made two-handed putbacks that looked like volleyball sets. "Sorry, sir," one of our forwards said after failing to spot a wide-open Karma Lam at the top of the key. But I was most struck by the shooting, which appeared to be free of Western influence. There was a formal, almost archaic quality to the way players raised and cocked the ball, brought their bodies into alignment, and let a shot go. It looked to be taken from a template—but surely helped explain the frequency with which each shot found its target.

This wasn't one-on-one with His Majesty, but to run full with two members of the royal family—cousins once removed to the king—wasn't your garden-variety package tour experience, either. No one kept score, so we played with a whimsy that pleased the steadily growing crowd, including two clean-headed monks in maroon robes who watched from the top row of the bleachers. Thimphu sits at 6,960 feet, and after 20 minutes the thin air began to singe my lungs. I waved Sherub in to spell me. He bounded from the sidelines, peeled his national costume down to his waist in Wangchuck style, and moments later scored on a feed under the basket from Karma Lam—a give-'n-*gho*, if I wasn't mistaken.

The Pawos's best player was a tiny point guard who liked to outrun the rest of his team, leap into the air with the ball, and toss heavily spun shots off the backboard and through the hoop. Regardless of the awkwardness of the angle or the abandon with which he barreled toward the goal, the ball always seemed to glance off the board with a preprogrammed intelligence. Benjo didn't do much more than trail on the break, adding cackling commentary to each of these baroque shots. *"Spiiiiiiiin doctor!"* he'd yell.

Benjo's brother was different. Toby was no talk, all walk. Twice he leaked out for breakaway dunks. I wondered: Was Toby being groomed to be aide-de-camp to the crown prince because of the wise counsel he'd provide? Or because he was a kind of Chocolate Thunder Dragon, able to throw it down for the Pawos? It dawned on me that I might have found my way to the world's only hoopocracy.

After the game Sherub and I accompanied Karma Lam to the Sports Complex on the other side of town, site of Bhutan's lone indoor basketball court, where all action moved during the monsoon. The air was pungent with varnish. As workmen applied one last coat, Karma Lam took a ball and pounded it into a dry corner of the parquet. I was hearing the report of a leather basketball on a wooden floor for the first time in the history of Bhutan.

Sherub surveyed the scene approvingly. "Looks like Boston Garden!"

For every game involving the crown prince and his Pawos team during the forthcoming tournament, a royal bodyguard would be in the gym with a cell phone, relaying updates every five minutes to His Majesty back at the palace. The king could hardly come to watch in person, for the protocol and security requirements would overwhelm Karma Lam and his handful of volunteers.

"When he's in Thimphu, the crown prince sometimes calls me after midnight," Karma Lam said. "He'll challenge me to a game of one-on-one, and I'll have to leave my wife and kid to meet him. It happened last year, the very day he arrived from the States. He wanted to show me how he had improved, all his new moves. He had no worries about jet lag. He called his friends and they came, too. At 3 A.M. we had a full-court game going. Can you imagine?

"He plays anywhere on the court. He likes to make moves in the center position—Olajuwon moves—and sometimes three-point shots, like his father. And he can drive pretty well, too. He's a very similar player to his father, except that his three-point shots are contested. It's changed from the old way of thinking, you know. We treat His Royal Highness differently from His Majesty. We dive for loose balls against him, and roll over and over in pursuit.

"In fact, a friend of the crown prince told me just the other day of a phone call he got from His Royal Highness. He called from Massachusetts to say that he didn't want Pawos to have any ringers from the army for the Silver Jubilee Cup. 'Let's see what we can do ourselves,' he said. 'Let's see what we can do if we train hard and fight hard.'"

Before leaving New York, I had tracked down Steve Nycum. Bhutan's original basketball aid worker now lived in Singapore, covering the Pacific Rim for Kidde International, the fire protection company. In exchange for background information and practical dope about hoops in the Himalayas, he asked only one favor. He made me promise to pass along greetings to his old teammate, the original court jester himself, Benji (C.J.) Dorji. "If anyone can get you an audience with His Majesty," he added, "Benji can."

Deal, I said.

Whether serving as consigliere to the king or as His Majesty's court jester, Benji—Dasho Benji in the proper form of address—was by all accounts an extraordinary man. He had studied law in England and graduated from Sandhurst, Great Britain's West Point. He had served as Bhutan's environment minister as well as its chief justice, even delivering an address at the Rio Summit in 1992 to an assembly of world leaders that included U.S. president George Bush. And he came from an equally notable family: His father, Jigmie Palden Dorji, had been the current king's uncle—the brother of the third queen of Bhutan—and, until his assassination in 1964, the country's first, and for a long time only, prime minister.

The story of how Benji's dad received that appointment actually explains how basketball came to Bhutan. In 1958 Jawaharlal Nehru, India's prime minister, agreed to make a state visit, but on one condition: that he be met at the border by a Bhutanese of equal or higher rank. This posed a problem. The Buddhist kingdom didn't have a prime minister. The journey from Thimphu to the border took a week, and King Jigme Dorji Wangchuck had no desire to spend days negotiating by horse and yak the rutted, muddy, leech-infested horsepaths that passed for roads, even to please a powerful neighbor and critical ally. So His Majesty turned to his brother-in-law and said, more or less, "Pack your bags. You, my man, are prime minister."

At the time Jigmie Palden Dorji took that post, his son Benji was off at a Jesuit boarding school in Darjeeling, where several Tibetan classmates introduced him to basketball. The game enchanted him. He shot hoops whenever he could, and after a Canadian priest screened for the students an 8mm film of Bob Cousy dribbling behind his back, Benji made of his father an urgent request: During his now frequent travels abroad, representing the Dragon Kingdom as its head of state, could he bring back a Bob Cousy–autographed basketball? His dad came through, and Benji made that ball his treasure. After finishing boarding school he continued to play in England, at law school and at Sandhurst. Back in Thimphu he shared his ball, and the rules of the game played with it, with friends and relatives. Ultimately he made a proselyte of his cousin the crown prince, who was a dozen years his junior.

So the arrival of basketball in Bhutan might be attributed to Nehru's ego, to the incumbent Druk Gyalpo's ingenuity, to Cousy's legerdemain, to a priest's passion, to the far-flung duties of Jigmie Dorji's job, as well as to a boy's imagination and a father's willingness to oblige it. But at root, basketball penetrated Bhutan precisely because of a chain of events set in motion by the country's very impenetrability. Hoops can be subversive that way.

Having now met and played with two of his sons, I had no qualms about calling Dasho Benji at home. I could hear Benjo in the booming, playful voice that answered the phone. He agreed to meet me for lunch.

Striding through the double doors of my hotel, Dasho Benji cut a magnificent figure. The dimensions of a yeti filled out a dashing gray *gho*. The young waiters in the restaurant all recognized him, and I could sense their nervousness as they took our orders and served our food. "Ah, basketball," Benji said. "And did you know? The king attributes it to me! The princes all say, 'Our father says you brought basketball to Bhutan!' And I can't argue with what the king says, can I?

"Perhaps you know my nickname. 'C.J.' really did mean court jester as much as chief justice. I did all sorts of crazy things. Put the ball behind my back and shot it from there. Shot it from behind the half-court line. Hid the ball inside my costume. A stand-up comic, I was. I missed my vocation. But the king always seemed to like me, I think, because I made him laugh."

I asked if His Majesty really had been the finest player in the kingdom—a delicate query, which Benji fielded as diplomatically as one might expect a prime minister's son to do.

"There was a short chap from the Royal Bhutanese Army, retired now, and he was *very* good. But I think His Majesty was the best. He was always working his way inside, then popping out for his three-point shots. We had a tough time keeping up with him. He was excellent—and not because we let him excel. The crown prince, he is very good, too. But I think he has a ways to go to catch up to his father."

Bhutan is a nation enraptured of target games. Every Olympics includes several Bhutanese who excel at archery, the national sport. In *daygo,* a game similar to boules, horseshoes, and even duck on a rock, a round stone is tossed at a twig stuck in the ground. In an indigenous dart game called *khuru,* participants try to distract the shooter with verbal harassment not much different from the woofing to be heard on any playground in the States. Taekwondo also has a following in Bhutan, and while it's not strictly a target game, it requires the same contained formalism that many target games do. You could argue that it involves finding bull's eyes both within and beyond oneself. It seemed natural that basketball would find a home here. I asked Benji why the Bhutanese enjoyed range-finding pastimes so much.

"In our history we've had to be warrior types. We were always being invaded by the Tibetans or the British and had to defend ourselves with bows-and-arrows and flintlocks. And we did so quite admirably, I might say. We remain one of the few countries in Asia never to have been colonized. Never!"

The bond Dasho Benji forged with his cousin through basketball hadn't kept him from being relieved of his ministerial duties a year earlier, when His Majesty asked for the resignation of his entire cabinet. So my lunch companion was no longer well-positioned to make a request of His Majesty on my behalf. Nonetheless, I asked him how a foreigner went about getting an audience with the king.

"Why, by asking, of course! Get in touch with Ugyen

Tshering, the foreign secretary. The foreign ministry is next to the Tashichhodzong. He is accessible." Benji laughed the laugh that had so delighted the king. "In Bhutan, you will find that every government minister is accessible."

I was homing in. My task here had amounted to penetrating a series of concentric circles—peeling the onion, advancing through stages, finding a target. So why did I feel as unsure as ever of seeing the king?

God bless Sherub. He must have thought I was nuts. He knew I was committing an act of chutzpah frowned upon in a deferential culture. He even knew that our errand would be futile, for he had spotted the king's motorcade leaving town early that morning, headed toward the airport in Paro. Still, he led me to the foreign ministry, to the threshold of the office of the foreign secretary, and, when an aide asked if I had an appointment, confessed that I did not. But would the foreign secretary be so kind as to see this visitor from New York?

Ugyen Tshering waved me into his office, where I lost myself in the pillows of his sofa.

The foreign secretary was no mere *dasho*. He was a *lyonpo*, which represented a whole new order of titular magnitude. Ordinary Bhutanese men wear a white *kabne*, or ceremonial shawl, over their shoulders in public buildings and formal situations; he wore a red one, only one color removed from the yellow *kabne* reserved for the king and the chief abbot.

Lyonpo Ugyen's assistant brought out an extravagant tea service of bone china, and for 15 minutes we discussed the kinds of things a foreign secretary might discuss with a disheveled tourist if the disheveled tourist were to show up unannounced at his door. We spoke about my neighborhood in Manhattan, which includes the United Nations, where Lyonpo Ugyen had been recently posted as chief of the Bhutanese mission. We touched on the recent cabinet purge that had left a number of ex-ministers playing a great deal of golf at the Royal Thimphu Golf Club. I believe I mentioned the weather. After a while the pointlessness of this small talk became too obvious to ignore.

"Now," the foreign secretary said. "How may I help you?"

I explained. I mentioned where I'd been—Bosnia and Brazil, Ireland and Israel, Poland and the Palestra. I mentioned whom I'd talked to—Kareem, Bill Bradley, the inventor's grandson, even the head of another sovereign state. I'd done all this, I explained, to riddle out the meaning of a game adored by millions around the world, the Druk Gyalpo among them. I would be ever so grateful for a few minutes of His Majesty's time.

"I am afraid you have asked me for the one thing I cannot grant. His Majesty does not give personal interviews."

"Well isn't this our lucky day! Because it's not really an interview I want. All I really want is to *hoop* with His Majesty! Promise, no questions besides, 'Show me what Your Majesty's got, *la*?'"

Actually, I said none of that. I said "I understand" and nodded pathetically when Lyonpo Ugyen confirmed what Sherub had suspected: that the king had indeed left that morning, for Delhi, to tend to unspecified personal business. He wouldn't be back for 36 hours. By then I'd be far away, in Paro, spending my last day in the kingdom.

"Is there anything else I may help you with?" the foreign secretary asked. He had a remarkable way of packing rejection in the foam peanuts of solicitude.

I thought for a moment, and decided that I didn't really want to ride every ride in Deportationland. "No, thank you very much. And thank you, too, for being gracious enough to see me on such short notice."

The foreign secretary took one last sip of tea, and as he raised the cup to his lips, his arm caused the hem of his *gho* to hike up ever so slightly. On his hip I saw the flash of a scabbard.

I could take no for an answer.

A broad valley cut by a roiling river; a vault of sky, boundless, blue, edged with ruffs of cloud—these formed the floor and ceiling for my last day in Bhutan.

Sherub drove me up the Paro valley until we could glimpse the Tiger's Nest monastery, where Guru Rimpoché alighted 13 centuries ago. It had been badly damaged by fire several years earlier, but still clung to the sheer face of a cliff, as if supported only by the faith of the monks who kept butter lamps burning inside. I could scarcely imagine arriving there on the back of a tiger, much less on one's stomach as the faithful were said to do, inchworming up a roundabout trail with prostration upon prostration, in a pilgrimage that can take weeks.

We watched an archery match play out in the floodplain of the Paro River. The archers took aim more than a football field away from their targets, nearly double the Olympic distance. A traditional Bhutanese bow is made of bamboo and strung with hemp, but some archers now used high-tech American bows, fashioned of composite materials. "The new bows are stronger," Sherub said. "But we get more accuracy with our traditional ones. An arrow shot from a traditional bow is more like shooting a basketball, where you have to take into account the arc of the shot."

If an archer could bring himself into equilibrium, Sherub explained, if he could calibrate stance, breathing, and release, a bull's-eye became inevitable. "Hitting the target is not the objective," he said. "It is only a consequence of form and balance." I know Hirohide Ogawa never actually said anything, but he couldn't have said it better.

Beyond the archery range we passed others engrossed in sighting a target and finding it. Kids chucked stones at crows along the roadside. A troupe of soldiers played *khuru*, the dart game. Everywhere I saw the principle underlying basketball's most fundamental act. Like the Apache lands, this, too, was shooting country. It was a stretch, I knew, to retrofit so young a game into a culture centuries old. But basketball found such kindred company here, it was hard to resist doing so.

I was booked for an early-morning flight to Bangkok, so it made no sense to return to Thimphu. Sherub and I checked into a guesthouse overlooking the valley, and after dinner, during a pass through the gift shop, I spotted a book about Bhutanese political history. At our lunch several days earlier, Benji had made a passing reference to his father's assassination. It seemed gauche to follow up at the time. Still, I wondered: Who killed Bhutan's first and only prime minister—the brother of Queen Kesang Dorji Wangchuck? Why? Had agents of India or China made mischief, hoping for a strategic land grab? I asked Sherub. No, he said, Jigmie Palden Dorji's murder had been a domestic political matter. But Sherub was so reluctant to elaborate that I began to entertain new suspicions. In a culture virtually free of media, answers weren't easy to come by. As Karma Lam had told me, "Many things aren't talked about here."

I took the book back to my room, and slowly the blanks began to fill in. I read a story of almost unfathomable intrigue, made all the more engrossing because it had played out in a country all but shut off from the world.

Like his son Benji and grandson Benjo, the late prime minister was direct, caustic, and worldly. Jigmie Palden Dorji had taken a Tibetan wife, sent his children to schools overseas, and begun the spadework that would ultimately deliver Bhutan into the United Nations seven years after his death. But while the course he charted may seem commonsensical today, in the early 1960s the prime minister's style and policies made enemies among the army and the clergy, two conservative and influential camps in Bhutanese life. Yet with the king suffering from heart disease, Jigmie came to exercise more and more power, if only by default.

On April 5, 1964, with His Majesty in Zurich for medical treatment, Jigmie paid a visit to the Bhutanese border town of Phuntsholing. After sharing Sunday dinner in a rest house with family and friends, he joined in a game of cards. Just as he flicked his lighter to fire up a cigarette, the report of a shot came from an open window 10 feet away, and Jigmie slumped forward. In this land of targetfinders, an assassin's bullet had found its mark. Jigmie's last words were these: "Tell my king I served him as best I could. I take refuge in the Buddha."

The king returned immediately from Switzerland to reassert his authority. An investigation implicated one of the monarch's uncles, who served as His Majesty's liaison to the army, and he was tried, convicted, and put to death. But all sorts of potentially scandalous details began to emerge. The murder weapon not only belonged to the king's Tibetan mistress, but it had been a gift to her from His Majesty himself. Moreover, the queen had to that point not known of her husband's affair, much less that the mistress, Yangki, had borne His Majesty a son—a potential rival to her own son, the crown prince. Now she learned all this as a result of the murder of her brother.

Because of Yangki's ties to the weapon, and the meager official efforts to probe her possible complicity in the crime, Thimphu seized up in a tangle of speculation. Was the crown prince to be eliminated, too, to clear a path for Yangki's son to ascend to the throne? Border guards, unsure of the king's wishes, failed to seize Yangki and her son when they fled south to India. A rumor began to circulate that enemies of the prime minister had persuaded His Majesty to get rid of the entire House of Dorji. Regardless of whether this was true, events were to make it moot. In December 1964, the king survived an unsuccessful coup. There was no evidence that any Dorjis were involved, but three siblings of the late prime minister believed they would be blamed and fled to Nepal.

Their sister the queen—the crown prince's mother and Benji's aunt—had nowhere to go. She had long since ceased being intimate with her husband in any consular or connubial sense, but she could only remain in Thimphu, listening to her husband liken the flight of those siblings to "the dropping away of a few rotten grains from a bag of rice." Meanwhile, in Delhi, Yangki and her son began to attract courtiers of their own. By now the king realized that only an orderly succession could assure the future of the monarchy. He began feverishly to groom young Jigme Singye, then all of eight, to succeed him. It was a good thing, for the ascension of the crown prince took place sooner than anyone expected—in 1972, upon the king's death, at 44, of a heart attack.

At 16, the new Druk Gyalpo was the youngest monarch in the world. His formal enthronement didn't take place until 1974, after a two-year transition period. But he moved to end the family feud, in accordance with the wishes of his one surviving parent. He rehabilitated the Dorjis, sending for Benji's exiled uncles in Nepal. He found Benji a place in his court. Benji found His Majesty a place on *his* court, as it were. And soon laughter rose from the old Changlimithang battlefield every afternoon.

I wasn't going to meet the king, not in this life anyway. But I now understood how splendidly he had been served by this game that turns, after a fashion, on "the delicate art of hastening slowly." Basketball had kept him vigorous. It had been a diversion, in the way some monarchs hunt foxes and others collect Fabergé eggs. But most of all the game had helped repair the breach between the houses of Wangchuck and Dorji, and thereby done its part to save the Bhutanese monarchy.

The next generation will use the game to cinch those ties tighter still. The king and his cousin had played together for all those afternoons, but always on opposite teams. By contrast their sons, Crown Prince Jigme Gesan Namgyal Wangchuck and Dasho Toby Dorji, were more than just the future king and his aide-de-camp-in-waiting. They were more than mere blood relatives. As fellow Pawos, they shared what I'd come to regard as the most consanguineous kind of kinship. They were teammates.

"Because it spins, it must develop," the old coach Bai Jinshen had told me in Shanghai. In his wise man's way, he spoke at once of the ball and of the game. Now it was time to figure out where the ever-spinning game was going.

SUMMER

Fast
Break
to the
Future

TWENTY-THREE

Washington, D.C.

Going to the Next Level

After several weeks of exotic encounters and nonencounters in the Near and Far East, I didn't expect to return home to melodrama. But I could hardly pass through the lobby of my building without hearing the latest in the lives of the Suarez family, including Johnny, the neighbor who had tutored me in the crossover dribble.

Johnny was still living at home, still playing pickup ball, still hoping to return to college in Puerto Rico, where he had played half a season and his coach was eager to have him back. But the health of his father, Angelo, had taken a turn for the worse just as Johnny was planning a return to the island. His college coach had arranged a tryout with Coamo, a club in the intensely competitive Puerto Rican professional summer league, the Liga Superior de Baloncesto. To make the LSB would mean instant money, celebrity, and perks. Though he was only 5'10", though he had quit his high school team before playing a game, though his incipient college career had been on hiatus for more than a year, Johnny spun this opportunity into an Archimedean moment in his life. If he made the team, he could buy his parents a house and they could retire to the tropics, spending their dotage watching him play. "That's if I make it," he said. "If, God forbid, I don't make it . . ." His voice trailed off into vapors of unmentionability.

On the face of it, there was no reason Johnny should have had any expectation of making a living playing basketball. Marooned in New York without any direction, he struggled to motivate himself to work out, and he would sometimes say things that betrayed the gaps in his schooling in the game. When I saw Johnny one Monday after he returned from a weekend tournament, I asked how things had gone.

"So-so," he said. "We reached the semifinals. I scored 23 and hit four threes, but we lost because my teammates didn't do the job."

On another occasion he said with a scowl, "The ball they play in Puerto Rico is all defense and passing." And then, beaming: "They like me because I bring *chispa.*" He used the Spanish word for "spark." "I bring New York, excitement."

I had to remind myself: How would he know any better? He only knew what he had picked up from TV and the back pages of the *New York Post:* the fame, the money, the idolatry, the props—all the gaudy end-products that obscure the sacrifice, cooperation, and fundamental work elite basketball requires.

Like many of his NBA heroes, Johnny had become a father prematurely, at 17. But his relationship with his daughter's mother, Ana, soon foundered, and within a couple of years he had taken up with a new girlfriend, Jovanka, who soon gave birth to a son. She and their boy, Brandon, lived in the Bronx with her Nicaraguan émigré family, and neither she nor her parents much cared for Johnny's obsession with basketball. Why didn't he return to school, earn his degree, find a job, and meet his responsibilities as a father, if not as a prospective husband? Johnny felt the disapproval of his would-be in-laws so palpably that he waited until the last moment to tell them of his plans to try out with Coamo.

With his mother, Carmine, heroically discharging Angelo's duties around the building, and with Jovanka working as a paralegal to help support their son, Johnny felt the tugs of polar desires: accommodating those people closest to him, and chasing his basketball dream the same way he played the point and lived his life—heedlessly, rakishly, *con chispa.*

I tried to turn myself into Johnny's own minister of the game. Basketball—or at least college basketball—needn't be the indulgence that Jovanka and her family made it out to be. If it weren't for the game, Johnny might not be in school at all. Hoops could help him get a free education and learn volumes about industry, patience, discipline, and responsibility, courses of study he hadn't shown much evidence of taking. But before I could offer any advice, I needed to know some basic facts.

"If you go to this pro tryout in Puerto Rico and the team doesn't offer you a contract, can you still go back to play at Universidad Interamericana?" I asked. "In the States, if you even sniff around pro ball, the NCAA declares you ineligible."

Johnny had no clue. Nor did he have any sense of what it would mean to go straight from pickup ball to the Puerto Rican pros, hurdling high school and any meaningful college experience in the process. In the weeks leading up to the tryout, Johnny made his way to the Y every day and duly passed along updates on how he had played. "I was unstoppable," he might say, or, "I was on fire." I didn't doubt him. But I knew the competition over at the Y—sometimes I *was* the competition over at the Y—and anyone could combust in one of those ragged pickup games.

One afternoon I joined Johnny and his younger brother, Christian, at the Y. Johnny and I wound up on the same team; Christian, a bony 17-year-old with long arms, played on the other. Twenty minutes in, each Suarez decided he was going to take the other to school, and the game ground to a halt. Three times in a row Johnny tried to break Christian's ankles, and three times in a row Christian stripped him or forced him to fumble the ball away. The rest of us might as well have been statuary. Johnny's misadventures left us trailing 16–13, and though we wound up winning when he sank a jumper at game point, I had as hard a time as ever imagining him submitting to structure. His inconsistency could relieve a coach of all patience. Yet he had a passion, an apparent eagerness to learn, and just enough raw talent to make harnessing it all seem worth a coach's while.

In many ways, Johnny's was the oldest of clichéd New York City stories—that of an underclass kid blinkered in his determination to use the vehicle of the game for social mobility. His tale departed from the stereotype only in that he still had a father around, albeit barely, and that, as a dual national, he could set his sights on the LSB, a marginally more realistic goal than the NBA.

On the morning Johnny was supposed to leave for his tryout, Angelo had to be rushed to the hospital and hooked up to a respirator. The Suarez family gathered at his bedside. "Do you want me to go?" Johnny asked his father.

His mouth clogged with tubes, Angelo couldn't reply. But Johnny saw assent in his father's eyes, and that night, with the rest of the family adding their blessings, he flew to San Juan.

For years I'd been fascinated by the particular species of basketball tenderfoot who suffers from a *folie de grandeur*. When 39 members of the Heaven's Gate cult committed mass suicide in San Diego in 1997 as the Hale-Bopp comet made a pass of the earth, I couldn't help but notice the parallels. They too made a fetish of Nikes. They too spoke obsessively of "going to the next level." They too performed inexplicable acts of self-destruction.

By law, the NBA can't exclude anyone from making himself available for its annual draft. Among those to do so in 1996 was Taj (Red) McDavid, a high schooler from Williamston, South Carolina, who, acting on the expert opinion of his family— including an uncle who reputedly said, "There's nobody in the NBA who can stop Red"—declared for the draft even though no college recruiters, much less any pro scouts, had a clue who he was. Red went unchosen, and a year later his high school coach was heard to say, "If you're looking for him, go to the Anderson Mall. He always hangs out at Foot Locker."

The tale of Taj McDavid should have been a cautionary one, yet a year later the number of early entrants increased. The monomaniacal way Johnny Suarez focused on his dream seemed to be distressingly universal. Why was reality so elusive for so many to grasp? What characterized this particular rite of passage? To find out, I headed for the MCI Center in Washington, D.C., site of the 1999 NBA draft.

I'd last attended the draft in 1985, when it was still held in the Felt Forum in Manhattan, a foul antechamber of Madison Square Garden usually reserved for mediocre boxing cards. In those days the draft hadn't yet become basketball's answer to Oscar night. Fans could stumble in off the street and heckle a team for its latest blunder. That year the Dallas Mavericks held three picks in the first round, at eight, 16, and 17, and after the Mavericks spent the first of these on Detlef Schrempf, the polyvalent German, reporters could sidle up to him in the scrum of players, agents, and executives around the stage and ask anything they wanted. I decided simply to hang around Schrempf as his new team prepared to choose at No. 16.

"Dumars!" Schrempf stage-whispered to no one in particular. "Pick *Dumars!*"

Schrempf had played with and against Joe Dumars, a guard from McNeese State, in a couple of all-star games several months earlier. He knew, in a way no front-office suit could know, the many virtues of Dumars's game. Schrempf nonetheless soon heard David Stern intone, "With the 16th pick of the 1985 NBA draft, the Dallas Mavericks select . . . Bill Wennington of St. John's University."

A ghostly look flashed across Schrempf's face. What passed through his mind was probably much like what an avenging Micheal Ray Richardson would yell at Virtus Bologna coach Ettore Messina years later: "W-w-w-wennington's not a b-b-ballplayer! H-h-he's a . . . *l-l-l-lumberjack!*"

But the Mavericks had the next pick, too, their final choice in the first round and No. 17 overall. Schrempf held out hope. "Dumars," he mouthed, more urgently now, as five more minutes passed. "They've gotta pick Dumars!"

"With the 17th pick of the 1985 NBA draft, the Dallas Mavericks select . . . Uwe Blab of Indiana University."

Schrempf looked as if someone had just doused him with

sauerkraut brine. If anyone knew what an irremediable stiff Uwe Blab was, it was his fellow member of the German national team. And if anyone knew that Detroit would soon win two NBA titles, it was Schrempf, when the Pistons snapped up Dumars with the very next pick.

I've often thought back to that scene, wondering how Schrempf could have even entered into contract negotiations with a front office for which he justifiably had so little respect. And I've never forgotten the enduring lesson of that day: If you want to know who can play, it's best to ask those who do play.

As I took the shuttle flight to Washington, I knew better than to expect a moment as revelatory as the one I'd glimpsed at the Felt Forum 14 years earlier. The NBA had long since turned the draft into a slick, prime-time production, rotating the event from one sold-out arena to the next. As prospective draftees waited to be selected, they were now sequestered with their families and agents in a room—it was actually called the "green room"—where they sat at tables with faux-flower center-pieces and sweaty glasses of ice water. All the while, TNT's cameras recorded the hope and dread on their faces. After Stern called his name, the draftee would rise from his seat. His frame would go slack with relief beneath the fabric of his well-tailored suit. A factotum would hand him the cap of his new team and convey him from the green room to the stage. There he would shake Stern's hand, then exit stage right to a series of tightly controlled interactions with the press.

The entire process was now a ritual so stylized that, to make sense of it, I had enlisted the help of an expert: Rick Olsen, a professor of communication studies at the University of North Carolina at Wilmington. While watching the draft six years earlier, he began pondering a question his wife had put to him: How come you like watching this so much? He started to sketch out plot lines during the telecast, and realized that what seemed to be a purely informational event was in fact a finely scripted drama, which he went on to analyze in his doctoral dissertation.

While reading Olsen's *Drafting a New American Dream: An*

Analysis of the NBA Draft Using a Triangulated Approach to Rhetorical Criticism I was fathoms out of my depth. I stumbled over the distinction between polysemy and metonymy, and never did sort out heuristics from hermeneutics. But I got the gist of his point: that the draft functions as a coherent and effective piece of television. To attract a prime-time audience TNT has to bait the hook with drama. Moreover, the NBA has ideological messages it wants to send. In the hands of the league's entertainment division, the broadcast becomes a powerful "rhetorical text," as the pointy heads would say.

A few hours before the draft I found Olsen in the lobby of the Washington Renaissance Hotel. Nattily turned-out families and girlfriends of likely draftees clotted its length and breadth, filling the hall with expectant buzz. Olsen—in his thirties, not quite six feet, with sandy hair and glasses—stuck out in this crowd. He had isolated a range of passages that would take place that evening, from boy to man, from poor to rich, from amateur to professional, from regional figure to national (and, increasingly, international) one. As the night sanctified transformation, it would also celebrate hope. "Not just the hopes of the players," he told me. "The hopes of the franchises and their fans, too. It's the only time the Clippers and Vancouver matter—the only time they're on TV all year."

The draft also served as a Trojan horse for the NBA's ideology. "A few years ago the broadcast kept emphasizing how these kids' lives would radically change because of the money they'd make, and there was no disadvantage to a kid's eagerness to get to the NBA," Olsen said. "Now the telecast puts a more cautionary frame around the narrative. The NBA has decided it wants to discourage early entrants, so it's happy with the more realistic appraisal of the talent. In their commentary Rick Majerus and John Thompson dwell on the stay-in-school thing and allude to myths that pertain to the work ethic, to overcoming the odds. So on the telecast, watch—we'll see a lot of rusty fences outside playgrounds, lots of kindly grandmothers."

Olsen pointed out how TNT's telecast borrowed from every form of televised event. The suspense echoed the Oscars. The set and podium, hung with red, white, and blue NBA heraldry, looked like those of a political convention. There was even an element of the Barbara Walters special, thanks to TNT interviewer Craig Sager, who famously removed the Milwaukee Bucks cap from Stephon Marbury's head at the 1996 draft so viewers could better see his tears.

As we walked the several blocks to the MCI Center, I told Olsen a little bit about Johnny Suarez. For every obstacle that crossed his path, Johnny liked to cite some professional player who had faced a similar vicissitude. It was as if he carried with him an official NBA authorized edition of *Life's Little Instruction Book*. Some excerpts from this volume were endearing, such as the way Johnny approvingly pointed out how Mark Jackson coped with the death of his father. Another player helped Johnny stare down the long odds he faced as he dreamed of fulfilling his fantasy: "Dennis Rodman, he didn't play high school ball and he still made the NBA," he had told me. "That gives me hope." But one comment he had made—in reference to pressure he was getting from Jovanka—left me chilled, for I could hear him deploying it in arguments with the mother of his son: "After he finished playing, that's when Michael Jordan said it was time to spend more time with his family."

Rick nodded as if he had known Johnny his entire life. "Stories help us cope, and our culture provides them—shared fantasies or ideals that encourage us in certain ways. Nike ads tell us to Just Do It. Canon tells us Image Is Everything. The press covers Dennis Rodman instead of a variety of other, more worthwhile stories. Johnny is looking to the media for tools for living, for ways to cope with what reality sends his way. In the case of Mark Jackson dealing with his father's death, he's picked a fairly good mediated example. But a lot of boys take tools for living from Arnold Schwarzenegger roles. A lot of girls take them from Madonna. And while many kids can throw up a fourth wall between themselves and a mediated example and say, 'That's just entertainment,' many can't.

"It's interesting to watch the norms and attitudes of pro sports trickle down into the culture. And to see how the culture at large responds. I've seen one study where 51 percent of adolescents surveyed in Chicago said they could make it in pro sports if given the right break."

In a few hours we would be watching a blitz of propaganda on behalf of that myth. Despite the caveat of the Taj McDavid case, despite the NBA's attempt to "put a more cautionary frame around the narrative," the spectacle of the draft would seduce more and more Johnnys into entertaining the most fanciful hoop dreams.

On the floor of the MCI Center we positioned ourselves so we could follow both the live pageantry and TNT's commentary on a nearby monitor. That prophet of bootstrapping African-American ambition, Jesse Jackson, sat just behind us.

A year earlier, broadcast host Ernie Johnson and his hall-monitor commentators—Majerus, Thompson, and Hubie Brown—had pounded away at the stay-in-school message. Perhaps that's why the number of underclassmen to declare for early entry had stabilized. Here the TNT crew sounded the same theme, even after the Chicago Bulls made an underclassman, Elton Brand of Duke, the first pick. With the second choice, the Vancouver Grizzlies chose another nonsenior, Maryland guard Steve Francis, who scowled after being chosen by a Canadian doormat. "As soon as I can take it off, I will," he said, indicating the team cap that had been placed on his head. Francis would ultimately force the Grizzlies to trade his rights to the Houston Rockets.

After the Charlotte Hornets chose Baron Davis of UCLA, yet another underclassman, at No. 3, the narrative reached a turn—the fourth pick, which belonged to the Los Angeles Clippers. It was a moment Olsen had been waiting for. Like all television serials, the draft needs strong characterization, and the hapless, clue-free Clippers are as well-drawn a character as any in sports. They are the Joe Bfstplks of June. As soon as the commissioner announced their choice—"With the fourth pick of the 1999 NBA draft, the Los Angeles Clippers select . . . Lamar Odom of the University of Rhode Island"—Olsen nodded. Odom was an underclassman who had disappeared from campus in the midst of the school year. He put his name in for the draft, then pulled it out, then put it in again when he discovered that the NCAA wasn't likely to restore his eligibility. After all that, he blew off invitations to work out with two NBA teams, and on the eve of the draft was left to insist, Nixonlike, "I am not a cancer."

After Stern announced the pick, I half-expected Jesse Jackson to say, "Keep no-hope alive!"

"Of course the Clippers choose Odom," Olsen said. "That's what makes them the Clippers. They need stability, so they pick Lamar Odom. Year after year, you can count on it. They're like the fool in the Shakespeare play who relieves the tension. We laughed about the Clippers, but everybody else was laughing, too. People may wonder why women follow soap operas and men follow sports. In fact, they follow them for the same reason. Both have compelling, fleshed-out characters and trackable plot lines."

As the first round moved into the teens, the MCI Center turned into a huge souk of humanity. Rod Thorn, one of Stern's top aides, began to announce trades. Most were apparently trivial transactions—a second-round choice tonight for a similar one next year, or some arcane flip-flop in draft order. None carried with it the fate of a franchise. But every time Thorn took the stage and said, "We have a trade," a cheer went up from the crowd.

"The crowd always applauds a trade, even before they know what it is," Olsen said. "It's on all the videotapes I've studied. That's because they want a plot twist. It's human nature for people to get pleasure out of deriving meaning from uncertainty. It's why mystery is the most popular genre. I can turn to my buddy and argue, 'That was stupid.' Or, 'That was great.'"

After the 21st pick, only Jumaine Jones, a 6'7" small forward from Georgia, remained in the green room. His gray suit began to look as if it were stitched of ashes, and you could almost hear that old Janis Ian song, the one about "those whose names are never called, when choosing sides for basketball." Jones had led the Southeastern Conference in scoring, but he was only a sophomore, and on TNT Thompson thundered his disapproval. "It's a pitiful thing," he said. "Stay in school!"

"Most initiation rites involve some kind of indignity," Olsen said. "Of course, this is a pretty gentle form of humiliation, given the money Jumaine will get if he's picked in the first round. But right now he's stuck between worlds. He's neither boy nor man, neither amateur nor professional. He's in that limbo of temporary demotion before promotion. A prospective draftee is neither a BMOC nor an NBA player. No one wants to *stay* a prospective draftee. Which is what Jumaine has been for a long time now."

Jones was finally delivered from his purgatory, at No. 27, by the Atlanta Hawks. At the podium he greeted Stern with a handshake and a wan smile through tears—of relief, he'd later say. Then he faced the press, exerting himself to say how excited he was to be headed to the Hawks, to stay in his home state, to have a chance to hook up with a buddy from summer ball, fellow draftee Dion Glover of Georgia Tech, and to play for Lenny Wilkens, "one of the best coaches in the league."

Minutes later the Hawks traded his rights to Philadelphia. Jones was trotted out again to reiterate all the obligatory niceties, only now about the 76ers. He pulled this off with remarkably little awkwardness. "It's a better situation for me in Philly. Less forwards. I feel like I can get a little playing time. I feel like it's a steal for Philadelphia." He knew the notes to sound: transformation and hope.

Toward midnight the crowd began to thin. Thorn had replaced Stern in the pulpit. "It's the deep fan experience now," Olsen said. Intoxicated men in Starter team jackets crept down to the railing by the floor, hoping their tasteless catcalls—"Rod Thorn's got chlamydia!" and "I want to bear Glenn Robinson's love child!"—would make air. These hardcores understood the plot and knew the characters better than the typical fan, but all that knowledge didn't correlate with decorum. "With the 42nd pick of the 1999 NBA draft," Thorn began, "the Minnesota Timberwolves select . . ."

"*Yo mama!*"

What we'd seen conformed with trends Olsen had already begun tracking several drafts ago. With few exceptions, the newly rich draftees spent interviews invoking a mother or grandmother, not a male counterpart. (There had been only one father in evidence all night: Wally Szczerbiak's dad, Walt, a former star with Real Madrid whose son, the story line went, hoped to redeem his father's failure to play in the NBA.) Five of the six pure centers chosen had been non-Americans. But more than anything, we had heard two notes besides transformation and hope struck over and over. One celebrated the value of hard work; the other heralded the unproven teenager who hits the jackpot. Together they made a dissonant sound.

"We put these guys in a double bind," Olsen said. "The American Dream was once to work hard and make money. Now it's make money and glide over the working hard part if you can. But when we push the dream hard and some people fail at it, we still moralize about their choice. The guys who declare early for the draft are only choosing what the culture is telling them to choose. Tonight the work ethic was exalted, but it was also being undermined. It couldn't help but be, when a first-round pick is guaranteed almost $1,800,000 regardless of performance."

Olsen and I missed TNT's signoff. But during his doctoral research, Olsen had studied enough telecasts to know the outcue. "Right at the end of the broadcast Hubie Brown tries to console those who weren't chosen. He's the perfect guy to do it, because you can imagine him growing up with a picture of the Blessed Mother tacked over his dresser. He'll retell the story of John Starks, the guy who bagged groceries and played in the CBA before making it to the league. Hubie makes Starks seem like some patron saint to pray to—St. John of the Undrafted."

The Gospel According to John was already in Johnny Suarez's personal breviary.

By the time Johnny returned home from Puerto Rico, his father had passed away. My wife and I invited him by, to offer our sympathies and hear how the tryout had gone. When we opened the door to our apartment, he was cradling Brandon in his arms. It was the first sign that he might not be the same person who left.

Johnny had played well. He survived the first round of cuts, from 50 players to 20, even though others were in better shape and quicker to pick things up. And though Coamo didn't offer him a contract, representatives of the club told Johnny's college coach that they'd liked what they'd seen. He needed seasoning, but the team would be closely following his progress. In perhaps the most encouraging development of the week, Johnny took this in stride. The entire experience had been his first reality check in months. "We did a four-man weave," he said. "I didn't even know you could *do* a weave with four guys. And you know how many plays there were for the point guard to learn? Fifteen!"

He betrayed no dread while recounting all this, no echo of "If, God forbid, I don't make it"—only exhilaration at how much better he might become. Nor had the tryout jeopardized his collegiate eligibility. In fact, he could play in the university league during the winter and, if the call came, in the LSB during the summer. In Puerto Rico, a permissive attitude on such matters prevailed.

The family would soon fly to the island for Angelo's burial. Johnny, Jovanka, and Brandon would stay there, she to find work and Johnny to return to school. Johnny was still Johnny, snatching from the basketball ether any mediated tool for living he could use. "When Michael Jordan quit basketball after his father died, I was like, 'What's up with *that?*'" he said. "Being in his shoes, now I can understand how he felt." But my wife and I were struck by what seemed to be the sober turn in his attitude and the responsibility implicit in his plans. "He left a boy," my wife remarked. "He came back a man."

The loss of a parent can leave a child feeling suddenly mature—terribly, unnaturally so. It can also leave him bereft of good advice. Good advice is like a parachute—of little use unless you're favored with it at just the right time. If Johnny continued to embark on his flights of fantasy, I only hoped someone would be there to make sure he packed a chute, lest he end up like Declan Kelly Jr., or Taj McDavid, poltergeist of the Anderson Mall. Basketball exhilarates in the heights to which its practitioners aspire and sometimes ascend. But when the falls come, they can be long and hard.

TWENTY-FOUR

France

The "I Love This Game" Theory of Conflict Prevention

In a spare moment I'd asked Rick Olsen why he chose to study the NBA draft. He could have easily examined some ritual from baseball or football, fields that scholars of American sport have long preferred to plow.

"Basketball is a more fluid game with less-defined rules," he told me. "It emphasizes versatility and initiative. In that way, it best reflects current trends in our society. The other day I was talking with a neighbor who works in education. She said there's a new buzzword in her field: holonomy. We all know about autonomy. It's well-integrated in our culture because we're so individualistic. But we also have an interest in emphasizing team goals, and that's where autonomy meets the group. You can see the duality between individualism and collectivism best in basketball. Players don't just play offense or defense, or regroup after every down to have instructions dictated from the top, the way they do in football. And basketball doesn't have narrow, skill-specific positions, as baseball does. In basketball, everybody has to be able to do everything, and that fits in with today's corporate culture—with downsizing, with 'intrapreneuring,' with employers 'cross-training' employees so they can do two or three jobs at once.

"It's the same way outside the corporate world. We're more

mobile than ever. More and more of us are less and less likely to
have an extended family around, so we end up internalizing a
lot of things—being our own family, in a way. Home might not
be a physical space, but a psychological one. This may not seem
connected to basketball, but to an extent, a ballplayer has to
build a home for himself, too. He has to be able to score,
rebound, defend, pass—to be his own best friend. Everything
has to be autonomized, 'self-contained in me.' Why else the
exaltation of the triple double as a stat? It's a way of saying, 'You
did everything.'

"Yet at the same time we do have a need to connect. As much
as we exalt individualism, we don't celebrate the monk as a cultural ideal. Even monks form communities in monasteries. So
basketball's ideal lies somewhere between autonomy on the one
hand, and a complete absence of individualism on the other.
Kobe Bryant gets chastised for being too individualistic, and
Derrick McKey gets criticized for being too unselfish—for not
being autonomous enough. Holonomy is a safe way for a capi-
talist society to recognize the benefits and uses of collectivism.
I don't know if the word will catch on, least of all in basketball.
But it's a good way to articulate our need to reconcile our individualistic nature with our quest for connection with others."

I wondered how far Olsen's observations obtained beyond
the U.S. With basketball having advanced to the far reaches of
a world growing more integrated and Americanized by the
hour, perhaps the game's popularity reflected a trend toward
holonomy on a global scale.

To fly from Washington to Paris is normally simple enough:
You choose from among several nonstops shuttling between
those old statesmen, Dulles and de Gaulle. But 10 months on
the road had trained me to economize, so I cashed in fre-
quent-flyer miles for a ticket routing me from D.C. to Paris
by way of Miami and London. It was a witless decision.
What might have been a trip out of E. M. Forster ("Only

connect . . .") turned into something booked by Kafka Tours and Travel.

I got as far as Miami. For six hours mechanics there tried to coax a light on the control panel of our 747 to account for itself. For six hours they failed. With the pilot unwilling to go wheels up in defiance of that stubborn illumination, I and several hundred other cranky passengers were herded into an Embassy Suites near the airport. Even if my plans had gone off without this hitch, I would have barely reached Paris in time to catch the last two rounds of the European Championships. Now, re-booked to fly out 24 hours later, I'd miss the semifinals completely and, barring any more delays, only just make the final.

The next morning, marooned in Miami with a day to kill, I logged on to the Web site for the Eurobasket. Every country pared away from Tito's old South Slav state had qualified for the final 16 in France—Bosnia, Croatia, Slovenia, even little Macedonia. But only the Serbian and Montenegrin leftovers, still known as Yugoslavia, remained. As bytes filled up the screen of my laptop, I couldn't decide what was more remarkable: that I could follow every basket of the semifinal between Italy and Yugoslavia in real time, or that the *azzurri* were in the midst of putting a 40-minute hurt on the defending world champions. I wasn't counting on reaching Paris in time to see it, but Spain, which had just eliminated France, would be playing Italy the next day for the title.

It had been some time since I'd last looked in on basketball in the Balkans. NATO had begun its bombardment of Yugoslavia in late March, in response to Belgrade's aggression in Kosovo. The attacks had ended only a few weeks before the Eurobasket was to tip off. Sitting in the shade-drawn gloom of a room in a tropical airport hotel, with jet fumes leaking through the window frames, I surfed to another site, and there discovered how the war had thrown Yugoslav basketball into chaos.

The arena in Leskovac, 150 miles south of Belgrade, had taken a direct hit from a NATO bomb. To limit the risk to crowds, the Yugoslav league had moved tip-off times for all league games to 2 P.M., and eventually canceled the playoffs.

Ballplayers in the capital liked to hang out at a pizzeria called New York New York, but in light of events, the place had changed its name. It was now known as the Baghdad Cafe.

Despite the bombing, the national team had tried its best to prepare for the Eurobasket. But by mid-May the Yugoslavs' usual training site atop Belgrade's Mount Kopaonik had been destroyed. The team was forced to train in the Greek city of Thessaloniki, and the Spanish government refused to permit its nationals to play several scheduled exhibition games. Strapped for funds and support staff, coach Željko Obradović was left to do everything from fetching food to taping ankles. Nonetheless, everyone connected with the team spoke bravely, defiantly. "It is not in our nature to cry," Obradović said. Sasha Djordjević, still the team's point guard, sounded like the same leader he had been in Bormio a dozen years earlier. "I don't see anyone challenging us in France," he said. "We're so outraged by what's gone on in our country, we could wind up beating everybody by 100 points."

In fact, Djordjević would bruise an Achilles tendon and fail to play. The star of Yugoslavia's run to its world title, center Željko Rebrača, would also sit because of injury. The Yugoslav team that limped into Paris was ill-prepared and below full strength, and its loss to Italy shouldn't have been a surprise.

One posting on the site impressed me more than any other. Four days after NATO began to target Belgrade, a handful of players were working out at Pionir, the home court of Red Star, where Vlade Divac had briefly played during the NBA lockout. In the midst of a game of three-on-three, air-raid sirens began to wail. Most of the players scattered. But a stalwart of the national team, a forward with Red Star named Milenko Topić, refused to head for the exits.

"Pionir is the safest place in town," he said.

Someone asked what made him so sure.

"Because NATO knows it's full of NBA prospects."

Flying into Paris at last, I should have had haute cuisine on the brain. Instead I found myself reflecting on how much of the past year had been overhung with golden arches.

A McDonald's occupied the sacred plot in Springfield. The player revolt that helped do in Mike McCollow had been hatched at a McDonald's in the Polish boondocks. McDonald's sponsored my old club in Switzerland. Buzz and Michael cemented their friendship at the McDonald's High School All-America Game. I could have just as easily found Aulcie Perry at a kosher Mickey D's. Sometimes my travels struck me as less a grand tour than a succession of trips to the drive-thru.

When I began my journey, I subscribed to a vague belief that basketball somehow made the world smaller. *New York Times* foreign affairs columnist Thomas Friedman has a theory that dovetails with that premise. He believes the world shrinks as markets expand, and nations that share a stake in the global bazaar are loath to engage in anything as disruptive as war. To make his point, Friedman has developed the Golden Arches Theory of Conflict Prevention, which holds that no two countries with at least one McDonald's franchise have fought a war since each opened its McDonald's. "When [a country] has a middle class big enough to support a McDonald's, it becomes a McDonald's country," he has written. "And people in McDonald's countries don't like to fight wars."

Friedman's theory had been shaken by NATO's action in the Balkans, for a McDonald's sat in downtown Belgrade. But Milenko Topić's brash assertion at the Red Star gym—that NATO might spare Yugoslav basketball in the name of hoops—had led me to try to fit Friedman's theory with new particulars.

Swap out the golden arches for the NBA's promotional tagline, and you have the "I Love This Game" Theory of Conflict Prevention: No two countries with at least one citizen in the NBA have fought a war since its citizen joined the NBA. When a country places a player in the NBA, it gains a stake in a kind of international movement, and people in NBA countries would rather watch and play ball than fight wars. A corollary might hold that any two countries whose citizens play in each other's national leagues are less likely to engage in hostilities than any two countries whose citizens don't.

I'd argue that basketball's potential to be an intercultural epoxy exceeds that of McDonald's or any other mass-market retailer. First, the game isn't really an objectifiable product. Anyone can partake of it, no purchase necessary. The beggar in Bombay who happens by the open door of a café with satellite TV, the schoolgirl in Tanzania who has a ball roll her way during recess, the bellhop in Bali whose eye is caught by the Miami Heat T-shirt worn by the tourist he has just led to the front desk—all have been touched by its influence. The NBA may be as slick and rapacious as any multinational corporation, but the league doesn't come off as being so because its product is a pageant of human striving, not some comestible that disappears into the alimentary canal. Further, basketball took root around the world long before the NBA's founding. So years later, when the league began to export its version of the game, the NBA came to be regarded less as a force of cultural imperialism than as an elite version of something essentially familiar. French farmers, Chinese students, British environmentalists— they've all rioted against McDonald's. It's hard to imagine anyone rioting against the NBA.

Of course, my theory didn't do much better than Friedman's when faced with the example of Yugoslavia. But during the NATO bombardment, no one but the odd ethnic heckler targeted Vlade Divac as he plied the NBA trail for the Sacramento Kings—and anti-American vandals *did* shatter the plate glass of that McDonald's in Belgrade, forcing it to close. Indeed, what distinguishes basketball is that people now migrate virtually everywhere to play it. There may be no better example of North Korea's status as a pariah state than its failure, despite strenuous diplomatic efforts, to secure a work permit for 7'9" Ri Myong Hun to play in the NBA. And there may be no better hope for Yugoslavia's reconciliation with Europe in the aftermath of the Kosovo conflict than this: At the time of the war, more than 160 Yugoslavs played beyond the borders of their country, most of them for club teams in NATO member states. Even as Slo-bodan Milošević dragooned Serbia further and further beyond the pale, every one of those ballplayers, consciously or not, served as a counterweight to Milošević's ideology of ethnic sep-aratism simply by playing an international game internationally.

As soon as my flight landed at Orly, I grabbed a cab and rushed to the Palais Omnisports in the Parisian quarter of Bercy. The ride began through the sprawl that rings the city. Few tourists are aware of this "circular purgatory," as French social critic François Maspero calls it, "with Paris as paradise in the middle." In the Parisian suburbs you'll find high-rise apartment blocks, women in *hejab*, branch offices for Crédit de Maroc, long-distance phone shops that allow menial workers from francophone West Africa to keep in touch with home. Here émigrés from the Ivory Coast, Senegal, Guadeloupe, and other points *outre-mer* turned the game that Americans know as an inner-city pastime inside out, creating a thriving, outer-city playground basketball culture. This helped explain why blacks made up half of *les bleus*—why the press called the French national team *les Américains d'Europe*.

The Palais Omnisports is a huge bunker on the banks of the Seine with grass growing on its roof, which makes it look like a plot in a cemetery. Stumbling inside midway through the bronze medal game between France and Yugoslavia, I had expected to hear hostility, or at least feel it. I could discern none. The fans were chauvinistic enough to provide a reminder that the word "chauvinist" is French in origin, but they applauded the Yugoslavs just the same. Players on both teams showed one another sportsmanship. A small knot of Serbs in the upper mezzanine broke out into occasional chants about Kosovo, but the rest of the crowd ignored them with a we're-okay, Eur-okay blitheness.

Late in the second half, finding himself alone with the ball at the top of the key, Vlade Divac sighted and sank a three-pointer. He stuck three fingers in the air in a configuration that matched the Serb salute. The French called a timeout. And the PA doused the whole scene with the sonic wash of "Papa's Got a Brand New Bag."

Given France's central role in the NATO alliance, it would have been easy to impute a political motive to Divac's gesture. But along press row I found Ailene Voisin, who covered Divac and the Kings for the *Sacramento Bee,* and she told me that in NBA games Divac routinely raised those three fingers after sinking a three. She had asked him about it, and he had told her the gesture had no ulterior meaning.

After the Yugoslavs' victory, and before Italy defeated Spain for the title, Divac said much the same thing he had told me back in 1996. He disputed that he had come to Paris with any motive beyond the sportsman's purest one. "We know most of our opponents personally. We play with each other, as I do with [French star and fellow Sacramento King] Tariq [Abdul-Wahad]. When you go beyond that, you quickly get into politics, and I detest politics. We're athletes, not criminals or government officials, even if people sometimes have a hard time making the distinction. I've never wanted to be implicated in politics. It's part of my character. I've had bad experiences with all that. All over the world, governments spend their time manipulating their people. I would live wherever's best for me and my family, and at the moment, that's in Los Angeles. People are going to question me about my nationality, but that's of no importance to me. I am a Serb and a citizen of the world."

No, Divac could no longer count Teo Alibegović and Toni Kukoč and Dino Radja as national teammates. But he did share a team with Chris Webber and Jason Williams and Abdul-Wahad, a devout Muslim. And tomorrow he could very easily be traded to, say, the Philadelphia 76ers, where he might be teamed up anew with Kukoč, a Catholic and a Croat. Collecting players of every nationality, then recombining them regardless of origin, the NBA really could create a new world order, virtually on a whim.

Perhaps Divac had us conned. Maybe he was giving expression to some crypto-Chetnik bravado every time he flashed three fingers after a three-pointer. I had no way of knowing for sure, and I probably shouldn't have been so naive as to think that basketball could promote brotherhood among men when it couldn't even sustain friendship among the Boys of Bormio. But I'd come to learn enough about Divac to take him at his word. He blamed the political crisis alienating him from his old junior teammates for killing off a part of himself. He still funded a charitable foundation that funneled clothing, food, and medicine to Balkan children at orphanages and hospitals, regardless of nationality. So long as he shunned the ethnic cleansers, so long as he claimed the citizenship of the world, every time he sank a three and flashed his fingers, perhaps a few more noxious scales fell away from the Serb salute. I wanted to believe that if he were to keep doing so, and if kids playing in driveways in Sacramento and around the world came to mimic him, the gesture might someday wind up having all the political meaning of a high five.

One raw Parisian spring morning in 1918, Doc Naismith left his hotel and headed down the boulevard Saint-Michel for his office with the American Expeditionary Forces. He was ahead of schedule, and the cold and damp of the day caused him to duck into a small shop stacked floor to ceiling with books. There a small volume with a red cover caught his eye. Curious, he cracked it open. He was surprised and delighted to find a chapter devoted to his invention.

The book, published in 1897, was called *Les Sports pour Tous*. Back then, basketball surely merited a place in a book entitled *Sports for All*. But a century later, *le basket hot* was no longer one game of many. On the cusp of the 21st century, it was poised to become the sport for all.

TWENTY-FIVE

Angola

*Lasme's Plane Will Be
Arriving Shortly*

For all the open wounds at the European Championships, Paris was at least at peace. The Eurobasket's African counterpart took place in the midst of war. The U.S. State Department warnings were explicit and grave: Do not go to Angola. The country hosting the Afrobasket was replete with peril, "renewed military conflict," and "continuing violent crime." Visitors could expect bandit attacks, undisciplined soldiers, and unexploded land mines. Those who insisted on going were to avoid crowds and steer clear of demonstrations, and under no circumstances go to the police for assistance, for they were underpaid and unpredictable. If this weren't enough, the Centers for Disease Control reported a polio epidemic in Luanda, the capital, that was further driving down a life expectancy already so modest that nearly one in every three children died before turning five.

There was no complying with any of these admonitions, not if I were to take the measure of the game on its most untapped continent. And so I waded into an atmosphere for which the locals had a well-worn word: *confusão*, a multipurpose Angolanism indicating chaos, danger, and uncertainty, of multiple sources and indeterminate length.

It would be impossible to avoid crowds. All the capital was a crowd. Luanda was once a sunbaked Portuguese colonial port city, built in the 16th century to accommodate about 30,000 people. Now it had swollen to 3.5 million with refugees from the 25-year-old war, a truculent, almost medieval conflict exacerbated by plague and famine. A fragile cease-fire had broken nine months earlier, and since then more than a million people had fled their homes in the country's interior, most of them flocking to Luanda. I was going in late July, the middle of the dry season, when both the government forces and Jonas Savimbi's UNITA rebels promised to launch offensives that were certain to kill and displace many more. This was Savimbi's latest strategy: Flush civilians out of the countryside and the provincial cities, drive them into the capital, then bring down the government by making its seat of power ungovernable. At least this had a kind of chilly logic to it. Normally, in the spirit of *confusão*, the fighting followed a more absurdist line, never more so than in 1988, when Cuban troops defended American refineries in the oil-rich Cabinda enclave from UNITA attacks funded by the CIA.

Nor were demonstrations to be avoided. Every day at the Afrobasket would be a demonstration, for every day would feature the favorite, Angola's national team. Most Luandans hated Savimbi and resented the government. "The rebels kill us with weapons," a young Luandan would tell me, "and the government kills us with starvation." But they were also at one in their love for the team and desire to see their homeland's suffering mitigated, however fleetingly, with a championship. Another African title would be Angola's fifth, vaulting the host country into the company of Egypt and Senegal as the only nations to pull off the *penta* and thereby retire the trophy. A homemade banner overhanging the court at the Pavilhão Gimnodesportivo turned miseries into points of pride. COM GUERRA E FOME O PENTA SERA NOSSO! it read—"With war and hunger, a fifth title will be ours!"

Finally, there was no avoiding the police, as I discovered at the *pavilhão* my first night in town. Every entrance was barricaded by a brace of cops, each outfitted with German shepherd, riot shield, nightstick, sunglasses, and AK-47. If their mission was to maintain order, they succeeded: Perfect coffles of fans filed through metal detectors and presented their tickets, for which scalpers were getting up to 25 million kwanza, eight months' salary for the average Angolan—an empty comparison, for the average Angolan rarely held a job and even more rarely got paid.

From watching a wispy young man I learned that you could indeed approach the police with a question, but only by performing an elaborate ritual. He stood 20 paces away from guard dogs straining at their leashes, then brought his hands together in the universal timeout sign. Only when he was sure the policeman had acknowledged him did the man advance close enough to be heard.

You tried to make your peace with the police, if only because the alternative was to leave yourself to the tender mercies of UNITA. Luandans widely assumed that Savimbi's men had already infiltrated the city. Only 10 days before my arrival, 80 rebel troops had swanned into Catete, a town not 35 miles from here, before dawn. Catete is the birthplace of Augustinho Neto, Angola's first president and a forefather of the MPLA, UNITA's longtime adversary and the party now ruling the country. The rebels shot up the town, killing civilians and murdering the police chief and two government administrators. By 9 A.M. they were gone. There seemed to be no military purpose to the raid. A diplomat in Luanda told me that it appeared designed to do only one thing: put on notice the players, coaches, and fans of the dozen nations participating in the African Championships.

Angolan president José Eduardo dos Santos was just as determined to prove that life went on, so he forged ahead with the Afrobasket, as much to spite Savimbi as in spite of him. The government was running a $12 billion debt and had to set aside 40 percent of its budget to wage war, yet it somehow found $7 million with which to stage the tournament and another $2.5 in annual support for the national team. In its effort to bag the prize the *penta* would bring, Africa's lone bid to the Sydney Olympics, Team Angola had pinballed around the world to train and tune up. The players' equipment and warmups were top-of-the-line. Their well-credentialed Portuguese coach, Mario Palma, had a handsome contract. While the 11 visiting teams were billeted at a sort of motel court verged by shantytowns at the edge of the city, the Angolan players stayed in Western-style opulence at the Presidente Meridien, on the promenade overlooking Luanda Bay. They ate meals served on white tablecloths by blazered waiters and drank from $7 bottles of mineral water. Nothing disturbed their air-conditioned slumber except the occasional gunshot from the adjacent port, where the police shot thieves on sight. I'd heard about governments falling over a lost soccer match, but here was a case of a regime that seemed to be staking its standing on a basketball title.

Angola was magnificent in the first game I saw, defeating Mozambique 104–47. Coach Palma had studied with both Arizona's Lute Olson and the Yugoslav defensive shaman Bozidar Maljković, and it showed. The Angolan post men poached over from the weak side to block shots. When defending the ball, the guards seemed to know where a dribbler wanted to go even before he did, and scuttled around to seal off a path before it could be taken. There was a high-end Division I American collegiate quality to the Angolans' spacing, ball movement, depth, and devotion to their roles. Everyone in the building could sense how determined they were to win, if only for the $23,000 bonus each had been promised for the *penta*.

Yet something struck me as strange. I had never sat among a crowd so willing to defer to the judgment of the officials. The fans were far from passionless; they had brought along a rummage sale's worth of noisemakers—gas canisters and serving spoons, bongos, snares, metal trays, pot tops, coffee cans. They made a rumpus after every flight of the team's 24-year-old star guard, Edmar (Baduna) Victoriano, and after every muscled layup from Jean-Jacques Conceição, who had been discovered in one of Luanda's squalid *musseques* and, at 35, was playing in his last international tournament. They celebrated lustily after the home team scored its 100th point, on a free throw by Herlander Coimbra, the 6'7", 168-pound forward whom Charles Barkley had famously elbowed to the floor during the original Dream Team's opening game at the 1992 Olympics. And they jumped on opponents, like the Mozambican who, after dunking on a breakaway, was hooted down for his presumption. But the derision we're conditioned to hearing from a juiced-up crowd at a bad call or no call or any bang-bang judgment that goes against the home team—offensive foul, over-the-back, whatever—never materialized.

I asked an American diplomat about the crowd's unwillingness to take on the referees, and he launched into a summary of Angolan history. "This country began as a source of slaves," he said. "There was forced labor—virtual slavery—as recently as 1961. Then came Portuguese fascism under Salazar, followed by the Cuban-Soviet model. This is a society with a 500-year history of totalitarianism. People simply don't speak their minds to authority."

Nor did Angola's merciless attitude toward its rivals much surprise him. Watching on TV with an Angolan friend two nights earlier, he had seen the hosts defeat South Africa 85–25 in the Afrobasket's opener. South Africa was no great favorite of the Luandans. The old apartheid regime was reviled for its open alliance with UNITA and 1975 invasion of the country. But even after the ascension of Nelson Mandela, Angola felt the new South African government hadn't shown sufficient gratitude for Luanda's support during the many years Mandela's African National Congress spent in the wilderness. "The score was 61–19 and Angola still had four of its five starters in, pressing," the diplomat told me. "I asked my friend if it wasn't time to send in the towel boys. He looked at me as if I'd suggested heresy. It was so extraordinary, I actually sent Washington a cable about it. But it was very Angolan. Victory here is defined as total victory, as the complete destruction and humiliation of your opponent. And that's why this whole conflict has an 'Emperor's New Clothes' quality to it. Because UNITA will never take the coastal cities, and the government will never completely wipe out UNITA.

"This is a terribly dysfunctional country, and the Afrobasket is an obscene misallocation of resources. But how can you not hope Angola wins after what they've been through? Basketball is all they have. Their soccer team recently lost 3–0 to Mauritius at home. Angolans are quite disciplined people, but they're incredibly fun-loving, too, and they could use some good news."

The next afternoon I found the president of the Ivory Coast Basketball Federation in the bar at the Meridien, gazing out over the bay as he nursed a Coke and whacked a pack of Winstons against an oak table. Alphonse Bilé is the son of a French mother and an Ivoirian father, and on the streets of Paris he's so often mistaken for the actor Billy Dee Williams that friends call him Bilé Dee. But today there was nothing smooth in his mood. For two nights he had been unable to sleep. The Afrobasket was already into its third day and the Ivory Coast national team still hadn't shown up.

The delegation had been booked from Abidjan on Air Gabon, scheduled to connect through Libreville. But at the airport the team was told that its plane would not be departing. The players showed up the next day with the same result. Bilé wanted to believe that Air Gabon hadn't sold enough tickets to make either flight profitable, but he wasn't ruling out something more sinister. The president of the Ivory Coast, Henri Konan Bédié, owed his power in part to UNITA's financial support, and his regime was openly pro-Savimbi. As a result, the Angolan government desperately hoped to lure the Ivory Coast to the Afrobasket, if only as a propaganda coup. Over the previous months Bilé had fielded anxious calls every few days from officials with the Angolan Basketball Federation, who offered to pay the Ivoirians' way if that's what it would take to get them to Luanda. Meanwhile Bilé's own government made it clear that his team couldn't accept the Angolans' money, even as the Bédié regime itself refused to fund the trip.

In the end Bilé was able to scrape together enough from private sponsors and the federation's meager treasury to cover the cost. But with tip-off approaching for that night's game against Tunisia, which had already been shifted and delayed, Bilé still didn't have confirmation that the team had even left Abidjan. "I am *traumatisé*," he told me. "These last days in Abidjan, going back and forth to the airport, we have no chance to practice. If the team arrives tonight, the players will have time only to put on their shoes. Yes, I know de Coubertin and all, that we're supposed to be happy simply to take part. But this is so difficult. In the future, if there is only one plane left in the world, only then do I take Air Gabon."

The problem may indeed have been nothing more than Air Gabon's skinflintedness. But I ran alternative theories past Bilé—that authorities in Abidjan might have delayed the plane; or that UNITA itself might have made clear, to the Bédié government or to Air Gabon, that it couldn't guarantee the plane's safety. "I don't know," he said, clearly entertaining their plausibility. "All I know is I asked the government to help send us here. And the government was willing to help junior soccer, but not us."

I mentioned that, from what I'd seen so far, Angola appeared to be a desperately poor country. Bilé did not agree. Angola was lavishly rich, he said, and in that wealth lay its misery.

"Too rich!" he said. "Oil! Diamonds! In Côte d'Ivoire we have nothing like that. Only coffee, cocoa, and bananas. That's why we don't have war. Angolans *think* we're rich. They see that Abidjan is clean, it has freeways, it has skyscrapers. But no. We are not rich. We just have peace. Africa, it is a pitiable continent."

A heron swooped over the bay. Catching it out of the corner of his eye, Bilé jumped with momentary excitement.

"Ughhhh," he said, slumping back down in his chair. "I thought that was Air Gabon."

On my first full day in town a man had bounded up to me in the lobby of the Meridien. He wore well-tended black hair and a bright red polo shirt embroidered with the letters FDU.

"Rob Orellana," he said with a Rotarian's confidence. "Assistant coach, Fairleigh Dickinson University." His handshake redirected my blood flow.

"Are you the only recruiter here?" I asked.

Orellana grinned. "Perry Watson was gonna come with me," he said, referring to the head coach at the University of Detroit. "Spent $2,900 on his plane ticket. Then the week we're supposed to go he called and said his travel agent had written him a letter with 30 reasons not to go to Angola. Said his wife was gonna divorce him if he went. I said, 'Perry, what are you scared of? You're from the streets of Detroit!'

"He said, 'Yeah, but at least I *know* the streets of Detroit.'"

The only other American to defy the State Department warning figured to be one so frisky. But then Orellana had reason to walk with a bounce in his step. At that very moment hundreds of his peers were back in the States, herding themselves from Hasbrouck Heights, New Jersey, to Augusta, Georgia, to Las Vegas, putting in face time at the summertime pageants where the next class of college recruits primped and preened. During the July "observation period," NCAA rules didn't permit coaches to do much more than nod at these prospects, the very best of whom were often controlled by slithery traveling-team coaches on the make, if not on the take. Still, few recruiters dared to leave this very narrow, well-worn trail. Here, Orellana could scope out African talent at a time the number of foreigners playing at U.S. colleges had more than doubled since the Barcelona Olympics. He alone was buttering up the coaches and federation functionaries whose goodwill he'd need to get those players past customs. And so far as anyone in Luanda knew, Fairleigh Dickinson's campus in Teaneck, New Jersey, was the Vatican City of American college basketball, and Orellana its African nuncio.

Orellana came naturally by his interest in overseas hoops. Though he grew up in Los Angeles, both his parents were Peruvian immigrants. He hooked on as a manager at UNLV at just the right time, as the glint from his 1991 NCAA championship ring made clear, and thanks in part to his fluent Spanish, he did brief turns coaching in Venezuela and the Canary Islands. Then one of coach Jerry Tarkanian's assistants on that Runnin' Rebels title team, Ron Ganulin, took over as head coach at St. Francis of Brooklyn of the Northeast Conference. He hired Orellana to find him some players. Rob-O, those in the business called him. I came up with a name of my own: Roborecruiter.

"I knew two players from Venezuela and got 'em to come to the States," he said, describing his maiden signees at St. Francis. "Then I got two more to come from the Canary Islands—eventually, 10 foreign kids in all. Before I got there, St. Francis had won 28 games in four years. After that they won 13, 15, and 20. Not bad for a campus where the only grass is what the students carry in their back pockets. We never even had to give 'em a tour of the campus. We'd take 'em right off the boat."

In 1998 he had crossed the river to join Fairleigh Dickinson, another Northeast Conference team. The Knights now had six foreign players, and based on the business Rob-O expected to do in Luanda, they might soon have several more. "Two here I'd take right now. One from Tunisia, and one from the Ivory Coast, from everything I've heard.

"I'll give you an example of what I'm looking for. Did you see number 10 on Mozambique? He's 21, maybe 6'2", with a good frame. But he's never been coached. Give him three square meals a day, get him working with weights, and you've got a player. That's an Atlantic 10, Big East body, and you can't get that body at our level."

I'd read that more of the slave labor making its way to the New World came from hereabouts than from any other part of Africa. Rob-O was culling from the same precincts. "With any five players from here you could win our league—allowing for a year or two to adapt, to get on a diet and hit the weights, of course. But you'd win any mid-major conference. The proof is St. Francis. Last season they were 16-4 in conference, 20-8 overall. Us, we're looking for a point guard for next year. We could go after one in New Jersey, but there'd be nine or 10 schools in the hunt. The kid from the Ivory Coast, he's only 16. He'll be 17 in December. He's a very, very good player. And now, with the relationships I've made here, I could get him with the snap of my fingers.

"The All-Africa Games are September 9 through 18 in Jo-burg." He winked. "'Jo-burg'—that's Johannesburg. Be there or be square."

That night for dinner I joined Rob-O and Arnaud, a French stat-head who had flown in from Paris to work the scorer's table as a gesture of international goodwill. Though he was a pharmacology student and should have known better, Arnaud somehow forgot to bring his international immunization card. At many African airports this can lead to nightmarish scenes. But in Luanda, airport officials simply asked him to cough up $50.

"Extraordinaire!" Arnaud cooed, clearly more impressed with the efficiency of the solution than the brazenness of the tariff.

"You better believe *extraordinaire,* Frenchy," said Rob-O. "When I went to Cameroon, I didn't even know you needed one of those yellow cards. A rent-a-cop hauled me off into a room and inoculated me himself."

Soon Rob-O was off, telling stories of where he'd gone in the name of player procurement: To Venezuela, where soldiers outside the arena fired rounds into the air to quell a restive crowd; to Cameroon, where to avoid offending officials who would help him pry loose two players he had supped on porcupine stew; to Colombia, where a bus driver wrapped his U.S. passport in a garbage bag and hid it under the hood, lest rebels jumping the bus finger him as a ransom-worthy gringo.

For all the rush he got from the road, Rob-O said he wanted to bail out of college coaching in a couple of years to set up a basketball academy, somewhere in Africa or the Caribbean, that would provide the instruction, diet, and organization that so many Third World prospects lacked. "Six of the top centers in the NBA are from Africa or the Caribbean," he said, ticking off the names of Tim Duncan, Patrick Ewing, Dikembe Mutombo, Hakeem Olajuwon, Michael Olowokandi, and Olden Polynice. "Basketball is where baseball was back in the fifties and sixties. Then you had, what, 22 guys on a team, and 19 had names like Jones and Smith and Johnson, and there'd be the odd Cepeda and Clemente and Marichal who were All-Stars. Now baseball is ruled by Latinos. Well, today in the NBA there's the occasional Olajuwon and Mutombo. But the day someone builds a basketball academy here, it'll be like the day they opened up Puerto Rico, Venezuela, and the Dominican Republic to the major leagues. I mean, puh-*leeease*. Nigeria only has 110 million people. South Africa only has 43 million. *That we know of*. Because how can you take a census in Africa?

"That's where pro basketball is going, toward development. The NBA's level of play has gotten so bad because there's not enough talent to stock the teams night in and night out. Only there is. It just hasn't been found and developed yet."

I asked Rob-O if he had a lead on any other prospects.

"Know that guy Belem?"

Mamadou Belem, the president of the Burkina Faso Basketball Federation, was an amply convex man with whom I'd already shared several cramped elevator rides.

"He comes to me and says, 'Maybe you can help me. At home I have a 16-year-old who's two meters six.'"

"I say, 'Oh, don't worry, *I* can help you!'"

Finally, three days late, the Ivoirians stumbled into town. They had forfeited their game with Tunisia, but they would still get to play Nigeria, South Africa, and Angola, and Mozambique agreed to reschedule for the tournament's rest day. I soon discovered why Rob-O had been up till three in the morning, buying the disconsolate Bilé Dee drinks.

That Ivory Coast point guard was easily the most riveting player in the tournament. Michel Lasme wasn't much to look at before tip-off. He stood barely six feet, with shorts that crept well below his knees. But he could fake his man by sending a tremor down a limb. He could spin forward with the ball cuffed close to his body, as if he were Earl Monroe brought back to action. He could drive with Iversonian fearlessness, only with what seemed like more control. And the ball kindled to his hands. He could yo-yo it, stutter it, cross it over, send it forward or backward through his legs, throw it no-look. His wraparound passes were like wraparound shades, a fashion statement. Though his game still had a few of the pimples of adolescence—he didn't have much conception of defense, and his body went too slack on his jump shot—I was left to think that Abidjan might as well be Peoria. If Lasme really was only 16, he had to be the most skilled 16-year-old point guard on the planet.

Nigeria's point guard, Kingsley Ogwudire, was a Nigerian-American who had grown up dueling with NBA stars Jason Kidd and Gary Payton in the Bay Area, so he had been on the business end of a few moves in his time. But he made the mistake of challenging Lasme at midcourt, and Lasme, in the open floor, sent a dribble *through* Ogwudire's legs. From that moment until the end of the week, the crowd belonged to Lasme. *Catorze!* the fans called out, shouting his uniform number, 14.

Bilé had played on the national team with Lasme's father. Lasme's mother had been the center on the Ivory Coast women's team. "I saw him born," Bilé told me. "From the age of four he has played *basket*. He was on the court all the time when we practiced, and he has come through all of our levels, from mini to cadet to juniors to seniors. There's a playground maybe 100 meters from his parents' home, and he is there all the time. We call him *la perle de la Côte d'Ivoire*."

Panathinaikos Athens, the wealthy club team that regularly turned up in the European final four, had tried to abscond with the Ivory Coast's jewel. Bilé knew enough of how the Greeks operated to veto their generous offer. "If he goes to Panathinaikos," Bilé said, "he'll be Greek in a week."

I found Lasme outside the Ivory Coast locker room. He said he had never been to the U.S., though he would like to go to school there. He also said that his game, while honed at that Abidjan playground, was inspired by TV.

"Are there any particular NBA players you model yourself after?"

"Iverson."

"Anyone else?"

"Iverson," he said, adding a smile. *"C'est tout."*

Lasme went on to tell me he was 17. But he also told me his birthdate was December 14, 1982, which would have made him 16. That Lasme's math didn't compute left me doubting his purported birthdate that much more. But then a birth certificate could surely be ordered up as easily—*extraordinaire!*—as an immunization card.

Rob-O materialized in the corridor, hoping to get what recruiters call a "bump" with his quarry. "You see Lasme's game? The way he *abused* that Nigerian? He could be straight out of Brooklyn. I'm telling you, satellite TV coming to Africa has changed everything. Until satellite TV, all short kids with talent played soccer. And that halftime show tonight?" Five kids in hip-hop garb had entertained the crowd with a routine of lip-synced rap and jerky gesticulation. "Ahhhh," Rob-O said, heading off to find his mark. "Las-me en-ter-*tain* you."

Michel Lasme stood for the game's future and this continent's promise. There were hundreds, perhaps thousands like him in Africa, eager to take off for faraway points where audiences were just as eager to see what they could do. But for every one of its Lasmes, Africa seemed to throw up some obstacle, an Air Gabon determined to keep him from landing.

I first encountered African basketball in 1988, at the Olympics in Seoul, when the Central African Republic played the host South Koreans in a game suffused with the warm-and-fuzzies. The Central Africans had qualified for the Games even though there was only one covered court in their entire country, and most of the two dozen basketballs that existed in all of "Centrafrique" had been a pre-Olympic gift of the South Korean government. The team featured only three pedigreed players,

Freddie Goporo, Bruno Kongawoin, and Anicet Lavodrama, all of whom had played at tiny Houston Baptist University. The Central Africans nonetheless won their first-ever Olympic game, defeating their hosts and benefactors, 73–70, in one of those stories that all by themselves make the Games worth staging.

Few in the press knew anything about the C.A.R., other than it had recently been not a republic but the Central African Empire, presided over by a sanguinary autocrat, Jean-Bedel Bokassa, who reputedly engaged in cannibalism. One of my more oafish colleagues asked Goporo whether he and his teammates shared Bokassa's taste for *Homo sapiens* sustenance. Goporo met this inquiry with better humor than it deserved. But then good humor was the order of the day: That night a member of the C.A.R. delegation got on the phone back to Bangui and read the game's entire play-by-play live over state radio.

Proof of the remarkable quality of Central Africa's accomplishment lay in its fragility. Over the next decade Lavodrama fled to Europe, making a tidy living playing professionally in Spain, while his homeland stumbled into unrest of its own. The C.A.R. quickly became irrelevant in African basketball, failing even to qualify for three of the four most recent championships.

After that, stories about the game on the continent came to me in tantalizing fragments, some almost too good to check. I tossed them into a mental folder. Had Senegal really shown up at the 1978 World Championships in Manila expecting to play barefoot? Did the national team of Mali really feature the most picturesque player imaginable—a seven-footer from Timbuktu? And what was up with the players' ages? Lasme's wasn't the only apocryphal birthdate. I would ask a reporter with *Le Soleil* of Dakar about this. He smiled and said, "In Africa, to the age, you must add VAT."

With Olajuwon and Mutombo having journeyed from Nigeria and the former Zaire, respectively, to become NBA All-Stars, African basketball had to be taken seriously. But what accounted for its bright success in some cases, and in others its petering out in the night sky? The case of the home team would provide some of the answers. So at the *pavilhão* I sought out the father of Angolan basketball.

As a white Angolan, Victorino Cunha wears the facial hair that has long distinguished members of his tribe. He might have fled Angola in 1975, shortly after the country was granted its independence; in the space of six weeks some 350,000 other whites of Portuguese descent left in a panic, as a transitional government broke down and the country sank into civil war. The refugees included most of Angola's adult basketball players and virtually all of its coaches. But Cunha, then a 30-year-old phys ed teacher, knew no other land. He had lived in Luanda since he was four. When UNITA troops and their South African allies mounted an offensive in the fall of 1975, Cunha took up a rifle and joined in the defense of the city. Soon after helping to secure victory he took over a reborn Angolan national team that shouldn't have been much more than a still-born one. Cunha had no more than 20 candidates to choose from. No team in Africa had a lower average weight. In 1977 the team took its first trip, to Bulgaria, and lost by 78 points.

"We not only had to start a new country, we almost had to start a new sport, from zero," Cunha told me. "Other coaches went to Bulgaria, Romania, and the Soviet Union to study their sports. The government wanted to send me to Yugoslavia to learn more about basketball. I told them, no—that if we were serious, we had to learn from the best. And in basketball the best was the United States."

Cunha's role in helping to defend the fledgling MPLA government gave him standing. An eight-year stint as President dos Santos's personal trainer gave him influence. So in the fall of 1980, just as American-Angolan hostility was to be enshrined with Ronald Reagan's election as president, Cunha flew to New York. He spent three months at St. John's, watching and learning from coach Lou Carnesecca. Two years later he prevailed on Carnesecca to bring a group of Big East all-stars to Luanda for a series of exhibitions.

During the early 1980s Cunha set about implementing what

he had learned, only with an intensity that isn't permitted at American colleges. He put his players through 700 hours of practice a year. The basketball federation made arrangements with restaurants in Luanda so the players could ingest 5,000 calories a day. And he introduced weight training, something theretofore unheard of in Africa. In 1985 the Angolans placed second in the African Championships. The following year, at the Worlds in Spain, they beat Australia. In 1989 Cunha brought Team Angola to the U.S. for the first of several exhibition tours. By the time he quit coaching the national team, in June 1995, Angola was the preeminent program on the continent, "founded on sound principles," Cunha told me. "Work hard, play defense, use flex motion on offense. Pass quick, cut hard, respect the opposing team." Thus this very week, in besieged cities like Huambo and Malanje, though people didn't have food, they were watching on TV and listening to the radio. Even the rebels, Cunha believed, were pulling for Angola. "I think, yes," he said. "And I hope so. One thing is war—political shit. The other thing is sport."

I asked Cunha to clear up a mystery for me. The Afrobasket featured a most bizarre mascot. The many-tendriled creature on posters and brochures, and which gamboled across the floor during timeouts, looked like an extra from *Little Shop of Horrors*. Over years of covering international sports events I'd seen just about everything pressed into service as a mascot, from anthropomorphized animals to cubist cartoon characters to the loathsome creature that blighted the Atlanta Olympics. But most all were fauna of one sort or another. Other than Stanford's Tree, this was the first floral mascot I'd come across. "It is the *Welwitschia mirabilis*," Cunha explained. "It survives in the desert on nothing. It represents the hard life in Angola. It's a symbol for the entire country. It stands for what you must do to win the *penta*."

Clearly Angolan basketball was surviving on more than nothing. There's no way to implement the principles Cunha ticked off without good coaching, ample diet, and extensive logistical support, none of which come without cost. The truth of this lay in Angola's counterexample. South Africa was represented here, but barely. It would finish 12th of 12. I turned up at one of South Africa's games and sidled up to a man who sat in the first row behind the bench, cradling a clipboard, barking encouragement to the team as it was being waxed again, this time by scraggly Mozambique.

John Domingues was South Africa's national junior coach. Like Cunha he was of Portuguese descent, only he had been born in Mozambique and in the mid-seventies emigrated to Johannesburg rather than remain in Maputo after independence. But he had impeccable bona fides for the new multiracial South Africa, as he had spent his first five days in his adoptive country in jail, for having joined a pickup game with three blacks at an outdoor court—unbeknownst to him, an imprisonable offense under apartheid.

"South Africa is a sleeping giant," Domingues told me. "We call basketball the Rainbow Sport. There are 30 million blacks in our country, and five million whites, and Indians and Chinese play, too. There are 15 to 20 18-year-olds between 7'2" and 7'4" in South Africa playing basketball right now. I have five of them. Not in my home—my wife would divorce me—but in a flat I pay for out of my own pocket. I feed them, too.

"Seventeen of our kids are in the States, where they excel and everything is free. Some of them are from the townships. But they get a girlfriend, then a green card, and never come back. We don't mind if they go off to the U.S. to better themselves. We just want them to play for the national team. If we could have only 12 of those 17 for just two months before a competition like this, we could prepare and do well. But we can't afford to fly them over. All we need is money—one company that wants to do business in South Africa, just one, to underwrite us."

For four years beginning in 1994, the South African federation had a corporate partner, and both parties benefited handsomely. Schweppes sank millions of dollars into promoting basketball, underwriting the erection of more than 200 baskets in the black townships. The company's name graced every backboard, and Schweppes quickly became the drink of choice among young people, overtaking even Coca-Cola. "Suddenly everybody wanted to play basketball," Domingues said. "Rugby and cricket officials were furious." But having achieved what it wanted, Schweppes pulled out of the sport and allocated its marketing resources elsewhere.

In 1997 Basketball South Africa thought it had eluded its problems with the hiring of a refugee from Sarajevo as national coach. Zoran Župčević had taken over the Bosnian national boys' cadet team in June 1992, after the shelling of his hometown had already begun. Using volunteer ham radio operators, as well as friends in Tuzla and Zenica, Župčević nonetheless put together a team, and in April 1993, 19 Muslim, Croat, and Serb teenagers, following the same route taken by Samir Avdić and Damir Mirković, escaped over the Sarajevo Airport tarmac. With the help of an attorney in suburban Chicago, Župčević had placed each of the boys at a high school in Illinois by the following summer.

Župčević brought the same determination to his job in Johannesburg. But with his coaching on display at the Under-22 African Championships in Cairo, several North African countries began bidding for his services. Tunisia made an offer no one could match. Not even a year into his stint with the South Africans, Domingues told me, "Boom! He was gone."

To watch the Tunisians for five minutes was to see the impact Župčević had already made. Their style was organized but fluid—characteristically Balkan. They worked the ball inside and kicked it out for open jump shots. Only three of their players were stars in Tunisia's national league; most were young role players whom Župčević had to jawbone the federation into letting him choose, but who helped form a cohesive team, one that would finish an impressive fifth here and beat its archrival, Algeria, for the third time in a month. Tunisia was already in transit between the fortunes staked out by South Africa at one extreme and Angola at the other. All it took was money, and the savvy coaching that money could buy.

A few days later I would ask Župčević about the national

team he had briefly led. "If South Africa starts to organize basketball at all levels now, in 10 years it could be at the top of Africa, with Senegal, Nigeria, and Angola," he said. "But they still have the idea that at 19 someone is a young player. He is not. At 19 he is a young man. You must start him at age eight. Then by the time he's 20 he's had a dozen years with structure and coaching. But one thing South Africa has going for it is its mixture of people. You have all different types. Small people and large. Fast people and strong. Different backgrounds, different mentalities."

"You sound like a man from Sarajevo," I said.

He smiled. "That's what I believe. One of the most powerful things in the former Yugoslavia was that mixture. Some guys who were calm, some who were temperamental. Some who were tall, some who were fast. Mixed together on a team, that was good. And that's what they could have in South Africa."

Domingues didn't begrudge Župčević for leaving after only nine months. "He has a wife and family to support," he said. In fact, Župčević was a useful exhibit in the case Domingues was trying to make—that South Africa stood only one benefactor away from a breakthrough. "Last year *we* beat Tunisia," he said. "Now Zoran is there, and Tunisia not only beat us, they beat Mozambique and Algeria.

"I know it can be done, because 25 years ago I was a guard on the Mozambique team that helped dedicate this arena. Can you believe that we destroyed Angola, the same country that beat Mozambique by 57 the other night? But the government here, it pumped money into basketball. The national team played hundreds of games, practiced thousands of hours. For this Afrobasket they trained for eight months. Of course if they don't win, their coach will be hanged. But they should win. They've done everything they need to do to win."

Domingues let a few beats pass, then said, "Tomorrow, you know—it's Savimbi's birthday."

As much as we know the birthday of anyone here, I thought. Then I realized how serious he was.

"See all the police? It's a very dicey situation."

The blue cops alone couldn't be trusted with Savimbi's birthday. The next day they were supplemented by the Rapid Reaction Force, a.k.a. the Ninjas, Angola's black-bereted specials, muscular specimens in jumpsuits and knee and elbow pads whose notion of rapid reaction I could only imagine. The German shepherds now had Dobermans to keep them company. But Michel Lasme was worth facing down even the Ninjas and Dobermans to see, especially against Angola's sophisticated defense, which would be his stoutest test yet.

Angola won by 24, but Lasme put on another show, scoring 20 points in 21 minutes and directing his team as if he were 25 years old. I slipped out with two minutes to play to avoid the *confusão*.

Back at the hotel I ran into Rob-O. "You see what our guy did at the end?" he asked.

I confessed that I'd ducked out early.

"Ahhhh! The final minute. Lasme's on the break. He swings to approach from the baseline, gathers steam, there's an Angolan coming at him, and he rises—then turns 270 degrees under the basket and throws down a reverse *dunk*. Saw Bilé Dee afterward. He said that one dunk made the whole Air Gabon ordeal worthwhile. *Mmmmm—Las-me tender!*"

I had somehow missed the play of the Afrobasket, and Rob-O was rubbing it in. I couldn't resist needling him back. I asked whether he had factored the VAT into Lasme's birthdate. He shot me a look that seemed to say, Details, details. And he returned to the thing that made me feel like a fool for doubting that he'd someday open that basketball academy. He returned to the big picture.

"Lasme's the perfect example of what I was telling you," he said. "So far, you talk Africa, you talk seven-footers. But you've seen these guys. They're unbelievable athletes. Why wouldn't there be a point guard among them? Or all sorts of twos and threes? *Because people don't want to think in those terms yet!* Believe me, someday a smaller kid will make it big in the States and change the whole mentality. And the first kid to do so might be this kid."

He was right. One day out at the *pavilhão* I'd kept my eyes half closed for several minutes of action, so the players became amorphous silhouettes moving before me. Between the foul lines their movements looked anarchic and ungainly. But whenever play came within range of the basket, the shadows converged on the goal with the kind of suddenness that basketball ultimately rewards. I opened my eyes to find arms plumb with the backboard, hands above the rim.

Rob-O knew he'd made a convert and fairly skipped off. "He Las-me; he Las-me not. He Las-me; he Las-me not. . . ."

Before the most recent fighting broke out, Oliver, my driver, had worked as a truck driver, plying Angola's main east-west highway, between Kuito in the interior and Benguela on the coast. Now those roads were a gauntlet of death for anyone foolish enough to drive them, especially in one of the aid convoys that tried to deliver food to the besieged cities. Each day, twice a day, we had made a safer journey, the round-trip from the hotel to the *pavilhão* and back. But Oliver always seemed to take his white Daewoo on a slightly different route, as if he were working for a kind of parallel tourism bureau determined to show off Luanda in all its motley desperation.

The Malthusian basics of what we saw hardly changed. We might take rua Comadante Che Guevara, or avenida Lenin, or rua G. Dimitrov—in Luanda, even the jayvee Communists had streets named after them. But every one would be choked with *deslocados*, flushed-out peasants strictly observing the division of what little labor could be had. The men waded into traffic to hawk car fresheners or packs of batteries. The women stayed on the curb, but sold just as wide a variety of goods, from eggs to toothpaste to ice cream, while balancing bananas on their heads and children at their breasts.

Every day some new feature seemed to pop out from the

same numbing backdrop. Grim variety amidst stasis: This too was *confusão*. Stopped at an intersection, we'd hear the hiss of a *kinguila,* one of the women who change money on the sly, riffling her wad of kwanza, which went now for just short of three million to the dollar. Or we'd see a land-mine victim who couldn't gimp along on crutches, but used a tricycle contraption to hand-pedal in and out of traffic. Or we'd pass the Hotel Turismo, now a Sarajevoesque husk, where in October 1992 government forces massacred several thousand holed-up UNITA troops marooned in the capital after Savimbi decided to ignore the results of free and fair elections, which he had lost, and retreated to the provinces to take up arms again.

Two years after renewing hostilities that fall, UNITA suffered heavy losses and sued for another cease-fire. The 1994 Lusaka Accords called for UNITA's disarmament and integration into the regular Angolan army, and a Government of National Unity and Reconciliation that would install Savimbi in the vice presidency. But the Lusaka Accords were a false peace. They only provided UNITA with a grace period to use its extravagant wealth from illegal diamond trading to rearm. The country quickly descended once more into war. Within six months UNITA took back 70 percent of the country, and Angola returned to the stalemate that obtained as this Afrobasket played out. UNITA was Team Diamonds, the government was Team Oil, and corruption was so rife that diplomats described reports of flight crews, ostensibly resupplying government forces, splitting their cargo between the Angolan army and UNITA right there on the tarmac, as if to say, Okay, here's your gear and here's ours, now let's play ball. No wonder people said the war wouldn't end "until dos Santos's widow attends Savimbi's funeral."

One afternoon Oliver and I drove past a schoolyard with three full courts, and there I saw the scene by which I'd remember the game in Africa. Only one of the six basket standards still had a hoop attached, and of course a half-court game raged there. But next to it, wearing school whites and a backpack, one irrepressible boy played all by himself, launching a ball again and again at a rimless backboard. James Naismith had wondered "what there was about goal-throwing that would keep a boy at it for an hour." And here the boy keeping at it didn't even have a goal at which to throw.

It was not, however, hard to project a basket onto the scene before me, and extrapolate from there the impact tens of thousands of hoops would have throughout the continent. In virtually every respect, the world had passed Africa by. But Africa was where the game was going.

My return flight left the night of the final. I was disappointed to discover that I'd have to be at the airport before tip-off at 7 P.M. But my mood improved after I learned the plans of others.

Oliver had game tickets but wouldn't be going. *"Muito confusão,"* he said. He would catch the final on TV.

Abdu, a Paris-based sports agent of Senegalese descent who used to play professionally in France, was booked on my flight to Brussels, and he was grateful to be missing the game. "I think Nigeria will win," he said. "They are so big and so strong, and there is so much pressure on Angola. The money at stake, the president in the stands—if Angola loses, there will be a riot. Believe me, it is better that we leave tonight."

At the airport I scribbled a few postcards in haste and franked them with the requisite postage, but there was no letter box in the terminal. Asking a security guard if he'd post them for me, I fanned the cards out in one hand so he could see the five-dollar bill I'd slipped in their midst. Angolans call this sort of bribe a *gasosa*—literally, a "fizz." Nothing gets done without a *gasosa*. The guard pulled me aside.

"Ten dollars," he said.

I pulled out my wallet and handed him another fiver.

This was a mistake. A minute later I heard a hiss behind me. "Amigo," a man said. He spoke no English and wore no badge, but from Portuguese cognates and insistent gestures I could tell he wanted a *gasosa* of his own—and he seemed ready to turn me in for something or other if I failed to pony up.

I had successfully negotiated the entire week, only to be felled at the threshold of departure by a hazard that probably hadn't even made Perry Watson's travel agent's Top 30 Reasons Not to Go to Angola. Yet if I paid my amigo off, who was to say someone else wouldn't see me do so and demand a *gasosa* of his own? And then another? I envisioned an endless loop of lubrication, an Escher sketch of baksheesh, and the week's only flight to Brussels going wheels up without me.

I lit out wordlessly toward customs. My amigo turned out to have been bluffing, but the departure lounge was no sanctuary. It was lousy with drunk Scandinavian oil workers on their 28-day shift change. One shattered a whiskey bottle on the floor. Another, passed out, would have to be carried aboard the Airbus 320 by a buddy.

Out on the tarmac I chatted up an American diplomat who was headed home after a two-year hitch. I asked him about Savimbi's birthday. "In fact, nobody knows exactly when he was born," he said. "But they say it's August third, and my problem is, August third is also my father's birthday. And since the embassy's phones are bugged, I had a terrible time figuring out how to wish him happy birthday without the Angolans thinking I was somehow sending coded greetings to Savimbi."

Days later I heard: That night police confiscated a bomb at the gate of the *pavilhão*. Angola won its *penta*, beating Nigeria 79–72. Several Ninjas fired off triumphant rounds from their AK-47s. Two civilians died in the postgame *confusão*.

Leaving Africa to return to Afro-America, I remained uncertain of Savimbi's birthday. I wasn't sure of Lasme's, either. But I knew my own, and counted myself lucky that I'd be celebrating another.

TWENTY-SIX

Kansas City

To Rest, Rather Than to Mischief

When James Naismith arrived in Paris in the fall of 1917, the YMCA put him in charge of its Bureau of Hygiene— "hygiene" of course being what people said back then when they meant "sex."

Doc Naismith's mandate was to warn the troops of the perils of promiscuity, and he did this by cowriting a sex-education booklet that every member of the American Expeditionary Forces received upon arriving in France. *The Basis of Clean Living* is a remarkable 32 pages of straight talk, debunked myths, and risqué Q's parried with unflinching A's. In a chapter called "Setting Right Some Wrong Ideas," Naismith restates beliefs that must have been widely held among American men of military age during the early 20th century, then summarily strikes each down. Lest a doughboy believe that *one will lose the powers of the organs unless they are exercised,* or that *it is the manly thing to indulge,* the good doctor demurs: "The manly thing is to overcome temptation, not to be overcome by it. Man is good by reason, not by appetite."

Yet to combat the brothels that sprang up near the barracks, Naismith knew better than to play the bluenose. He doubted that young men could be tricked into mistaking patently pleasurable things for unpleasurable ones. But he had long believed you could outwit the devil by steering young men toward sports. So he set up a boxing ring near the gate to the camp, and on Friday nights, just as soldiers began to file out of the barracks for a night on the town, he stationed himself by the entrance. "Fellows, we've got boxing here tonight," he'd say. "Six great bouts. Why don't you stick around?"

Naismith later described their reaction. "They stopped to watch; then begged for a chance to participate; and the next thing they knew it was time to be back in quarters." As a carny barker for Christ, Naismith kept scores of soldiers from "going into a near-by town and getting into all kinds of devilment. Prize fights may sound like strange preaching, but they did the work."

A place like Angola is too far gone for sports to make much of a difference. But Stateside, basketball has proven that it can right the lives of teetering youth. Nearly 70 years after Naismith made his observations, an army vet from Tennessee would take that notion of sport as social palliative, marry it to the good doctor's invention, and touch off a movement.

By the mid-1980s tracts of low-income housing had transformed much of Prince Georges County, in the Maryland suburbs outside Washington, D.C., from sleepy bedroom territory into a kind of exurban Dodge City. No incident better emblematized that change than the cocaine overdose that killed Len Bias, the star at Maryland, hours after the Boston Celtics made him their No. 1 draft pick in 1986. Both Bias's obituary and the press coverage of the trial of the dealer who supplied him carried a Prince Georges dateline.

G. Van Standifer was town manager of Glen Arden, Maryland, a community at the epicenter of those changes. Though home to only 4,500 people, Glen Arden had been the site of some 1,900 violent crimes the previous year, most committed between 10 P.M. and 2 A.M. by men 21 and under. Within four years of Standifer's opening the Prince Georges Midnight Basketball League, crime in the county dropped by 60 percent. Word of Standifer's success spread across the country. Organizers took the basic concept and added features of their own, from draconian penalties for trash talk or rough play to mandatory classes in life skills. In Boston, the Peace League made a point of recruiting gang members who had a history of clashing with one another in the streets. In New York, which launched a statewide program, no one without a high school diploma could play unless he agreed to pursue a GED. The leagues weren't conceived to send kids to college, only to keep them out of trouble, but some rudderless young men—like Marshall Phillips, Buzz Peterson's star at Appalachian State—found themselves by playing at the bewitching hour, and recruiters in turn found them. More than 50 cities around the country introduced some variation on the Prince Georges theme, and in 1991 President George Bush visited Glen Arden to honor Standifer and his league with a "Point of Light" award. "The last thing midnight basketball is about is basketball," read the president's citation. "It's about providing opportunity for young adults to escape drugs and the streets and get on with their lives."

The movement found one of its most evangelical followers in Kansas City with the election of a Methodist minister, Emanuel Cleaver, as mayor in 1991. Mayor's Night Hoops would drive down crime by 25 percent in those neighborhoods with a venue, and during the nineties the program expanded to include girls and young women. Games ran every night but Wednesday, for that's when participants gathered for workshops on such topics as job interviewing, conflict resolution, and—*pace* Doc Naismith—sex ed. Eventually, Cleaver launched the Mayor's Urban Symposium and Tournament (M.U.S.T.), inviting players from midnight leagues around the country to Kansas City to try out their basketball skills and, because hoops could take them only so far, discuss other moves they'd need to make in life.

Kansas City spent about $200,000 each summer to cover the supervisors, gym rental, and security staff required to run Night Hoops. Seeing as it cost $30,000 for the criminal justice system to cope with a single juvenile offender, midnight basketball paid for itself if it could keep out of trouble only seven of the 1,200 at-risk adolescents who enrolled in the program each year. Despite this persuasive arithmetic, Night Hoops constantly grasped for funds. Cleaver was able to prevail on the city's municipal court to increase the cost of a parking ticket by five dollars and earmark the additional revenue for Night Hoops. Only half kiddingly, the mayor urged Kansas Citians to park illegally so the program might continue. "We've done this without one penny of federal funds," he said in his appeal. "If we had federal money, there's no telling what we could do."

In cities around the country where midnight basketball had taken root, Cleaver's counterparts found themselves saying much the same thing. If you did the cost-benefit analysis— a few hundred bucks per kid per year now, versus tens of thousands of dollars annually for every one to become a ward of the system later—it was hard not to become a booster. That's why the comprehensive crime bill to come before Congress in 1994 included $40 million over five years to fund midnight basketball nationwide. Yet despite the imprimatur of a high-profile Republican like George Bush, a band of GOP no-men in Congress fought midnight hoops. The bill called for the funds to be spent in areas addled by crime, drugs, joblessness, and sexually transmitted disease—the whole point, after all. But opponents howled that this somehow constituted "pork," or worse, "quotas." Though midnight basketball had a track record of both cost- and crime-fighting effectiveness, a representative from Texas, Lamar Smith, called it "vague social spending" that was "based on the theory that the person who stole your car, robbed your house and assaulted your family is no more than a . . . would-be basketball star." Another congressman, Martin Hoke of Ohio, demanded to know, "Is this some sort of legislative blackmail that would suggest if they are not playing basketball they are going to be committing crimes?" Only insofar as *any* preemptive strike against crime—a bill that would put more cops on the beat, for instance—was "blackmail." But basketball's enemies were either unable or unwilling to grasp the concept. I couldn't imagine a more constitutionally Republican character than James Naismith of Lawrence, Kansas, devotee of family, exemplar of self-reliance, tribune of rectitude. Nor could I imagine anyone being more disappointed than he had he lived to see the debate and vote that killed midnight basketball in Congress.

In the final chapter of *The Basis of Clean Living*, Naismith asks, "What is the relation of recreation and athletics to morals?" There's a didactic, Victorian quaintness to both the way he frames the question and the way he answers it. I pictured the good doctor on a Sunday morning toward the end of his life, in one of the modest sanctuaries on the circuit he rode, responding in that Scottish-Canadian burr. "The athletic field furnishes one of the best laboratories for self-restraint and moral training," he'd say, as he once wrote. And, "Absorption in athletics occupies the mind along natural and helpful lines, and furrrrrtherrrrmore is a continual incentive to good living."

Both could be reprised today as arguments for midnight hoops. But neither is more persuasive than this: "By using up our surplus energy, we invite to rest, rather than to mischief."

I flew to Kansas City in high summer. The place has had its civic quarrels, but at the time of my visit the merit of midnight basketball was not among them. Although term limits had recently returned Mayor Cleaver to the pulpit of St. James United Methodist Church, his successor, Kay Barnes, was continuing Night Hoops, and for an argument Kansas Citians were left to revive a perennial: Which baron of barbecue served up the best stuff, Ollie Gates or Arthur Bryant?

Seeing as Mr. Gates had recently served as the city's commissioner of recreation, the rec department official showing me around considered the matter settled. Mark Bowland turned his Chevy Corsica past the sign reading HI! and into the lot outside the Gates Bar-B-Q outlet on Main. As we ambled in for dinner, he explained: "When I joined the department, Ollie made me sign a pact that I'd never eat at any other barbecue place."

Mark was compact, feral, sharp-witted. He had the darting eyes of the street kid he once was, before his parents plopped him down on the University of Missouri campus one day, begging him to give college a try. "I wasn't groomed, I wasn't mentally aware, because of what I was doing in the streets," he told me. But he stuck with school and delivered himself from a fate he's loath to imagine. A man back in the neighborhood took him under his wing, much as ministers of the game like Mister J and Doctor James had taken in others. Now he was acting superintendent of the city's department of parks and rec.

Over platters of Gates's finest, I asked Mark if he knew of Doc Naismith's belief in salvation through sport. He didn't, but in light of his own experience, and what he had seen over a decade of Night Hoops, it made perfect sense to him. "People are so spent after they play, they just go home and chill out." He turned to look out the window. "See that thing?" He gestured at a lone, illegally parked Caprice soon to be enfolded by the gloaming. "Now, that's money for Night Hoops right there."

I mentioned that a few honorable gentlemen had risen to their feet in the well of the House to denounce midnight basketball. To lambaste it as pork.

"Pork?" Mark said. "No. *This* is pork." He jabbed a fork into the short end of ribs on his plate. "Come to Kansas City—come to Gates and Night Hoops—and we'll be glad to show you the difference."

When we left Gates—pulling out past the sign that read BYE!—the night lay before us. It was a Friday, the same evening Doc Naismith once posted himself outside the barracks in France. We picked up the Night Hoops administrator, a long-boned, solemn-tempered man named Coleman Russ, and as the three of us made our way through the city, I felt as if I'd been dropped into a Spike Lee remake of a Jim Jarmusch film. With each venue, the players got gradually older, the ball progressively hotter.

"That first year we had guys mother-thissing and motherthatting," Coleman said. "Guys shooting dice in the rest rooms. Drugs in the parking lots. Not anymore." When we pulled up to Clymer Community Center, I could see why: Several uniformed metro police officers stood outside, and a few more lingered within. There we caught the very end of a game among 10-, 11-, and 12-year-olds, on a floor fashioned from recycled basketball shoes. Two kids had a brief flare-up over a loose ball. "Kum-ba-*ya!*" a mom yelled from the stands.

One of the coaches came by after the buzzer sounded. He was a thickly built black man in a broad-brimmed white hat, with a left hand that listed sharply to one side. The cause, I discovered, was the Super Bowl ring he had won years ago as a defensive back with the Chiefs. "One thing about kids," said the coach, Jim Kearney, "is that if they don't join a positive organization, they're gonna join a negative one."

By 9:30 we had reached Don Bosco Community Center, where the boys were a little bigger, 13 and 14, but the court was not. Thus each team threw a press at the other, leaving kids no choice but to work together to break it. Players wore shirts reading THIS NIGHT THING IS THE RIGHT THING, while a banner on one wall proclaimed OVERTIME IS BETTER THAN SUDDEN DEATH. Many more people filled the stands here than at Clymer, or so it seemed from the way voices reverberated off the tile floor. Each breath came thick from the lack of air-conditioning, and every exhalation contributed to the soupy heat. "This is Night Hoops," Mark said. "AC is for sissies. With every point scored, the temperature rises one degree."

For all games involving kids 14 and under, organizers tried to finish up by 10 P.M. The older boys were at greater risk, so their games pushed later into the night—through the next several hours and into prime crime time. Within 15 minutes we reached the gemstone of the city's public schools, Central High, a huge, brightly lit plant featuring an amply air-conditioned field house that would have done a land-grant university proud. More than 70 percent of these kids, aged 15 to 18, didn't play on their high school teams. They nonetheless received a structured experience in the game, with coaches and referees—adults whose influence is most critical when kids are at their most malleable. Supervisors kept an eye out for anything amiss, even something as apparently benign as baggy shorts. "We have a rule," Vickie Shelton, who ran Night Hoops at Central, told me. "You can't sag. If they're saggin', we put 'em out the very first week."

I asked Melvin Hawkins, a Kansas City police sergeant who headed the security detail at Central, what the streets would be like without Night Hoops. He shook his head slowly and said, "I don't even want to think about it."

It was well past midnight by the time we reached Hillcrest Community Center on the city's southeastern fringe. These were the wizened veterans of Night Hoops, aged 19 to 25. Two out of three hadn't had, and wouldn't have, any exposure to college. "This is the group I'm most concerned about," Mark said. "They're the most likely to get into trouble, if only for something like driving with expired tags."

The crowd was sparser here, and tougher, too: fewer parents and family, more homeys and girlfriends. The game was frenetic in pace, headlong in style. Onlookers serenaded with derision anyone who muffed a dunk—and three did so in the first 10 minutes. Perhaps it was the hour. I wondered if the door to a janitorial closet would swing open, and out would pop the Executioner, that strict enforcer of standards from Amateur Night at the Apollo. But I couldn't imagine keeping up in this game and then hunting down any kind of trouble.

Coleman caught me stifling a yawn. "You know, that first year, we wouldn't let anyone play zone," he said. "They had to play man-to-man. We wanted 'em so tuckered out they couldn't even *think* of doing anything once their game was over."

From his perch on my shoulder, I felt Jiminy Naismith stir. No wonder the inventor hated that "stratified transitional defensive system." And good for so many of my acquaintances of the past year for recognizing what Congress couldn't—the purpose for which the game was invented. Midnight basketball sprang from the same truth enshrined in Niall O'Riordan and Liam McGinn's Neptune Stadium in Cork, and Verdell Jones's

Ft. Sooy in Peoria, and Dennis Villanueva's NBA in Villa San in Manila, and Mister J's Dunbar, hard by ground zero in Springfield: a frank acknowledgment of human nature. Young men will be doing something. Better that they be doing this.

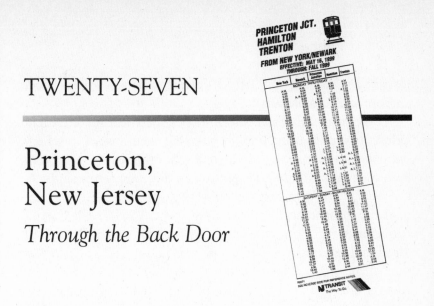

TWENTY-SEVEN

Princeton, New Jersey

Through the Back Door

In Kansas City I'd seen the game trying to perfect the world. But to revisit the perfectibility of basketball itself, I had to go back where I'd started. I had to return to Princeton, to the back door—a.k.a. "change of direction," "pulling the string," or (as those junior-high girls at the Celebration Macker called it) "Danielle high."

The play that "people always get faked out by" had figured in every one of Princeton's appearances on the national stage after Bill Bradley's departure. From their NIT championship in 1975, when that title still meant something; to their one-point loss, as a No. 16 seed, to top-seeded Georgetown in the 1989 NCAA tournament; to their upset of UCLA in the '96 NCAAs, the Tigers under Pete Carril used an adaptation of the old "pivot play" popularized by Dutch Dehnert and the Original Celtics back in the 1920s.

Moments before his game-winning layup against the Bruins, Princeton forward Gabe Lewullis had tried to sell UCLA's Charles O'Bannon on a backdoor cut. O'Bannon wasn't buying. But during the previous timeout Carril had urged Lewullis to try a second back cut if he failed to free himself with the first. On that second cut O'Bannon suffered a lapse of mental discipline, the back door swung open, and

Carril clinched the last of 514 career victories in the most appropriate possible way.

At the heart of what Princeton does sits a feature of human nature besides that inclination of young men toward mischief. All players are attracted to the ball. On offense, the Tigers try both to suppress and to accommodate this urge. They suppress it because four teammates all converging on the ball isn't a particularly constructive basis for an offense. (You'll recall Carril's condemnation: "Guys who come around to the ball only feed greed and ignorance.") Yet it's okay to indulge your desire for the ball as long as a teammate has decided to share it, either by passing it to you or, if that's not possible, dribbling over to you to hand it off. And it's when one of them dribbles over that the Tigers exploit that same human tropism for the ball, only on the part of the defense. The man defending the intended recipient of this handoff is conditioned to help stop the approaching dribbler. He'll likely shift his weight toward the ball, or at least turn his head to track its progress. That's when the offensive player bolts behind him for the basket.

Carril himself—feisty, clever, resourceful—embodies the traits you'd expect in someone who had devoted his life to so subversive a style of play. He grew up a steelworker's son in Bethlehem, Pennsylvania, playing games with his friends in a coal yard across the street from his home. He had been a run-and-shoot guard at Lafayette, in nearby Easton, and during his early seasons at Princeton, when his teams included professionals-to-be like Brian Taylor and Geoff Petrie, he had been a run-and-shoot coach. But he came to rely on the counterpunch of the back door more and more over the years, as circumstances restricted the kind of athlete he could attract. From the time he arrived on campus in 1967, Carril himself played "the Princeton style" during pickup games over his lunch hour, sometimes with a stogie hanging from his lip. That noontime game was like hundreds of noontime games on campuses around the country, and at the same time like none of them. It had survived Carril's decision, after the UCLA valedictory, to join the Sacramento Kings as an assistant coach. Ever since Princeton's epic 1997–98 season, the school's sports information director, Jerry Price, had urged me to come by Jadwin Gym, at least to watch. "But if you really want to understand the system," he said, "you've got to play."

And so I began taking the midmorning train down to campus. The games included the odd professor and grad student, a local sportswriter, and bodies culled from the athletic department's offices along the Jadwin mezzanine, among them Jerry and his assistant, Matt, as well as Becky, an assistant coach with the women's team who was renting Carril's vacated home near campus and showed no adverse effects from breathing years' worth of stale cigar smoke. Bill Carmody was an occasional participant, but two of his assistants, John Thompson III and Joe Scott, both of whom had played for Carril during the eighties, were regulars and strict enforcers of the principles.

John, whose namesake father is the TNT commentator and former coach at Georgetown, had passed for more assists than any forward in school history as a Tigers co-captain. "Drift!" he would yell in the middle of a game, or "Curl!" At first the words made little sense to me, but regulars seemed to know just what to do, so I watched and imitated. John was so much the coach that he would call out these commands to players on the opposing team, too. Nothing escaped his notice from his accustomed spot on the wing. He'd make quite a head coach one day, I thought, especially after an incident during my first noontime visit. A loose ball ran out of bounds and several of us took the obligatory couple of hard steps in pursuit before giving up. I could hear the wry tone of his father in John's interjection: "Nice fake hustle!"

Joe had been a Princeton captain and passer, too, only as a point guard. At law school in South Bend he had twice played on the team that won Notre Dame's storied Bookstore Basketball Tournament, and he still had the feet and competitive spirit of someone in his early twenties. "Stay wide!" Joe would tell anybody—usually me—who saw the cavity of the lane as a place to post up and call for the ball. I'd scramble out to the wing. But

I'd soon drift back into that beckoning expanse, and Joe would shout, louder: *"Stay wide!"*

Fearing Joe's wrath, I learned quickly not to linger in the post, but to circle back out, and cut hard, and circle back out again, and cut hard again. Sometimes our numbers forced us to play three-on-three, which left plenty of space for all this statutory cutting, and exposed anyone dogging it. I could feel blisters rise on my feet from the repeated jab-stepping. I wished for wind and calluses. But even as my body screamed for relief, my mind came to appreciate negative space and positive space—how we who occupied the latter had to pour ourselves into the former, over and over again.

One day I arrived early. Jadwin was hushed and dark. I took a seat on the edge of the floor to stretch and, hoping to forestall another blister, pull on an extra pair of socks. That's when I noticed a figure filling the doorway from the lobby. There was no way to make out the details of its features, for it was backlit by sunlight spilling through the lobby. But the silhouette was of a man—short, rounded, dressed in loose-fitting clothing—I thought I knew.

"Hey Alex."

The voice I definitely knew.

Pete Carril has a favorite story from his time at Princeton, a story James Naismith would have loved. Carril goes back again and again to a game at Virginia in 1975, when a referee ejected him moments into the second half. One assistant was off scouting, the other was coaching a freshman game, so Carril turned the team over to a junior reserve named Peter Molloy. Princeton went on to a victory that would have its echo 23 years later, against Niagara at the Garden, when Carmody told his players during that timeout, "You're smart guys. You figure it out."

It may be surprising that a coach would take such pride in his own expendability. But in our neo-Prohibitionist age people are even more surprised to learn that Carril, believing beer to be restorative, encouraged his players to drink, even in season. He winced when he saw them eating candy. Kids eat candy; he wanted his players to be men, and men drink beer. Andy's Tavern was the dive, literally on the other side of the railroad tracks from campus, where Carril once took his lager. If he had been looking for a sign that the time had finally come to leave, he surely found it in the fate of Andy's, which by the mid-1990s had become a sushi bar.

On a summer's day long before that apocalypse, Carril was on his way out of Andy's, headed for a basketball clinic where he was to speak on offense. He asked the barflies what he should tell the campers. A half-in-the-bag regular known as Whiskey Steve piped up with an answer that Carril came to regard as the perfect summary of the system. "Tell 'em," Whiskey Steve said, "to watch where they're going."

The man who strode from the doorway onto the floor was now pushing 70 and receding from five feet seven inches. Nonetheless, back in town to have his teeth cleaned, he was tan and trim, and he had an ebullience at odds with the doleful old countenance I remembered. Perhaps this was a result of the Kings having led the league in scoring the previous season, or of Sacramento playing so well in the playoffs. Most coaches would be ready to give themselves credit for such things, but Carril usually scowled at praise. "The cheapest kind of reward," he called it. Late in his final season, after Princeton beat Dartmouth by holding the Big Green to 39 points, someone asked Carril what he thought of his team's opponent that evening. Carril sensed a trap. Dartmouth deserved no praise, but he didn't believe his own team deserved any, either. His response was perfect: "They have guardable players. And we guarded them."

I fed him the ball at the foul line. *Bang bang bang bang bang:* Five free throws in a row he sent through the net, every one with his left hand—his off hand. He made a crack about the lousy free-throw shooting of one of his players, Chris Webber. But he had uncharacteristic kindnesses to say about the Kings.

"It's not the system. It's who you have running it. And we do have some fellows who can pass and shoot." He singled out the man who held down the middle, the Serb I'd followed for much of the past year, Vlade Divac. "The perfect Princeton center," he called him.

By now several of the noontime crowd had drifted in. Still, we barely had a quorum. Though he acted like a man reluctant to play, Carril was dressed to do so—swaddled in sweats, wearing basketball shoes. "If you've got five, I'm the sixth," he said. "If you've got seven, I'm the eighth."

We had five. He had to play—with Joe and me, against Jerry, Matt, and Becky.

He hardly cut back door. He hardly cut at all, preferring the safety of the perimeter. His favorite tactic was a sudden hooked skip pass, usually to Joe on the wing for an open jumper. On defense he guarded Becky, who was only a few years out of college and much too spry for him. "No respect!" he shouted at her when she sagged off him. "No respect!" he mock-scolded himself, when he, from old age, failed to get out to challenge her, and she knocked down shot after shot.

Someone passing through the gym recognized him. "How you doing, Coach?"

"Getting drilled. Went to the dentist yesterday and it hasn't stopped."

Midway through the game he held the ball just to the right of the key. I moved aimlessly from the left wing toward the circle. That's when I realized I was committing a sin against the game. I was coming around to the ball. Hellfire! *I was feeding greed and ignorance.*

"Go behind him!" Carril yelled.

It had worked for Gabe Lewullis. I cut off Matt's back and down the left spine of the lane. As I did so, time suddenly slowed down. Looking up I found the ball, plump and soft, seeing its way into my hands.

The old coach had thrown it perfectly. I took the permitted step and a half. Torquing my body just so, the back of my right hand to the glass, I flicked in the layup.

Once I thought I knew the game. At times over the past year I doubted whether I knew the game at all. Now, in this gym I'd hardly played in, with this coach I'd never played for, I knew it as I'd never known it before. To Matt's firmly planted oak, I'd swayed like a willow. And in that gesture of counterweight, in the space of that moment, a year of moving about came unclouded into view.

Basketball is really nothing but an ongoing quest for balance. Balance: It's embodied in Doc Naismith's "agile, graceful and expert" athlete, not the "massive muscular" specimen or the "cadaverous greyhound." It's what Frankie Williams and Johnny Suarez and Michel Lasme are all trying to deprive you of, so they can beat you. It lies in the personalities of a couple of Geminis, Šarūnas Marčiulionis and Scott (Gus Macker) McNeal, who are forever playing off others. It's the path a sky-hook describes, tracing faith and will in equal measure. It's the keel you must keep so last-in-the-power-ratings Yale doesn't do to you what the hubris of Penn's students did to the Quakers at the Palestra. It's what Carril brought about by imparting coal-country lessons on an Ivy League campus, what Buzz Peterson sought to strike when he tossed an *Andy Griffith* episode in with a few game tapes, and what John McLendon found after sticking that Dr Pepper in his blazer pocket. It's a swaying hip and a falling three in Brazil; an aroused temper and a "Kum-ba-ya!" in Kansas City; a bustling street and a stillwater garden in Japan; a scabbard and a teacup in Bhutan.

The game's numerology underscores this immanent equilibrium. The cutter who beats an overplaying defender back door; the "holonomous mean" between Kobe Bryant and Derrick McKey; the yin and yang of Bai Jinshen's peelable basketball; the split distance between No Whiskey Naismith and Whiskey Steve—all speak to twos, and the proposition that there's a theory of the game in game theory, in the teeter-totter principle of zero sum. Yet these pairs exist alongside the game's store of trinities, from triple-threat position, to the perfect Macker complement of three-on-three, to the Bulls' triangle offense, to Bill Bradley's "third leg" notion of governance, to the straight

Springfield line from Doc James through Mister J to Doctor J, to Naismith's degrees in phys ed, medicine, and divinity, which echo so perfectly the YMCA's fundaments of mind, body, and spirit. The game, it seems to me, lies in sturdy, covalent two, and in flexible, dynamic three. Add them up and you have a team.

Moments after scoring that backdoor layup, I had to turn around to play defense. Except in a few precincts where make it, take it still rules, basketball demands this of everyone who scores. But I went slack in a moment of self-congratulation. I turned my head, felt the ball whip past it, and an instant later knew that feeling of vertigo that comes from looking up into a hoop through which a ball is being flushed. Matt had snuck back door on me and Jerry had found him. Just as Hirohide Ogawa predicted, I'd imitated the tiger and been hunted in my turn. But this too underscored the primacy of balance. No wonder basketball found a following in Bhutan, a country pledged to Buddhism and its Middle Way. If you win, you'll get complacent; if you get complacent, you won't win. If he lays off you, shoot the jumper; if he overplays you, go to the hole. Basketball is full of these sturdy causal relationships. Like Aulcie Perry's rabbi, the game has an answer for everything.

"What is it to make a mistake?" Ogawa asked. "Does it lie in not scoring? No, for perhaps it was correct not to score that time when you were off balance. For, if you had scored then, what would be the merit in right balance?" Thankfully, that's not the credo taped over the monitor of the techies who log highlights for *SportsCenter*. But for someone who never existed, Ogawa was on to something. Basketball's great merit, and the elusive key to its mastery, is that it demands of its players an ever-retrievable equipoise. This isn't meant to reduce the game to little more than an exercise of alternately agitating and stilling the heart and the head. Then basketball would be little more than biathlon. But as you play the game—as you keep your feet moving and get your feet set, calibrating *want to do* with *what to do*—there's a point at which hustle and smarts sit in optimal proportion. It's a sceptered place, where you can do your very best with an effortless, unawares marshaling of effort and awareness, and I'd found it in Jadwin Gym that noontime. A journey that began in those stands, at the sight of Mitch Henderson's pass, had ended on that floor, with the observer become participant, taking a pass for a layup. Another fulcrum found: Watching is okay, but sometimes you have to go, too.

I'd set out believing the game was conquering the world. But that's far too aggressive a verb for how hoops works. It beckons, woos, *courts*—and only the rare monastic, the Shelly Pennefather, can resist its seductions. Like the globe that basketball has enraptured, like the globe that a basketball is, the game will forever draw us in, gravitationally, as it spins. In the meantime, take it from me: There's no limit to what you can learn about these endlessly beguiling spheres—the one we occupy, and the one that occupies us—if only you watch where you're going.

EPILOGUE

I didn't go everywhere I'd have liked. I somehow missed Spain, home to the Asociación Clubs de Baloncesto, the slickest professional league beyond the NBA. I bypassed Indiana, for I'd written often about Hoosier basketball and felt tapped out. Nor did I make it to Australia, or Kentucky, or Greece, or North Korea, where dictator Kim Jong Il was reputed to be a fan of Wangchuckian enthusiasm. But I'd met so many people in so many places that news washed up in New York long after I came off the road. (More extensive updates than those that follow may be found at biggamesmallworld.com.)

John Gosset and his Canadian allies finally succeeded in establishing a shrine of permanence and prominence to the Naismith legacy. After years of politicking and five months of renovations, the Naismith Museum and Hall of Fame opened in Almonte's old town hall in June 2000.

Žalgiris Kaunas came a long way from the loss I'd watched in that Vilnius sports bar called Men's Joy. Lithuania's top club team went on to defeat Virtus Bologna in the EuroLeague championship game—a result that delighted fans of Fortitudo Bologna, which had lost to Virtus in the semifinals. Nine months later Šarūnas Marčiulionis launched his Northern European Basketball League, and CSKA Moscow won the inaugural title by beating Lietuvos Rytas, the commissioner's old team, in the final.

But Lithuania would celebrate a far more significant basketball achievement at the 2000 Olympics in Sydney. After he and his teammates lost in preliminary-round play to a U.S. "preen" team of NBA players, Šarūnas Jasikevičius, the guard I'd watched in that dingy gym in Klaipėda, was asked when he thought the American professionals themselves might finally lose. "They're gonna lose *here*," he predicted with summary confidence. A week later Jasikevičius all but made himself a prophet. He barely missed a three-pointer at the buzzer of an 85–83 U.S. victory in the medal round. The game caused a sensation back in Lithuania and quickly established itself as a historical marker. From that point, people would no longer speak of a world "catching up" with the American game, only of a world caught up.

Richard Dumas, Mike McCollow, and Steve Wojciechowski all left Poland within weeks of my visit. Pekaes gave Dumas his release and he returned to his hometown of Tulsa, where police soon picked him up in a motel room on a cocaine charge. He was convicted the following August, but a judge deferred his two-year sentence after he completed a treatment program and vowed yet again to remain drug-free. The following season he played in Bosnia until he suffered a knee injury; in August 2000 the Fargo-Moorhead (S.D.) Beez of the International Basketball Association added him to their roster. "He's in good shape and at the top of his game," said Beez coach John Jordan, who doubled as Dumas's agent. "He's clean and sober."

I could only imagine Mike McCollow's reaction upon learning that Jordan, citing "health reasons" and violations of team rules, released Dumas two games into the Beez's season. Mike and his family had moved back to the Twin Cities after his firing. He found work as a personal trainer for several Minnesota Timberwolves during the late stages of the NBA lockout, then took a job in a store that sold running shoes. Soon he and Katie had bought out the owner. He still worked camps and clinics and hoped to get back into coaching.

Within a month after Wojciechowski returned to the U.S. and signed on as an assistant coach at Duke, his application for Polish basketball citizenship somehow came through. Pekaes officials spent several weeks frantically but unavailingly trying to lure him back. In April 2001 Wojo must have been able to look back with a smile at his brief Polish sojourn, for his third season in Durham ended with the Blue Devils winning an NCAA title.

STV Luzern played out the next two seasons in Switzerland's second division before striking a deal with its crosstown rival, TV Reussbühl, to merge into a single team. The river that flows through Lucerne and into the lake is called the Reuss, and at first, André Porchet told me, the plan was to call the new club the Reuss Rolls. But a lawyer warned the club's directors that they'd be open to a lawsuit for trademark infringement, so they settled on the Reuss Rebels. André described the merger as "one last chance" for Lucerne to ascend to a secure place in the Swiss first division. To that end the Rebels had hired a Yugoslav coach. His background, André assured me, had been thoroughly checked out.

The Macker staged another All-World Championship in Celebration, Florida, in the fall of 1999, then moved the event across the state to Titusville on the Space Coast. As of 2001, all four of the Whitney Point Eagles were still playing high school and summer traveling team ball.

Even though Virtus wound up advancing to the 1998–99 EuroLeague final, Fortitudo won five of that season's six Derbies. Bologna's working-class team also signed a 20-year lease to move back into the PalaDozza, the old arena in the center of town, even though the club had to sacrifice several thousand seats of capacity to do so. As Enrico Comastri told me, "We'd rather lose money than pay rent to Cazzola," the Virtus owner who had built the suburban Palasport. The following season Fortitudo defeated Varese for its first *scudetto,* and the Fossa dei Leoni celebrated by singing a ribald song that recapped the club's history. One verse hailed "Santi Puglisi, who pulled the *paletta* down."

Bosnia remained a country divided, but basketball had begun to effect a tentative reintegration of several of the federation's opposed parts. Beginning with the 1999–2000 season, for the first time since the war, Bosnia's national league included clubs from the Republika Srpska, and one of them, Borac Nektar of Banja Luka, won the title.

The following September, in the weeks leading up to elections that would depose Slobodan Milošević from power in Belgrade, the Boy of Bormio most wary of politics finally took a stand. Vlade Divac criticized the regime in an interview with a Yugoslav weekly. Soon after his comments were published, officials with the Yugoslav National Olympic Committee insisted that they had no idea how Divac's credentials to stand for an election of his own—to the Athletes Commission of the International Olympic Committee—had become lost in the mail between Belgrade and Lausanne. A short time later Divac's face began to appear on T-shirts alongside the clenched-fist logo of Otpor, the student-led resistance movement.

With a new regime came a fresh breeze, and that wind carried on it several familiar characters. Divac, with recently retired Virtus star Predrag Danilović, bought the club for which he had once played, Partizan Belgrade. The Yugoslav Basketball Federation hired Svetislav Pešić to coach the national team for its campaign for the 2001 European Championship. And over a summer weekend in Treviso, Italy, the United Nations and the NBA co-sponsored a gathering that embodied at least the spirit of the reunion that Pešić and Teo Alibegović had quixotically imagined for me. Basketball without Borders brought together 50 campers aged 12 to 14—10 each from the Yugolsav Federation and its four successor states—for a camp that emphasized tolerance and leadership as much as basketball. Divac, of course, was among the pros from all five entities of the ex-Yugoslavia who served as counselors. That Toni Kukoč joined his old junior teammate, however, indicated that even someone once dismissive of reconciliation could be persuaded to reconsider, at least in the service of a new generation.

By the summer of 2001, Shaun Livingston, the point guard prodigy from Peoria, had sprouted to six feet three inches. He had completed his freshman year of high school, though he had done so at Richwoods High, not Manual High, the alma mater of crossover conjurer Frank Williams. Manual nonetheless had much to be proud of: Williams and high school buddy Sergio McClain started for Illinois's 2001 Big Ten co-champions, and Williams was voted the league's Player of the Year. Meanwhile, Verdell Jones was determined to bring Ft. Sooy to points beyond downstate Illinois. Shortly after returning from my visit, I'd sent Verdell a note urging him to "keep holding down 'the Fort.'" A few months later I caught up with him on the phone. "You know that slogan of yours?" he said. "'Hold down the Fort?' Got a guy working on a T-shirt with it *right now*."

Several months after I'd left him in Lawrence, Ian Naismith felt his double heartbeat turn over to normal once again. John McLendon wasn't so fortunate with his health. On September 30, 1999, Ian drove from Chicago to McLendon's home in Cleveland, where the old coach was suffering through the late stages of pancreatic cancer. "Well, little brother," John told Ian, in a voice weakened by the loss of 38 pounds, "the enemy's got me pinned down." He died nine days later, at age 84.

I'd also chosen an auspicious time to visit Don Haskins, for the Bear wouldn't coach another season. Doctors implanted a pacemaker in his heart several months after I saw him, and when he announced he was calling it quits, he said, "This is it. I'm off the hot seat." His old assistant Tim Floyd hired him to be a consultant to the Chicago Bulls.

In February 2000, 11 months after the Alchesay High Falcons lost in the first round of the Arizona Class 3A state tournament, the Los Angeles Clippers hired Kareem as an assistant coach. But in June he and the Clippers parted ways, and a month later a Los Angeles police officer arrested him on a charge of driving under the influence of marijuana, a drug he had previously said he sometimes used to dull the effects of migraines. The charge was eventually dropped. Kareem was devoting his time to speaking and lecturing, often about the history of the American West.

Bigger schools continued their annual attempts to lure Buzz Peterson from Appalachian State. In the spring of 1999 he accepted an offer from Southwest Missouri State, only to change his mind 12 hours later. But when Tulsa came calling the following year, Buzz couldn't resist. The third paragraph of the Associated Press report of his hiring mentioned whom he had roomed with in Chapel Hill. A year later, only days after he had led Tulsa to the NIT title in his first season with the Golden Hurricane, Tennessee lured him away, and the AP's mention of Michael Jordan vaulted to an appositive clause in the very first sentence. By taking a job in the Southeastern Conference, Peterson was no longer a man afraid to "step out on a limb and go for it," as his old friend had long urged him to do. But I couldn't help but notice that the old geography major had found a comfort zone of sorts: Despite those two additional moves, he never left the same 36 or so degrees of latitude.

Thanks in part to new rules that permitted Irish clubs to add two Americans and a continental European to their rosters, crowds were beginning to flock back to Cork's Neptune Stadium for something other than Tuesday Night Bingo. Meanwhile, on January 7, 2000, Edward T. Hanley abruptly stopped enjoying his $310,000 pension from the Hotel Employees and Restaurant Employees International. He was killed in a car accident near his vacation home in northern Wisconsin. He was 67.

Frustrated by the deteriorating business climate on Tel Aviv's Dizengoff Street, Aulcie Perry decided to shutter his Burger Ranch outlet in May 2000 and open another, in a suburb 20 minutes outside the city. "It's doing fantastic," he told me over the phone. Steve Kaplan was doing better, too, and not just because he no longer had to drive past that billboard of his snarling nemesis. His son Tom was in Steve's native state of New Jersey, on a basketball scholarship at Monmouth University, which won the Northeast Conference tournament and a bid to the NCAAs in Tom's freshman season. And Kap had become a sort of food mogul in his own right, baking cookies and selling them in espresso bars around the city.

In the Philippines, the upstart Metropolitan Basketball Association was struggling. "The games hardly rate on TV," Quinito Henson told me. "Money isn't coming in. Owners are losing their shirts. Too many big-name players have deserted to the PBA, and others have gone to court asking to be paid by teams that refuse to honor contracts." He still hoped the MBA would survive, if only as a second-echelon feeder for the PBA, and might supply fans in the provinces with creativity, action, and surprises. Meanwhile, Bobby Jaworski never did suit up again after my trip through Manila. He was concentrating on his work in the Philippine Senate, where he served on 11 committees and chaired two, including the Committee on Games, Amusements, and Sports. Though he and Robert Jr. never played together in a PBA game, the Little J now served his father as chief of staff.

On the eve of the 1999 playoffs, Beijing temporarily banned the NBA from Chinese TV as a result of the NATO bombing of China's embassy in Belgrade. In the meantime, after playing one more full season for Winston Li and Ao-Shen at a 50 percent cut in salary, Ma Jian decided to ease himself into a career as a sports marketing executive. He had long since accepted that he wouldn't become the first Asian to play pro ball in the U.S. But thanks in part to Ma's trailblazing, the Dallas Mavericks prised seven-foot Wang Zhizhi from the army team, the August 1st Rockets, in April 2001. In his debut Wang took a pass from Canada's Steve Nash, rose, and sank a short jumper for the basket that gave the Mavericks their 100th point of the game and thereby qualified everyone in attendance to collect a free Taco Bell chalupa.

As this distinctly 21st-century moment played out—a Chinese, set up by a native of the country of James Naismith's birth, scoring the point that fed Mexican food to more than 18,000 Americans—the Chinese government was holding 24 U.S. Navy crewmen and their spy plane against their will. The crowd in Dallas nonetheless offered Wang a warm welcome, and this time Chinese TV thought nothing of broadcasting the events to a domestic audience of 300 million. For the moment, basketball seemed to have gotten the better of geopolitics. Nonetheless, the directorate of the Shanghai Sharks refused to release Yao Ming for the 2001 NBA draft. And a correspondent for *TIME* magazine, interviewing a patron at a Beijing sports bar during Wang's debut, collected a comment with implications as much for the future of Sino-American relations as for the balance of power in international basketball: "We will learn all the things you Americans teach us. And then we will use what we learned to beat you."

I'd witnessed one historic comeback during my visit to the Palestra. Fourteen months later came the announcement of another: The round-robin City Series involving Philadelphia's Big Five would return. To be sure, not every game was to be staged at the Palestra, and the schools wouldn't split ticket and concessions revenue equally as they had once upon a time. But La Salle agreed to play its home game with St. Joseph's in the Palestra. St. Joe's pledged to take its home games with Villanova, Temple, and Penn there, too. With all of Penn's home games of course scheduled for 33rd and Walnut, the doors of the Quaker meeting house were to be flung open once more.

The news came just before the graduation, at age 57, of Palestra custodian Dan Harrell, who had taken advantage of a program available to all university staff to earn his B.A. in American civilization. At commencement he marched with Quaker seniors Michael Jordan and Matt Langel, carrying a maroon-and-blue dust mop.

In January 2000, on the eve of the Brazilian women's league season, Magic Paula announced that the forthcoming campaign would be her farewell. BCN Osasco put together the league's best record during that regular season, but Paula's team lost in the semifinals of the playoffs after she missed the game's last shot. In retirement she hoped to become manager of a team of her own, which meant her rivalry with Hortência was likely to be renewed once more.

The effectiveness of Bill Bradley's presidential campaign waned as it played to bigger and bigger audiences and Al Gore began throwing elbows. Nonetheless, for a November 1999 rally at Madison Square Garden, a score of basketball characters showed up to offer their support, including longtime Bradley rival John Havlicek.

Sister Rose Marie of the Queen of Angels was still cloistered at the Poor Clare monastery in Alexandria, Virginia.

Shortly after I left Bhutan, the regime celebrated the king's silver jubilee with great ceremony. In Changlimithang Stadium, as citizens packed into those same concrete bleachers from which Sherub and I had watched three of his sons play, the Druk Gyalpo led celebrants in the *tshilebey*, a traditional Bhutanese dance. Several days earlier, the crown prince had led the Pawos to a 13-point victory in the finals of the Silver Jubilee Cup, no ringers required.

On a summer afternoon in Puerto Rico, on his way to the car wash, Johnny Suarez took a turn too fast. His car glanced off a concrete retaining wall and spun back across the road, slamming into a tree. He was lucky: There was no oncoming traffic, and he got away with little more than 20 stitches in his knee and a few more between his lip and chin. But his island sojourn turned out to be a rough one. That fall he found out he wouldn't be academically eligible to play at Universidad Interamericana until the following season. Discouraged, he soon returned with Jovanka to New York, where they had another child and moved into an apartment in the Bronx. He took a job working the night shift at a social club in Washington Heights. Though he no longer dreamed of playing pro ball in Puerto Rico, Johnny would still sometimes pop up at the Vanderbilt Y.

The French national team, so feckless at the Eurobasket it had hosted in Paris, somehow advanced to the gold-medal game at the Sydney Olympics. The French daily *Libération* offered this explanation for the loss *les bleus* suffered there to the U.S.: "Very early in [the lives of American players], mothers pull forcibly on the legs of their small boys. Then, when they have finished stretching them on the clothesline, they force-feed them with a funnel. French mothers do this as well, but usually to geese."

Michel Lasme—now well-known to college recruiters as

Mike Lasme—had polished his English and surfaced as a high schooler at Life Center Academy in Burlington, New Jersey. His great suitor, Rob Orellana, now back in his home state as an assistant coach at Cal State–Fullerton, had no choice but to cede the hunt to big-time recruiters from such schools as Cincinnati, Connecticut, and Florida. In the summer of 2000, before he enrolled as a junior at Life Center, Lasme had captivated onlookers at the Eastern Invitational Basketball Clinic much as he had won over Angolans at the Afrobasket. "He got off the floor like no guard you'll ever see," camp director Rob Kennedy told me. "You could be two courts away and he caught your eye." The following December, during a holiday tournament at the Pyramid of Memphis, Lasme had, according to a report in the Memphis *Commercial Appeal*, pulled off several "acrobatic moves that got people out of their seats."

At least Lasme made it to the States. Despite that *gasosa* to a security guard at the Luanda airport, my postcards never did.

In Jo-burg, John Domingues had two reasons to be excited about the future of South African hoops. He had discovered a superbly agile 17-year-old of Afrikaner descent who stood 7'3" and was prepared to give up rugby for basketball. Meanwhile, as a result of negotiations that had begun, unbeknownst to me, at the Luanda Afrobasket, Domingues had lured Zoran Župčević back from Tunisia in May 2000 to coach the national team once more. "I felt I hadn't finished what I'd started," Župčević told me after he had been on the job for a year. Still, he despaired at the country's lack of resources. "If we don't find a sponsor, which is a good possibility, we won't participate in this year's Afrobasket in Morocco. That would be sad. But to just 'show up' would be wasting money. Better to spend that money on youth programs and the future. Our goal is to participate in the Olympics in 2012."

A new administration at the Kansas City Parks and Recreation Department, under orders to eliminate $1.5 million from its budget for the 2001–02 fiscal year, weighed 45 possible cuts, including Night Hoops. City officials could have saved $100,000—almost half the annual cost of midnight basketball—by ordering that municipal fountains spout water for only four months of the year instead of seven. "Not gonna happen," Mark Bowland had predicted. "We're 'the City *of* Fountains.' There'd be a huge public outcry." Night Hoops ultimately took a $55,000 hit, which forced the program to shut down for one night a week.

In September 2000, after having pledged that he wouldn't be going anywhere, Northwestern coach Kevin O'Neill bolted to take a job as an assistant with the New York Knicks. Northwestern hired Bill Carmody away from Princeton to replace him. And thus did the alpha and omega of my journey—the profane and the sacred, in a sense—circle past each other. As John Thompson III took over at Jadwin Gym, where he would hatch an Ivy League title in his first season, I was reminded anew that this is indeed an ever-spinning game.

In August 1999, just as I was winding up my trek through the country of basketball, Big Xu passed through Manhattan. I was delighted to be able to offer him some of the hospitality he had shown me. Together we caught the WNBA's New York Liberty at Madison Square Garden, and afterward made a pilgrimage to the cage at West Fourth Street in Greenwich Village, where we took in Ken Graham's West Fourth Street Pro Classic, the summer league that has been a fixture of Village life since the 1960s.

The scene mesmerized Xu as much as the basketball did. Spectators pressed two and three deep against the chain link. A bullhorn served as the PA system. Employees at an adjacent McDonald's, he discovered, cheerfully lent players a push broom to sweep the court after it rained. Xu took pictures and notes and vowed that, upon returning home, he'd publish an account of all he had seen.

"I want to show Chinese people that you can start your own tournament," he told me. "You don't need the government to do it for you. All you need is a ball and a court. Preferably near a McDonald's."

In Kansas City, basketball didn't have enough government support. In Beijing, it still suffered from too much. Between those poles the game whispered its byword once more: balance.

ACKNOWLEDGMENTS

If you've read this far, you know how many people helped in the making of this book. That's one of the benefits of the travelogue: Acknowledgments nest naturally in the text. But I'd like to recognize others whose help isn't so obvious and cite some of the sources I turned to along the way, all of which I recommend to anyone interested in learning more about the places I went and people I met.

Parts of the manuscript had their genesis in assignments for *Sports Illustrated, Sports Illustrated for Women, PhillySport,* the *Princeton Alumni Weekly,* and *Attaché,* as well as in my books *The Back-in-Your-Face Guide to Pick-Up Basketball* (with Chuck Wielgus), *Raw Recruits* (with Armen Keteyian), and *Basketball: A History of the Game* (originally published as *100 Years of Hoops*). Editors I worked with on those projects—Morin Bishop, Jerry Gross, Jay Heinrichs, Jim Merritt, Abigail Seymour, Leslie Wells, Tim Whitaker, and Linda Belsky Zamost among them—helped lead to this book.

Because of the collaborative way we work, current and former colleagues at *Sports Illustrated* will find their labors reflected here, too, particularly senior editor Greg Kelly. When I shared with him a proposed itinerary for this project, Greg challenged me, telling of an old woman he met on a trip through the Irish countryside. The woman asked where he was going and didn't much like his answer. "You must go *beyond!*" she admonished him, and Greg's citation of this advice resounded through my own journey. Managing editor Bill Colson cheerfully made available the time to do the project justice. Gabe Miller and Richard Demak and their copy and research departments have kept me from making innumerable mistakes. Other *SI* staffers and contributors, past and present, to whom I owe thanks include Kelli Anderson, Lars Anderson, Sandy Bailey, Chris Ballard, David Bauer, Lisa Twyman Bessone, Mike Bevans, Trisha Lucey Blackmar, Ed Burns, Marty Burns, Peter Carry, Brian Cazeneuve, Kevin Cook, Seth Davis, Frank Deford, Rob Fleder, Mark Godich, Sally Guard, Hank Hersch, Chris Hunt, Lynn Johnson, Roy S. Johnson, Kostya Kennedy, Curry Kirkpatrick, Moritz Kleine-Brockhoff, Heinz Kluetmeier, Stefanie Krasnow, Franz Lidz, Jack McCallum, Miriam Marseu, Bob Martin, Chad Millman, Mark Mulvoy, Craig Neff, Merrell Noden, Rich O'Brien, Sandy Padwe, John Papanek, Steve Robinson, Bob Roe, Steve Rushin, Natasha Simon, B. J. Schecter, Gary Smith, Chris Stone, Phil Taylor, Rick Telander, Ian Thomsen, Anita Verschoth, Grant Wahl, Linda Wachtel, Jon Wertheim, Kelly Whiteside, Paul Witteman, Steve Wulf, and Don Yaeger.

I owe my understanding, such as it is, of Princeton basketball to many people, including Sean Gregory, Matt Henshon, Tom Odjakjian, Jerry Price, Gary Walters, Bruce Wood, and Chuck Yrigoyen, but particularly to Harvey Yavener, who has covered the Tigers for the *Trenton Times* through parts of at least four decades. When I was a college sophomore, Harvey trusted me to cover Princeton's appearance in the 1976 Kodak Classic when he had no reason to do so. Others whose coverage of the Tigers helped me include Jeff Coplon, whose take on the 1997–98 team appeared in the *New York Times Magazine;* and Webmaster Jon Solomon and the many contributors to princetonbasketballnews.com.

The Naismith trail took me to two states and one province in two countries, and I found blazes in Robin Deutsch, Glenn

Kappelman, Howard Campbell, Marilyn Campbell, and Paul Virgin. For the contours of Naismith's life, I turned to Bernice Larson Webb's *The Basketball Man,* as well as *Almonte's Brothers of the Wind* by Frank Cosentino. In Almonte I consulted archives at the Naismith International Basketball Centre and the Almonte Public Library. The good doctor's life became clearer thanks to Andrea Hendig of the YMCA of the U.S.A. Archives at the University of Minnesota, and Springfield College's Babson Library, where Eleanor Corridan and Rachel Naismith provided invaluable help. Doug Stark, the librarian and archivist at the Naismith Memorial Basketball Hall of Fame, set me up with its material, and Ian Naismith graciously shared his grandfather's unpublished correspondence, as compiled and edited by Ian's mother, the late Frances Pomeroy Naismith.

In Lithuania, I owe thanks to Šarūnė Galickaitė, Zita Marčiulionytė, Greta Rimkienė, Rytis Sabas, Milda Sabienė, and Linas (Little Priest) Kunigelis. Violeta Gaižauskaitė finagled for me 15 minutes with President Adamkus. In Poland, Marcin Gadziński taught me about Pruszków, and Wojciech Michałowicz showed me Warsaw—and fronted me a 20-złoty bill. In Lucerne, I'm indebted to Pius Portmann and his wife, Priska Fischer, and to their son Julian for the use of his room.

For their welcomes in both Celebration and Belding, I thank Cla Avery, Tim Manes, and the entire Macker family, especially Scott and Mitch McNeal's parents, Dick and Bonnie McNeal. Thanks, too, to Jennifer Wing of the Celebration Company, and to the authors of two insiders' looks at life in the Osceola County petri dish—Andrew Ross (*The Celebration Chronicles*) and Douglas Frantz and Catherine Collins (*Celebration, U.S.A.*). I also went back often to a dog-eared copy of Don Sicko's seminal *Gus!*

Giorgio Gandolfi began tutoring me in Italian basketball long ago, and Enrico Campana steepened my learning curve. But I'm particularly indebted to the staff members of *Super-Basket* who made me welcome in Bologna, Roberto Gotta, Enrico Schiavina, and Stefano Valenti foremost among them. I'd also like to thank Simonetta Santini, Fabrizio Pungetti,

Michele Forino, Carla Minnicelli, and Marco Angrisani for their help and kindness. Giampiero and Giulio Hruby, whose names you'll find in their magnificently monikered Jump & Julius Scouting Service, set me up with their *J&J Basketball Registers,* while Giamp provided transportation, too. Meanwhile *J&J* collaborator Dan Peterson, the expatriate American turned Italian coaching immortal, was a font of information and opinion, all the more authoritative for his having coached Virtus Bologna for five seasons. A copy of the Gallimard guide to Bologna helped me understand *la grassa.*

The Balkans have called out to me from the time I first heard my stepgrandmother sound out the name of Skopje, the city of her birth. Over the years, through conversations with Neven Bertičević, Richard Brody, Ivica Dukan, Zoran Radović, and Drenka Willen, I've moved fitfully toward a better understanding of that part of the world; thanks to Maja Nikolić, I have a better understanding of its names. Filmmakers Peter Gilbert and Steve James joined me in bringing the story of Svetislav Pešić and the Boys of Bormio into focus, literally and figuratively. Others who helped in that undertaking were John Black, Sue Chung, Chris Clarey, Paulette Douglas, Tom Smithburg, and David Zuccaro. For her translation assistance, I thank Sally Guard. Meanwhile Stefano Valenti fortified me for my trip to Sarajevo, while Alan Kontić and Emir Jesenković introduced me to their city once I got there. Among the accounts I drew on were Robert Kaplan's *Balkan Ghosts,* Roger Cohen's *Hearts Grown Brutal,* Peter Maass's *Love Thy Neighbor* (which I'd recommend even if its author hadn't been a frequent teammate in a weekly pickup game), Miroslav Prstojević's *Sarajevo: The Wounded City,* and *The Death of Yugoslavia* by Laura Silber and Allan Little. Thanks also to David Berman of the University of Pittsburgh, and to Miguel Angel Forniés, who took the famous picture that opens chapter seven.

In Illinois, Gary Childs of the *Journal-Star,* Percy Baker Jr. of Carver Community Center, and Reggie Livingston welcomed me to Peoria, just as Barbara Butler of the University of Illinois sports information office welcomed me to Champaign.

In Kansas, I relied on the hospitality of Dean Buchan, Renée DiGiulio, Amy Perko, Rick Perko, and Miles Schnaer, as well as the help of Deb Graber and Carol Leffler at the University of Kansas, and Blair Kerkhoff, whose biography *Phog Allen: The Father of Basketball Coaching* provided additional background on Naismith's life. Diana Giddens and Chris Burkhalter, stalwarts in UTEP's basketball and sports information offices, respectively, helped me in El Paso, as did Darren Hunt and Joe Muench of the *El Paso Times*. I also consulted Frank Fitzpatrick's *And the Walls Came Tumbling Down* and Dan Wetzel's prizewinning profile of Don Haskins for *Basketball Times*. Kareem's own book, *A Season on the Reservation*, answered a number of questions that nagged after my visit. Bill Dyer, Melissa Hill, Steve Kirschner, Andrew Marannis, and Kelby Siler all helped fill me in on the Buzz Peterson story, as did David Halberstam's *Playing for Keeps*, the last word on Michael Jordan.

In Ireland, thanks go to Michael Finn for the transportation, Joe Boylan for the pints, and Tony Keane, Noel Keating, and Scott McCarthy for their time and attentions. Dan Doyle and his crew at the University of Rhode Island's Institute for International Sport—over the years, Wally Halas, Patrice Jones, Lorna Prout, and Chris Stiepock among them—were their usual helpful selves. To flesh out both Ed Hanley and his legacy to Irish basketball, I relied on the reporting of John Gearan in the *Worcester* (Massachusetts) *Telegram;* Eugene Methvin in *Reader's Digest;* Stephen Franklin in the *Chicago Tribune;* and Victoria Corderi of *Dateline NBC*.

In Israel, Eli Groner, Mike Karnon, and Arie Rosenzweig helped me develop Aulcie Perry's story; Andrew Jackson of the U.S. Federal District Court clerk's office in Brooklyn and Rabbi Stephen Lerner did the same closer to home.

Asian basketball was almost entirely new to me, but many people helped in my orientation, as it were. They include Yeo Choo Hock of the Asian Basketball Confederation in Kuala Lumpur, as well as his colleagues Ng Swee Fong, Tan See Wah, and M. P. Haridas; and in Hong Kong, Tom McCarthy of ABC

Promotions, Mike Chinoy of CNN, as well as the NBA's able China hands, Cheong Sau Ching and Cindy Ng. In and around Manila, Menchu Genato-Henson was as lavishly hospitable as her husband, Quinito. Nic Jorge, Angelina Jorge, and Monica Jorge, as well as Sonny Santos and the entire staff at the Best Center Sports Foundation, have created Asia's finest basketball school and showed me hospitality on the same high level. Thanks, too, to the Bautista family, Julian Malonso, Rhea Navarro, Tito Panlilio, Bobby Rius, Carlos A. Velez, Kathryn Grace Tan and her parents, Rubin and Virginia, and the executive staff of the Philippine Basketball Association. Much closer to home, a *salamat* to José Vidal for his attentions to a draft of chapter 16.

I couldn't have explored China without the help of Jimi FlorCruz, who with his wife, Ana, fed and counseled me in Beijing, and hooked me up with Huang Yong, who was an indispensable interpreter and guide. Judy Polumbaum served as a sounding board Stateside; her symposia on sport and cultural distinctiveness at the University of Iowa weave fabric whose hem I've barely touched. Richard Avory, Paul Tsuchiya, and Zhang Weiping of IMG all helped me riddle out Chinese basketball, as did John Anthony Spencer and Xia Song. Deng Li Li addressed the Qiao Dan phenomenon. And two hoteliers— Tina Castillo in Beijing and Louis Spataro in Shanghai—cut me much-appreciated price breaks.

Over the years Dan Baker, Paul Baker, Joe Cassidy, Fran Dunphy, Dick Jerardi, Les Keiter, John McAdams, Tom Schneider, Bob Vetrone, Dick Weiss, and Chris Wyche have all shared with me their passion for the Palestra. To inform my retelling of the 1999 Penn-Princeton game there, I drew on accounts by Wes Tooke in the *Princeton Alumni Weekly* and Rich Hoffman in the *Philadelphia Daily News*. Shaun May provided the most valuable thing of all: a seat in the stands. And to Jack Scheuer and the regulars, thanks for welcoming a stranger to your game.

My trip to Brazil depended on a daisy chain of people, beginning with David Duckenfield, who worked the Latin

American beat for the NBA. Dave put me in touch with Alex Teixeira of Curitiba's *Gazeta do Povo,* who provided logistical support and hospitality, and introduced me to Adriana Freitas, an invaluable interpreter and guide. Thanks, too, to Grego Bozikis and Roberto Beck of the Brazilian Basketball Confederation for a warm welcome to Santo André, and to Deniz Albino Fantin, for feeding me. Alma Guillermoprieto's *Samba* is essential to an understanding of music, movement, and religion in Brazilian culture, and the central role of women in each, and I consulted it often.

Among Bill Bradley's staff, Emma Byrne, Eric Hauser, Matt Henshon, Sara Howard, and Rick Stengel all helped smooth my way. John McPhee's *A Sense of Where You Are* remains the basic Bradley text, and I dipped often into the candidate's own books *Life on the Run, Values of the Game,* and, especially, *Time Present, Time Past.*

Kelly Whiteside first alerted me to the extraordinary transit of Shelly Pennefather, while Shelly's mother, Mary Jane Pennefather, put me in touch with Sumiyo (Pipi) Iida. Yumi Tanabe was an interpreter of great stamina. I'd like to thank Professor Yutaka Mizutani, who may be the foremost scholar, Western or non-Western, of James Naismith's life and work, for his time and help, and extend the same gratitude to Yuji Wada, Shelly's coach in Japan. At Villanova, Harry Perretta and Dean Kenefick joined all of Shelly's former teammates in sharing their recollections, as did an old Villanova opponent, Doris Burke. I enlisted many people in my search for Hirohide Ogawa, among them Nike's John Patrick, the NBA's Yoko Nakamura, and John Gaustad and Rob Bagchi at Sportspages, the sport specialist bookshop in London, and I thank all for their forbearance. In the end, however, I'm most grateful to Phillip Ward of Oleander Press, who confessed to the provenance of *Enlightenment through the Art of Basketball* and thus spared me a fruitless chase through the backwoods of Japanese basketball. *Enlightenment* is no less rewarding for having a fanciful author—it's still "true" in at least some sense of the word. Those interested in a less chimerical take on basketball and

Eastern thought might nonetheless consult, as I did, *The Tao of the Jump Shot*, whose author, John Fitzsimmons Mahoney, actually lives in Newark.

Pico Iyer is an evangelist of the faith that cultural truths can be found in sport, and he supplied both encouragement, before I lit out for Bhutan, and wisdom in the form of his essay on the country, which appears in his collection *Falling off the Map*. Marie Brown got me to the Dragon Kingdom, and Dick Nycum, Ruth Nycum, Heinz Valtin, and Tom Valtin all helped make sure I was well informed upon arrival. Thanks also to Leo Rose and to Barbara Crossette, who, along with Sreenath Sreenivasan and others in his South Asian Internet newsgroup, helped lead me to a copy of Nari Rustomji's *Bhutan: The Dragon Kingdom in Crisis*, the most authoritative account of the events described at the end of chapter 22.

Evan Silverman of the NBA helped make it possible for Rick Olsen to join me to explore the June draft as ritual. Jean-Pierre Dusseaulx of the French Basketball Federation welcomed me to the Eurobasket, where I could once again plumb the finest basketball minds in France: François Brassamin and Jean-Luc Thomas of *L'Équipe*, and Didier Le Corre of *Basket Hebdo*. For years, *SI*'s Agathe Dumond has been a valued colleague and friend in Paris, no less so this time, when I showed up on my own project.

In Angola, Tundé Aina, Pius Ayinor, Mamadou Diouf, Bi Figueiredo, Manuel Mateus Figueiredo, Phil Ives, Alex Laskaris, Tito Muamba, Russ Schiebel, and Tony Sofrimento all welcomed a stranger. José Alberto de Sousa and Fernando J. Andresen Guimaraes of the Portuguese Mission to the United Nations provided essential background before I left. Jere Longman of the *New York Times*, who passed through Luanda for the *Philadelphia Inquirer* during the cease-fire in 1992, prepped me, too; the *Inquirer*'s Mel Greenberg tracked down a copy of Jere's account of that visit. Doug Cress helped fill me in on basketball in South Africa. And Miles Bredin and Ryszard Kapuściński—authors, respectively, of *Blood on the Tracks* and *Another Day of Life*—survived a Luanda much more perilous than the one I visited, and I relied on stories they lived to tell.

For background on midnight basketball, I consulted *Pickup Artists* by Lars Anderson and Chad Millman, as well as Chris Ballard's *Hoops Nation*. Thanks are due to Rosetta Harris and all the Night Hoops supervisors in Kansas City, as well as Arzelea Gates and the congregation of St. James' United Methodist Church, all of whom warmly welcomed me to their town. Denise Gottfredson of the Department of Criminology and Criminal Justice at the University of Maryland clarified questions about midnight basketball's effect on crime.

Dan White's two collaborations with Pete Carril, *Play to Win* and *The Smart Take from the Strong,* are definitive on the former Princeton coach's life, and I drew on both. Thanks, too, to Penny Bassett Hackett of New Jersey Transit, and to all the noontime regulars at Jadwin who let me crash their game.

Between the stopovers recounted in these pages I sometimes stumbled down alleys that didn't lead to chapters in the book. At other times I simply paused to catch my breath. Friends and relatives who took me in during these fits and starts include Mart Smeets and Karen Mulder in Haarlem, and in Munich, Christiane and Christoph Clemm, Sibylla and Peter Schliep, and Adelheid and Jon Baumhauer. In Holland, Henry Smith let me in on his weekly run, while Jay Goldberg was an extravagant host in England, as were Julie Boden, Chris Finch, Jennifer Nurse, Nick Nurse, and Ian Whittell.

The NBA's Kim Bohuny, and the league's international public relations staff, directed by Terry Lyons and Brian McIntyre, never failed to help. The press officers at the FIBA secretariat in Munich—Marcos Beltrá, Jon Ingram, Joanna Sutherland, Romain Vez, and Florian Wanninger—were every bit the NBA's equal. My gratitude also goes to FIBA general secretary Borislav Stanković; his deputy, Patrick Baumann; and Shaheen Haunschild, all of whom made time for me.

My parents, Mary and Nikolaus Wolff, and my sister Katherine Wolff, gave careful attention to the manuscript, as did Rob Goldberg, Greg Kelly, Bruce Musgrave, Merrell

Noden, Roland Ottewell, and Steve Rushin. Pete McEntegart gave the manuscript both an edit and a fact check. I'm grateful to all for their time and counsel, as well as for the encouragement that Gerald Couzens, Steve D'Amato, Rainer Dressler, Jason Folkmanis, Ann James, Robert James, Jay Jennings, Michael MacCambridge, Ethan Mann, Steven Mann, Eva Mantel, Ed Markey, Bradley Naples, Jim O'Connell, Charlie Pierce, Leslie Robinson, Robert Sullivan, Chuck Wielgus, and Bob Wright all supplied, too. For the use of their photos I thank my sister Stephanie Wolff and my colleague Heinz Kluetmeier. And I took inspiration from Simon Kuper and his book *Football against the Enemy,* which examined soccer much as I've tried to look at basketball. Simon was generous in sharing advice both on how to go and how to make sense of the going.

My agent, Sloan Harris, and editor, Rob McMahon, intuitively understood why I had to write this book, made it possible for me to do so, and brought the manuscript home through several shaky incarnations. Careers in midwifery await both should either choose to impoverish the book trade by abandoning it.

Finally, I thank my wife, Vanessa James Wolff. To follow basketball around the world is a crazy way to begin a marriage, yet her pickup spirit exceeded mine. She saw, heard, and teased out much of what appears here, and along the way taught me the virtue of being an unburdened traveler: The lighter you pack, the more you can bring home. Let my debt to her, explicit in the dedication, be reiterated here. It extends to every page in between.